Showdown Against RAF Terror

"I just want to tell the German government that it's their fault if we die. And we will die. I know they will do it; they have already prepared everything. (...) They do care about us. But the German government doesn't care about our lives. (...) Seize every opportunity, I beg you, try, please try. Think of the children, the women, think of us! Think of the people who have already died. Can you reconcile this with your conscience, can you really live with such a conscience until the end of your life? (...)"
—*Radio message from "Landshut" stewardess Gabriele von Lutzau (née Dillmann) to the Mogadishu airport tower on 17 October 1977*[1]

"Someone who knows that he will be burdened with failure and guilt regardless of his efforts, will not want to say to himself that he has done everything and everything has been right, no matter how he acted. He will not try to blame others for his failings and omissions, because he knows that others are facing the same inevitable entanglement. But he will be allowed to say: We decided this and that. We failed to do such and such a thing for such and such a reason. We are responsible for all of this. God help us."
—*Federal Chancellor Helmut Schmidt in a government statement to the German Bundestag on 20 October 1977*[2]

---

[1] Hermann 1977, p. 177.

[2] Plenary record of the German Bundestag, 8th electoral term/50th session, pp. 3756–3760.

Martin Rupps

Showdown Against RAF Terror

Helmut Schmidt's Crisis Management in the German Autumn

Martin Rupps
Mainz, Rheinland-Pfalz, Germany

ISBN 978-3-031-76249-9   ISBN 978-3-031-76250-5   (eBook)
https://doi.org/10.1007/978-3-031-76250-5

© The Editor(s) (if applicable) and The Author(s), under exclusive license to Springer Nature Switzerland AG 2025

This work is subject to copyright. All rights are solely and exclusively licensed by the Publisher, whether the whole or part of the material is concerned, specifically the rights of reprinting, reuse of illustrations, recitation, broadcasting, reproduction on microfilms or in any other physical way, and transmission or information storage and retrieval, electronic adaptation, computer software, or by similar or dissimilar methodology now known or hereafter developed.
The use of general descriptive names, registered names, trademarks, service marks, etc. in this publication does not imply, even in the absence of a specific statement, that such names are exempt from the relevant protective laws and regulations and therefore free for general use.
The publisher, the authors and the editors are safe to assume that the advice and information in this book are believed to be true and accurate at the date of publication. Neither the publisher nor the authors or the editors give a warranty, expressed or implied, with respect to the material contained herein or for any errors or omissions that may have been made. The publisher remains neutral with regard to jurisdictional claims in published maps and institutional affiliations.

Cover Illustration: The photo on the book cover was taken on October 18, 1977 in front of the Federal Chancellery in Bonn. Chancellor Helmut Schmidt is waiting for the British Prime Minister James Callaghan to receive him as a state guest with military honors. During the night, the passengers and crew of a Lufthansa plane that had been highjacked by a Palestinian terrorist commando and taken to Mogadishu (Somalia) had been freed by members of the German border police GSG9. Shortly afterwards, the leading members of the left-wing terrorist group Red Army Faction, Gudrun Ensslin, Andreas Baader, and Jan-Carl Raspe, took their own lives in Stuttgart-Stammheim prison.
Source 'J. H. Darchinger/Friedrich-Ebert-Stiftung, 6/FJHD015210'

This Springer imprint is published by the registered company Springer Nature Switzerland AG
The registered company address is: Gewerbestrasse 11, 6330 Cham, Switzerland

If disposing of this product, please recycle the paper.

For the children, women and men in the Refugee Accommodation Centre "Housing Area" in Mainz-Gonsenheim

Foreword

Martin Rupps' new book on Helmut Schmidt is characterised by its extensive use of sources and numerous interviews with contemporary witnesses. The result is an extremely lively and multifaceted picture of the events of the "German Autumn", which not least provides new insights into the decision-making processes of the time and offers a deeper insight into the thoughts and actions of Chancellor Schmidt.

It becomes clear, for example, that Schmidt went into the deliberations of the *Großer politischer Beratungskreis* (Large Political Advisory Group) in the firm conviction that he could under no circumstances give in to the blackmailing demands for the release of the imprisoned RAF terrorists. He was aware that he would have to convince the representatives of the political system assembled there of his line at the very first meeting. He achieved support for his position essentially through two arguments: The Lorenz kidnapping case had shown that giving in to the kidnappers' demands by the state would only lead to further serious criminal offences. The population also expected the government to take a tough stance in the fight against terror. However, he would use all police and intelligence resources to free the hostage, and unusual proposals word would also be considered to save Schleyer's life without having to give in to blackmail. The Chancellor was well aware of the risk of murdering the hostage - that much I know from my conversations with him. This had to be accepted in the interests of a defensible state.

Nevertheless, it was clear from the outset that the Chancellor would not give in. In the case of the hostage (and later the hostages of the "Landshut"), he could only hope that the rescue attempts would succeed—which they did in the latter case, but not in the former. Schmidt held on to this unyielding stance to the end. Nor did he seriously pursue proposals for solutions such as those put forward by the "Ruhnau Group". One of these proposals involved flying the detainees out to a third country willing to cooperate, which, upon the release of Hanns-Martin Schleyer, would have been tasked with re-incarcerating these RAF members. Such an opportunity would have arisen if the passengers of the "Landshut" in Mogadishu had been included. Such an agreement could have been reached with President Siad Barre, who incidentally was honored for his support, as I had publicly demanded at the time. Instead, the "Chancellor of Strength" ordered the deployment of the GSG9, in which the risk of numerous casualties among the passengers was extraordinarily high. Schmidt was aware of this. In the end, human lives did not count in this situation, nor did the fact that the hostage Schleyer had been held captive for many weeks in constant fear of death under unacceptable circumstances.

I knew from my father's letters to the government and also from conversations we both had long before the time of his abduction that he would have accepted a quick decision of any kind from the German government, but not such a long period of inhumane suffering. This also prompted me to seek a decision from the Federal Constitutional Court after the Federal Chancellor refused to make such a decision. The court then announced what I consider to be an inherently contradictory decision. Over many pages, it convincingly justified the state's fundamental obligation to comprehensively protect the life of a citizen who is specifically at risk, but then, in a brief final passage, granted the Federal Government its own discretionary powers in the "Schleyer kidnapping case". In a later conversation, the then President of the Federal Constitutional Court, Ernst Benda, conceded to me that the deliberations on this decision had been under a certain amount of pressure from the Federal Government.

I am convinced that Schmidt sacrificed one human life and endangered many out of an understanding of the state that was characterised by very personal experiences. In doing so, he was in no way able to prevent the RAF from committing further acts of terror and murdering people. With the murders of Siegfried Buback and Jürgen Ponto in 1977, the RAF had already aroused growing doubts among many of its supporters about the justification of its "political struggle" against the structures and representatives of the Federal Republic of Germany at the time. (Consequently,) the "secret sympathies" for the terrorist group and their violence against individuals were also increasingly publicly rejected by opinion leaders. The political and moral debate that Schmidt called for in the first Bundestag debate after my father's murder had thus long begun and ultimately, albeit years later, led to the dissolution of the RAF.

At the latest when my father was taken hostage, the Federal Chancellor could have seized the opportunity to make a humane and constitutionally required decision in favor of the hostages and at the same time make joint resistance against the threat to the liberal order the subject of his political action. Talks and public discussions with personalities from the worlds of science and culture, especially those to whom left-wing extremist groups had referred, proved their willingness to participate in and shape a political and moral debate.

In the fight against terrorism, Schmidt retreated to primarily applying legal and policy measures. Even though he spoke of the humanisation of politics, of understanding young people and their questions of meaning and the necessary willingness to find common solutions to differing social positions, he developed little political leadership on these pressing issues during his time in government. Martin Rupps' book is an impressive demonstration of the fact that, although he was preoccupied by these problems, he was nevertheless convinced that his decision was the right one and took full responsibility for it.

Munich, Germany Hanns-Eberhard Schleyer
May 2024

Acknowledgments: A Word of Thanks

I would like to thank the hostages of the "Landshut" abduction flight Gaby Coldewey, Beate Keller (née Zerbst), Beate Knauff (née Brod), Gabriele von Lutzau (née Dillmann), Daniela Müll, Birgitt Röhll, Stefan Röhll and Jürgen Vietor for their friendly support of my work. Also to their liberators Ulrich Wegener (died on 28 December 2017) and Dieter Fox.

Ruediger von Lutzau, Lufthansa co-pilot of the flight from Frankfurt am Main to Mogadishu on 17 October 1977, died on 2 August 2021. The conversations and email exchanges with him were always valuable. Ruediger von Lutzau was a dedicated editor of my first book manuscript on the subject, "The Survivors of Mogadishu". Ruedeger, you are missed!

Dorothea Hauser made her interviews with contemporary witnesses, which she conducted as part of a research project by the Helmut and Loki Schmidt Foundation, available to me. I would like to thank her for this and for important information and categorisations.

Ludwig Hildebrand provided me with the transcript of Lufthansa's internal radio traffic between Frankfurt and Mogadishu.

Karin Ellermann from the Helmut and Loki Schmidt Foundation and Sven Haarmann from the Friedrich-Ebert-Stiftung's Archive of Social Democracy actively and patiently supported me during my visits.

Karlheinz Viehmann has been tirelessly collecting information about the identity and subsequent lives of the former "Landshut" hostages and their liberators for years. Thank you for this meticulous research work!

Sophie Hartmann, Laura Nührenbörger, Robert Jung and Christian Stücken read the early manuscript and provided valuable feedback.

Laura Nührenbörger helped with the translation of the manuscript into English.

Thank you Christina, Christine, Doris, Elvira, Ute-Beatrix, Renata, Hans-Jürgen, Marc and Robert for your friendship.

I owe the episode "And then I had enough. The decision was final not to go there again. The next morning, I went back." to Björn.

Thank you Bülent and your team at "Caipi": Anastasia, Carina, Eda, Fiza, Meli, Rama, Sabrina, Albert and Tom. Especially Rosl and Mani.

Thank you, Maja and Vedran, for your wonderful "Hartenberger Treff".

Mainz, Germany
May 2025

Contents

1	**Olaf Scholz and Helmut Schmidt**	1
	Editorial Notes	12
2	**Crime with an Announcement**	15
	Cologne	15
	Stuttgart	17
	Bonn	20
	Stuttgart	44
3	**The Brutality of Chance**	61
	Palma De Mallorca Airport	61
	Rom	66
	Larnaka	69
	Bahrain	73
	Dubai	78
	Aden	113
	Mogadishu	126
4	**A Night of Life and Death**	159
5	**On the Catwalk**	165
6	**Mr Vietor, We Make You Captain**	175
7	**Congratulations on Your Rebirth**	183

8	**Guinea Pig**	191
9	**A Red Bicycle from Mr Federal Chancellor**	199
	Helma Van Dreumel	208
	Livia Vamos	210
	Edelgard and Everhard Wolff	212
10	**Our New Friends, the Sheikhs**	217
	Great Britain	217
	Palestine Liberation Organisation (PLO)	219
	Souhaila Andrawes	223
	Arab Emirates	226
	Saudi Arabia	227
	Israel	229
	South Yemen	230
	Mogadishu	231
11	**Triumph and Decline of a Generation**	235
12	**Expansion**	243
13	**State Raison**	249
Bibliography		265

Abbreviations

AdsD	Archive of Social Democracy of the Friedrich-Ebert-Stiftung, Helmut-Schmidt-Archive
Archiv BK	Archive of the Federal Chancellery
BArch	Federal Archives Koblenz and Potsdam
BGS	Federal Border Guard
BK	Federal Chancellor/Federal Chancellery
BMI	Federal Ministry of the Interior
BND	Federal Intelligence Service
BRD	Federal Republic of Germany
CDU	Christian Democratic Union of Germany
CSU	Christian Social Union in Bavaria
FDP	Free Democratic Party
GDR	German Democratic Republic
GSG9	Border Guard Troop 9 of the Federal Border Guard
HSA	Archive Helmut and Loki Schmidt Foundation
LH Archive	Archive of German Lufthansa
OEG	Victim Compensation Act
OTB	Operation diary
PA AA	Political Archive of the Federal Foreign Office
PFLP	Popular Front for the Liberation of Palestine
PLO	Palestinian Liberation Organisation
SPD	Social Democratic Party of Germany
StM	Minister of State
Sts	State Secretary

1

Olaf Scholz and Helmut Schmidt

On 24 February 2022, Russian President Vladimir Putin launches a war of aggression against Ukraine. In doing so, he brings death and devastation to the neighbouring country in the middle of Europe. Many thousands of people on both sides are killed, millions of Ukrainians lose the roof over their heads and flee. Germans are also reacting fearfully to the war (almost) on their doorstep.

On 23 February 2022, Social Democrat Chancellor Olaf Scholz makes a government statement in the *German Bundestag,* the parliament, in which he calls the Russian attack a *Zeitenwende* ("turning point"). Nothing is as it was, he says. The great power Russia is no longer predictable. And dangerous for its neighbours, for Europe and the world.

At the same time, the Federal Chancellor announces a 100-billion-euro package to modernise the *Bundeswehr*. The army had been heavily economised on for years on the assumption that conventional weapons technology would become superfluous with the end of the Cold War. Germany and Russia were forging ever closer economic ties, for example in the gas business. Surely, Russia would never politically abuse its new role!

Social Democrat outsider Olaf Scholz owed his surprising election victory to the weak CDU and CSU candidate for chancellor, Armin Laschet, who messed things up for the government-spoilt CDU/CSU. The Social Democrat Olaf Scholz formed a government with the Greens and the FDP, the Liberal Democratic Party.

Olaf Scholz is a politician without charisma, a functionary type who does not know how to explain his policies and tends to be arrogant. His intellectual brilliance and excellent expertise were a stroke of luck in his previous position as Federal Minister of Finance. In the most important political office, he cannot really succeed at any time.

Dissatisfaction with current top politicians such as the Federal Chancellor creates fertile ground for the glorification of former ones. Since the outbreak of Covid-19, the Russian attack on Ukraine and the energy crisis, many German citizens have been wishing for a supposedly "strong man" in the chancellery to return.[1] Someone like Helmut Schmidt. He was the self-declared crisis manager during the Hamburg flood disaster of 1962 and in the German Autumn of 1977, when the left-wing terrorist *Rote Armee Fraktion* ("Red Army Faction"), abbreviated RAF, sought a kind of decisive battle with the representatives of liberal-democratic West Germany.

This longing is reinforced by the cult status Helmut Schmidt acquired in the 2020s during his political retirement. In speeches, articles, books, but above all in the talk shows on public television. As a guest of TV talk shows with Sandra Maischberger or Reinhold Beckmann. The former chancellor spoke plainly without regard for those in power. Helmut Schmidt did something that had long been forbidden in a television studio or restaurant—he smoked.

"He does his thing", was the favourable opinion of many spectators, quoting singer Udo Lindenberg.

Helmut Schmidt died on 10 November 2015. Olaf Scholz, also a Hanseatic citizen, spoke as Hamburg's governing mayor at the funeral service for the fifth Federal Chancellor. He called Helmut Schmidt a "giant" and added: "It may sound pathetic, but it's true." This is how social democrats create legends for each other.

After Helmut Schmidt's death, the German Bundestag approved money for a Federal Chancellor Helmut Schmidt Foundation. Several million euros a year. Unfortunately, the members of parliament did not reserve the right to have a say in the organisation and personnel of the foundation—just as they had no say in foundations for former chancellors.

The SPD candidate for chancellor, Peer Steinbrück, who was once personally proclaimed by the former chancellor but failed, is the chairman of the board of trustees of the foundation. The chairman of the board and managing director, Meik Woyke, is always able to hire new employees with social democratic views. Not for traditional historical research and scientific debate into Helmut Schmidt's life's work, but to continue the uncritical image of Schmidt

---

[1] "Vaccination disaster in nursing homes. Where is Helmut Schmidt?" was the title of an article by Hans-Jörg Vehlewald in Bild am Sonntag on 27 January 2021.

that the weekly newspaper "Die Zeit" painted during the former chancellor's many years of service. A legend was created for its own journalistic glory.

Authors of the Federal Chancellor Helmut Schmidt Foundation like to write about the "crisis chancellor" Helmut Schmidt, totally making the protagonist's self-portrayal their own. The book uses the example of Helmut Schmidt's greatest political challenge, the German Autumn of 1977, to take a new look at his actions in crises.

In the 2021 election campaign, the SPD is confidently advertising with the label of "crisis chancellor" Helmut Schmidt. An election commercial announces that Olaf Scholz will not only demonstrate the same sense of duty as Helmut Schmidt as Federal Chancellor, but also the same strong leadership.

Olaf Scholz has failed to deliver on this promise in the second half of the legislative period until the coalition broke up in November 2024.

The subsequent reference in the advert that Olaf Scholz joined the Social Democrats as a young man at the very time "when Schmidt was leading Germany out of the crisis" seems rather contrived. That was 1975, the year of a global economic crisis.[2] In other words, it was not Helmut Schmidt but fate that made Olaf Scholz join the SPD.

Olaf Scholz is leading the German government in crisis mode, just like his Social Democrat predecessor Helmut Schmidt once did. The crisis since the Russian war of aggression on Ukraine and the crisis in the German Autumn of 1977 have different causes. Nevertheless which, then as now, represent a test of strength for the political community of the Federal Republic. And situations that trigger fears in many people and make them doubt the state's ability to protect their security.

"It all depends on the chancellor" was the slogan of the CDU/CSU in the 1969 Bundestag election campaign, which appeared on the election posters of incumbent Kurt Georg Kiesinger. At the same time, the phrase is a reminder of a constitutional fact: According to the Basic Law, a Federal Chancellor has less power than it generally seems. He or she determines the policy guidelines, but not the government's actions. The latter is done by the cabinet, the federal ministers. The *Ampelkoalition* also came to an end because Olaf Scholz could not become the basta chancellor under the Basic Law.

In a crisis, quite a lot depends on the tone a Chancellor chooses; on the statements made in the German Bundestag and in front of the television nation. This gives the population an impression of the extent to which he or she fulfils the expectation of political leadership. How he or she deals with

---

[2] See Kellerhoff, Sven Felix: Führung in der Zeitenwende. Continuities between Helmut Schmidt and Olaf Scholz, in: Kellerhoff/Stubbe da Luz 2024, pp. 248–261.

the fear that has gripped many people. During the German Autumn, it was the fear that violent criminals could destroy the free and democratic basic order. With the war in Ukraine, the fear arose of a war in Central Europe and its economic consequences.

The question of how Chancellor Helmut Schmidt governed during the German Autumn is a topic of contemporary historical research. At the same time, he provided an example of political action from which conclusions can still be drawn to the present. Some of what Helmut Schmidt did was due to the moment or his political personality. Much remains a successful or unsuccessful government management, regardless of cause and time.

Although the crisis of 1977 and the consequences of the Russian war of aggression are not comparable in terms of the facts of the case, there is a historical similarity: In both cases, a federal government was or is facing an unprecedented challenge. Both events were and are unique in their own way.

Today, contemporary historians agree that the German Autumn was a kind of second birth of the state of the West German Republic. Because of the tragic-happy brokenness of its beginning. And the beginning of the examination of its prehistory. This also included the examination of the motives of the murdering perpetrators. There is no question that they were ruthless criminals. Some of them had surprising backgrounds. The terrorist Gudrun Ensslin, for example, was a student scholarship holder of the German National Academic Foundation before her time in the RAF. She came from a Swabian pastor's house.

Those born later have no idea of the collective fear that grips the country in 1977, the year of terror, and especially in its autumn. Fortunately, not. In all major cities, there are police checkpoints on transport routes or in front of bridges. Respectable citizens are taken out of cars and trains, put up against a wall and frisked. Armoured vehicles patrol the government district in Bonn. In the foyers of government offices and post offices, wanted posters are displayed with photos of the wanted terrorists. After one of them is arrested, someone crosses out their portrait with a felt-tip pen.

Intellectuals such as Golo Mann and journalists from the "Frankfurter Allgemeine Zeitung" newspaper bring up the introduction of the death penalty. Asked by a television crew citizens in Stuttgart-Stammheim, where the first generation of leaders of the *Rote Armee Fraktion* are imprisoned,[3] want to "shoot RAF members as they flee" or "hang them from the nearest

---

[3] A court building was erected specifically for the terrorist trials on the grounds of the Stuttgart-Stammheim prison.

tree". The Lord Mayor of Stuttgart, Manfred Rommel, is asked in a retirement home "whether we old people can be protected from the terrorists and be allowed to live a little longer".[4]

News programmes of ARD and ZDF, the West German main channels, show video messages from Hanns Martin Schleyer, the kidnapped president of the employers' association, who appears both calm and distraught in his hostage situation. Weeks later, images of a hijacked Lufthansa plane go around the world. It stands in the scorching heat at the airport in the Emirate of Dubai. Flight captain Jürgen Schumann is sitting at the open door at the front left, the leader of the terrorists is pointing a pistol at him. A scene like in a movie. Indeed a violent crime committed before the eyes of the world.

Days later, the Boeing 737 "Landshut", which was only built for short-haul flights, reaches the Horn of Africa. The airport of Mogadishu, the capital of Somalia. At 6.32 a.m. German time, something is lowered down the emergency chute at the rear right-hand door of the aircraft. It turns out to be the body of Jürgen Schumann. The leader of the terror squad had shot him in cold blood. After dark, members of the GSG9, ("Border Guard Unit 9"), a special unit of the Federal Border Guard, storm the plane and free all the hostages. Three of the four members of the terrorist commando are killed during the operation. A female terrorist survives with serious injuries.

The year of terror, 1977, strikes at the very heart of the identity of the only 28-year-old Federal Republic of Germany. Since the 1960s, it has been regarded as the scene of an unprecedented "economic miracle". The rump state from the former Western occupation zones recovers unexpectedly quickly from the devastation of the world war. Despite two economic crises in the mid-1960s and early 1970s, West Germans have more money in their pockets every year. Their weekly working hours are steadily decreasing. At the same time, there are more and more holidays for the proverbial best weeks of the year, for example in Italy, the former Yugoslavia or on the Spanish island of Majorca.

Consumerism and prosperity create opponents. Enemies. Since the end of the 1960s, members of the Rote Armee Fraktion, men and women who want to bomb away this democratic, liberal, economically successful state, have appeared on the scene. In the guise of a crude left-wing extremist theory—the country's labour force is to be won over to the revolution through acts of violence—they set off bombs in department stores, the supposed temples of consumption. Later, they kidnap or murder representatives of this state. In 1977, they do so with unprecedented frequency and brutality.

---

[4] Rommel 1998, p. 268.

In this situation, where politics and the public are looking into an abyss, Helmut Schmidt, as the book will show, is not the crisis manager in the sense of a lonely, tough decision-maker. Never before and never since has the Federal Republic been governed as consensually as in the German Autumn. The Federal Chancellor decides nothing alone. Contrary to his personal impatience in meetings ("No jellyfish fat, please!"), he allows discussions to take place in the crisis teams. Helmut Schmidt, described as "the lonely pilot", "the fearless helmsman"? Myths that political friends attributed to him, and journalists from Die Zeit, for example, attributed to him for decades, and which he himself will nurture throughout his life.

Helmut Schmidt's achievements in the German Autumn lie elsewhere. He takes politics and the public with him emotionally. He moderates, calms the frightened people with his rationality of expression and action. He is the best of his time at this. His moderating style of leadership, which includes his cleverly applied "muzzles" for opposition politicians, remains a historic achievement.

The narrative can draw on many previously inaccessible and even unknown sources. These include very early, highly authentic sources such as the board minutes of German Lufthansa on the handling of the "Landshut" drama. It also draws on conversations held immediately after the event with those for whom the event is still fresh in their minds, full of fear.

The "Landshut" stewardess Gabriele von Lutzau (née Dillmann) and co-pilot Jürgen Vietor, for example, talk directly after the event in an interview with "Stern"[5] reporter Gerd Heidemann and in individual and group discussions in front of Lufthansa executives out of palpable dismay. In the following year, Monika Schumann, the widow of the murdered captain, authentically characterises her husband's personality and thus provides a key to Jürgen Schumann's behaviour on the hijacked flight. Freed "Landshut" hostages give interviews to Südwestfunk editor Ebbo Demant in 1981 with an atmospheric density that will not be repeated in later years.

There are also previously unreleased interviews with contemporary witnesses and decision-makers in Bonn during the German Autumn. The historian Dorothea Hauser led them for a research project at the request of the Helmut and Loki Schmidt Foundation. With one exception, these interviews, in which the interviewees did not mince their words, were included in the manuscript.

I myself was also lucky enough to meet people affected by the German Autumn—members of the Schleyer family, former "Landshut" hostages and

---

[5] One of the leading West German magazines.

their liberators—for book and film projects. In 2017, after years of preparatory work, I succeeded in persuading the German government to bring the hijacked plane back to Germany from Brazil. When it arrived in two Antonov planes a few days before the 2017 federal election, many of those affected were also there.

This sheds lighter than ever on the perpetrators and victims of the crimes during the German Autumn, on the actions of the Federal Government and their political friends and opponents. How exactly does the Federal Chancellor lead in the thick of it? Who supported Helmut Schmidt in his toughest test, who let him down? Where do those responsible in Bonn show clear-sightedness, what do they misjudge? The book provides answers to these questions—surprises included.

At the same time, it provides an insight into the government apparatus of the Federal Republic of Germany at that time. In the age of dial telephones, telex machines and IBM ballpoint *(Kugelkopf)* typewriters—decades before computers, mobile phones and the Internet will become part of the technical armoury in Bonn and Berlin. All government action took place under the conditions of the technology available at the time, with its possibilities and limitations, opportunities and dangers.

Even in 1977, contemporary technology ensured that the events surrounding the kidnapping of *Arbeitgeberpräsident* ("president of the employer's association") Hanns Martin Schleyer and the "Landshut" aircraft were well documented. Schleyer's kidnappers contributed with video messages from their hostage, along wirth numerous written messages and phone calls, to the documentation.

The radio traffic between the airport tower and the hijacked "Landshut" in Mogadishu is not only recorded by the Somalis (on West German Uher tape recorders), but also by the American foreign intelligence service, the CIA. Because the Somalis do not want to give the Germans any copies, the Americans step in. "I have just received from Washington copies (…). I hope you and your colleagues will find them of some use."[6] Shortly after the event, this transcript of the talks is sent to the magazine "Stern". The magazine will print it in full.

Lufthansa's internal radio traffic between Frankfurt and Mogadishu has remained unknown to this day. It is a document of despair that found by chance its way onto a tape recorder belonging to hobby radio operator

---

[6] Letter from George A. Carver Jr. (member of the American Embassy in Bonn) to Horst Herold dated 9 December 1977, in: BArch 136/16982.

Ludwig Hildebrand. He has made a transcript of these disturbing dialogues available for this book for the first time.[7]

The extensive documentation of the "Landshut" drama and the German Autumn is helped by another rather sad circumstance: the division of Germany into two states. When schoolboy Franz Joepgen—his grandparents were on the hijacked "Landshut"—ordered the Stasi files on the "Landshut" hijacking from the now defunct "Birthler Authority", he received a thick parcel weeks later—including many documents that can also be found in Helmut Schmidt's legendary "War Diary" (more about this later).

The documents show that the Stasi read along enthusiastically and in an alarming amount during the German Autumn. Employees in Helmut Schmidt's office passed on documents—scenarios or criminal reports—from Bonn directly to East Berlin. Decades later, Georg Bönisch and Sven Röbel provide a fact-filled and exciting account of this chapter of German-German espionage.[8]

The book also sheds light on the dual nature of the Federal Republic of Germany at the time—economically a world power, politically a dwarf. In the German autumn, Chancellor Helmut Schmidt embodied toughness and determination. On the international stage he was a supplicant who was rebuffed. The Italian government wanted to get rid of the hijacked "Landshut" as quickly as possible after it landed in Rome, while the British government refused to allow the GSG9 task force onto one of its military bases. While German Chancellor Helmut Schmidt is on the phone to an Arab sheikh to detain the "Landshut" at Dubai airport, the sheikh signals that the aircraft may take off.

Thanks to years of hard work and lively consumer behaviour, the West Germans may have successfully suppressed the fact that their state was only 28 years young in 1977—but the rest of the world does not. Helmut Schmidt leads a rump Germany under the supervision of the victorious Western powers of the Second World War. In official parlance, they are called allies. In reality, they are occupiers. In terms of foreign policy, a German Chancellor has to coordinate every significant step with them.

Against this historical background, the Federal Republic of Germany is not diplomatically represented in many places in the mid-1970s. There is no West German ambassador in the United Arab Emirates, one of the "Landshut" hijacking destinations. In Aden, the penultimate stop of the hijacked "Landshut", there is an ambassador from the GDR. In Somalia, where the

---

[7] Hildebrand 1977.
[8] See Bönisch/Röbel 2021.

"Landshut" ends its odyssey, the entourage of Minister of State, Hans-Jürgen Wischnewski, has to hand in their passports.

The hijacking of the Lufthansa aircraft "Landshut" has an international dimension because of the Palestinian hijackers. It makes frequent stops on its errant flight on different continents. Pope Paul VI offers himself as a hostage in exchange for the women, men and children on the plane. Towards the end of the hostage drama, the whole world knows the fate of the kidnapped people.

The book also examines the foreign and domestic policy consequences of the German Autumn. "Mogadishu" unexpectedly opens the door to new regions of the world for the small Federal Republic. The Federal Republic makes peace with Yasser Arafat's Palestine Liberation Organisation, which leads to a rift with the Israeli government. Helmut Schmidt travels to the Saudi Arabian capital Riyadh, where the sheikhs express their interest in the German "Leopard II" tank. (Helmut Schmidt is in favour of the armour project, Federal Foreign Minister Hans-Dietrich Genscher is against it—finally, it won't materialise.) The Federal Chancellor secures arms deliveries to Somalia from Egyptian President Anwar es-Sadat, as Somalia is at war with its neighbour Ethiopia. In the negotiations for the release of the US embassy staff in Iran, German diplomats—including the German Chancellor himself—are playing a meditating role.[9] After the German Autumn, "Bonn" finally dances on the world political stage.

In terms of domestic policy, the alleged restriction of fundamental rights in the German Autumn turns into its opposite. The Federal Minister of Justice, Hans-Jochen Vogel, obtains funding from the cabinet to have the motives of the RAF terrorists scientifically investigated for the first time. The resigning Federal Minister of the Interior, Werner Maihofer, is succeeded by the free-thinking, more talented politically Gerhard Baum. Under him, the President of the Federal Criminal Police Office, Horst Herold, soon resigns.

As the book will show, the German Autumn forced the Helmut Schmidt generation to retire early from top political offices. In the long term, the consequences are even epochal. Decades later, a Federal Foreign Minister Joschka Fischer (Greens) would presumably not have been possible without the intellectual and constitutional debate that followed the German Autumn. Similarly, a Federal Minister of the Interior like Otto Schily (first Greens, then SPD), once a defence attorney for terrorists in the Stammheim trial, would not have been possible.

---

[9] See Bötsch 2015.

In the way the German government deals with the freed but traumatised hostages and their relatives, the decision-makers in "Mogadishu"—Minister of State Hans-Jürgen Wischnewski, the head of the Federal Chancellery Manfred Schüler, even Chancellor Helmut Schmidt himself—remain children of their time. They treat those affected as insurance cases. With little to no empathy. After all, according to the prevailing opinion, we had them taken out of the machine at great risk—what more do they want?

This book is therefore also about the triumph and tragedy of the Helmut Schmidt generation. Her members were the last ones with nerves of steel. The triumph could not be achieved without the tragedy. At the moment of their greatest achievement, their either/or thinking is proving to be a hindrance to a successful political future. A political drama that only life itself can write.

In almost five decades, legends have overgrown the events of the German Autumn like weeds in a garden that has never been tended. Even at the very beginning, there were bad publications that were hastily cobbled together, such as the "Stern" magazine series of articles and the later book by Kai Hermann and Peter Koch[10]. The "Stern" book, which became the reference book, is teeming with factual errors, as "Landshut" co-pilot Jürgen Vietor[11] and the purserette of the hijacking flight, Hannelore Brauchardt (née Piegler)[12] will prove early on.

After the German Autumn, the German government and German Lufthansa quite understandably want to create the impression that they have done everything right. Over the years, former hostages will remember events differently or not anymore. The surviving terrorist Souhaila Andrawes will minimise her guilt in court. Journalists add new stories every few years so that their book or feature film will also be a success.

The decades-long myth-building culminated in the 2008 feature film "Mogadishu", produced by Nico Hofmann with a screenplay by Maurice Philip Remy. The public-sector spent millions of euros on the film. Nico Hofmann, who is well connected with the TV film decision-makers in public television, is allowed to make the film without any external reason—such as a round date or a retelling based on previously unknown sources.

It is not contemporary history speaking to Hofmann and Remy, but rather the two speaking to it. The plot for presumably high viewing figures is that Lufthansa captain Jürgen Schumann had to die for his heroic behaviour on

---

[10] Cf. Hermann/Koch 1977.
[11] CF analysis of the "Landshut" hijacking of 19 December 1977, p. 2f.
[12] Letter from Hannelore Piegler to Christa Schmiedl FRA NB 54 dated 23 January 1978.

the hijacking flight. Jürgen Schumann knowingly took high risks, as the book will show.

This book provides a clear view of the actual, historically documented events. I leave nothing out, despite the drastic nature of some of the sources. Contemporary history must tell what happened. The hostages experienced an ordeal on the border between life and death. It was even worse than the image we have of it so far.

The following pages are guided by my deep respect for the victims of the German Autumn and their families. For the Schleyer family's ability to suffer and her great loss. For the Schumann family with her great loss. For the will to survive of the children, women and men in the hijacked "Landshut". And in continuing to live with the trauma afterwards.

Hopefully the book will reach many readers from generations who did not experience the German Autumn themselves. Those who were spared the fearful experience of the German Autumn should know the facts as younger people. They provide information about the continuing terrorist threat to which the old Federal Republic was exposed then as now. And about the vulnerability of the free and democratic basic order then as now.

This makes it all the more incomprehensible that the Federal Government is still allowed to keep important sources secret, such as the minutes of the Bonn crisis teams *Kleine Lage* ("Short Briefing") and *Großer politischer Beratungskreis* ("Large Political Advisory Group"). This is regularly confirmed by judgements of the Federal Court of Justice. Stereotypically, the court cites as a reason that these protocols supposedly reveal the reaction of politicians and the police to a terrorist threat situation.

I do not like to believe that. The decision-makers responsible in the autumn of 1977 didn't have mobile phones, they had rotary dial telephones. No PCs, but mechanical or electric typewriters. No Internet, but telex for transmitting documents. Modern technology allows for modern and therefore incomparably better routines. A lot has also changed in terms of police tactics in almost 50 years.

I was able to reconstruct quite a lot that is under lock and key. The head of the Federal Criminal Police Office, Horst Herold, for example, discussed in all seriousness in the Short Briefing and the Large Political Advisory Group whether and which suspicious homes should be under surveillance or raided. He turned the gentlemen in the meeting room into fellow investigators. That was clever. This meant that failures in the manhunt did not go home with him alone. And the co-investigators were busy, felt important. They didn't leak information, as is the common practice today.

The investigation files of the Federal Criminal Police Office in Wiesbaden are also not accessible. The then-President Horst Herold handed them over to the Karlsruhe Federal Public Prosecutor's Office in the year following the German Autumn. Provided with a list of file numbers. These files, too, are off-limits to anyone with the stereotypical reasoning that it is an ongoing investigation. The Federal Prosecutor could close the case after almost 50 years. However, he either does not want to or is not allowed to.

In my opinion, the sovereignty and self-confidence of a democratic constitutional state is also expressed in the willingness of the federal government and federal authorities to disclose past actions. Politicians must have the last say here, not the police.

Editorial Notes

The spelling of personal names, such as those of political leaders in Dubai or Aden, may differ from the spelling in other articles or books.

The leader of the "Landshut" terror commando is mentioned once by his full name. I then use the pseudonym he chose himself, "Captain Machmud". Freed hostages used this name immediately after their liberation, and most of them still do today. The pseudonym makes it clear that those affected remember the head of the terror squad less as a person with a first name and surname than as a diabolical monster.

The women from the liberated "Landshut" are referred to by their names after their marriages. This is followed in brackets by the maiden or married name from 1977, which places the narrative in the present but makes it clear that the traumatic events are in the past.

The hijacked "Landshut" has flown through various time zones. All time references in this book are based on Central European Time. This takes account of the fact that Chancellor Helmut Schmidt naturally held talks and made decisions in West German time. Where the time difference between Central Europe and the Arab or African region is significant, this is mentioned. Co-pilot Jürgen Vietor, for example, tries to stay as long as possible in Aden with the "Landshut" so that the aircraft with broken landing lights can reach the next airport in daylight.

Some sources are reproduced verbatim as they have been handed down. Telegrams, minutes. This is intended to shed some atmospheric light on the transmission of messages at this time.

The so-called Operation Diary of Federal Chancellor Helmut Schmidt is, in terms of file technology, a case of "cabbage and turnips". The Chancellor had the material compiled but not further organised. Some of it, including the important cover pages of the files, is difficult or even impossible to decipher after almost five decades. I received two data carriers several years apart, and the problem occurs with both. Apparently, pages are lost due to the poor quality of the paper. Early reproduction techniques proved to be perishable.

The manuscript has been compiled over many years from studies of files in archives, conversations with protagonists and accompanying academic research. Nevertheless, it cannot be free of factual errors and personal mistakes. I would like to apologise for them.

2

Crime with an Announcement

Cologne

The year 1977 begins badly for Helmut Schmidt. After the parliamentary elections in October 1976, the social-liberal coalition can only continue with a narrow majority. Right at the beginning, it makes a serious mistake with the "pension debacle"—a promised pension increase is cancelled by Helmut Schmidt due to new figures. Later, under pressure from his own parliamentary group, it finally materialised. At the turn of 1976/77, the federal government's poll ratings are in the basement.

During his winter holiday on the island of Marbella, the Federal Chancellor gathers his thoughts for a new start. Helmut Schmidt writes "Considerations for 1977",[1] as he calls his paper, in which he analyses the role of the Federal Republic of Germany in the world and outlines future government tasks. Initially, only the SPD chairman Willy Brandt and Herbert Wehner, chairman of the SPD parliamentary group, receive the "Considerations". Helmut Schmidt incorporates their comments and sends the papier to the members of the SPD parliamentary group on 10 April 1977.

There is not a word about internal security in the "Considerations". Apparently, the Federal Chancellor did not see any terrorist threat at the beginning of 1977. Fortunately, there were no attacks by left-wing terrorists in 1976. They were preparing actions for 1977, as will become clear in the spring.

---

[1] HSA 1/HSAA006567, typescript.

On 7 April, members of the Red Army Faction shot and killed Federal Prosecutor General Siegfried Buback, his driver Wolfgang Göbel and the head of the Federal Prosecutor's Office's motor pool, Georg Wurster, in Karlsruhe. On the open road, at a red light. Georg Wurster had spontaneously got into the car as a passenger. The images of the bodies on the road, covered with makeshift covers, caused grief and horror. At Siegfried Buback's funeral, Federal Chancellor Helmut Schmidt reaffirmed the defence of West German democracy against its enemies.

On 30 July 1977, Jürgen Ponto, CEO of Dresdner Bank, was abducted from his home in Oberursel near Frankfurt am Main. His goddaughter Susanne Albrecht had announced her visit and arrived at the door with flowers. She brings two friends with her, in reality RAF members like herself. There is a scuffle with Jürgen Ponto, during which he is shot. Two hours later, he succumbs to his injuries in hospital.

5 September 1977, 5.28 p.m. Hanns Martin Schleyer, President of the Employers' Association, is on his way to his official residence in Cologne. Sitting next to him in the S-Class Mercedes is his driver Heinz Marcisz and police officer Reinhold Brändle in the back seat. Behind them, they are accompanied by a Mercedes W123 with police officer Helmut Ulmer as driver and Roland Pieler as co-driver. The cars reach Vinzenz-Statz-Straße. They then want to turn onto Aachener Straße to the building where Hanns Martin Schleyer, his driver and the bodyguards each live.

It doesn't come to that. A blue pram is rolled onto the road in front of Schleyer's car. Heinz Marcisz brakes sharply, the small Mercedes hits the big one. Five people form a semi-circle around the two cars and shoot at Schleyer's escort with submachine guns. Another one drags the 62-year-old out of the car to a white VW bus waiting at the corner of Friedrich-Schmidt-Straße. The seventh person involved in the crime is at the wheel. Schleyer is injected with a tranquiliser. Then it's a breakneck drive to his first hiding place.

Schleyer's driver and the two policemen have no chance of survival, given the brutality of the perpetrators. However, the policemen in the escort car can offer little resistance. Their submachine guns are in the boot. Roland Pieler is 20 years old, Helmut Ulmer 24. Reinhold Brändle, 41, does not appear to have asked the two of them to carry their weapons in their neighbourhood. Yet their protégé Hanns Martin Schleyer has been classified as security level 1 ("seriously endangered; an attack is to be expected") since 2 August 1977.[2]

---

[2] The failure of police officers, their own part in their tragic deaths, was not addressed back then.

A massive police failure, which the highest police officer in the country, the head of the Federal Criminal Police Office Horst Herold, will of course deny. He will be told by Hanns Martin Schleyer himself, from his captivity. For good reason, the employer president felt that he had been amateurishly protected before and during his kidnapping.

A passer-by has memorised the registration number of the white VW bus, K–C 3849, and the "heute" news programme is searching for the car. The car has long been parked in an underground car park in Cologne, far away from where Hanns Martin Schleyer is being hidden. A passer-by notices the bus and alerts the police. Officers find the kidnappers' first message in the car:

"to the federal government.

You will ensure that all public searches are cancelled or we will shoot schleyer immediately without any negotiations about his release. raf."[3]

The terrorists want to use Schleyer's abduction to free eleven of his comrades from prison: Andreas Baader, Gudrun Ensslin, Jan-Carl Raspe, Verena Becker, Werner Hoppe, Karl-Heinz Dellwo, Hanna Krabbe, Bernhard Rössner, Ingrid Schubert and Irmgard Möller as well as Günter Sonnenberg, who was seriously injured during his arrest and is unfit to stand trial.

Baader, Ensslin and Raspe are among the RAF founding members. They and Becker are imprisoned in Stuttgart-Stammheim. Journalism therefore writes of the *Stammheimer* ("Stammheimers").

The capitals of Somalia, South Yemen and Vietnam are named for their deportation. Nevertheless, the "Stammheimers" are to decide for themselves where all those released are to be flown out to.

Stuttgart

Hanns Martin Schleyer's wife Waltrude and their four sons, Hanns-Eberhard, Arndt, Dirk and Jörg, gather in their house on Ginsterweg in Stuttgart after hearing the shocking news. The 32-year-old lawyer Hanns-Eberhard Schleyer, considerably older than his brothers, knows that he must now take responsibility. Speaking for the family.

The Schleyers are deeply shocked by the kidnapping of their father, but not really surprised. Unlike the murders of Federal Prosecutor General Siegfried Buback and his companions, unlike the attempted kidnapping

---

[3] Press and Information Office of the Federal Government 1977, p. 13.

of Jürgen Ponto, Hanns Martin Schleyer's abduction is a crime with an agenda. According to police information, the employer president is one of the most endangered persons in the Federal Republic of Germany as mentioned. The residential building was fitted with bullet-proof windows for the occasion/for this reason, against which Hanns Martin Schleyer's wife protested unsuccessfully.

When the Schleyer family is on holiday in their own holiday home on Lake Constance in the summer of 1977, unknown people appear in the neighbourhood. Residents thought this was strange and alerted the local police. There are no consequences. In fact, Mr and Mrs Schleyer and their four boys are under round-the-clock surveillance by RAF terrorists.

Former members of the police service in the 1970s tell us why: poor training, poor commitment to duty, sloppiness in investigations. The West German police see themselves as "your friend and helper". In fact, they have the clout of a cucumber squad.

There is a mixture of guilelessness and repression in the family on this last holiday together. "We just couldn't imagine it",[4] the eldest son Hanns-Eberhard Schleyer would say decades later, referring to the threat to his father. He remembers his summer holiday in Meersburg on Lake Constance in 1977 as peaceful and relaxing as ever.

Hanns Martin Schleyer devotes all his time on holiday to his family. Even if the beefy man with the puffy lips doesn't look it, Hanns Martin Schleyer has a big heart. Not just for his wife and children. He helps wherever he can. He is completely devoid of arrogance.

The endangered person himself can very well imagine a kidnapping or an attack. He is one of the leading representatives of West German business. Politics is a compliant accomplice of big business, not a few leftists and left-wing extremists are convinced of this at the time. They count the president of the employers' association, Hanns Martin Schleyer, among the real powerholders in the country.

Schleyer does not hide his thoughts about this from his family. Just as he is not afraid to talk about his time under National Socialism. In terms of age, only Hanns-Eberhard is old enough to fully engage with his father.

Hanns Martin Schleyer reveals to Hanns-Eberhard that he would like the German government to make a quick decision in the event of a kidnapping. He doesn't want to be held off for long, but rather a short period of uncertainty, whatever the outcome. That is how he thinks this summer, and that is how he will think in the German Autumn.

---

[4] Conversation with the author on 25 August 2022.

It is possible that the outward calm of the holidays intensified Hanns Martin Schleyer's inner turmoil. Back in Stuttgart and Cologne, he tries to take his fate into his own hands. Hanns Martin Schleyer travels to Chancellor Helmut Schmidt, who is on holiday in his own holiday home at Lake Brahmsee in Schleswig–Holstein. The two are not political friends, but reliability is an important virtue for both of them. Once a commitment has been made, it stands! Both also share a tendency to speak plainly.

Hanns Martin Schleyer reveals his fear of being kidnapped in a conversation with the Federal Chancellor. He asks Helmut Schmidt to arrange an appointment for him with the President of the Federal Criminal Police Office, Horst Herold. The employer president wants to talk to the highest German police officer about his own protection.

Back in Bonn, Helmut Schmidt follows this request and informs Horst Herold's office. It is summer. Holiday time. Appointments are more difficult to make than earlier or later in the year. Horst Herold is also on holiday in Bavaria.

On 5 September 1977, Helmut Schmidt—as Horst Herold would later report—wrote: "Talk to Herold."[5] Hours later, Hanns Martin Schleyer is already in the hands of his kidnappers. Horst Herold breaks off his holiday and hurries to Bonn.

Once in the first hiding place, Hanns Martin Schleyer has to move into a cupboard. The terrorists had built it especially for him—spacious enough to line with mattresses. No sound from Schleyer may escape. The kidnappers and the victim live in a spacious high-rise flat with many parties, where things are anonymous.

The 62-year-old is now sitting or lying in his prison and willingly provides information to the men and women who question him about the "shitty state" of the Federal Republic of Germany. Not out of opportunism, but because that's how he "ticks". Communicative, self-critical, a good listener. He will not turn out to be the political lord of the manor that his kidnappers thought he was. And he shows the father who longs for his family.

"So I'm still here", Hanns Martin Schleyer was allowed to write laconically to his son Hanns-Eberhard the day after the kidnapping, on 8 September 1977.

---

[5] Herold/Hauser, p. 17.

Bonn

The first emergency call on the day of the attack is received at 5.33 p.m. The Federal Chancellor is informed shortly after 6.00 p.m. In the following hours and on the following day, Helmut Schmidt consults with Federal Foreign Minister and Vice-Chancellor Hans-Dietrich Genscher, Federal Interior Minister Werner Maihofer, Federal Justice Minister Hans-Jochen Vogel, Minister of State Hans-Jürgen Wischnewski, the Head of the Federal Chancellery, State Secretary Manfred Schüler, the Government Spokesman, State Secretary Klaus Bölling and the President of the Federal Criminal Police Office, Horst Herold.

It could have remained with this handful of technically responsible individuals. But between the evening of Hanns Martin Schleyer's abduction and the afternoon of the following day, Helmut Schmidt devises a different approach. He presumably fears that his time and energy would henceforth be taken up not only by Hanns Martin Schleyer's kidnappers, but also by CDU/CSU politicians on the opposition bench in the Bundestag.

Opposition leader Helmut Kohl (CDU) has already delivered a foretaste. On the evening of Hanns Martin Schleyer's kidnapping, he made a statement on Second German Television at 9.00 p.m. It's tenor: "We must all realize now that it is five minutes to twelve (...) to finally put an end to this intolerable danger (of RAF terrorism, editor's note) to our internal freedom."[6]

The statement may have been personally motivated—Hanns Martin Schleyer and Helmut Kohl are friends. At the same time, it seems inappropriate at this point (in time). Before Chancellor Helmut Schmidt knows it—his televised speech is broadcast at 9.30 p.m.—Helmut Kohl has beaten him to it.

Helmut Schmidt's statement on television is nothing less than great statesmanship. Plain-text sentences to the point, delivered with horror and determination. Helmut Schmidt looks serious and menacing. He comes across as authentic. Helmut Schmidt as the man who was at war. Now it's war again.

He addresses "the enemy", as he calls the terrorists in the Short Briefing, directly. "As I speak here", Helmut Schmidt says verbatim, "the guilty perpetrators are certainly listening somewhere. (...) They should not be deceived. (...) Not only the will of the state organs stands against terrorism, but the will of the whole people also stands against terrorism."[7] This is reference

---

[6] Press and Information Office of the Federal Government 1977, p. 13.
[7] Ibid. p. 3 of the appendix section.

to the crude RAF strategy of using terror to incite the people against the government.

The Federal Chancellor sets up two advisory bodies: [8] Helmut Schmidt's closest advisors, including the head of the Federal Chancellery, Manfred Schüler, his government spokesman Klaus Bölling, Justice Minister Hans-Jochen Vogel, the President of the Federal Criminal Police Office, Horst Herold, and Federal Prosecutor General Kurt Rebmann, belong to the *Kleine Lage* (Short Briefing). He appoints the party and parliamentary group chairmen of all parties represented in the German Bundestag to a *Großer politischer Beratungskreis* (Large Political Advisory Group) as well as the minister presidents of the states in which RAF terrorists who are to be released are imprisoned. Journalists soon dubbed these meetings as mentioned Short Briefing and Large Political Advisory Group.

Both advisory boards are inventions of Helmut Schmidt. The Basic Law provides for a so-called Federal Security Council for special security policy situations, which advises the Federal Chancellor on matters of external, not internal, security. It is an irony of history that Helmut Schmidt's office has been planning an exercise for a military emergency since the spring of 1977. The members of the Federal Security Council were to be called into the bug-proof NATO room of the Federal Chancellery to test communication under alarm conditions. The staff of the Federal Chancellery had recently moved into a new building, the security technology was ultra-modern, but not yet fully tested.

Files in the federal archives in Koblenz prove that there are exact alarm plans with prepared telephone numbers. The exercise is due to take place in late summer this year. The actual "Offensive 77" by the Red Army Faction renders the simulation obsolete. Reality catches up with it in a bloody way.

Federal Chancellor Helmut Schmidt prepares decisions in the Short Briefing. In the Large Political Advisory Group he virtually integrates the second political ring around the Federal Chancellery. The construction is intended to silence day-to-day political disputes. Presumably Helmut Schmidt fears that debates in the Federal Parliament about his government's decisions could fuel the agitated public mood. At the same time, the Federal Chancellor holds political friends and opponents accountable. They must remain silent so that the so-called news blackout against the press and radio—one of several decisions on the verge of constitutionality—holds.

The advisory groups are created in the spirit of carrots and sticks—involving political Bonn and at the same time holding it accountable.

---

[8] For a detailed critique of Schmidt's approach, see Kraushaar 2006.

Allowing debates and channelling them at the same time. Emphasising one's own role as the final decision-maker and at the same time shifting some of the responsibility. In a nutshell, the Federal Chancellor is putting political friends and opponents to the test.

Kaiser Wilhelm II's exclamation at the beginning of the First World War inevitably comes to mind: "I no longer know any parties. I only know Germans."

Only a "trained democrat"[9] could come up with the idea that two advisory groups that do not comply with the Basic Law help to protect the constitutional state from its enemies. (This also applies to the de facto restriction of fundamental rights, which will be discussed later. Helmut Schmidt holds an important office in a democracy, but he was politically socialised in a dictatorship. As well as he later learns and practices the craft of a democrat, deviating thought patterns remain. In this case, he quickly reorganises the political Bonn for his crisis management.

It is up to Federal Minister of Justice Hans-Jochen Vogel to justify the *Kleine Lage* and the *Großer politischer Beratungskreis* as being compatible with the Basic Law. The only suitable defence for this justification is to point out that the legal assessment of political action never takes place in a vacuum, but always in a specific situation. This will also apply weeks later to the Federal Constitutional Court's decision on an urgent appeal by the Schleyer family.

Helmut Schmidt's invention of two crisis teams does not cause any offence in Bonn, on the contrary. Most of the decision-makers at the time are "trained democrats" and therefore free of scruples. The chairman of the CSU parliamentary group in the German Bundestag, Friedrich Zimmermann, sees the crisis task force, as the committee will soon be known, as "a kind of experiment—and probably also for the government."[10] Why would Friedrich Zimmermann refuse? Although on the opposition bench, he now has a strong political voice.

There are only doubts and objections in Helmut Schmidt's inner circle. His most important colleague, the head of the Federal Chancellery Manfred Schüler, advises against this strategy. Manfred Schüler is an intellectually brilliant mind who runs the government apparatus quietly. An introverted, cautious man. He argues that the search for the Schleyer kidnappers should remain in the hands of the responsible cabinet members, Federal Minister of the Interior Werner Maihofer and Federal Minister of Justice Hans-Jochen

---

[9] Cf. Stephan 1988.
[10] Hauser/Zimmermann, p 2.

Vogel. By virtue of his office, the Federal Chancellor is to remain in charge of the investigation. The manhunt for the kidnappers may succeed or fail, Hanns Martin Schleyer may come out of the affair alive or dead—politically, this should not go home with the Federal Chancellor.

Helmut Schmidt's party colleague Heinz Ruhnau, State Secretary in the Federal Ministry of Transport, also warns: "You must not make yourself the nation's detective commissioner here."[11] Heinz Ruhnau fears that the Federal Government will be mainly preoccupied with the Schleyer kidnapping case in the coming period. That important domestic and foreign policy issues will be neglected.

Heinz Ruhnau is right with this prediction. Helmut Schmidt's Minister of State in the Federal Chancellery, Hans-Jürgen Wischnewski, will concede after the German Autumn that "we have largely let our government work slip".[12]

Helmut Schmidt sticks to his opinion. He knows about his political leadership in crises. And that the Germans trust him, since he is known as the crisis manager. Regardless of his behaviour at the time, they regard him as a multiple lifesaver in the Hamburg storm surge of 1962, as a reformer of the Bundeswehr and a saviour of the state finances (as Federal Minister of Defence and as Super Minister of Economics and Finance).

Added to this is Helmut Schmidt's strong self-confidence: He considers himself to be the best in Bonn (and presumably not only there). Why leave it to weaker men in the field? He would be fuming if Maihofer and Vogel mess it up.

As far as the Federal Minister of the Interior is concerned, Helmut Schmidt's assessment seems justified in retrospect. Werner Maihofer was not a man of action, his successor in office, Gerhard Baum would say decades later. "Meetings took a very long time. It was no coincidence that the Federal Chancellor took the reins out of his hands. That would never have happened to Genscher (Federal Foreign Minister, previously Federal Interior Minister, editor's note) as Interior Minister."[13]

Hans-Dietrich Genscher is originally a member of Helmut Schmidt's Short Briefing, together with his FDP party colleague Burkhard Hirsch, the Interior Minister of North Rhine-Westphalia, where Red Army Fraction members were also imprisoned. Both names disappear from the list of participants after

---

[11] Ruhnau/Hauser, p. 6.
[12] Wischnewski/Hauser, p. 37.
[13] Interview Baum/Treuter 2017b.

a few days.[14] Helmut Schmidt does not want any FDP colleagues in his inner circle.

The chairman of the FDP parliamentary group in the Bundestag, Wolfgang Mischnick, is allowed to be a member of the Large Political Advisory Group. Schmidt trusts Mischnick, considers him reliable unlike Genscher and Hirsch.

Helmut Schmidt himself is the "nation's crime commissioner". He makes not the Federal Minister of the Interior, but BKA chief Horst Herold, a member of the SPD, his most important advisor. The joint task is nothing less than waging and winning a war.

Over the years, the RAF has waged a civil war against Bonn politics, and now—according to most of the players in Bonn—a kind of decisive battle is about to begin. "The enemy" even gives his troops a name. The RAF members who prepare and carry out Hanns Martin Schleyer's kidnapping call themselves *Kommando Siegfried Hausner* "Command Siegfried Hausner." Siegfried Hausner was one of the RAF terrorists who occupied the German embassy in Stockholm. He was seriously injured and later died of his injuries in the prison hospital in Stuttgart-Stammheim.

Andreas Baader and co, the RAF prisoners there, do not see themselves as criminals or even murderers, but rather stylise themselves as freedom fighters who want to destroy—as they see it—a capitalist, inhumane state order. In their view, the end justifies all means. "And of course it's okay to shoot" is one of the most famous sentences of RAF terrorist Ulrike Meinhof. The aforementioned submachine gun (MP5 model from the West German company Heckler & Koch) is emblazoned in the centre of the RAF logo. This is not an attitude but expresses the RAF members' willingness to kill.

This clearly criminal viewpoint suits the decision-makers in Bonn. The members of Helmut Schmidt's generation got, to use a casual formulation, the full brunt of the Second World War. They took part in it for several years and made a career as non-commissioned officers or officers in the Wehrmacht. They started out as ordinary soldiers. Later they became officers and were assigned to units.

The war was hell on earth and their own personal hell. The soldiers of the Wehrmacht—including later top politicians of the Bonn Republic—took stimulants so that they could advance for days and nights without sleep. They were killed in combat and saw their comrades die. They know the feeling of fear of death. They know the damned duty of not going crazy as superiors, even though their nerves are on edge and their minds threaten to go blank.

---

[14] Note from Division 131 dated 13 September 1977 to Mr Chief BK. Subject: Participants in the discussions on the Schleyer kidnapping, in: Archiv BK 13–211 20 (3) Additional file 3, no p.

After the war, former soldiers will keep to themselves who exactly experienced what. Many won't even talk about it within their own families. In their future top positions as entrepreneurs, lawyers or politicians, they establish language rules so that all questions are silenced for the rest of their lives.

There is a pragmatic reason for this—no politician, scientist or journalist wants to jeopardise their career in the new, democratic state. At the same time, this silence presumably serves as a protective mechanism for the soul. It is concreted over so that it doesn't make a sound. Sometimes the concrete becomes brittle with age. Never in Helmut Schmidt's case.

Eight of the ten members who belonged to the Short Briefing in the German Autumn were in the war. Some of them exercised military command. In detail:

- Klaus Bölling, government spokesman, born in 1928, anti-aircraft helper, released after the arrest of his Jewish mother.
- Günther Erkel, State Secretary in the Federal Ministry of Justice, born '24, soldier, lieutenant.
- Siegfried Fröhlich, State Secretary Federal Ministry of the Interior, born '20, Captain.
- Hans-Dietrich Genscher (Federal Foreign Minister), born '27, private in the last days of the war.
- Horst Herold, President of the Federal Criminal Police Office, born '23, lieutenant, seriously wounded in the war.
- Otto Graf Lambsdorff, born '26, officer candidate (Federal Minister of Economics from 7 October 1977).
- Georg Leber, Federal Minister of Transport, born '20, non-commissioned officer.
- Werner Maihofer, Federal Minister of the Interior, born '18, First Lieutenant.
- Wolfgang Mischnick (Chairman of the FDP parliamentary group in the Bundestag), born '21, Lieutenant.
- Kurt Rebmann, Attorney General, born '24, seriously wounded at the age of 19.
- Helmut Schmidt, Federal Chancellor, born '18, First Lieutenant.
- Franz Josef Strauß (CSU Chairman and Bavarian Minister President), born 15, First Lieutenant.
- Hans-Jochen Vogel, Federal Minister of Justice, born '26, non-commissioned officer, wounded twice.

Back then as soldiers in the world war, in 1977 as defenders of a free and democratic constitutional state, they have to bear responsibility in borderline situations. Functioning in political office. There is no doubt that the personal biographies of these men characterise the atmosphere in the Short Briefing and the Large Political Advisory Group. "As he did during the Hamburg flood disaster, Helmut Schmidt once again spread a general staff atmosphere around him that even the most die-hard civilians could not escape."

As mentioned, there is talk of the "enemy" and the "operational situation". The military-anonymising term "opponent" also appears several times in written notes made by Chancellor Helmut Schmidt during the meetings of the Short Briefing and the Large Political Advisory Group. In doing so, he invokes an old pattern of thought. At the same time, he anonymises the members of the Red Army Faction so as not to feel human compassion.

The perception of the acting politicians and former soldiers in the Wehrmacht of being in a war may appear to be a very male one. In fact, there is not a single woman in the Short Briefing and The Large Political Advisory Group who could weaken such a view or dissuade the men from it. The few women in Bonn politics at the time were concerned with "fuss", as a party colleague and Helmut Schmidt's successor in office, Gerhard Schröder, would say disparagingly years later. About supposedly less important areas of politics.

Meetings—the first of the Large Political Advisory Group late in the evening on day two of Hanns Martin Schleyer's abduction—always follow the same course, labelled with military terms. "Situation of own forces" and "Communication situation with the enemy" are fixed items on the agenda of former First Lieutenant of the Wehrmacht Helmut Schmidt.

In general, the choice of words seems coloured by the tension of these weeks. To describe the later "Landshut" kidnappers, the Federal Chancellor will choose hefty words such as "stupid sheepdogs", "trained sheepdogs" and "trained sheepdogs" in telephone conversations with Minister of State Hans-Jürgen Wischnewski.

The head of the Federal Criminal Police Office, Horst Herold, and Federal Chancellor Helmut Schmidt use the two crisis teams for—to use a modern word—brainstorming. Horst Herold in terms of police tactics, Helmut Schmidt in political terms. They present their personal considerations and put them up for discussion. They listen, weigh up, discard ideas or take them up.

Most of the time, the focus is on measures to trace Hanns Martin Schleyer. Horst Herold reads out messages—if available—from the Schleyer and "Landshut" hijackers and makes suggestions for answers. He reports on the terrorists' movement profile and their possible whereabouts. The police have seized RAF documents and are following up countless tips from the public. The question comes up again and again: Observe a property? Storm it? Horst Herold gets the go-ahead from "Bonn" for every action.

Unfortunately, not for the storming of the flat in Erftstadt-Liblar, Zum Renngraben 8 (flat 104, third floor). The reference to the first Schleyer hiding place, telex 827, never reaches "Soko 77", the responsible investigation team. And thus never Herold. Someone must have taken the Telex out of the box through official channels. This "someone" will probably never be identified.

After Horst Herold's presentation in the crisis units, Helmut Schmidt describes the situation from his point of view. He reports on past telephone conversations with heads of state, has his ministers speak and discusses the next steps for action.

The Short Briefing and the Large Political Advisory Group also serve as discussion forums for fundamental issues. Federal Minister of Justice Hans-Jochen Vogel is having his office examine the possibility of "temporary laws"—meaning temporary laws for a kind of state of emergency, in this case a terrorist threat. They would possibly temporarily suspend laws that affect fundamental rights. A scenario about more than what the German government will allow itself to do in the German Autumn.

Hans-Jochen Vogel's ministry concludes that "temporary laws" are legally possible, but politically difficult to imagine as "emergency laws."

Another study from Hans-Jochen Vogel's ministry lists the legislative levers available to the German government in the fight against RAF terror. For example, the interception of conversations between prisoners and defence lawyers. The list of measures is long. If they were all implemented, the Federal Republic would presumably become a different country.

Helmut Schmidt and Co. act in the light of their political experience. In the first terrorist action during Helmut Schmidt's chancellorship, the kidnapping of the Berlin CDU politician and candidate for the office of governing mayor, Peter Lorenz, in the spring of 1975, the German government gave in. Five imprisoned terrorists were allowed to fly out to the southern Yemeni capital of Aden so that the hostage could be released. Helmut Schmidt would later attribute this decision—which turned out to be wrong—to his limited ability to act during those days. "I (…) had a fever of 40 degrees, and in reality, others in my place had already made the decision when I was made fit to negotiate for a short time with the help of medical tricks and injections."[15]

---

[15] Helmut Schmidt in conversation with the author on 17 May 1995.

The fact that the Federal Chancellor was presumably confined to bed at the time appears to be just one of many factors in the decision.[16] Neither the Federal Government nor the West Berlin Senate has a hostage scenario on their radar. A general sense of helplessness characterises the actions of politicians and the police—partly because of the location of West Berlin, where the Western Allies were in charge. The terrorists released for Peter Lorenz would return to Germany and commit new crimes.

Only weeks later, terrorists occupy the German embassy in Stockholm. This time, Helmut Schmidt stays firm against the advice of Swedish Prime Minister Olof Palme, whom the Chancellor greatly supported. For Helmut Schmidt, it is no longer a question of the pros and cons of a police operation, but of a battle of wills "in which the strongest prevails in the end."[17]

From then on, Helmut Schmidt and many other fellow politicians use words such as "toughness and determination", "intransigence", "duty" and "sense of duty" or even "willingness to make sacrifices" against terrorists. As if the aim was not to prosecute political offences, but to wage and win a war. This history must be considered in order to understand the rhetorical armament between the German government and terrorists in the German Autumn.

With each additional day that Hanns Martin Schleyer is in the hands of his kidnappers, the pressure on political Bonn, the German government and the members of the crisis teams increases. They are pressurised by political friends and the public to give in in letters and public appeals. The most effective way to do this is via the press and radio.

With every day that passes since Hanns Martin Schleyer was kidnapped, the responsibility for the life of the employer president—and later the "Landshut" hostages—weighs more heavily on the shoulders of those politically responsible. They remain steadfastly in crisis mode, or more precisely: in war mode.

On the evening of Hanns Martin Schleyer's kidnapping, Chancellor Helmut Schmidt decides not to give in to the terrorists' demands. The brutality of the perpetrators, who shot people in cold blood to achieve their goal, rules out any kind of political concession. Releasing imprisoned terrorists would create the impression that the German government was condoning the murders in Cologne, Oberursel, Karlsruhe and the others with the benefit of hindsight.

From the outset, the Federal Chancellor asks the participants in the Short Briefing and the Large Political Advisory Group, how the kidnappers can be

---

[16] Cf. Dahlke 2007.
[17] Metzler 2014, p. 1f.

stalled until Hanns Martin Schleyer is captured and—in the lucky event—freed. The Federal Government wants to gain time and avoid short-circuiting reactions from Hanns Martin Schleyer's kidnappers.

Helmut Schmidt courts the CDU and CSU opposition not only in the Large Political Advisory Group but also in the Federal Parliament. In his first government statement on the Schleyer kidnapping case on this Thursday, 15 September 1977 [18], he complies with the CDU/CSU's request to "exclude from my statement the topics of foreign policy, growth and employment that were planned for today (…)."[19] A little later, he emphasises: "I don't want to give any cause for controversy this morning."[20]

Helmut Schmidt thanks the public, the Schleyer family, the editorial offices of the media, the members of the police and the judiciary for their constructive attitude. He makes special mention of the party and parliamentary group leaders and the members of the German Bundestag—"whether opposition or coalition."[21] He then thanks the Minister Presidents concerned and their state ministers. The Federal Chancellor expresses his confidence "that this all-round cooperation will continue until the dire predicament is resolved (…)".[22]

Helmut Schmidt calls on all the social groups mentioned to continue "not to miss anything and not to go into debt".[23] And once again he addresses Hanns Martin Schleyer's kidnappers directly: "You are wrong: we will not be infected by your madness. (…) You are wrong: the masses are against you."[24]

In the end, Helmut Schmidt, contrary to his usual reticence, mentions what personally characterised him, the war participant, and the members of his generation in general. "We older people, who experienced dictatorship and violence, prisons and expulsion, misery and hardship, we know what war is."[25]

The historian Golo Mann, who saw West Germany in a state of civil war after the Cologne attack, would call Schmidt's statement in the Bundestag "highly dignified and convincing".[26]

---

[18] Cf. plenary protocol of the German Bundestag. 42nd session of 15 September 1977, pp. 3164–3166.
[19] Ibid, p. 3164.
[20] Ibid.
[21] Ibid.
[22] Ibid.
[23] Ibid. p. 3165.
[24] Ibid, p. 3166.
[25] Ibid.
[26] Letter from Golo Mann to Hans-Martin Gauger dated 12 October 1977, in: Lahme/Lüssi 2006, p. 244.

By this time, Federal Chancellor Helmut Schmidt is no longer in contact with Hanns Martin Schleyer's family. He spoke to Waltrude Schleyer on the phone the day after her husband's abduction. He also received Hanns-Eberhard Schleyer—together with Hans-Jochen Vogel—for a meeting in the Chancellery.[27] Afterwards, only Hans-Jochen Vogel maintains contact with the family on behalf of the Federal Government. The Minister is keeping quiet about the fact that the Federal Government has already decided against exchanging the terrorists for Hanns Martin Schleyer.[28]

The Schleyer family does not remain in passive waiting but begins a kind of public life. Coordinated by son Hanns-Eberhard, Waltrude Schleyer turned to politicians and the public via the "Bild" newspaper, the powerful West German tabloid of the time. She even will publicise letters from her father to his eldest son in order to exert pressure on the decision-makers in Bonn.

Schleyer's kidnappers in turn inform their victim about the family's news and activities. Following an appeal by Waltrude Schleyer in the "Bild" newspaper to release her husband, Hanns Martin Schleyer responds in one of his messages: "Above all, I would like to thank my wife, who certainly did not find yesterday's appeal easy."

Hanns-Eberhard Schleyer, who is about to celebrate his 33rd birthday, is growing beyond himself (during) these weeks. He not only seeks contact with influential journalists, but also utilises his father's political network. Eberhard von Brauchitsch, the strong man in the Flick Group, provides him with a sum in the millions for the kidnappers. The German government prevents the money from being handed over so as not to jeopardise Hanns-Eberhard Schleyer's life.

Hanns Martin and Hanns-Eberhard Schleyer share a kind of code of honour. Despite their desperation, they always remain in control. They shy away from escalation. Hanns Martin Schleyer could threaten to spill the beans, just like the Italian politician Aldo Moro, who will fall into the hands of the Red Brigades next March.

The 62-year-old, who is not even given fresh clothes by his kidnappers, appears increasingly helpless and desperate in the video messages. But he always speaks or writes rationally in his letters. He leaves it at sentences like: "If Bonn refuses, then let them do it soon, although man would like to survive as it was in the war."

---

[27] Cf. draft memo for Mr Federal Chancellor. Subject: Abduction of Hanns Martin Schleyer. Here: conversation with the son of the abductee. O. D., in: Archiv BK 13–211 20 (2) Additional file OTB vol. 2, pp. 40–44.

[28] Hanns-Eberhard Schleyer in conversation with the author on 25 August 2022.

Hanns-Eberhard Schleyer could intensify the family's tone towards the Federal Government. To stir up the already alarmed public. He, the correct jurist, in need of harmony at heart like his father, does not. His sharpest sword, which he announces to the Federal Chancellor early on, is a legal one: going to the Federal Constitutional Court in Karlsruhe.

Hanns Matin Schleyer shows discipline and acumen at the same time. Politically a fox, he repeatedly plays the psychological card. "The kidnappers' goal", the father writes to his son Hanns-Eberhard, "will only prompt them to go after the next victim if they reject my demands and liquidate me. (…). Helmut Schmidt should know that (sic!) as well as Helmut Kohl + (sic!) HD Genscher."

A few days after his abduction, Hanns Martin Schleyer sends letters to Helmut Kohl and Flick boss Eberhard von Brauchitsch. He hopes that they—one politically, the other economically powerful—would exert pressure on the Chancellor. Hanns Martin Schleyer does what he can to prick the consciences and hearts of the decision-makers in Bonn.

For weeks, messages between Hanns Martin Schleyer's kidnappers, the German government and, indirectly, the Schleyer family go back and forth as if in a kind of war of position. The German government regularly demands proof that Hanns Martin Schleyer is alive. These proofs are provided.

"How lucky that the mirror that fell into ARND's (sic!) cot in our Offenburg flat didn't hit him."

"Today would be my cousin Anny Müller's birthday. She was born in Würzburg in 1904."

This war of position reflects the gloom of Hanns Martin Schleyer's weeks of abduction. On the one hand, he reveals personal details to prove that he is alive. On the other hand, he makes this personal information immediately as public as possible. The man, who is in a hidden place, is read, heard and seen by millions of people.

And so is the German government's reaction to this. The President of the Federal Criminal Police Office, Horst Herold, personally formulates every communication to the hijackers. He agrees them with the Federal Chancellor in private, in the Short Briefing and the Large Political Advisory Group. Everyone should support the line he chooses, right down to the choice of words.

The tension barometer between the warring parties goes up and down. "We will not make any further statements until the prisoners have flown out", reads an early communication from the Command Siegfried Hausner. Three days later, the terrorists demand that one of the terrorists to be flown out appear on German television.

Horst Herold, who has nerves of steel and is psychologically adept, skillfully lets the immense pressure that the kidnappers want to build up come to nothing.

The head of the BKA is sometimes placatory, sometimes brash towards the terrorists. "It is unreasonable", he writes in one of his messages, "to release the prisoners (sic!) without knowing for sure that Hanns Martin Schleyer will not be murdered by the kidnappers."

The kidnappers have complicated their task by letting the "Stammheim prisoners" decide on their destination themselves. This has led to a dialogue that must flatter Baader and Co., because they are now presumably negotiating on an equal footing with their main opponent, Chancellor Helmut Schmidt. But these negotiations unexpectedly open up a window of opportunity for the federal government during which they can question the detainees and "go from door to door" with Minister of State Hans-Jürgen Wischnewski and other affected governments. The goal is a "no" requested by all of them. This buys more time to search for Hanns Martin Schleyer's kidnappers. The British historian Thomas Skelton-Robinson considers the decision of the "Siegfried Hausner commando" that the "Stammheim prisoners" should name possible flight destinations on behalf of all terrorists to be released, a serious strategic mistake.[29]

Hanns Martin Schleyer's kidnappers and the RAF prisoners presumably see through the German government's stalling tactics—they cannot prevent the manoeuvre. At best, they could use coercive measures against their hostage. But in doing so, they are jeopardising the life of Hanns Martin Schleyer as a pledge for their demands.

In the meetings of the Bonn crisis teams, it is Federal Minister of Justice Hans-Jochen Vogel who justifies the Federal Government's position not only legally but also morally. He does so in his sober, analytical diction. Time and again, he weighs up the presumed danger to people who could become victims of the Red Army Faction in the future against the acute danger to Hanns Martin Schleyer's life. Hans-Jochen Vogel comes to the conclusion that, politically and morally, further deaths are more serious than the loss of a single, directly endangered person. The Federal Minister of Justice will also defend this judgement before the Federal Constitutional Court.

The terrorists put the German government's attitude to the test, as they have the most modern technology available at the time. They send Polaroid instant pictures: photos that do not need to be developed in a laboratory. With the help of a black-and-white video camera, they record Hanns Martin

---

[29] Cf. Skelton-Robinson 2006.

Schleyer's messages in words and pictures. The abductee is also allowed to discuss compact cassettes that are sent to selected people.

In this way, the political decision-makers and the public follow the suffering of a kidnap victim more authentically than ever before. The poor photo quality and the black-and-white film with its many wobbles and image disturbances make Hanns Martin Schleyer seem painfully distant and yet close. With each week of the kidnapping, the employer's president appears more personally distressed, his tone more pleading. His kidnappers share this with the public.

Hanns Martin Schleyer. A man from "those up there". He serves his kidnappers as a representative of a corrupt state that has been seized by an economic and political elite. All of them men with obscure pasts who did their thing in Hitler's Germany and later in the Federal Republic. Supposedly unscrupulous representatives of a world capitalism that misuses all politics for its own ends.

Hanns Martin Schleyer is not particularly well known or popular with the Germans. He would be intellectually brilliant and endeavoured to establish a constructive relationship between employers and trade unions. But he cannot be called a media talent. He seems to be a type of functionary who gives the impression of spending his life in talks and meetings.

Hanns Martin Schleyer's public image changes abruptly with the kidnapping. The videotapes with statements by the kidnapped man, who had to appear on camera in his vest, stirs up the public. The kidnappers demand that the tapes to be broadcast not only on German television, but also in other Western European countries. The German government can prevent broadcasts abroad. In its own country, viewers of the first and second television programmes are shown excerpts of the leaked video material. This selection alone is shattering.

Recordings in which Hanns Martin Schleyer appears particularly distressed do not even leave the Federal Criminal Police Office and are consigned to the poison cabinet for all time. Who, apart from Horst Herold and his staff, even sees the video tapes? It is quite possible that the Federal Chancellor and the specialised ministers are among them. Perhaps also the participants in the two Advisory Groups. Nevertheless, nobody of them will later say how much of the material they have seen.

Despite the infamy of their motives and the crimes committed before and after, the members of the Red Army Faction also act highly professionally in another respect: the logistics of keeping Hanns Martin Schleyer's hiding place secret and communicating with the German government. They appear well prepared and focused at every stage. They are women and men, mainly from the student milieu. In other words, intelligent minds using their intelligence for a terrible cause.

In 1977, there was no mobile phones and no internet. But the dual task of remaining undetected for weeks and changing hiding places with the hostage several times was already complex back then. More complex than any Red Army Faction terror operation before.

The members of the Command Siegfried Hausner and their helpers will write and send no fewer than 139 letters during the German Autumn. Each letter is sent from the place where it was written or at another place where a courier had taken it. Couriers also sometimes leave mail in easy-to-find places, such as hotel lobbies.

Almost all letters are error-free in terms of expression and spelling. And correct grammar. Only one addressee is written to twice. This is a brief summary of an analysis of the messages by the Federal Criminal Police Office, which is included in Helmut Schmidt's War Diary. The report describes German precision work for the worst possible purpose.

The analysis proves: Hanns Martin Schleyer's kidnappers and later murderers maintain a complete overview of what needs to be done and what has been done at all times. They always know who is doing what. Nothing is done carelessly. No mistakes are made.

Speaking out but leaving no trace—the RAF obviously practised this principle long before the "Offensive 77" was carried out. Messages to the federal governments are received by newspaper editors, the German Press Agency, in hotels or parsonages. They do not allow any conclusions to be drawn about the whereabouts of Hanns Martin Schleyer and his kidnappers. There is no doubt that Hanns Martin Schleyer's kidnappers knew that they would have to plan and organise for weeks. And they do it with staying power.

Obviously, they are also aware of the intellectual brilliance of some of their opponents. Historian Dorothea Hauser would call the duel between the imprisoned head of the RAF and Horst Herold, the head of the Federal Criminal Police Office and Chancellor Helmut Schmidt's most important advisor, "Baader and Herold."

The historian does not resort to any dramaturgical means here. She tells the story of a real-life duel. Andreas Baader did in fact call for "Offensive 77" through various communication channels and accompanied its planning together with the terrorists Gudrun Ensslin, Irmgard Möller and Jan-Carl Raspe, who are as mentioned together imprisoned in Stuttgart-Stammheim. The extent of this leadership and control will be revealed in the police investigation after the German Autumn.

A memo from the kidnappers, which reaches the Federal Criminal Police Office immediately after the first demand paper, is quoted here in full. It shows the perfidy with which Schleyer's kidnappers proceeded and their hatred of the West German state.

It is a supposedly invented "interrogation" of Hanns Martin Schleyer by his kidnappers. The note "Identification: cassette" is supposed to testify to its authenticity, but some of the employer president's answers seem less credible given his knowledge of the abductee's personality and political thinking.

Hanns Martin Schleyer's alleged interrogation is reproduced here in the order and spelling in which the individual pages were included in the Operation Diary.[30]

"It is not a question of morality for us to fulfil certain wishes that the prisoner h.m.schleyer had expressed in the event of his execution. On the contrary, we assume that the executed man had personal enemies among his peers, which are of interest to us now.

We will therefore follow with the greatest attention what YOU make of the enclosed statements by h.m. schleyer and then decide whether we will send YOU further copies and transcripts.

Identification: Cassette

kommando siegfried hausner

raf.

recording of o. k. schleyer, 10.9.77

…

Schleyer: …I want to answer directly: you need martyrs, and now it's my turn

…

Question: are kohl and strauß really dancing to schmidt's tune?

Schleyer: …if YOU survive me for a few days, this dramaturgy will become obvious to YOU by then at the latest …

Note: you have great political friends, but you wouldn't do anything different with them…

…

Recording o. k. schleyer, 11.9.77

---

[30] Archiv BK 13–211 20 (3) vol. 1, pp. 135–139.

…

Question: why are YOU only telling us this now? we would have told YOUR son, for example -

schleyer: and you think schmidt gets it when we allude to herold with kohl?

Schleyer: I hope so… but I'm still worried about my family …

Note: …but well: even if we have nothing in common with YOU, we can assure YOU of one thing: even the most sophisticated meier bulls will not succeed in tricking one of the raf into turning YOUR family into a heroic family like the kennedys.

Recording o.k. schleyers, o. d.

…

Note: … here is also the confirmation that the first three cassettes have arrived.

Your guarantor has accepted our conditions as requested, so that the initiative is now left to us. Almost everything is now settled … on the german wine route.

Schleyer: thank you … if you make use of this, I can only ask you to omit the explanation of my motives ni (sic!) -

They have clear security guarantees, so what should … however …

Schleyer: … I have to take that risk … did he have any other concerns?

Note: concerns and recommendations. Concerns above all about the … address. He thinks, as we do, that the csu is rummaging around in … and if the tapes fall into the hands of strauss, neither YOUR nor our bill would be half right …

Schleyer: it should only be a temporary storage until the material is complete

…

Question: by the way, in this context he wanted to know if maybe YOUR son knows one of the addresses, is that so?

Schleyer: no, just … YOU and I … but YOU also spoke of recommendations -

Note: right, I have written a few things down -

Schleyer: wait, I'll make a note of that too, you know my powers of concentration ...

Note: yes, yes, just do it—so:

1. the thing with meier and herold, the accusations against schmidt, maihofer etc.—nope, that's fine...
2. about the dickwurst: in the case of the so-called suicide of the giant, YOU should state more precisely what role the ostrich woman and the tandlers played in this -

Schleyer: mm. Yes.

Note: further to strauß: YOU would like to explain in detail, if possible, where the lockheed bribe money went—who is in possession of evidence, including YOUR own—also: why heubl first wanted to sell his lockheed knowledge to wehner, but then preferred kohl—also as precisely as possible: when, everywhere and how kohl used this information against strauß. -

Schleyer: this is now on the fourth cassette.

Note: aha—but there's more:

What biedenkopf knows about the whole story -

Schleyer: Difficult, I only know that he knows something ...

Note: then YOU just give YOUR informants -

like this:

3. the story with the bribes, sorry, of course donations of the business associations for the individual parties is clear—oh no: YOU should give a programmatic reason why the business associations favour dregger as federal chancellor candidate ...

schleyer: everything?

Note: yes, just one more little thing: YOUR ss number is missing from YOUR CV. Don't YOU remember it? You will remember ...

Schleyer: ... well, I'll try to finish by ... then.

Hint: you have to, because we have received good news from our comrades ... besides, we are hardly here to organise grand revenge campaigns ...

...."

The kidnappers of Hanns Martin Schleyer obviously want to use this message to spread discord among the decision-makers in Bonn. Helmut Kohl and Horst Herold are to be played off against each other. Hanns Martin Schleyer could "spill the beans" about scandals and scandalous figures in the Federal Republic of Germany during the course of his abduction. The Chancellor, the kidnappers presumably calculate, would sooner or later put an end to these revelations by fulfilling their demands.

The German government remains silent about the announcement. And keeps it secret from the media and the public. It remains with this one attempt to drive a wedge between top politicians in Bonn. Apparently, Hanns Martin Schleyer's kidnappers come to the conclusion that nothing could be achieved in this way.

After the first few days of the kidnapping, the dialogue between the German government and the kidnappers of Hanns Martin Schleyer comes to a standstill as mentioned. Neither side has anything new to report. Neither side has any new information to report. A Geneva lawyer, Dennis Payot, offers himself as a mediator in a newspaper interview. The Schleyer kidnappers had already mentioned his name. Together with the former governing mayor of Berlin, pastor Heinrich Albertz, Payot was supposed to accompany the released prisoners on the flight to a destination of their choice.

Not much is known about the man, except that as president of the Swiss League for Human Rights he had met the mothers of Gudrun Ensslin and Andreas Baader—tireless defenders of their daughter and son respectively.

There are risks involved in this personnel decision. Dennis Payot does not speak German. This can lead to linguistic misunderstandings. Dennis Payot looks at the Federal Republic of Germany from the outside, so he doesn't know the conditions in Bonn. As little as his law firm's associates whom he needs for this task. The head of the Federal Criminal Police Office (BKA), Horst Herold, takes the hint from the Geneva lawyer, and so do the terrorists.

What is the respective interest? From the terrorists' point of view, a mediator makes it unnecessary to negotiate directly with the German government. He can remain better hidden. The German government, on the other hand, may be happy to have a contact person. It will need the media less in future. The mediator also ensures a kind of orderly procedure. Short-circuited actions by the kidnappers seem less likely. And presumably time is gained. Horst Herold is constantly looking for ways to stall the kidnappers of Hanns Martin Schleyer.

In autumn 1977, Hanns Martin Schleyer is a member of the Board of Management at Daimler-Benz, responsible for human resources and social affairs, and leads two powerful associations, as President of the Confederation of German Employers' Associations (BDA) and as President of the Federation of German Industries (BDI).

Not all representatives (no female representatives in 1977) of these organisations stand by him now.

"The Presidium of the BDI (Vice-Presidents)", writes Manfred Schüler, Head of the Federal Chancellery, in a note to the Federal Chancellor on 6 September, "is meeting in Cologne and is concerned that Wolf von Amerongen (President of the Association of German Industry and Commerce, editor's note) is asking you for support for a public statement by the Joint Committee. The BDI does not want this at present (...). The BDI first wants to await the further progress of the investigations".[31]

A few days later, Manfred Schüler receives a visit from Johannes Niemeyer from the Commissariat of Catholic Bishops. "The Catholic Church is being pushed by the Schleyer family to influence the government and the public to free Schleyer by releasing the prisoners", reads a note from Schüler dated the same day.[32] "The Catholic Church was not prepared to do this." Niemeyer "tippes off" Schüler that the Bishop of Rottenburg—the diocese in which the Schleyer family lived—wants to make an appeal to the kidnappers later that day. Manfred Schüler immediately informs Hans-Jochen Vogel, who immediately dissuades the surprised bishop.

Mention should be made of an emerging conflict between two leading politicians who are also brothers. Hans-Jochen and Bernhard Vogel belong to different parties. One is the Social Democrat Federal Minister of Justice, the other is the Christian Democrat Minister President of Rhineland-Palatinate.

Hans-Jochen Vogel maintains political contact with Schleyer's family at the request of the Federal Chancellor. He has to stall them. He remains silent about the decision Helmut Schmidt has already made. Bernhard Vogel, on the other hand, is not only a personal friend of Hanns Martin Schleyer, but also from Schleyer's family.

Bernhard Vogel keeps in close contact with Waltrude Schleyer and the four children during the weeks of the kidnapping. He often travels from Mainz after work for a visit to Stuttgart and then back again at night. Bernhard Vogel is interested in personal support. He has nothing to report on the matter, as he has no contact with the German government or members of Helmut

---

[31] Note from the Head of the BK to the Federal Chancellor dated 6 September 1977, in: Archiv BK 13–211 20 (3), Additional file 3, no p.
[32] C Note from the head of the BK dated 13 September 1977, in: Archiv BK 13–211 20 (2), Additional file OTB vol. 2, p. 53; Archiv BK 13–211 20 (3), Additional file 3, no p.

Schmidt's crisis team during this time. And only sporadically with his brother Hans-Jochen. They avoid each other.[33]

Hanns Martin Schleyer has been held hostage for nine days when the "Stern" magazine reports that the German government and the opposition were in agreement that an exchange of terrorists was out of the question.[34] The same applies to the Federal Minister of the Interior, Werner Maihofer, and the President of the Federal Criminal Police Office, Horst Herold.

There is no doubt that a member of the Short Briefing or the Large Political Advisory Group has "spilled the beans". The facts are true, but, as the saying goes, he can't stand the huffing and puffing. "Stern" magazine's boss Henri Nannen can be assumed to be aware of his journalistic responsibility in the German Autumn. He lets his magazine fire to make clear: We are well informed. And we can do things differently. After this "warning shot" to the German government, Nannen remains journalistically silent.

Presumably for something in return, a promise. At the end of the German Autumn, "Stern" magazine will have exclusive information and photos of the events like no other medium. For example, it will print pictures taken by officers of the Federal Criminal Police Office in the stormed "Landshut".

Chancellor Helmut Schmidt reportedly asked the members of the two crisis teams to think the supposedly unthinkable. A working group set up by the head of the Federal Chancellery, Manfred Schüler, also takes this intellectual freedom. It owes its name "Ruhnau Group" to its leader Heinz Ruhnau, State Secretary in the Federal Ministry of Transport and later Chairman of the Executive Board of German Lufthansa. The group also includes Dieter Posser, Minister of Justice of North Rhine-Westphalia, as well as the Head of Department 2 (Foreign and Internal German Relations, External Security)[35] in the Federal Chancellery, Jürgen Ruhfus, and the Head of Department 3 (Internal Affairs) [36], Gerhard Konow.

The Ruhnau Group devises scenarios as to how Hanns Martin Schleyer can be released without letting the terrorists go.

Its simulation game envisages cooperation between the German government and the President of Togo. The West African country was once a German colony. Since January 1967, President Gnassingbé Eyadéma runs the country like a dictator. Human rights violations and the persecution of political opponents are part of everyday life in Togo.

---

[33] Cf. Bernhard Vogel in conversation with the author on 25 August 2022.
[34] Cf. statement by StS Bölling and letter from StS Bölling to Henri Nannen dated 15 September 1977, in: Archiv BK 13–211 20 (2) Vol. 1, Annexes to Protocol 2.
[35] Busse/Hofmann 2010, p. 116f.
[36] Ibid.

At the end of the 1960s, the president has an idea to attract companies from Europe with branches. This means many new and well-paid jobs in the poor country.[37] Gnassingbé Eyadéma lifts the religious ban on eating pork. The CSU chairman and Bavarian Minister President Franz Josef Strauß gets wind of this and senses big business. Strauß, himself a butcher's son, persuades the Rosenheim meat products millionaire Josef März ("Marox—for the joy of eating") on investments in Togo.

The example will set a precedent on the African continent. The dictator of the Congo, Mobutu Sese Seko—known to Germans as the organiser of the "Rumble in the Jungle", the heavyweight boxing match between George Foreman and Muhammad Ali on 30 October 1974 in Kinshasa—comes to Rosenheim to visit Josef März's factory. The two men reach a trade agreement. The Congo also gets Bavarian meat factories.

Franz Josef Strauß and members of his state cabinet travel to Togo several times to cultivate the new, heartfelt friendship. There, Strauß and Co. experience the—as they see it—deserved fame for their political genius, which they are denied in West Germany—quite unjustly, as they also find.

For a visit to Togo in March 1977, CSU chairman Franz Josef Strauß even skips a speech at a CDU federal party conference. In the Togolese capital of Lomé, he is given an almost triumphant welcome. A huge banner bears the inscription: "PRESIDENT STRAUSS BE AT HOME IN TOGO". A "Stern" magazine reporter accompanies Franz Josef Strauß on his journey. Later in his article, mockery and amazement are in equal measure.

The hopes of the "Ruhnau Group", a secret brain pool of Federal Chancellor Helmut Schmidt, rest on the dictatorial regime of this country, which is friendly to the Federal Republic of Germany. The scenario of Heinz Ruhnau and Co. is that all the governments of the countries to which the *Stammheimer* want to be flown refuse to accept them. At the request of the German government, only Togo should be prepared to do so. The imprisoned RAF terrorists agree nolens volens—on the condition that "the character of the regime in Togo is not seen through. The actual content of the operation must remain secret from prisoners, kidnappers and escorts."[38]

The eleven terrorists are taken from the prison to an airport, where they board a supposedly scheduled flight with tourists. In reality, they are armed police officers in plain clothes. Alternatively, only the crew—pilots

---

[37] Cf. Schwarzes Patenkind, in: Der Spiegel No. 11 of 7 March 1977; cf. Ein Schwarzer in Afrika, in: Der Stern No. 13 of 17 March 1977.

[38] Operation "Lomé". Triggered by the Federal Government to end the kidnapping or by ultimatum from the kidnappers, in Archiv BK 13–211 20 (2) Additional file vol. 7, no p.

and accompanying personnel—are on the plane. Police officers only come out of hiding in the air.

The plane flies to Lomé. President Gnassingbé Eyadéma makes a credible-sounding statement that the terrorists will be granted political asylum after the code word is given to Hanns Martin Schleyer's kidnapper—the signal for his release. After the release of the employer president, the terrorists are "collected" again.

The authors of the simulation game themselves doubt the success of their idea. On the one hand, they should think the supposedly unthinkable. On the other hand, they cannot believe that the fake, to use a modern word, will remain secret. The operation would involve two governments. The logistics would be complicated.

There are also doubts about the credibility of the Togolese dictator among Hanns Martin Schleyer's kidnappers and the *Stammheimer*. The ladies and gentlemen are concerned with international politics, but do they know where the African state of Togo is located?

It is quite possible, according to Ruhnau and Co., that the plan will fail in another way. That no Lufthansa crew will agree to fly the aircraft to Lomé with terrorists on board.

Despite all doubts, the "Lomé Enterprise" is included in the "Ruhnau Group" paper, which develops various scenarios for the Federal Chancellor.[39] On 10 October 1977, Minister of State Hans-Jürgen Wischnewski writes a statement on the Ruhnau paper, including a proposal for cooperation with the Republic of Togo. It is sceptical, but not negative. The time spent in Lomé could be considerably reduced "if two aircrafts were used".[40]

Chancellor Helmut Schmidt presumably receives the paper from the "Ruhnau Group". Heinz Ruhnau is a friend of the SPD party and thinks highly of Jürgen Ruhfus. There is no record of him or Franz Josef Strauß actually approaching the Togolese president for a "Lomé undertaking".

At the beginning of October 1977, Hanns Martin Schleyer let it be known in a letter to his wife how much the uncertainty about his fate is weighing on him. He writes of "vegetating for over a month now". This state of affairs is "no longer bearable for me".

---

[39] The other scenarios cannot be fully deduced from the pages contained in the OTB. They are schematic depictions of if–then scenarios without further explanation. They attempt to describe the presumed consequences for the hostage and the public if the German government or the kidnappers of Hanns Martin Schleyer were to act. It is interesting, indeed revealing, that the German government always considers the public impact of its decisions.
[40] Stm (Wischnewski, as signed by him in his own hand): Note to the Federal Chancellor dated 10 October 1977, in: ibid., no p.

The kidnapped man senses that the confrontation between the German government and the terrorists has reached a dead end. In the meantime, the kidnappers of the employers' president let days pass before Hanns Martin Schleyer spoke again and showed signs of life. Mediator Denis Payot can only pass on what reaches him.

Helmut Schmidt's most important advisor, Horst Herold, assumes that Hanns Martin Schleyer is no longer in the Federal Republic and that the prospect of tracking him down and freeing him is dwindling. It seems less likely that Hanns Martin Schleyer's kidnappers will be caught with each passing day. On the other hand, the terrorists maintain their demands. They need the employer president as a bargaining chip.

A document of this mentally demanding interim period is the speech with which Federal Chancellor Helmut Schmidt opens a national conference of the Junior Circle of German Business on 6 October 1977.[41] Both the Chairman of the Junior Circle and Helmut Schmidt himself address the topic, which is depressing people in the Federal Republic of Germany like no other. The thoughts of all those gathered in the "Harmonie" festival hall in Heilbronn are centred on the man who they do not know whether he will escape alive from his hostage situation.

In Heilbronn, the Federal Chancellor confesses that he had been "on friendly terms" with one of this year's terror victims, Jürgen Ponto, for many years. "I think it's been a quarter of a century since my wife taught one of his sons at school." He also speaks of a "very intensive contact and exchange of views with Hanns Martin Schleyer" before his abduction. He feels personally affected by these two crimes "and not just as one of 60 million citizens and not just as the Federal Chancellor".

Then Helmut Schmidt addresses his hosts. "I must warn you. I have no opportunity to give you a speech. I have had no opportunity to prepare for this in the last 14 days." The Federal Chancellor then talks about what he sees as an intact relationship between company management on the one hand and works councils, staff councils and trade unions on the other. This is followed by the proverbial "world economic opera" typical of Schmidt, an analysis of the national economy and its global causes.

The Federal Chancellor speaks for an hour as usual. At the end, he once again comes back to the kidnapped employers' president Hanns Martin Schleyer. Helmut Schmidt recounts "the last conversation we had together before the crime against him, very detailed, two or three hours (…)". Very

---

[41] Federal Press Office. Steor. Dienst. Poles of 6 October 1977, in: AdsD, 1/HSAA010350.

indirectly, very awkwardly, the Chancellor expresses how much he appreciates Hanns Martin Schleyer. And now fears for him.

Stuttgart

In the late stages of Hanns Martin Schleyer's kidnapping, Attorney General Kurt Rebmann asks the head of Stuttgart-Stammheim prison, Horst Nusser, to talk to Andreas Baader. The Attorney General wants to overcome the deadlock in the dispute between the Federal Government and the Schleyer kidnappers. Nusser is to ask Baader if he would like to make a statement. It doesn't happen to many inmates at Stuttgart-Stammheim that the top boss of the prison receives them for an interview.

Andreas Baader informs Horst Nusser that he would like a meeting with the head of the Federal Chancellery, Manfred Schüler. Nusser presumably assumes that Baader, the self-proclaimed guerrilla fighter, wants to satisfy his own vanity. Something like this: If I'm going to talk to a representative of this pig state, it has to be Helmut Schmidt's closest colleague!

Of course, Horst Nusser does not know that Andreas Baader has a pistol in his cell. The Minister of the Chancellery would presumably have it held to his head during his visit. The federal government would suddenly be vulnerable to blackmail in another prominent case. The world would laugh at "Bonn" for its negligence. And another person would be in mortal danger.

After the conversation, Horst Nusser first telephones Manfred Schüler, then Federal Prosecutor General Kurt Rebmann. Federal Chancellor Helmut Schmidt has the minutes of the two telephone conversations recorded in the Operation Diary. They are quoted here.

Nusser to Schüler: "Baader had said "it would be very important to talk about the situation with someone who is competent, who can decide and who is not a policeman (Hans Nusser is not a policeman, but a lawyer, but is identified with police work, M. R.'s note)." (…) He then said—this was perhaps the only suggestion that could be somewhat critical—well, if Mr Schüler doesn't come soon, he might have to travel a long way. When I asked him if he could tell me what he wanted to say, he flatly denied it (…)."

Schüler: "And the one remark, if he doesn't come soon, then he might have to travel a long way, he said, so that's an implication that they didn't want to take him there either, or how is that to be understood? Or does he reckon that the second option would be that he expects to be flown out and that he would then be taken to his destination—is that how you understood it?"

Nusser: "Yes."

"Yes, that's interesting that they still reckon with it." (…).⁴²

Days later, Schüler and Nusser will know what Baader meant by the "long journey". After Baader's suicide, Nusser had to visit the realm of the dead for a "reunion".

Here are excerpts from the following telephone conversation between Federal Prosecutor General Kurt Rebmann and Horst Nusser.

Rebmann: "This is Rebmann. Could it be that they've been informed by radios that others have in their rooms?"

Nusser: "You can't rule that out. (…) You know this courtyard, it's very reverberant. So you can definitely hear it when the radio is some distance away. (…) I was with Baader. (…) In his opinion, the overall situation required a conversation with a competent man from Bonn, which he should conduct, but not by telephone. (…) The conversation he wanted now, if it did not take place soon, then it could be that the right person would have to travel a long way. I also told all this to State Secretary Schüler (…)."

Rebmann: "Okay, good. Thank you very much, Mr Nusser."⁴³

The head of the Federal Chancellery, Manfred Schüler, agrees to talk to Andreas Baader. In other words, to go to Stuttgart-Stammheim prison. The Large Political Advisory Group gives the green light. Everything that can contribute to the rescue of hostage Hanns Martin Schleyer is to be done.

When a helicopter lands in the garden of the Federal Chancellery to fly the head of the office to Stuttgart, Federal Minister of Justice Hans-Jochen Vogel vetoes the decision. "We need to talk about this again."⁴⁴ Days later, Manfred Schüler will thank Vogel more than once.⁴⁵

Not only Andreas Baader, but also Gudrun Ensslin and Jan-Carl Raspe hint at suicidal ideation. The police officer responsible for the RAF prisoners draws up verbatim records of conversations with Baader and Co. They are forwarded to the federal government via the prison warden.

---

⁴² Telephone minutes of an undated conversation between StS Manfred Schüler and Hans Nusser, in: Archiv BK 13–211 20 (2) Additional file OTB vol. 8, no p.
⁴³ Telephone minutes of an undated conversation between GBA Kurt Rebmann and Hans Nusser, in: ibid., no p.
⁴⁴ Vogel/Hauser; p. 21.
⁴⁵ Ibid.

The police and politicians know about the terrorists' suicide threat for a total of two weeks before the prisoners at Stammheim carry out their threat. More on this later.

Decades later, in an interview with Dorothea Hauser, the then Federal Minister of Justice Hans-Jochen Vogel would say that hindsight is always wiser. "There was not a single case of someone from this group of people who, if they had really killed themselves, would have spoken about it beforehand" [46], Hans-Jochen Vogel says verbatim.

> *"dpa reports to CvD that strange calls were made to various dpa offices in the evening hours. dpa has not yet reported this."*
>
> *Frankfurt: 8.40 p.m. "The mouse is dead"*
>
> *Trier: 8.53 p.m. "The hedgehog is dead"*
>
> *Hamburg: 9.25 p.m. "The mouse is dead"*[47]

Time and again, as in the meetings on 7 and 21 September, the crisis teams discuss cooperation between the federal and state authorities. What can and should the police, who are subordinate to the federal states, do, and what should the federal Border Guard Force 9 do? In 1977, there was still little experience of this. And jealousies, then as now. Ulrich Wegener's GSG9, which still has its baptism of fire ahead of it, is involved in routine tasks such as personal protection for the Federal President and storming flats and houses. It has a difficult standing before "Mogadishu".

The Short Briefing and the Large Political Advisory Group are not provided for in the Basic Law. Therefore, a trick is needed to document the course of discussions—not formal decisions!—to document the course of discussions. On 13 September 1977, Helmut Schmidt asks the head of the Federal Chancellery, Manfred Schüler, to appoint "a capable civil servant (…) to be responsible for complete documentation (…)". In a bundle that Helmut Schmidt would sometimes call a *Kriegstagebuch* ("War Diary"), sometimes an *Operationstagebuch* ("Operation Diary", OTB for short), minutes from the Short Briefing and the Large Political Advisory Group were to be collected, supplemented by important documents—letters from the Schleyer family, statements from the terrorists imprisoned in Stuttgart-Stammheim, telephone logs, forensic investigations. A collection of files documenting an exceptional

---

[46] Vogel/Hauser, p. 42.
[47] Note by Chief of Service Dr Liebau for StS dated 5 October 1977, in: Archiv BK 13–211 20 (2) Additional file OTB vol. 4, p. 321.

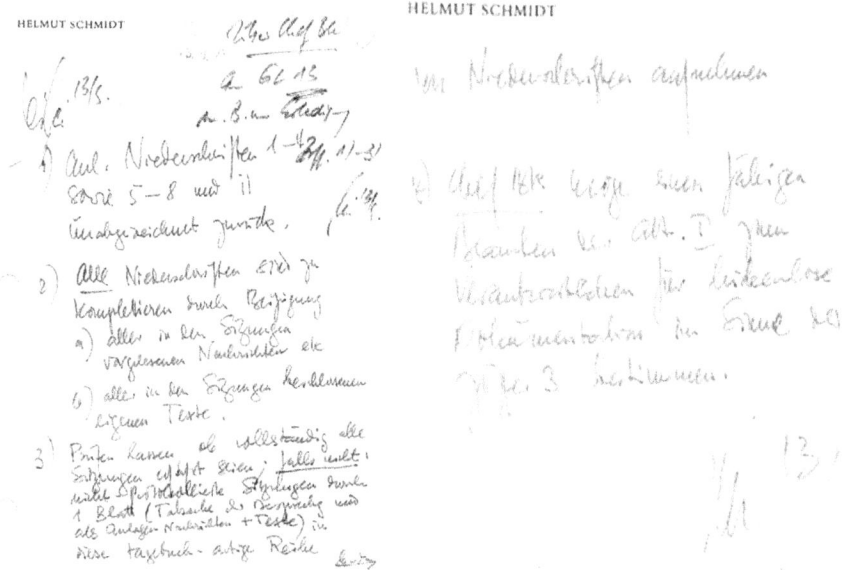

Fig. 2.1 a, b Handwritten note by Helmut Schmidt on his personal stationery (letterhead "Helmut Schmidt") *Source* Archiv BK 13–211 20 (2) and vol. 7

situation. Helmut Schmidt can say afterwards: "I made all my decisions after intensive discussions" (Fig. 2.1).

After the German Autumn, the War Diary is consigned to the proverbial poison cabinet. Not even the members of the crisis teams are given access to it on request. Neither the then Minister President of Baden-Württemberg, Hans Filbinger, nor Klaus Kinkel, then State Secretary in the Federal Foreign Ministry, nor the head of the CSU parliamentary group in the Bundestag, Friedrich Zimmermann. An exception is made for the CSU member of the Bundestag Hermann Höcherl as the author of an investigative report on mishaps in the manhunt for Hanns Martin Schleyer. He is able to inspect the logs of Schleyer's first days of abduction.

Only BKA chief Horst Herold is believed to have the entire material diary copied for a book he intends to write in retirement. He won't write it, but what happened to the copy after Herold's death in December 2018?

Years later, Helmut Schmidt will obtain permission for the historian Dorothea Hauser to view the complete diary. As mentioned above, Dorothea Hauser is supervising an eyewitness dialogue project of the Helmut and Loki Schmidt Foundation. With the help of the War Diary, she is good at preparing.

48 years after the German Autumn, documents from the Operation Diary comprising eight folders are accessible. An exception to this is a total of 122 crisis team minutes—one minute for each day of consultation. Minutes were also kept of meetings after the German Autumn. A table of contents compiled later by the Federal Chancellery is accessible to researchers and journalists.

It is quite possible that the 122 protocols will be "unlocked" at some point. It seems unlikely that they will shed new and different light on the behaviour of the political players in the German Autumn. As mentioned at the beginning, the published material allows many conclusions to be drawn about the closed material. The Federal Chancellor's room for manoeuvre in decision-making and the way in which he conducted politics are already in the open.

Apart from the operations diary, the Federal Archives in Koblenz and other archives contain numerous other freely accessible files from the German Autumn, for example all the telephone logs of the conversations between Federal Chancellor Helmut Schmidt and Minister of State Hans-Jürgen Wischnewski during the "Landshut" abduction. These are authentic, vivid testimonies to the thoughts and government actions of the most important players. After the embargo period expired, "Der Spiegel" and "Bild", among others, reported on her. This is the first time that they have been placed in the overall context.

Historic sources provide information about events, not emotions. Do the personalities shaped by the world war, such as Helmut Schmidt, Hans-Jochen Vogel or Werner Maihofer, feel fear during the German Autumn? Concern, certainly, but also fear for the life of Hanns Martin Schleyer? Fear of becoming a victim of a crime themselves (there are personal threats)? Fear of failing in office because they are not up to the responsibility imposed on them?

Later, in some cases much later, decision-makers at the time will reveal such fears. In the German autumn, they only emerged indirectly. BKA President Horst Herold quietly receives requests from top politicians, including Federal Finance Minister Hans Apel, for personal protection or, if such protection already exists, for it to be reinforced.

What unites the leading politicians in these weeks is their common view of things. There has already been talk of World War II as a foil for biographical memory in thought and speech. When Justice Minister Hans-Jochen Vogel arrives at the scene of the crime in Cologne on 5 September 1977, the "memory of the war, the dead and the fallen"[48] returned. The kidnap

---

[48] Quoted from Richter 2014, p. 241.

victim Hanns Martin Schleyer (born 1915, *SS-Untersturmführer* during the war) also draws parallels to the war. "If Bonn refuses, then they should do it soon, even though a person—as was the case in the war—would like to survive", reads a letter from the hostage situation dated 8 September.[49]

These men experience, to use the modern word, a flashback. The feeling of a maximum, almost superhuman challenge is back. "Their own self-sacrifice, their own experience of physical and psychological limits, reflected an almost soldierly ethos of duty that was intended to authenticate the cause of the state."[50]

In the "German Autumn" of 1977, Helmut Schmidt and his colleagues are convinced that they are the only ones who can master this difficult situation. Their actions were both a profession and a calling. "Herold was at war with the terrorists, he was a party to the war, it was his war. He gave the impression that this war had been declared on him personally",[51] says Dieter Schenk, a former employee of the BKA, about the former boss. The "war party" Horst Herold will not be sparing with self-praise in retrospect. "Officers in the old army had excellent training, a first-class polish. We knew the trade."[52]

In their flashback as world warriors, top West German politicians take the terrorists and their so-called sympathisers[53] far too seriously. RAF members detonate bombs, kidnap, murder, they commit terrible crimes, but fortunately these crimes are committed by very few people. In the worst year of terror, 1977, a dozen people.

These criminals are also few in number, supported logistically by a few hundred helpers. They stylise themselves as a kind of urban guerrilla, waging an armed struggle against the Federal Republic of Germany, which has become a slave to the USA and is intoxicated with consumerism. RAF manifestos are declarations of war. As imprisoned criminals, the terrorists claim the status of political prisoners or prisoners of war with corresponding rights.[54] There is of course a bed in Andreas Baader's cell, but he does not sleep in it. He lies on the floor like a guerrilla fighter who chooses to camp out in the open. The bed is seen as the sleeping place of personally bourgeois and politically toothless citizens in a supposedly fascist state.

---

[49] Quoted from ibid., p. 240.
[50] Metzler 2014, p. 4.
[51] Quoted from Hachmeister 2004, p. 325.
[52] Herold/Hauser, p. 144.
[53] SympathiSers were women and men who provided the members of the Red Army Faction with practical help for their lives in the underground. They provided them with passports or apartments, for example. Over time, the meaning of the term faded. Anyone who tried to understand the motives of the RAF members, like the writer Heinrich Böll, came under suspicion of being a sympathizer.
[54] Cf. Musolff 2006, p. 309.

"In paranoia, at least", Friedrich Christian Delius would write 20 years later, "the enemies were united. (...) Despite all the differences, there was a symbiotic relationship between the RAF and its opponent."[55]

Paranoia is not only a psychological finding between two "warring parties". It also guides the behaviour of former world warriors towards those who think differently and especially younger people. Representatives of other, differentiated thought patterns play no role in the consultations. SPD chairman Willy Brandt experienced the world war in exile, "from the outside", as former battery commander Helmut Schmidt would scornfully say in his old age. Willy Brandt, almost five years older than Schmidt, rarely attends the meetings of the Large Political Advisory Group and makes little contribution. Apodictic, military-influenced either-or thinking is not his thing. He lacks any form of soldierly demeanour anyway.

The German Autumn deepened the estrangement between Willy Brandt and Helmut Schmidt, these two men, presumably who are of such fundamental importance for German social democracy and the history of the Federal Republic of Germany, and who are so fundamentally different as individuals.

The members of the so-called war generation—Helmut Schmidt himself uses this term early on at[56]—also consider the members of subsequent generations to be sissies. CDU chairman Helmut Kohl, for example, already belongs to the "sceptical generation", as sociologist Helmut Schelsky called it. Their biographical imprint was formed in the final phase of the war, as the last contingent. As simple soldiers, not as non-commissioned officers or officers.

A Helmut Kohl, born in 1930, did not have to go through the "shit of war" (Schmidt's standing expression) for so long and so deeply in the perception of the former First Lieutenant Helmut Schmidt. Consequently, he could not have been sufficiently prepared for a challenge such as the German Autumn. After the Lorenz kidnapping in 1975, Helmut Schmidt mocked Helmut Kohl's behaviour, saying how he had begged for his political friend to be rescued.

Journalists and prominent publicists are also talking and writing about a special situation, a state of emergency, even a war. The historian Golo Mann explains in an article in "Die Welt"[57] that "we are at war; we are facing

---

[55] Delius 1997.
[56] Cf. Helmut Schmidt 1968.
[57] To this day, the daily newspaper "Die Welt" is the journalistically sophisticated, politically conservative flagship of the Axel Springer publishing house, which also publishes the tabloid newspaper "Bild".

enemies determined to kill. And Germany is as innocent as an angel in this war."[58]

These enemies are working on the Federal Chancellor personally as the most important political player in this country. They presumably need to fixate on one person in order to maintain their "fighting power". "We will never forget Schmidt's bloody deed", would be one of the statements made by the RAF after Bader, Ensslin and Raspe committed suicide. For a while before that, they consider placing the body of Hanns Martin Schleyer in front of the Chancellor's office. Only the fear of the massive police presence in the government district stop them.[59]

Helmut Schmidt makes threats in television addresses and speeches in the Bundestag like a general at war. His two crisis teams form a kind of Supreme Army Command—as did his staff during the Hamburg flood disaster in 1962. The boundaries between the federal government and the opposition appear to be blurred. In the course of the German Autumn, Helmut Schmidt takes all the powers of the state to task: the parties represented in the Bundestag, the Federal Constitutional Court, his own federal government, even the "fourth" power, the press and radio.

The political leadership of the Federal Republic of Germany believes it is at war. Nevertheless, the meetings of the Short Briefing and the Large Political Advisory Group are sober. The participants conduct focused, objective debates, as will emerge from the accounts of participants decades later. The files that have been made available to date paint the same picture.

Federal Chancellor Helmut Schmidt leads the meetings according to a fixed agenda. Horst Herold—there was a brief mention of this at the beginning—presents the latest news on the Schleyer and later the "Landshut" hijackers at the meetings.

Helmut Schmidt is more tolerant than usual in these meetings. He lets debates run their course for his own reflection and to serve the vanity of the participants. Only wafflers like Federal Minister of the Interior Werner Maihofer are called to order. Decades later, the head of the Federal Criminal Police Office, Horst Herold, would still be complaining about the law professor and educated citizen: "He started every problem with the Hittites, and an endless amount of time passed before he worked his way through Sumerians, Akkadians, Phoenicians etc. to the modern era. And Schmidt said: "Get to the point!"."[60]

---

[58] Quoted from Botzat 1977, p. 23.
[59] See Bönisch/Röbel 2021, p. 16.
[60] Herold/Hauser, p. 53.

According to Helmut Schmidt's calculations, the members of the Large political advisory should always be better informed than their few female colleagues and many male colleagues in Bonn. That binds them in. Makes them tame. Makes them bound to secrecy.

In historical retrospect, the tactics of Federal Chancellor Helmut Schmidt and the head of the Federal Criminal Police Office, Horst Herold, must be called "soaping up". They prepare decisions in detail. The gentlemen are supposed to agree in accepting decisions they seem to have made themselves.

The portrayal of the "lone decision-makers" Helmut Schmidt in political terms and Horst Herold in police terms is one of the myths of the German Autumn. There is no doubt that both were responsible. But they avoided going it alone. Everything they had planned was submitted to both crisis teams for approval.

Helmut Schmidt would later justify this collegial leadership style with the seriousness of the situation, in which there could be no room for party-political disputes. It was also a clever move, as it distributes the responsibility for the life of Hanns Martin Schleyer and later the "Landshut" hostages onto many heads.

Helmut Schmidt's plan will work out. After the assassination of Hanns Martin Schleyer and the end of the German Autumn, the parliamentary opposition will refrain from apportioning blame against the Federal Government.

Freedom of thought prevails in the Short Briefing and the Large Political Advisory Group. The situation should be scrutinised from as many angles as possible and even unconventional courses of action be discussed. The Federal Chancellor wants to have all options on the table at least once in this circle. He wants to maximise the collective intelligence of the participants.

As mentioned earlier, there are indications that Franz Josef Strauß "spoke of shootings" in the Large Political Advisory Group.[61] The literal translation of the alleged quote is: "We also have hostages." Franz Josef Strauß does not often attend the meetings [62], and when he does, it is at a high level. "But he was usually drunk, it was disgusting. He was so drunk every time that he could hardly speak properly."[63]

---

[61] Herold/Hauser, p. 96f.
[62] Cf. Hauser/Zimmermann, p. 3.
[63] Herold/Hauser, p. 96ff.

In 1980, the "Spiegel" magazine[64] publicises Franz Josef Strauß' statement as a Union candidate for the Bundestag elections in the same year.[65] The magazine wants to prevent the decades-long archenemy from becoming chancellor by any means necessary. The article once again triggers a debate about the impulsive Bavarian's suitability for the most important political office in West Germany. Strauß, the unpredictable one, who occasionally loses his cool.

It is quite possible that the tip with the Strauss quote came from the now retired President of the Federal Criminal Police Office, Horst Herold. He maintains a good relationship with the editorial team at "Spiegel" and gives interviews time and again—even after leaving office. He presumably has a copy of Helmut Schmidt's War Diary—or simply remembers the controversial word.

Even decades later, in conversation with the historian Dorothea Hauser, Horst Herold will leave no doubt that Strauß' has made this remark.

After "Der Spiegel" brought the quote into the world, Friedrich Zimmermann, head of the CSU regional group in the CDU/CSU parliamentary group in the Bundestag, demands a denial—but not from "Der Spiegel", but from the Federal Government. This puts the head of the Federal Chancellery, Manfred Schüler, in need of an explanation. In a letter to the editor of "Der Spiegel",[66] Schüler points out the informal nature of the recordings of the German autumn session. After reviewing them again, Manfred Schüler says that he cannot confirm such a statement by Franz Josef Strauß in the recordings.

At best a half-true answer. It seems unlikely that Strauß' remark found its way into the operation diary. Nevertheless, the discussions were much more than informal. As mentioned, there are result logs about it.

The fierce debate about Franz Josef Strauß' supposed remark—many media pick up on the topic—can only partly be explained by the 1980 Bundestag election campaign. "Bonn" has so far been able to keep under wraps how consistently the political decision-makers have followed Chancellor Helmut Schmidt's call for exotic proposals. In other words: borderline, radical, constitutionally problematic proposals.

Historical sources prove that other top politicians also made the Federal Chancellor's "homework". Wolfgang Mischnick, the proverbially liberal, because he is level-headed, chairman of the FDP parliamentary group in the

---

[64] The opinion-forming news magazine at the time.
[65] Cf. Exotic solution, in: Der Spiegel No. 7 of 11 February 1980, p. 27f.; cf. Archiv BK 12–211 20 (2), vol. 5, p. 122/9.
[66] Manfred Schüler: Vertrauliche Aufzeichnungen, in: Der Spiegel No. 8 of 17 February 1982, p. 7.

Bundestag, is in favour of a standardised federal police law. This would take away the police sovereignty of the federal states. Wolfgang Mischnick makes this proposal "without objection from the coalition circle", as stated in the minutes of a coalition meeting on 21 September 1977.[67]

"At the same time", the minutes continue, "it is clear within the coalition circle that there will be opposition to this proposal not only from the opposition, but also from the social-liberal side."[68] No doubt, the gentlemen know what they are doing.

This session also sees the birth of the so-called Contact Blocking Act, which is still referred to in the minutes as the "Preliminary Act on the Blocking of Defence Counsel".[69] Defence lawyers of imprisoned terrorists would no longer be allowed to visit their clients. This will also be discussed later.

Wolfgang Mischnick's proposal is civil compared to others this autumn. The proposals in a paper entitled "Reprisals" are different.[70] It contains no reference to the client(s) or the author(s). It was presumably created in the Federal Chancellery and came to the desk of its boss, perhaps even the Federal Chancellor himself, because it is included in Helmut Schmidt's war diary. The informal nature of the paper, which contains no handwritten entries, suggests that it was "sent" outside of the regular postal system.

The paper "Reprisals" lists possible punitive measures against the RAF terrorists who were to be released after the kidnapping of Hanns Martin Schleyer and later the Lufthansa plane "Landshut". It discusses ways of putting the detainees under psychological and physical pressure. This in turn is intended to exert pressure on the hijackers of Hanns Martin Schleyer.

The author (or authors) is (are) aware of the explosive nature of such ideas. It is the script for a kind of torture that has no pl in a free and democratic constitutional state. With good reason, the author(s) of the paper first discuss(es) the possible effect of the measures on the German and international public.

The following is a list of possible measures.

(1) "Change in prison conditions (including pre-trial detention)

    – Continued solitary confinement (additional primitive accommodation)

---

[67] O. A.: Re: Result of the coalition talks on issues of legislation to combat terrorism on 21 September 1977, in: Archiv BK 12–211 20 (2), vol. 7, no p.
[68] Ibid.
[69] Ibid.
[70] Archiv BK 13–211 20 (2) Additional file OTB vol. 7, no p.

- Prevention of all contacts
- Withdrawal of any information
- Court withdrawal
- Basic force-feeding
- No force-feeding
- Torture
    (a) Physical: deprivation of food, sleep, daylight Chastisements, mutilations
    (b) Psychic: light, sound, pharmaceuticals
- Forced labour

(2) Execution

   (a) Free pressing
   (b) uninvolved prisoners
   (c) Perpetrator

(3) Internment of family members and/or sympathisers
(4) Expulsion of sympathisers and supporting family members"

In the end, the author (or authors) of the paper reject(s) their exotic solutions. The paper concludes that "the number of people against whom reprisals could be directed is in any case negligible compared to the number of people who could be subject to reprisals by terrorists. Therefore: every repression triggers a spiral effect of brutality."[71]

In historical retrospect, the paper shows how little legal awareness one or more employees of the Federal Chancellery displayed during the German autumn. His or her proposals for the Federal Chancellor as the most politically powerful man in the state would suspend the free and democratic basic order of this state.

Another paper[72] in the war or operations diary goes beyond possible leverage against imprisoned RAF terrorists. It states that the death penalty would require a two-thirds majority of the Bundestag to amend the Basic Law and the Criminal Code. This poses the risk of "great polarisation, which works into the hands of terrorists. The introduction of the death penalty is described as having a positive effect on the public in Germany and a negative effect on the public abroad.

---

[71] Ibid.
[72] In the following ibid.

The paper also discusses the scenarios.

- "higher penalty for hostage-taking and criminal organisation"
- Introduction of the penal system "prison or forced labour"
- "Tougher pre-trial detention for terrorists" "preventive detention"

The author(s) come(s) to the conclusion that measures that remain within the framework of the Basic Law are unsuitable for a counter-ultimatum. "They have a rather negative effect on Schleyer's chances of survival". In the end, it is recommended that the introduction of the death penalty should be rejected because it could jeopardise the expected consensus on other counter-terrorism issues.

Almost 50 years later, such papers read in a different light. As evidence of the general hysteria that affects pretty much all West Germans, including countless ministerial officials in the federal capital Bonn. Obviously even the political decision-makers in top offices.

For the decision-makers, it is also a question of personal fitness. Federal Chancellor Helmut Schmidt had the committees meet ad hoc, with just a few hours' notice. The day-night rhythm of their members is suspended for weeks. Behind the meeting rooms there is—in the words of Hans-Jochen Vogel—"a reclining area".[73] A head of department in the Federal Chancellery had been out late at night with a lamp. "You were walking along the corridor at night and suddenly someone came round the corner."[74]

Not only are times are difficult, time itself seems to have been suspended. Federal Interior Minister Werner Maihofer would not sleep at all during the "Landshut" hijacking out of concern that it would be difficult to wake him up. Do other players in Bonn politics take wake-up pills like they once did as participants in the world war? Even Helmut Schmidt and Co. cannot override a person's biological rhythm. The gentlemen were obviously never asked this afterwards.

The Hanseatic sobriety of the Federal Chancellor characterises the culture of discussion together with the Short Briefing and the Large Political Advisory Group. The venue where the "Supreme Army Command" meets contributes to this atmosphere. The Federal Chancellery building, which had only recently been occupied, exudes the charm of a savings bank branch, according to its first employer Helmut Schmidt. The building complex is spacious but functional. The new building is a showpiece of German efficiency. There are no signs of political power at all. A place for frequent workers. Helmut

---

[73] Vogel/Hauser, p. 29f.
[74] Ibid.

Schmidt claims that his working day lasts 18 h. He likes to justify this with his sense of Immanuel Kant-inspired duty to the country. A man of the war generation cannot say that he enjoys political responsibility.

In addition to the increased sleep deficit in the German autumn, there was the enormous emotional strain, the concern for the life of Hanns Martin Schleyer and later the "Landshut" hostages. The enormous pressure from political friends and the public to give in to the kidnappers' demands. Or not to do so under any circumstances.

The perceived state of emergency in the Federal Chancellery has its counterpart on the streets and squares of Germany, where more police officers are patrolling than ever before. It feels like every German citizen is being stopped by the police at this time of year. They have to get out of their car, show their identity card and have their whole body frisked. They have to open the boot of their car. Queues stretch for kilometres because of the controls.

German Bahn passengers get off a train, are surrounded by police officers, placed against a wall and frisked. The policemen find nothing and leave without a word of apology. This experience in the German Autumn of 1977 will stay with many people.

Volker Busse, then head of the Internal Security Division and secretary of the meetings of the Short Briefing and the Large Political Advisory Group, recalls that citizens had written letters calling for RAF terrorists to be tortured or shot. A film team from the German *Süddeutscher Rundfunk* radio picks up the voices of angry citizens in Stuttgart-Stammheim, where the prison of the leading RAF terrorists is located. They demand that the terrorists should be "hanged from the nearest tree" or "shot under martial law".

Manfred Rommel carries a "loaded pistol"[75] with him at this time. Like many politicians, he accepts that police cars patrol in front of his house. The Lord Mayor of Stuttgart, Manfred Rommel, stops protecting the property after one of the police officers accidentally has shot himself with his own submachine gun.[76]

Not a day goes by without some kind of threatening call to a West German police station or federal ministry. The police have difficulty distinguishing between fake and real threats against prominent personalities and public institutions.

"Either the Ministry of Health pays a ransom of five million German mark, or we contaminate drinking water supply networks and swimming pools in a conurbation with cholera and typhoid pathogens. Large quantities of these pathogens have been

---

[75] Ibid.
[76] Cf. ibid.

produced by us and are just waiting to be used (...) If you don't want to pay, the pathogens will be used without further warning."[77]

At the end of September, the head of the Federal Chancellery, Manfred Schüler, receives notification "that there are signs of a threat to Mr Birnbaum".[78] Hans Birnbaum is General Director of Salzgitter AG. His secondary activities include chairing the Supervisory Board of Volkswagen AG. Mr Schüler asked Mr Fröhlich to inform the relevant authorities in the state of Lower Saxony in order to arrange for protective measures to be taken.

Loki and Helmut Schmidt are worried about their daughter Susanne. A year earlier, on 26 May 1976, the Federal Chancellery had received an "anonymous petition from Hamburg with a threat against the Chancellor's daughter".[79] By the German autumn, Susanne Schmidt is no longer living in Germany. She moved to Great Britain, her adopted country to this day.

Helmut Schmidt knows from seized RAF cassettes that the terrorists discussed his abduction but rejected it because of the extensive personal protection. The code name for Helmut Schmidt in the RAF papers was "Dwarf". Nevertheless, Loki and Helmut Schmidt take precautions. During a walk in the garden of the Federal Chancellery, they decide that no terrorists should be released in the event that one of them is kidnapped. Loki and Helmut Schmidt put this wish in writing. Only decades later, on the occasion of the 2013 NDR documentary "The RAF", will Helmut Schmidt talk about their joint agreement.[80]

The Federal Chancellor's ears prick up when the Large Political Advisory Group discusses RAF terrorists who are observing a property in Schleswig–Holstein. The Schmidts own a holiday home on nearby Lake Brahmsee. Helmut Schmidt asks Horst Herold to clarify whether the holiday home was under surveillance. After a short time, the Federal Criminal Police Office can answer in the negative.[81]

---

[77] Anonymous letter to the Federal Chancellery, posted on 8 September, midnight, in Mainz, in: Archiv BK 13–211 20 (3) Additional file 3, no p.

[78] Chief BK, St Dr M. Schüler of 23 September 1977. cf. 1) Note for State Secretary Dr Fröhlich. Re: Protective measures for Mr Birnbaum, Chairman of the Executive Board of Salzgitter AG dated 23 September 1979, in: Archiv BK 13–211 20 (2) Additional file 3, no p.

[79] BArch B 136/15632 The idea of kidnapping the Federal Chancellor was apparently rejected early on. In the 1970s the police found a note in a flat belonging to the RAF, stating that the risk of "getting close to the Chancellor" was too great. He was too well regarded. See Hella Kemper: Die Sache mit der Tasche. Otti Heuer was Helmut Schmidt's bodyguard for 26 years, in: Die Zeit. Helmut Schmidt on his 90th birthday, Hamburg 2013, p. 38.

[80] Cf. former Chancellor Schmidt. No exchange in the kidnapping case, in: Focus Online of 13 November 2013, accessed on 2 February 2023.

[81] Archiv BK 13–211 20 (3), vol. 1, p. 179.

The leader of the opposition in the German Bundestag, Helmut Kohl, recalls in his memoirs "that many men no longer sit in the car with me. For fear of assassins."[82] He was not only politically but also personally affected by the fate of Hanns Martin Schleyer. Both belonged to the same hunting party.

Helmut Kohl suggests to the Federal Chancellor that he offers himself to the kidnappers as an exchange hostage. The suggestion was presumably made by one of Hanns Martin Schleyer's corps brothers from the common student days, the Palatinate entrepreneur Fritz Ries ("Pegulan Werke Frankenthal"). He is a close friend of both Hanns Martin Schleyer and Helmut Kohl.

Helmut Schmidt rejects Kohl's offer out of hand. And may feel confirmed once again that the emotional Helmut Kohl is not fit to be Federal Chancellor.

Four years before the German Autumn, former Federal President Gustav Heinemann and his wife were already talking about the possibility of being kidnapped. "In the event that I fall into the hands of blackmailers (…)", says a letter from Gustav Heinemann to State Secretary Dieter Spangenberg in the Office of the Federal President,[83] "after careful consideration, I ask and expect all those concerned to make the decision *without regard to my person* (emphasis added by G. H., note M. R.)."[84]

After the kidnapping of Hanns Martin Schleyer, the Heinemanns return to this letter. In mid-September 1977, Hilda Heinemann asks the Office of the Federal President to pass on her husband's statement to the Federal Chancellor.[85] This is also done.

At the same time—or on Hilda Heinemann's initiative?—personal security for Gustav Heinemann's successor, Federal President Walter Scheel, is stepped up. Police officers are now stationed around the clock at his private home. Officers from Border Guard Force 9 supplement the Federal President's escort team when he keeps appointments outside his official residence.

The German autumn is also trying the patience of politicians in Bonn. Federal Interior Minister Werner Maihofer—there has already been talk of that—becomes a cause for concern in the eyes of his colleagues. In retrospect, Friedrich Zimmermann calls the FDP politician a "guileless skater" who gave the impression that "he had now been abruptly torn out of his young girl's

---

[82] Quoted from Bahners 1998, p. 178.
[83] Archiv BK 13–211 20 (2) Additional file OTB vol. 4, p. 23.
[84] Ibid.
[85] Cf. letter from the head of the Federal Criminal Police Office to the head of the Federal Chancellery dated 15 September 1977, in: ibid. p. 22.

dreams".[86] Werner Maihofer had hardened over time, "from an over-Saul to an over-Paul".[87]

Government spokesman Klaus Bölling also comes off badly in the retrospect of other members of the crisis team. "Bölling was one of those people who always wanted to give up. Bölling (…) is always out for consensus. That's his character."[88]

In a television documentary ten years after the German Autumn, the former government spokesman still seems personally shaken. He reproaches himself for not having insisted on the rescue of Hanns Martin Schleyer.[89] He thus remains an isolated case among the Bonn decision-makers during the German Autumn.

---

[86] Ibid., p. 11.
[87] Ibid., p. 14.
[88] Ibid. p. 3.
[89] Cf. Kienzle 1987.

3

The Brutality of Chance

Palma De Mallorca Airport

On the morning of 13 October 1977, the Lufthansa aircraft "Landshut", registration number D-ABCE, stands at Palma de Mallorca Airport. A Boeing 737–200, also known as "Bobby" because of its squat shape. The flight number is LH 181 and the aircraft had arrived in the morning from Frankfurt am Main. Captain Jürgen Schumann had flown it. In addition to him, co-pilot Jürgen Vietor, purserette Hannelore Brauchart (née Piegler) and stewardesses Annamaria Staringer and Gabriele von Lutzau (née Dillmann) make up the crew.

Part of everyday life at Lufthansa is that crew members are called to duty at short notice if necessary. There is a duty rota that often has to be knocked over. Instead of Jürgen Vietor, a colleague coming from Hamburg is supposed to be on duty in the "Landshut". But fog hangs over Hamburg and the colleague cannot leave. Jürgen Vietor, at home in Bensheim, Hesse, is called out of stand-by to fill in.

He gets out of bed late that morning. Rushed but on time, he arrives at the aircraft's take-off point at Frankfurt Airport.

Gabriele von Lutzau (née Dillmann) is also on stand-by that morning. And learns that she has to fly in place of a colleague. Her partner Ruediger von Lutzau, who has recently become a co-pilot for Lufthansa, drives her to the airport. Contrary to what authors would have you believe later, the two do not have a deep conversation on the way there. Not one about getting married or having children. On this supposedly normal day, Ruediger von

Lutzau says goodbye to his girlfriend as usual: "Have a good flight. See you tonight. I love you."

At Palma de Mallorca Airport, the small aircraft designed for short-haul flights is loaded with cargo. Airport employees push two zinc coffins with dead bodies to be transferred into the cargo hold. A cage full of exotic birds for a zoo. A tapestry by Pablo Picasso, the most important artist of the twentieth century. The valuable piece—Pablo Picasso did not design many tapestries—is to be exhibited in a German museum.

The women and men on this short-haul flight come from all directions. Cäcilia Meyer-Werner has been on holiday in her holiday home in Mallorca and wants to return to Hamburg via a stopover in Frankfurt am Main. The same goes for Hartwig Faby and his mate Rhett Waida, who is carrying his son Steffen, just under three years old, in his arms. Hartwig Faby has never flown before. Rhett Waida gave his wife her first days off after Steffen's birth with the holiday.

Julia Filius (née Sost) wears red patent leather shoes. Her handbag is made of genuine crocodile leather. Julia Filius and her husband Dietrich were on holiday in Ibiza, but they were bored of the island. They decided to return to Germany as soon as possible. They even took a stopover: from Ibiza they travelled to Palma de Mallorca and now to Frankfurt am Main.

Two Arab women and two Arab men check in quite late. A few passengers will later say that they thought the four of them were strange in the terminal. This happens at quite a few airports around the world that morning. In this case, passengers will remember their impression for life.

Last but not least, in a very literal sense, a group of young women want to join the "Landshut". Wilhelmine "Helma" van Dreumel, Jutta Knauff (née Brod), Nomi Wilkens Jensen, Diana Müll, Simone Regelmann (née Liedke), Dorothea Selter and Beate Keller (née Zerbst) spent a week's holiday in El Arenal and took part in a beauty contest in the "Graf Zeppelin" discotheque, with Jutta Knauff (née Brod) as the winner.

The barman, a German with the nickname "Otte", is supposed to collect them that morning and drive them to the airport. The young women had partied hard during the night and got out of bed too late and hungover. "Otte" knows he wouldn't be able to make the scheduled departure time of the "Landshut". He alerts his boss Manfred Riek, the operator of the "Graf Zeppelin" discotheque. Manfred Riek calls the Lufthansa airport desk and insists that the aircraft wait for the women. Otherwise, he threatens, he will advise future discotheque guests from Germany never to fly with LH again. And he won't either.

3 The Brutality of Chance

The threat is effective, Lufthansa employees ask the "Landshut" pilots to wait. What does it matter if a short-haul flight takes off later than planned?

Diana Müll and the others know nothing about Manfred Riek's initiative. They only find out about it 40 years later, during a visit to "Otte's" restaurant for a television documentary.[1] At first, the former "Landshut" hostages cannot believe that they almost slept through their own abduction. Diana Müll bursts into tears.

The aircraft doors are closed. The aircraft, with eight seats in First Class and 85 in Economy, is almost full. 86 passengers and five crew members take their seats. It is cramped in a Boeing 737–200 with a floor area of 73 square metres. The American aircraft manufacturer only designed the "Bobby" under pressure from Lufthansa Germany. The airline needed a short-haul aircraft to transport business travellers between European capitals. "Bobby" is a sales success right from the start, because not only in Germany, but throughout Europe, things are much tighter than in the USA.

In an almost full "Bobby", the confinement is particularly great.

What "Landshut" passengers don't normally realise: The aircraft can do even more. Heavy hauling. On some of Lufthansa's 737 s, the seats are removed in the evening in order to fly cargo through the night. The "Landshut" is one of these aircrafts, recognisable by the large cargo door at the front left. Thanks to its dual role as a passenger and cargo aircraft, the 737 has a robust design. It can take a lot. A small, faithful packhorse.

The "Bobby" is not beautiful, but it is reliable. A kind of VW Beetle of the skies. The "Landshut" will have to prove its phenomenal robustness.

Right after the start, a party atmosphere sets in.[2] Someone treats the "beauty queens" to a bottle of sparkling wine. The two stewardesses Eva Maria Staringer and Gabriele von Lutzau serve lunch.

When the "Landshut" passengers have almost finished, two women and two men jump up, shouting and waving weapons. Pistols, hand grenades, explosives. A man and a woman run to the front of the cockpit while throwing punches. There, the man declares the flight hijacked. He kicks the co-pilot Jürgen Vietor, who has to leave the cockpit. The second woman drives the stewardesses out of the galley.

The co-pilot and the female crew have to find free seats in the rear. The same goes for the First-Class passengers and the passengers in the first Economy row. The hijackers claim First Class for themselves. In rear Economy, men have to sit away from the aisle in a window seat. From there, they cannot spontaneously jump up to overpower the hijackers.

---

[1] Interview Baum/Treuter 2017b.
[2] Cf. Götschenberg 2022, p. 55.

The passengers don't put up any resistance, how could they? The tables opened up for lunch, with crockery on them, make resistance impossible. The hijackers obviously know their criminal trade.

The aircraft is flying at an altitude of 33,000 feet. Jürgen Vietor fears that the terrorist leader will fire a shot, "then there will be a rapidity compression (…), you have no chance of survival (…)."[3] Captain Jürgen Schumann is forced to change the plane's course. "Captain Machmud", as the leader calls himself, names Larnaca on Cyprus as the destination. Captain Jürgen Schumann calculates the fuel required to get there. No chance. The "Landshut", he explains, has to land earlier! Now Captain Machmud demands to fly to Rome-Fiumicino. Captain Jürgen Schumann sets course for Rome.

In the fuselage of the plane, the other terrorists reel off the routines they have been drilled in the weeks before. All the hostages have to hand over their passports for their personal incapacitation. The hand luggage is collected and stacked at the front right cockpit door. The passengers are only allowed to speak English so that the hijackers understand what is said. Anyone who wants to use the toilet has to raise the hand and wait for permission.

The kidnappers do everything they can to wear down the hostages down physically and mentally. They are supposed to fall into a state of apathy in which resistance is no longer possible. As a first measure, they are not allowed to go to the toilet for hours. This leaves them with little else to think about. And suspends social standards. A beauty queen says to someone next to her: "I can't hold it anymore". The neighbour replies: "Let it go."

Harassment follows harassment. Couples, families, people travelling together, the crew are put away from each other. Any sense of togetherness is to be suppressed. Men have to hand over combs, keys, penknives, pens and pen lighters. To prevent self-harm, as the kidnappers explain. Women hand over their hand bags. They are not supposed to be able to take care of themselves.

At 3.40 p.m., the "Landshut" touches down at Rome's Fiumicino Airport. The tower directs them to a secluded area surrounded by a high fence. The leader of the terrorists, who identifies himself to tower as "Captain Mohammed", demands that the plane be refuelled.

The leader knows he needs the pilots and crew to carry out his plans. He makes the two swear an oath not to try any tricks. "No tricks. No fools, otherwise, You will be executed, or the airplane will be blown."[4] "We promise

---

[3] Conversation Vietor/Salewski 1977. vol. S I, no page number, presumably p. 1.
[4] Gerspach Vietor/Salewski, Vol. S I, p. 14.

you: no tricks",[5] Captain Jürgen Schumann and co-pilot Jürgen Vietor assure him.

Bonn

At 2.38 p.m., the drama has begun. Air traffic control notices that flight LH181 is flying "uncontrolled turns"[6] over Alghero, a coastal town in Sardinia. At 3.00 p.m. over Cagliari (Sardinia). At 3.30 p.m., there is certainty that the "Landshut" is heading for Rome. Federal Minister of the Interior Werner Maihofer is informed. He in turn informs the Federal Chancellor—and already surmises a hijacking during this conversation.

BKA chief Horst Herold expected a follow-up action by terrorists to increase the pressure on the German government. With an attack on a German embassy abroad or the kidnapping of another person in Germany. But not with an operation by an international commando group to seize 86 passengers and five crew members of a Lufthansa scheduled flight.

A Lufthansa aircraft, of all things, the supposedly safest airline in the world. On the routine flight of a small plane, a better railway, except that it doesn't drive, but flies.

Deadly. There was mortal horror", is how Horst Herold would later describe the reaction in the Short Briefing and the Large Political Advisory Group.[7] "Ultimately", Helmut Schmidt's biographer Klaus Stephan will aptly state, "there was no way out of the matter with a triumph without any loss, possibly only with losses without any triumph.[8]

Women, men and children in the hands of unpredictable terrorists. A completely new "situation", to choose Helmut Schmidt's military terminology. Suddenly "Schleyer's life (...) becomes very small in relation to this large number of hostages", as Horst Herold will put it literally decades later.[9] The focus shifted away from the employer president to the rescue of many in the "Landshut". Every effort continues to be made to free Hanns Martin Schleyer alive. But the participants in the Short Briefing and the Large Political Advisory Group know that the national and international attention now belongs to the people in the "Landshut"—like their own personal attention.

---

[5] Ibid.
[6] German Lufthansa: Flight log, p. 1.
[7] Herold/Hauser, p. 103.
[8] Steffahn 1990, p. 10.
[9] Ibid, p. 104.

And the political success of their actions will be measured by whether and how many passengers will leave the aircraft alive.

The discussion quickly turns to "shooting the thing out", as one of the participants says, i.e. freeing the hostages with special forces. "What else?",[10] whispers the SPD parliamentary group leader Hebert Wehner, who says little in the meetings. Federal Chancellor Helmut Schmidt is happy to take note. He has deep respect for Herbert Wehner's political achievements after 1949 and for his sharp mind. "We can't execute eighty people because of one principle", is how Horst Herold would summarise the mood in both crisis teams decades later.[11]

Rom

Standing Time "Landshut": Thursday, 13 October 1977, 3.40 P.M. To 5.42 P.M.

At 3.40 p.m., the "Landshut" touches down at Rome-Fiumicino Airport. Rome. Italy. A close political ally of the Federal Republic of Germany. A difficult one. Italian politics is as temperamental as the people it is supposed to govern. Governments rarely last a full legislative period, coalition breaks, and early elections are part of everyday political life. The state cannot make ends meet. Back then as little as today.

In autumn 1977, a Christian Democrat, Mario Andreotti, governs without a majority in parliament, tolerated by the Communists of all people. This caused the most important allies—the USA, France, Great Britain and the Federal Republic of Germany—to distance themselves. During the Cold War, communists in the West are seen as outposts of the "Eastern Bloc". When the Italian government asked the Western industrialised nations for loans, it was rebuffed. Also, with the German Chancellor.

Terror rages not only in the Federal Republic of Germany, but also in Italy, where it comes from both the right and the left. Members of the "Red Brigades" commit acts of violence even more frequently than members of the Red Army Faction. The police cannot keep up with the prosecution of the many crimes.

It isn't just Italy and Germany that are experiencing unprecedented bloodshed in those years; the same is true of Northern Ireland. It would take decades before the conflict there was resolved politically. This accumulation of

---

[10] Cf. Wischnewski/Hauser, p. 27.
[11] Ibid, p. 104.

trouble spots in Europe presumably occurs at the end of the post-war period. Overcoming the political and economic consequences after 1949 took time and effort. Now conflicts are becoming domestic again. The Federal Republic of Germany gets off comparatively lightly.

Italy. Rome. The small Lufthansa plane "Landshut" with Palestinian hijackers on board evokes traumatic memories. On 17 December 1973, a five-man Palestinian commando caused a bloodbath at the same airport. Terrorists opened fire in the transit area, detonated two phosphorus bombs and hijacked a Lufthansa aircraft together with her crew. Over 30 people were killed and 15 were seriously injured.[12]

Domestic political reasons also mean that the Italian government during the "Landshut's" stopover in Rome-Fiumicino does not want to see, hear or say anything. And will days later add to the NATO partners' annoyance with contradictory statements.

The government, with a right-wing prime minister, Giulio Andreotti, and a communist tolerator, Enrico Berlinguer, is neutralising itself politically. Now that a hijacked plane is parked outside the capital, no top politician is really taking the initiative. The government could come to the aid of its German ally, but the domestic and foreign policy consequences seem incalculable. At this early stage of the hijacking, nothing is known about the identity and motives of the terrorists.

Italian Foreign Minister Amaldo Forlani is faced with the practical problem that the country's most important politicians are not within easy reach. Interior Minister Francesco Cossiga may also remember the political fate of his predecessor Paolo Emilio Taviani. He had to resign after the bloodbath of 1973.

At 5.39 p.m., the State Secretary in the Federal Ministry of Transport, Heinz Ruhnau, contacts the Italian Ministry of the Interior. Later, Federal Minister of the Interior Werner Maihofer and his counterpart Francesco Cossiga speak on the phone. Werner Maihofer asks that the aircraft not be allowed to take off under any circumstances. The Italian police is to shoot through the tyres of the "Landshut". What makes the minister think that? A draconian measure that could trigger a short-circuit reaction from the hijackers.

At the airport, German embassy staff get the impression that they are being held up by incorrect information, confusion about responsibilities and the inability to find the person they want to speak to. The Italians have the "Landshut" refuelled with 9,700 litres of fuel at 4.53 p.m. That is an

---

[12] See Terhoeven 2014, p. 506.

announcement. Later they will claim: We tried to delay the refuelling by positioning the tanker accordingly.

In fact, the Italian police had "arrived in full force, but did not intervene. (…)".[13]

Surprise, horror and an inability to manage the crisis characterise the situation. In the few pictures shown on German television in the evening, the "Landshut" stands in a bright, late autumnal light. Because of its characteristic snout, it is the "Bobby" and somehow not. Its stay in Rome is an interlude planned by the terrorists, to be followed by others.

The terrorist leader points his pistol in the direction of Jürgen Vietor's temple and says: "You take off now." The co-pilot pushes the throttle forward. At 5.42 pm, the "Landshut" starts to move. Without permission to take off. Her lights remain switched off. It taxis onto the runway and takes off.

Allegedly, an instruction from Interior Minister Cossiga to stop the plane did not arrive until two and a half minutes later. Chancellor Helmut Schmidt would later claim that Francesco Cossiga had promised Werner Maihofer that the "Landshut" would be held in Rome but reneged on this promise.[14]

Francesco Cossiga wants to explain the Italian government's behaviour in parliament on 20 October. Italy had the plane towed "because of the threatened reactions and the decision taken by the hijackers and the person in control of the plane, which left them with no other option than an extremely high-risk violent action, without it having been possible to apply the necessary measures—also in terms of psychological handling—in the short time available".[15]

German Chancellor Helmut Schmidt reacts with disappointment, even anger. Days later, he would express his indignation to British Prime Minister James Callaghan about the "negative experiences" with the Italians.[16] From Helmut Schmidt's point of view, "Rome" had failed to fulfil something that the German Chancellor and former soldier in the Great War places particular value on: Reliability.

---

[13] German Lufthansa, Event Log, p. 1.

[14] See Terhoeven 2014, p. 509.

[15] The State Secretary of the Federal Foreign Office. The personal advisor -. To the personal adviser to the Head of the Federal Chancellery, State Secretary Dr Schüler. Bonn, 24 October 1977: Italian behaviour during the hijacking of the LH aircraft "Landshut". Translation of the statement by the Italian Interior Minister Cossiga before the Italian Parliament on 20 October 1977, in: Archiv BK 13–211 20 (2) Additional file OTB Bd. 7, p. 133.

[16] See Terhoeven 2014, p. 509.

Larnaka

Standing Time "Landshut": Thursday, 13 October 1977, 8.40 P.M. To 10.50 P.M.

Holidaymakers and businesspeople. Picked at random—the main thing is that most of them have a German passport. Another violent crime committed by Palestinian terrorists to draw attention to their political lawlessness and terrible living conditions.

Memories of the assassination attempt in Munich come to mind. Five years earlier, Palestinian compatriots stabbed the heart of the Olympic Games by taking the Israeli athlete's hostage in the Olympic Village. The terrorists murdered ruthlessly. An amateurish rescue attempt by the German police at Fürstenfeldbruck airport sealed the catastrophe. One of the powerless witnesses was Ulrich Wegener, who was entrusted with setting up Border Guard Force 9 after the fiasco.

The "Landshut" hijacking strikes again at the heart of the Federal Republic of Germany in its 32nd year after the end of the war and the 28th year since its foundation. West Germany is one of the world's leading economies. As a result of an "economic miracle", wages rose sharply in the 1960s and early 1970s. By up to ten per cent and more every year. The so-called oil crisis of 1973 caused an economic slump, which the German government cushioned with debt—the beginning of a gigantic debt policy that continues to this day.

Germans live a consumer-orientated life with little interest in politics. The few female politicians and many male politicians in Bonn think that's just fine. They believe they can do everything better than the young and remain in top offices as long as their health allows. Herbert Wehner, Willy Brandt, Franz Josef Strauß, Helmut Schmidt—the same faces at the centres of power for decades.

The economic miracle after 1949 was no sure-fire success. The advocates of the so-called social market economy set out on a long, rocky road that put people's patience to the test. It was not until the end of the 1950s that the measures taken by the architects of the economic miracle began to take effect. The most famous of them, Federal Minister of Economics Ludwig Erhard, averted his political failure in the final metres.

This economic growth was helped by the fact that there are many production sites in the territory of the Federal Republic as the heartland of a née larger German Reich. Areas lost during the Second World War, such as Silesia and East Prussia, contributed comparatively little to the gross national product of the Reich.

In addition, many companies that had previously been in the so-called Eastern zone or the later GDR were newly established in the West. Schott, for example, or Zeiss. Nor did the Federal Republic of Germany suffer the fate of the GDR, whose industrial plants were often sent to the Soviet Union. The Western Allies treated West Germany better than the Soviets treated East Germany.

The bumpy start is quickly forgotten, and things improve with every year. With the help of above alle the Americans and through their own efforts. Work makes a decent life possible and numbs the pain of the soul. Traumas from Hitler's Germany and the world war. Cigarettes and alcohol help with this. The tobacco and spirits industry enjoys the prospering rump Germany.

On that October day in 1977, when a Lufthansa plane en route to Frankfurt am Main is diverted from its destination and hijacked to the Horn of Africa, Germans are living in great prosperity. In one of the kitchens of that time stands the orange-coloured "Moulinex", a forerunner of the current "Thermomix". In the living room, a television from brands such as Telefunken or Grundig. Most West Germans were already watching in colour. German consumer electronics are one of the leading in the world. So is the precision engineering of cameras and cameras. From Leitz, Rollei or Bauer.

Villeroy and Boch equips West German households with crockery. Normal earners choose the "Avocado" service, while higher earners go for the "Wild Rose". Never before and never again have such differences had such significance. AEG or Miele. Opel or Mercedes-Benz.

Germany is divided, the so-called federal territory occupied by the Western powers of the Second World War. In this squeeze, a rump Germany thrives and flourishes, which almost 50 years later will awaken nostalgic feelings in many older and younger Germans. The "old" Federal Republic of the 1970s is presumably experiencing its best period—politically a dwarf, but prosperous and modern. Musty and cosy. Simply great! As Hans Rosendahl puts it in a nutshell in his programme "Dalli-Dalli".

Speaking of television. The programme stands for comfort with only a small political component. On this Thursday, 13 October 1977, "Die Drehscheibe" starts at 5.40 p.m. on Second German Television, followed at 8.30 p.m. by "Tegtmeier's Travels—Jürgen von Manger in the USA". The following evening, at 9.55 p.m., ARD will show "Bericht aus Bonn" with Friedrich Nowottny. At 11.15 p.m., the "Tatort" episode "Kassensturz" with Inspector Franz Gerber (Heinz Schimmelpfennig) will be repeated.

In 1977, many West Germans can afford a summer holiday in Mallorca in addition to the good life during the year. Spanish and West German businessmen trade successfully between their countries. Horst-Gregorio Canellas, for example, at times president of the Bundesliga football club Kickers Offenbach and hostage in the "Landshut", sells fruit and vegetables in Germany with economic success.

The "Landshut" hostage Julia Filius (née Sost) wears her red patent leather shoes in the "Landshut". As a statement. The middle-class family can afford children, a house, holidays and fashion items. The fact that the holiday in 1977 was boring, as Julia Filius recalls in retrospect, is another matter. So what? After the holiday is before the holiday.

The leader of the terror squad instructs co-pilot Jürgen Vietor to target the Cypriot capital Larnaca. In this early phase of the abduction the atmosphere is tense. The hostages are not yet tired and could put up a fight. However, they are in shock and feel they have been transported into a nightmare.

At 7:11, Captain Schumann places a message in a position description: "2 men, 2 women, with pistols and hand grenades".[17] The captain of Lufthansa flight 640/13 is listening in and passing on the information so that it reaches Deutsche Lufthansa and the German government.

At 8.40 pm, the hijacked plane lands where "Captain Machmud" wanted it to be earlier in the day, in the Greek section of Larnaca Airport in Cyprus. The island republic's foreign minister, Ioannis Christophides, is currently in New York. He is there to assure the German ambassador to the United Nations, Ruedeger von Wechmar, of his support. Finance Minister Andreas Patsalides promises Federal Minister of the Interior Werner Maihofer on the phone that he will use force if necessary to prevent the "Landshut" from continuing its flight.

But the Greek Cypriots—the island is divided between Greece and Turkey—are doing as the Italians did before them. Say one thing, do another… Their diplomatic room for manoeuvre is small. In the constant confrontation with the Turkish Cypriots and the middle power Turkey, they need support from other parts of the world, for example from the Arabs. An Arab terror squad, which the German interior minister has asked to stop, does not suit them.

"Captain Machmud" demands that the aircraft be refuelled. The attaché of the German Embassy is coming to the Tower. The authorities want to gain time for negotiations with a representative of the Palestinian Liberation Organisation (PLO) in the tower. The PLO man talks for an hour with "Captain Machmud", who raves and shouts during the radio conversation. He has already realised that many of his compatriots disapprove of the kidnapping.

---

[17] German Lufthansa, Event-Log, p. 2.

In Larnaca, the pilots have their first opportunity to bunk off. The terrorist leader stays in the back for a while to wait for fuel. Captain Jürgen Schumann and co-pilot Jürgen Vietor are alone in the cockpit. Jürgen Schumann wants to get away. "He always wanted to leave."[18] Schumann says to his co-pilot: "Come on, let's get out of here. (…) We go through the cockpit windows (…)."[19]

You can climb out of the cockpit through the windows and jump onto the airfield or abseil down using a rope, which is part of the cockpit equipment.

Jürgen Vietor waves it off: "(…) You can leave, I'll stay on board. I'm not doing this. I'm staying with the passengers."[20]

Jürgen Vietor goes on to say that it was a conversation between the captain and him, "not an argument". "I gave my opinion on the subject, I said you can go, I'm staying."[21]

There are also only a few photos and television images of the Landshut's stopover in Larnaca—an aircraft is parked on an airfield in complete darkness, lights flashing. At 9.57 p.m., the terrorist leader becomes impatient and threatens to blow up the plane if a petrol tanker does not arrive immediately. At 10.27 p.m., the "Landshut" is refuelled. At 10.50 p.m., the "Landshut" takes off for Beirut despite the previous warning from the tower that Beirut airport was closed.

The Cypriot government will later claim that its security forces do not have suitable weapons to shoot out the tyres of an aircraft. Apparently, the German government—allegedly Federal Minister of the Interior Werner Maihofer—had expressed this wish not only to the Italian, but also to the Cypriot government.

The reluctance of the Cypriots to help the German government is evident in the handling of another aircraft. This aircraft is carrying officials from the Federal Criminal Police Office and Ulrich Wegener's Border Guard Force 9 to the British military airfield at Akrotiri on the south coast of the republic. From there, the plan is to continue to Larnaca, around 60 kilometres away.

The aircraft only receives permission to land in the capital at 0.54 am. By then, the "Landshut" had already been gone for almost two hours. Nobody on the BKA and BGS aircraft is allowed to disembark. Contrary to a promise to the German embassy that the aircraft would be allowed to stay in Cyprus for as long as it wanted, the authorities urge it to take off. The German aircraft takes off with an unknown destination. At this point, it does not

---

[18] Discussion Vietor/Salewski, vol. S I, p. 11.
[19] Ibid.
[20] Ibid.
[21] Ibid.

have permission to land from another country. It finally lands in the Turkish capital Ankara.

It is also unwelcome there. At the request of the Turkish government, its landing is to remain secret. Passengers and crew have to spend 39 h in the aircraft. Only smokers are allowed to disembark for the length of a cigarette.[22]

The solidarity of other states with the German government, which is facing an international hijacking, is definitely not very strong.

Bahrain

Standing Time "Landshut": Friday, 14 October, 01.52 h to 03.24 h

"'By early 1970, most Middle Eastern states had learned,' writes historian Thomas Skelton-Robinson in a highly illuminating essay, 'to fear the consequences of allowing a hijacked aircraft to land'. This explains why subsequent hijackings often involved agonisingly long flights to increasingly distant countries in order to find a 'friendly' one that would land the plane for 'humanitarian' reasons and at the express request of Western governments."[23]

This is also the fate of the hijacked "Bobby". Beirut airport, the capital of Lebanon, is effectively closed. Also, the Syrian capital Damascus does not want the "Landshut" either. Neither does "Jordan"[24]. On the orders of "Captain Machmud", the "Landshut" flies to the Kingdom of Bahrain. The tower is persuaded that the aircraft urgently needs fuel and transmits the frequencies for the instrument landing system. At 01:52, the hijacked "Landshut" lands in Bahrain—politically an absolute monarchy run by a clan.

The "Landshut" is not wanted here either. On the airfield, the aircraft is immediately surrounded by soldiers. A clear indication that political negotiations are not on the agenda. "Captain Machmud" demands that the tower withdraw the soldiers. He gives them five minutes. Otherwise, he will shoot Jürgen Vietor. In this first phase of the hijacking, his anger is directed at the co-pilot, not yet at the captain—perhaps because the leader has undergone pilot training himself and has respect for a German captain.

"Captain Machmud" sits in the first-observer seat behind the captain and presses the pistol to Jürgen Vietor's head. "I shoot you. You will be killed", roars "Captain Machmud". Jürgen Vietor begs the tower to carry out the

---

[22] See Herzog 2022, p. 197.
[23] Skelton-Robinson 2006, p. 839.
[24] German Lufthansa, Event-Log, p. 3, probably referring to the Jordanian capital Amman.

order. "I begged for my life", the co-pilot will later say to "Stern" magazine reporter Gerd Heidemann.[25] Jürgen Schumann also implores that Jürgen Vietor be allowed to live.

The five minutes are almost up. Suddenly there is movement among the soldiers. They retreat. Suddenly the "Landshut" stands alone on the airfield. The terrorist leader lets go of the co-pilot and pockets the pistol. What reads like the script of a crime thriller is a terrible reality.

Jürgen Vietor finds himself in danger a second time in Bahrain through his own doing. In an announcement to the tower, he calls the kidnap squad "terrorists". A loss of words. "We are no terrorists! We are peacefighters!", shouts "Captain Machmud" into the microphone. It again takes the energetic efforts of Jürgen Schumann and the crew to calm the choleric man down.

Even at this early stage of the kidnapping, it is clear that the two women and two men of the commando are well prepared for their task. They appear physically fit and have the psychological know-how to keep 91 people at bay for days. With carrots and sticks. Mental and physical humiliations are followed by friendly gestures, even cordiality. Then threats and harassment again. The hostages are never supposed to know where they stand with "Captain Machmud".

The command appears to have been carefully put together. "Captain Machmud" is in a relationship with the younger of the two terrorists, the woman adores him. The second female terrorist and the second male terrorist have no energy comparable to that of the boss. They loyally carry out his orders. At no time during the days of the kidnapping a proverbial piece of paper fits between the members of the kidnap squad.

Bahrain was both a necessary and politically useful stopover for the hijackers. The "Landshut", built for short-haul flights, has to land again and again to avoid running out of fuel. At the same time, every change of location produces new television images and makes headlines around the world. Take-offs and landings always cause new political upheavals. Presumably, the terrorist commando's strategy is to wear down the German government.

The "Landshut" remains in Bahrain for less than two hours. Further threats from the terrorist leader led to the aircraft being refuelled. At 03:24 am, the "Landshut" taxis onto the runway and takes off for an unknown destination. At this time, all airports in the Persian Gulf are already closed.

---

[25] Interview Vietor/Heidemann 1977.

Bonn

In Bonn, politic and police officials are in the dark about the identity of the terrorists. So far, "Captain Machmud" has only hinted that he shares the demands of the Red Army Faction for the release of terrorists. BKA chief Horst Herold wins over the Spanish police for a so-called dragnet search; 22,000 hotel registrations are checked for the authenticity of the names on Mallorca. That takes time.

Shortly after 1.00 a.m., the German government receives messages from the office of Geneva lawyer Denis Payot, who as told is mediating between Hanns Martin Schleyer's kidnappers and the German government. The Schleyer kidnappers confirm the connection between the two kidnappings. Once again, their professionalism in dealing with the most modern means of communication at the time is demonstrated. Your contact with the perpetrators of the "Landshut" hijacking seems to be going smoothly. Both groups threaten the federal government hand in hand.

"We have now given Helmut Schmidt enough time to change his mind (…)"[26], the kidnappers of the president of the employers' association Hanns Martin Schleyer once again address Federal Chancellor Helmut Schmidt directly in a statement. "The ultimatum of Operation Kofr Kadum of the commando 'Martyr Halimeh' and the ultimatum of the commando 'Siegfried Hausner' of the RAF are identical."[27] A letter of confession with the title "communiqué of operation kofr kaddum" appears.

Kaddum is a Palestinian village near Nablus that was destroyed by the Israelis. It is located in the area of the Israeli-occupied West Bank, which used to belong to Jordan.

Kofr Kadum. Martyr Halimeh. The terrorists themselves call the commando "martyr halimeh" ("Martyr Halima"). The German terrorist Brigitte Kuhlmann bore the code name "Halima" during the hijacking of a passenger plane of the Israeli airline El Al to Entebbe, Uganda, in June 1976. Brigitte Kuhlmann was killed during the violent liberation of the hostages by Israeli soldiers. In Arab countries, "Halimeh" (English spelling) is considered a martyr. The "Landshut" kidnapping is obviously also an act of revenge for the failure in Entebbe.

---

[26] Statement Commando Siegfried Hausner of 13 October 1977, in: Archiv BK 13–211 20 (2) Additional File OTB Bd. 5, p. 238.
[27] Ibid.

"Today, Thursday, 13 October 1977, our commando "martyr halimeh"[28] took complete control of the Lufthansa plane, flight No. 191, on its way from Palma de Mallorca to Frankfurt" begins the message from the "Landshut" hijackers.[29] This is followed by a vague condemnation of the Western states which, together with Israel, have allied themselves "against all Arab masses". The hijackers accuse these states of "world imperialism". According to this, the West—with the help of the "Zionists"—Jews—wants to rule over the Arabs.

The catalogue of demands includes the release of the eleven RAF terrorists, which the kidnappers of employer president Hanns Martin Schleyer already want to obtain, as well as two members of the extreme Palestinian wing PFLP (Popular Front for the Liberation of Palestine), who are being held in custody in Istanbul. More on the PFLP later.

In addition, 15 million US dollars in hand money. The so-called target countries to which the terrorists want to be flown are the Democratic Republic of Vietnam, the Republic of Somalia and the People's Democratic Republic of Yemen. If the demands were not met, Hanns Martin Schleyer's would be killed and plane would be blown up with passengers and crew.

The two-page declaration reveals the proximity, but also the distance to RAF terrorism in the Federal Republic of Germany. On the one hand, it reaffirms the demands of the Schleyer kidnappers. On the other hand, it makes it clear that the Palestinians are concerned with something completely different. The hatred of West Germany relates to its close political and economic cooperation with the Palestinians' main enemy, Israel. "In fact, the similar character of neo-Nazism in West Germany and Zionism in Israel is becoming increasingly clear."[30] Both states, so the argument goes, are fighting freedom fighters all over the world, in Germany against members of the Red Army Faction, in Israel against the Palestinians.

The connection seems artificial. The command ignores the fact that the German chancellors of the 1970s, Willy Brandt and Helmut Schmidt, was or rather is not so vehemently in favour of the interests of the Palestinian party as their Austrian counterpart, Chancellor Bruno Kreisky (a politician with Jewish roots). Nevertheless, their federal governments supported or rather supports international declarations on the Palestinians' right to

---

[28] Four years earlier, the connection between Palestinian and German terrorists had already become apparent. At the 1972 Olympic Games, a Palestinian terrorist commando stormed the accommodation of Israeli athletes. The hostage-takers' demands included the release of members of the "Baader-Meinhof gang", as the RAF was still commonly referred to at the time.

[29] Communiqué of Operation Kofr Kaddum, in: Press and Information Office of the Federal Government 1977, p. 88ff.

[30] Ibid, p. 90.

self-determination. The "Landshut" hijackers show solidarity with the RAF members in their terrorist struggle, but they also seize the opportunity to once again draw attention to their own, the Palestinian cause.

The "Landshut" hijacking is, as it soon turns out, not a political free ride. According to an unknown Palestinian source who contacted the German government (a corresponding note can be found in Helmut Schmidt's operations diary), the hijacking of an aircraft had been planned for some time. It was to begin at the same time as the hijacking of Hanns Martin Schleyer. It is still not clear why it did not come to that.

As mentioned, the President of the Federal Criminal Police Office, Horst Herold, had the hotel registrations on Mallorca combed through. With success. The comparison with the names on the "Landshut" flight shows that four people were staying on Mallorca under false names. Four false names—and the real ones?

The breakthrough comes when the aide to GSG9 commander Ulrich Wegener—disguised as a member of the supply crew at Dubai Airport—takes photos. He succeeds in photographing members of the terror squad at the left open cockpit door. The faces look familiar to employees of the British secret service, which is one of the organisations contacted by the Federal Criminal Police Office.[31] After further research, the identities of the commander members are established.

Zohair Yousif Akache alias Ali Hyderi, 23, born in Beirut. He chooses the name "Captain Martyr Machmud" for hostages and negotiating partners. In detail:

Nabil Harb alias Biza Abbasi, 22, born in Beirut. Secretly called "the boy" by the "Landshut" crew.

Nadia Shehadah Yousuf Duaibes alias Shahnaz Gholam, 22, born in Lebanon. Secretly called "The Little One" by the "Landshut" crew.

Souhalia Sayeh Andrawes aka Souhaila Sayeh aka Souhaila Sami Endrawis al Sayeh aka Soraya Ansari, 22, born in Hadath near Beirut. Secretly called "The Fat One" by the "Landshut" crew.

---

[31] See Herzog 2022, p. 181.

Dubai

Standing Time "Landshut": Friday, 14 October 1977, 5.51 a.M., to Sunday, 16 October 1977, 12.23 P.M.

The airport of the Emirate of Dubai has already been mentioned. The "Landshut" shows military vehicles and fire engines there during the approach. They block the airfield. The tower does not give Jürgen Vietor permission to land. "Aircraft will land!" yells "Captain Machmud" in English into the microphone.

Only when the Boeing runs out of fuel does a by chance British air traffic controller take the initiative and has the runway cleared. In doing so, he acts against government instructions. Co-pilot Jürgen Vietor is given a frequency so that the aircraft can land safely—one of the miracles that are to precede the "Miracle of Mogadishu".

The "Landshut" touches down at 5.51 a.m. Bonn time on 14 October 1977 at the airport in the sheikdom of Dubai. It is immediately ordered to an external aerodrome so as not to disrupt flight operations.

Dubai is a desert airport with intense heat during the day and freezing cold at night. The small Boeing stands unprotected in the scorching sun. Soldiers in the desert sand point their machine guns at it.

The kidnappers and abductees have finally left the Federal Republic's political zone of influence. Belgium, France, Great Britain, Japan, Austria and the USA maintain embassies in the capital of the United Arab Emirates, Abu Dhabi, but the German government does not. For them, it is a diplomatic no-man's land.

Helmut Schmidt must have it written down who is in charge politically there: "Head of State: His Highness Sheikh Zayed Bin Sultan al-Nahyen, President of the United Arab Emirates, Abu Dhabi. Head of Government: His Highness Sheikh Maktoom Bin Rashid Al-Maktoom, Prime Minister of the United Arab Emirates, Abu Dhabi".[32]

The Arab Emirates, founded four years earlier, form a loose union of sheikdoms in the region. Politically, the emirates remain sovereign, but they have joint ministries for their administration. The Emirates of Abu Dhabi and Dubai are considered the most developed by the federal government.[33]

The German government knows that it is now dependent on the support of its allies—France, Great Britain and the USA. However, as we will see, they

---

[32] Operation Diary, serial No. 289.
[33] Cf. telex to the Head of the Federal Chancellery dated 14 October 1977, subject: Situation United Arab Emirates (vae) here: Dubai, in: OTB, p. 291.

have their own interests. The members of the two crisis teams had an inkling of this. "There was initially a phase of perplexity as to what to do—outside our territory, in countries whose circumstances were not easy to assess", Hans-Jochen Vogel would say decades later.[34]

At 6.15 a.m., the "Landshut" cockpit requests that a woman bring soft drinks and sandwiches (not a man who could be a police officer disguised as an airport employee). German Lufthansa does not employ women in Dubai. Locals do not want to volunteer for the job.

Just ten minutes later, a man brings drinking water to the "Landshut". Captain Machmud wants the hostages to have enough water and food available at all times. Collapsing hostages or sudden deaths would be inconvenient for the terror squad. The mood could then also change in the Arab region.

When a "Landshut" hostage does not touch the delivered food—chicken with mayonnaise—"Captain Machmud" orders him to eat. He takes care of the "surveillance" himself, pointing the gun at the man.

A patient needs medication, which he receives. A doctor may bring insulin syringes for a diabetic to the machine. The medication that a family needs is not available in Dubai. "Captain Machmud" requests cough sweets for himself. The German psychologist Wolfgang Salewski sees this as an indication that the man wants to survive. In fact, the stewardess Gabriele von Lutzau (née Dillmann) urges "Captain Machmud" to do so.[35] His hoarse announcements on board and to the tower have recently become increasingly difficult to understand.

At 7.51 a.m., the Foreign Minister of the United Arab Emirates, Sheikh Mohammed Bin Rashid a-Maktoum, arrives at the Tower to negotiate with "Captain Machmud". He will do so for 55 h.

I our "Captain Machmud" gives the federal government an ultimatum until 1.00 p.m. on Saturday. Later that day, he will extend it until 1.00 p.m. on Sunday. Ultimatums are a blunt instrument in this middle phase of the abduction. That will change later.

The hijackers work through their checklist at the parking area at Dubai Desert Airport. They meticulously search the hand luggage of passengers and crew. They are particularly interested in whether there are any Jews on board. This can be deduced from passports or objects bearing the Star of David. "Captain Machmud" comes across a "Pfungstädter Bier" beer mat in a handbag. The logo shows a horseshoe, with small red stars underneath. "What's that?" he shouts and has to be calmed down with great effort.

---

[34] Hauser/Vogel, p. 17.
[35] Cf. conversation between Lutzau (née Dillmann) and Heidemann 1977.

On Saturday morning, the highly nervous, always suspicious terrorist leader notices Jürgen Vietor's wristwatch. Its dial shows an emblem, a kind of cogwheel that "Captain Machmud" thinks is the Star of David. In fact, it is the logo of the German watch company Junghans.

"What's your religion?", the terrorist starts shouting. "You are a Zionist! You have a Zionist clock! You are a fool that, I will shoot You. You are a Zionist and You will be executed. You will be killed!", Jürgen Vietor remembers. "Captain Machmud" presses his pistol to Jürgen Vietor's forehead. "Evangelic", stammers the insulted man. "Lutheran". When the terrorist doesn't seem to understand him, Jürgen Vietor asks the stewardesses for the right word. "What does Lutheran mean in English?" "Protestant", says one of them.

Captain Jürgen Schumann also talks to "Captain Machmud". In a calm, determined tone. Captain Machmud decides that co-pilot Jürgen Vietor can stay alive, but must destroy his watch. Jürgen Vietor throws the watch to the ground and stomps on it. It takes him a while to break it.

Jürgen Vietor expects "Captain Machmud" to shoot him at the next opportunity. He whispers in English to an airport employee who brought food to the aircraft: "I am the co-pilot of the aircraft, and I will be shot. Say all the best to my wife."

Back in the cockpit, Jürgen Vietor reaches for the logbook. If the machine explodes, he hopes that the flight log will only be singed, with the pages in the middle remaining unscathed. "Dear darling", writes Jürgen Vietor on a page in the centre of the book, "life was beautiful, but short. Greetings from Your Jürgen."

"Captain Machmud" spends a lot of time and energy identifying passengers of Jewish origin. Nevertheless, historian Sophie Hartmann does not consider the terrorist leader to be an ideological anti-semite. "His hatred of the Jews did not stem from any racist sentiment, but was characterised by the impact of Israeli policy on his living conditions as a Palestinian."[36] "Captain Machmud" does not rage against Jews, but against Israelis. He is fanatically convinced that the Israeli government is holding his people, the Palestinians, hostage.

Just as he is now doing to the "Landshut" passengers.

"Captain Machmud" demands that the hostages write postcards to their families. He needs the passengers' addresses so that, as he announces, he can pursue them personally if they "betray" him after an exchange. Hostage Karl Hanke also has to write a postcard. His family knows that Karl Hanke likes

---

[36] Hartmann 2009, p. 73.

to put a full stop after his signature in old German Sütterlin.[37] If there is no dot behind it, he has signed it under duress. The dot is missing on the postcard that Karl Hanke writes from the "Landshut."[38]

At 8.25 a.m., Captain Jürgen Schumann sends a telex to Bonn via the tower "To the Chancellor of the Federal Republic of Germany, Mr Helmut Schmidt." The wording:

"Mr Federal Chancellor,

the lives of 91 men, women and children on board the DABCE depend on our decision. They are our last and only hope.

On behalf of the crew and passengers.

Schumann, Captain."[39]

Gabriele von Lutzau (née Dillmann) informs "Captain Machmud" that it is her colleague Anna-Maria Staringer's birthday that day. She is 28 years young. Gabriele von Lutzau suggests having a cake brought for a special moment. "Captain Machmud" agrees on the condition that crew member Jürgen Vietor, whom he has relegated to a seat at the back, doesn't get from the cake. However, he will secretly receive a piece of cake later.

At 9.11 a.m., Captain Jürgen Schumann orders the cake from the tower. He also requests four cartons of cigarettes. When asked which ones, he replies: "Nothing, 2 plus 2."[40]

An ARD camera team films an airport employee carrying the birthday cake to the freight car. The images are shown in the evening programme "Tagesschau". The Lufthansa press spokesman concludes from them in the "Tagesschau" interview that the mood on the plane is good.

At 12.08 p.m., the commander of Border Guard Force 9, Ulrich Wegener, lands in Dubai together with four members of his troop.

Bonn

In a telex dated 14 October 1977, 2.10 p.m., to the head of the Federal Chancellery, Manfred Schüler, the name of the man allegedly responsible for the "Landshut" hijacking is mentioned.

"subversive activities of radical palestinian groups are mainly associated with supporters of wadi haddad. At the end of August 1977, a source reported on activities by members of the ppl in dubai aimed at terrorist preparations

---

[37] A typeface created by the German typeface designer Ludwig Sütterlin in 1911 to teach school beginners how to write. The Sütterlin letters were more curved than those of the Latin script.
[38] Cf. Hanke 1978.
[39] German Lufthansa, Event Log, p. 6.
[40] Ibid, p. 7.

in the federal republic in the event of the final failure of the Geneva middle east negotiations."[41]

Federal Chancellor Helmut Schmidt asks the political leaders in Dubai "not to allow the plane to take off. I therefore urge you to instruct them to block the runaway and to disenable the tires of the plane if the engines of the plane are started."[42] The aircraft is to be prevented from taking off—as it has been since it landed in Rome.

On this day, the Federal Chancellor telephones the heads of government of the most important allies in Europe, France and Great Britain. The conversation with British Prime Minister James Callaghan takes place at 2.15 p.m. Helmut Schmidt wants to know from James Callaghan whether he considers military action to be sensible and promising. Suddenly the line breaks down. The two men continue the conversation from 4 p.m. Now the Prime Minister declares that he too believes it is right not to give in to the terrorists' demands.[43] James Callaghan wants his statement to be understood as the personal, not official, opinion of his government. Callaghan continued: the ruler of Dubai has "a very independent position" within the United Emirates. In any case, he will make his decision independently of the opinion in Abu Dhabi.[44]

James Callaghan—a Clairvoyant at This Moment.

French President Valery Giscard d'Estaing also advised Helmut Schmidt to remain firm. Even now that 90 (sic) lives are at stake, he would not give up and would not hand over the prisoners.[45] The French President also emphasises that he was speaking as a personal friend of the Chancellor, not on behalf of all French people. He advises storming the plane. "But it is important that the military action is carried out by a good team. In this case, there may be some fatalities, but certainly not all the passengers will die."[46]

Helmut Schmidt wilfully ignores the loophole of the two gentlemen to speak only for themselves and not on behalf of their nations. On future occasions, he will emphasise that James Callaghan and Valery Giscard d'Estaing not only advised him to take a hard line, but urged him to do so.

---

[41] Archiv BK 13–211 20 (2) Additional file OTB vol. 5, p. 292.

[42] Ibid.

[43] Cf. recording of the telephone conversation between BK Schmidt and PM Callaghan on 14 October 1977, 14:15–14:30, in: ibid. p. 327.

[44] Ibid, p. 328.

[45] Note. Telephone conversation between the Federal Chancellor and President Giscard on 14 October 1977, 14.30–14.45, in: Archiv BK 13–211 20 (2), Additional file OTB vol. 5, p. 28Xf. (third number not legible).

[46] Ibid. On the following page.

The German Chancellor is thus instrumentalising the British Prime Minister and the French President for his central decision in the German autumn. On the one hand, this is clever as an appeal to higher authorities. On the other hand, it expresses a lack of courage. The Chancellor believes that he has to enhance his authority in office with the help of third parties.

In the popular understanding, a good crisis manager is characterised by qualities such as courage and determination. Helmut Schmidt himself portrayed this image throughout his political life. During the German Autumn, his greatest challenge, he shows no personal courage in the sense of: "I'm standing here and can't do anything else". He spends his time and energy on coordinating and reassuring his policies with others. The reassurance with Callaghan and Giscard d'Estaing may well have been embellished.

"Dear Chancellor", begins a letter that arrives at the Chancellery in Bonn on the morning of 14 October, "I do not know whether the idea of replacement hostages for the hijacked Boeing has ever been considered (...). Nevertheless, I would like to inform you that, in accordance with my fundamental rights, I would be prepared to board the hijacked aircraft at any time and without delay if at least the five children, and if possible, the women are let out."[47]

Federal Chancellor Helmut Schmidt decrees in green felt-tip pen that the letter is to remain secret. Head of Office Manfred Schüler has already seen it, and State Secretary and government spokesman Klaus Bölling is allowed to "personally"—this word underlined in each case—take note of it. Helmut Schmidt instructs Manfred Schüler himself to reply to the letter writer. This reply is not attached to the file.

At noon that day, at 12.55 p.m., the Permanent Mission of the Federal Republic of Germany in East Berlin receives a call. "This is the Red Army Faction. If the demands are not met, the permanent representation will go up (or 'blow up') on Sunday."[48]

Helmut Schmidt already wants a military solution in Dubai. On 15 October, 11.00 a.m., he telephones Hans-Jürgen Wischnewski—this time from a hotel, where there is a greater risk of eavesdropping on the telephone than in his office. To keep the conversation short, he reads out four points to the Minister of State and Hans-Jürgen Wischnewski takes notes.

---

[47] Letter from Hans-Roderich Schneider to Federal Chancellor Helmut Schmidt dated 14 October 1977, in: AsD 1/HSAA010016.

[48] Telex message from the Permanent Mission to the Federal Chancellery, Situation Centre, dated 14 October 1977, in: AdsD, 1/HSAA010016.

The Federal Government is thinking of a storming of the machine "tomorrow morning at dawn or before dawn. (…) But you have a free hand: especially if individual shootings take place locally, you would have to act."[49]

Helmut Schmidt's plan: 32 men from Border Guard Force 9, led by Commander Ulrich Wegener, are to arrive in Dubai by Saturday, 15 October, 7 p.m. local time at the latest and prepare the storming with the help of British or Israeli specialists. Ulrich Wegener has already received the map material for the airport from the British. Before then, the hijackers are to be persuaded to release the women and children.[50]

Desire and reality are two different things, even for a German chancellor. Helmut Schmidt asks his negotiator Hans-Jürgen Wischnewski in a telephone conversation late in the morning how likely it is "that you will do it the following night".[51] The Minister of State's answer: "I don't think so."[52]

Dubai

Hans-Jürgen Wischnewski and Ulrich Wegener ask the Foreign Minister of the United Arab Emirates for a GSG9 rescue operation. The Sheikh insists on using locals because of his country's sovereignty. Ulrich Wegener offers to train them and gets the go-ahead. The group of 30 paratroopers also includes British mercenaries. A Boeing 737 from Gulf Air, parked at random, serves as the training aircraft. The training takes place at the airport in public. It would be easy to warn the "Landshut" hijackers over the radio.

Ulrich Wegener quickly realises that the squad has never practised such an action before. You can't take them by storm. He says to Mohammed Bin Rashid a-Maktum: either your own people or none.

The sheikh is playing a double game. According to his assurance, he would personally give permission to the GSG9 if he were authorised to do so. Shortly afterwards, he actually broadcasts the news on Radio Abu Dhabi that a Lufthansa aircraft is on its way to Dubai with a special unit.

A rather unfriendly indiscretion. It makes clear that the sheikhdom will not accept a German rescue operation. Here too, as with the exercise at the

---

[49] Telephone conversation between BK Schmidt and StM Wischnewski 15.10.77, 11.00 a.m., in: Archiv BK 13–211 20 (2) Additional file OTBB d. 6, p. 156.
[50] Cf. BArch B136/16982.
[51] Telephone conversation between BK Schmidt and StM Wischnewski on 15 October, 11.00 a.m., in: Archiv BK 13–211 20 (2) Additional file OTB vol. 6, p. 158.
[52] Ibid.

airport, the young sheikh and minister accepts that the "Landshut" hijackers will find out about it. He puts the hostages at considerable risk.[53]

The double game does not go unnoticed by the German government. The Federal Chancellor reacted angrily. After the "fake Turks"—Helmut Schmidt's original words in the aforementioned conversation with Hans-Jürgen Wischnewski—he has to put the brakes on a GSG9 operation.

Hope dies last. The next day, a Saturday, Helmut Schmidt discusses a police operation "modelled on Entebbe" in the Federal Cabinet, as it says in a resolution note.[54] In the draft, the wording is "modelled on Entebbe", but the minute-taker, Helmut Schmidt's office manager Klaus-Dieter Leister, has to cross out the word "model" at the behest of the Federal Chancellor and write the word "example" above it.

In Entebbe, the capital of Uganda, Israeli police forced freed aircraft hostages against the will of the local government. The discussion in the Federal Cabinet is recorded as being in agreement that no comparable action should be carried out in Dubai at present. Only the Federal Minister of Agriculture, Josef Ertl, breaks ranks. "Reservation BM Ertl, who would like to keep this option open", it says in the minutes.[55]

On this Saturday morning, Captain Jürgen Schumann and co-pilot Jürgen Vietor are again alone in the cockpit at times. Once again, the captain suggests that they leave together. Jürgen Vietor responds again: "You can go, I'll stay."[56]

The "Landshut" captain also expressed thoughts of escape to purserette Hannelore Brauchardt (née Piegler) in Dubai. "I also write in my book", says the former purserette a year after the drama, "that Schumann definitely had the opportunity to jump out the day before in Dubai (…) because we were sitting all alone at the entrance". And then he said: "We could leave now. Then I said: Yes, we could."[57]

At a moment when none of the hijackers are in the cockpit, Jürgen Vietor speaks to his captain about giving out messages. "Jürgen, I wouldn't do it. We're in an unknown country here. We know that the PLO has its confidants

---

[53] Hartmann 2009, p. 31.
[54] Klaus-Dieter Leister, Head of the Federal Chancellor's Office (presumably, as the sheet bears his signature): Cabinet meeting of 16 October 1977, in: Archiv BK 13–211 (2.) Additional file OTB Bd. 6, p. 78.
[55] Ibid.
[56] Discussion Vietor/Salewski, vol. S / I, p. 11.
[57] Hannelore Brauchardt (née Piegler) in: Berliner Abendschau from 21 October 1978, Sender Freies Berlin.

everywhere, probably here too."[58] And so it remains. The pilots would not return to the subject.[59]

Captain Jürgen Schumann does not follow his co-pilot's advice, on the contrary. He instructs Jürgen Vietor to order FOUR English-language and FOUR Arabic newspapers. Later, the captain will place four unsmoked cigars on a rubbish bag without Jürgen Vietor's knowledge.

What is Jürgen Schumann's motive? On the one hand, as captain, he sees it as his responsibility to do what he can to help end the hostage situation. On the other hand, he is putting his own life in danger. His wife Monika will later provide an explanation for this. The submission prescribed by Lufthansa—for example in the LH-training film "Behaviour of aircraft crews in acts of terrorism in air traffic"—was contrary to his nature. The American passive command, a cautious resistance, suited him better.[60]

"And that you shouldn't get involved in arguments in the first place. And that's one reason why I think he had no choice but to act. It was a completely normal and important thing for him to try to get as much as possible out about the kidnappers. He would never really have made a pact with them. For him, these people were criminals."[61]

In his personal notes from 1995, Jürgen Vietor comes to a clear conclusion about Captain Schumann's behaviour. "The release of messages from the aircraft is of course of great importance for the measures to be taken, e.g. a rescue operation. In my opinion, however, the safety of the passengers is even more important. This is where Cpt. Schumann deviated from the recommendations in the film 'Behaviour during hijackings' and my concerns."[62]

The educational film from the mid-1970s was edited by the psychologist Wolfgang Salewski, who was therefore also invited to advise the federal government. Salewski will play an important role at the last stand in Mogadishu.

At 02.14 p.m. on Saturday, 15 October, the fuel rans out. "Captain Machmud" had requested new fuel immediately after landing, but did not get it. The little that remained kept the aircraft's own auxiliary power unit (APU) running. It supplies the aircraft on the ground with electricity and the air conditioning system with compressed air. Now, however, nothing works. A sweltering heat reaches the "Landshut' interior.

---

[58] Ibid, p. 3.
[59] Cf. ibid.
[60] Tumler 1978.
[61] Ibid, p. 3.
[62] Ibid., p. 13.

The fuel lasted longer than expected, but that doesn't matter now. After half an hour, passengers start to keel over in rows. An elderly man keeps wanting to get up and take his hat off. He asks his seat neighbour "when we'll finally get there on the bus". His seat neighbours make a joke out of it. The hostage in the seat behind puts a glass of water on the confused man's head. He hopes that the man will move and the glass will fall down. The old man notices the glass, takes it off his head and says to his wife: "Mum, Mum, when are we going to get there, I've got an appointment."

His wife has not been noticed so far. At some point, she also speaks in confused sentences. Unfortunately, she can't stay here any longer, she says, "I have to go to the hairdresser, I have an appointment at the hairdresser, I have to go there, my hair doesn't look right anymore." The stewardess Gabriele von Lutzau (née Dillmann) takes care of the couple and comforts them like children.

"Quite a scene is unfolding now", Jürgen Vietor will later say in an interview with "Stern" magazine reporter Jürgen Heidemann. The crew and hostages take immediate action. "Captain Machmud" allows the front and rear doors to be opened. At least there is now a light breeze blowing through the aircraft.

A broken aircraft with physically and emotionally exhausted hostages. The hijackers involved in coping with an emergency situation. Outside, everything is quiet. Not a soul to be heard, let alone seen. Now the "Landshut" could be stormed and the hostages freed, co-pilot Jürgen Vietor will later say to "Stern" magazine reporter Jürgen Heidemann. His hope is not realised.

At 5.47 p.m., the radio communication also goes down. Complete power failure. Jürgen Vietor remembers that he learnt Morse code in the navy. Even light Morse code. With a rod lamp ("jet light"), which every aircraft has on board for the external technical check, he morses lights into the dark night. He announces every word to the terrorist beforehand—in English, of course. Jürgen Vietor must ensure that "Captain Machmud" does not feel betrayed. "Now I light morse 'we'". He light morses 'we'. "Now I light morse 'need'". Now he's light morsing "need". And so on. His message: "We need communication."

Three or four times, the co-pilot lights up "We need communication." Nobody light morses back.

At some point, a refuelling truck pulls up to the aircraft. The men from the airport attempt a pressurised refuelling. It fails because the aircraft's electrical system has failed. The helpers then decide to perform an overwing refuelling. The refuelling crew fills the right-hand tank with fuel. What they obviously don't realise: A fuel transfer from the right to the left tank is not possible due to the lack of battery voltage of 115 V. The APU can only be supplied with fuel from the left-hand tank.

Jürgen Vietor points this out to the airport staff. They think it's a trick to get more fuel. They leave without leaving another gallon. Sometime later, the tanker returns. The locals now also fill the left wing. They have obviously made sure that Jürgen Vietor is telling the truth.

Meanwhile, Captain Jürgen Schumann is trying to start the APU despite the almost empty battery. This would use up the very last bit of power. Jürgen Vietor has previously advised the captain not to do this. Later, journalists would develop the theory that Jürgen Schumann had deliberately tried to create a hopeless situation. The idea was to create obvious chaos in the cockpit and cabin to make it easier to storm the "Landshut".

At 8.17 p.m., another vehicle approaches the aircraft to bring water. At the same time, two men steer a so-called Ground Power, a mobile power generator, towards the aircraft. One of them makes contact with the terrorist leader via megaphone. "I am a friend of yours. Talk to me like a gentleman." Whereupon Captain Jürgen Schumann lets out a laugh: "They're Germans!".

Right. Martin Gaebel, Director of Flight Operations and Chief Pilot at German Lufthansa, and his colleague Peter Heldt, Fleet Manager of the B 737 Pilot Department. "Captain Machmud" goes berserk. German agents! That's a trick! He fires four shots into the darkness. Martin Gaebel and Peter Heldt zigzag back towards the tower. They leave the ground power standing. "You must help yourselves!", Peter Heldt shouts to his colleagues.

What is not yet known: Martin Gaebel and Heldt stalked the "Landshut" between the sand dunes around the airport to within 20 metres of it that morning. And then from behind under the fuselage of the aircraft. Nobody in the cockpit can see this unless they cast a shadow. The action has been agreed with the defence secretary in the tower.

Martin Gaebel and Heldt have a headset and microphone with them. There are contact points under the fuselage to talk to the pilots in the cockpit. When the engines are started, the pilots and the mechanic on the tarmac use them to communicate. Gaebel and Heldt want to listen in on the conversations in the cockpit and the communication from the cockpit with the stewardesses.

It turns out that only one contact point on the right front side of the fuselage is operational. The advantage of these contact points—no light or display in the cockpit comes on when contact is made—proves to be a disadvantage in this case. Neither the pilots nor the terrorist leader uses this method of communication. Jürgen Schumann and Jürgen Vietor don't even think of listening in from time to time. Martin Gaebel and Heldt leave without having achieved anything.[63]

On this occasion, Martin Gaebel and Peter Heldt notice that fuel is dripping from the tank ("slight fuel leak").[64]

Efforts to listen in on conversations in the cabin are also being made by the German government. It is discussing the idea of people disguised as caterers attaching listening devices to the outside wall of the "Landshut". Technicians from the Federal Criminal Police Office dismiss the idea. There are no devices that could do that. Nevertheless, the office mobilises two men. They are to smuggle available devices into food containers so that the crew can secretly place them in the cockpit and cabin.

The local sheikhs are not allowed to find out about this. The two technicians are flown to Tehran on a special plane to board the next scheduled flight to Dubai. In Tehran, it turns out that there are no flights to Dubai for the time being. By the time the technicians land at the sheikhdom's airport, the "Landshut" has already left.

The mood in the tower at Dubai Airport is sour following the failed start-up of an emergency power generator. Minister of State Wischnewski is thinking aloud about mixing water into the fuel so that the "Landshut" can no longer take off. A Lufthansa employee points out to him the "futility of the plan".[65]

Jürgen Vietor asks "Captain Machmud" for permission to leave the aircraft so that he can connect the ground power unit (GPU) brought in by Gaebel and Held and parked some distance away. Consent Vietor uses a woollen blanket held by two hostages—teacher Hartwig Faby and boxing promoter Hans Hasse-Heyn—on the cockpit door to shimmy down to the airfield. Jürgen Vietor has never driven a GPU before, let alone connected it to an aircraft. Fortunately, there is a short instruction manual in English next to the steering wheel. Jürgen Vietor reads it, drives the GPU under the aircraft and connects the cable. He then walks to the left-hand open aircraft door.

Nothing works. Jürgen Vietor now tries out all the plug-in variants for the cables. Nothing works.

In between, the co-pilot remembers the exotic birds in the cargo hold. Canaries and parakeets. He briefly considers releasing the birds but refrains from doing so because the cargo hold door must be closed with force. The Boeing would have shuddered briefly, and "Captain Machmud" might have become suspicious. Jürgen Vietor lets himself be pulled back into the machine

---

[63] Cf. interrogation protocol Heldt, p. 3.
[64] German Lufthansa, Event-Log, p. 6.
[65] Ibid.

by Faby and Hasse-Heyn without having achieved anything. There he falls to the ground, exhausted. "Captain Machmud" asks him to rest first and has water brought to him.

Later, Jürgen Schumann and Jürgen Vietor analyse the situation. A voltage of 115 V is needed to pump fuel from the left tank to the right tank. The other problem: The on-board battery must have a minimum voltage of 24 V so that a relay is switched to transfer the voltage from the GPU to the aircraft.

After some time, four local airport employees drive up. This time, "Captain Machmud" does not fire. "We need a new battery", Jürgen Vietor tells them. The battery arrives after 1.00 a. m. The co-pilot is allowed to leave the aircraft once again. The locals swap the batteries. At around 1.30 a.m., the on-board systems are up and running again. Jürgen Vietor makes radio contact with the tower. It works.

In the "Landshut"

"For man is a wolf to man, not a man. This is true at least as long as you don't know each other." These words are attributed to the Roman comic poet Titus Maccius Plautus (ca. 254–184 BC). The 86 passengers and five crew members who fall into the hands of Palestinian hijackers at midday on 13 October 1977 do not know each other. They form a random community. Nevertheless, a "cross-section of the entire population", as the youngest stewardess on the plane, Gabriele von Lutzau (née Dillmann), likes to say. Young, old and elderly people, holidaymakers and businesspeople, Germans and non-Germans.

The people in "Landshut" reflect the *Zeitgeist* of the 1970s with their biographies and professions, their partnerships and lifestyles, their fashion and their hobbies. They include businesspeople who achieved prosperity during the economic miracle of the Federal Republic of Germany. Or civil servants like the teacher Hartwig Faby. Employees in industry or insurance companies. The "beauty queens" in the "Landshut" had to save up for months for their week on Mallorca. They will do it many times in their lives.

The West German lifestyle in the 1970s is also reflected in the "Bobby", which flies back and forth between Frankfurt am Main and Palma de Mallorca. Many of the "Landshut" passengers smoke. Their cigarette brand places them socially on a scale between "Marlboro", "HB" and "Peter Stuyvesant". Grounded. High earners. The well-heeled.

As told people drink a lot of alcohol in this West Germany. To party or to numb the mind of cruel images of war. Cognac, bourbon and whiskey also flow on television, in crime thrillers and feature films. In West Germany, alcohol and cigarettes can be advertised as freely as washing powder and jeans.

The images of war in their heads. German history is condensed in the biographies of the passengers flying from Palma de Mallorca to Frankfurt in the second half of the 1970s. Many passengers lived through Hitler's Germany and the Second World War. Some, a few, were able to escape the Holocaust as Jews.

One of the "Landshut" hostages is a Jewish woman who lost her relatives in the Holocaust. She herself experienced the fear of death in Hitler's Germany. This fear returns in the hijacked "Landshut". She probably owes her renewed survival to the stewardess Gabriele von Lutzau (née Dillmann), who deceives the hijackers during a passport check. Gabriele von Lutzau (née Dillmann) has Jewish roots herself and is aware of the danger. She repeatedly succeeds in calming the deeply frightened woman.

War and destruction were followed by years of economic hardship. Later the so-called economic miracle. Later still, the Federal Republic of Germany was accepted into the international community as one of two German states. Chancellor Willy Brandt receives the Nobel Peace Prize in 1971, Heinrich Böll the Nobel Prize for Literature a year later. Germany organises the Olympic Games in 1972 and the Football World Cup in 1974. West Germany is coming back.

West Germany is back on the world stage in terms of sport and culture. Two German bandleaders, Bert Kaempfert and James Last, are invited to give concerts in England, the former enemy of the war, and celebrate triumphs there. The Germans buy heaps of records by French artists. France was once the "arch-enemy". Now Mireille Matthieu ("the sparrow of Avignon") and Gilbert Becaud are singing in German living rooms.

The economic miracle creates careers that are unthinkable today. In the hijacked "Landshut" is boxing promoter Uwe Hasse-Heyn, who served as a soldier in the Wehrmacht during the war and then eked out a living with temporary jobs. He has since made a fortune as a businessman in boxing. But Uwe Hasse-Heyn drinks. As a gay man, he feels socially isolated. West German society in the 70 s is not tolerant of lesbians and gays.

The "Landshut" hostage Matthias Rath symbolises the many hard-working Germans who have climbed the career ladder with diligence and discipline. Matthias Rath is head of business administration at a company that produces car bodies. A stylish man in a shirt, tie and jacket. After the "Landshut" hijacking, he will no longer be able to do his job.

Young adults in the "Landshut" are the teacher Hartwig Faby and the innkeeper Rhett Waida. The two friends have been on holiday in Malle.

Rhett Waida owes his first name to the character Rhett Butler from Margaret Mitchell epic novel "Gone with the Wind". In it, Rhett Butler masters all dangers. He rescues his beloved Scarlett from the burning city of Atlanta.

Rhett Waida's almost three-year-old Steffen receives a special service when it comes to wee. Purserette Hannelore Brauchardt (née Piegler) takes a coffee pot from the galley. This way, Rhett Waida doesn't have to take the little one to the toilet.

Steffen Waida is too young to remember his abduction later, with one exception: The image of the crackers that someone hands him in the "Landshut" will stay in his head forever.

Julia Filius, the passenger with red patent leather shoes and a black handbag, and her husband epitomise the middle-class family in West Germany in the 1970s. Thanks to many years of hard work, they can now afford something. A little luxury and a holiday. Their common goal was to achieve something. And they have achieved it.

Still in the luggage compartment, the "Landshut" provides a reflection of West Germany as a cosmopolitan economic and cultural nation at the time. As mentioned, the luggage compartment contains cages with exotic birds for a German zoo. There is also the aforementioned tapestry by Pablo Picasso. Conversely, museums around the world exhibit art from the Federal Republic of Germany.

When the terrorists in Mogadishu announce that the plane is to be blown up, a hostage in the second row of aisles begins to cry. The women are often confronted with such an image. "The men are all crying", says hostage Iris Roggenkamp to her sister Kirsten. Men look to their partners for support. They openly tease the "beauty queens" while their own wives sit next to them. Diana Müll, for example, nicknamed "Snow White", feels "eaten up" by men's looks.

It doesn't stop at glances. Men in the hijacked "Landshut" paw women on their thighs.

Purserette Hannelore Brauchart (née Piegler) will write about the night of Aden that full water bottles were not passed through to the last row of seats. "People's greed made them collect and hoard the bottles so that not a single one reached the back of the cabin."[66]

The varnish of human civilisation is thin. People in borderline situations act reflexively for their own survival.

Iris Roggenkamp's neighbour only utters one word for a long time, "water". She gives him some of hers. A man two rows behind her is different. He

---

[66] Piegler 1978, p. 121.

reaches for his wife's glass of juice. And drinks it down in one go. The woman suffers a crying fit and has to be comforted by others while her husband looks away.

While still on the hijacked plane, the woman decides to separate from her husband. When they both descend the gangway in Frankfurt after the happy liberation, they do not look at each other. The wife will indeed file for divorce soon.

In the case of an elderly couple, it is also the man who helps himself to his wife's plate. The two have been married for decades. The woman no longer recognises her husband in the "Landshut". At home, a deep estrangement develops between the two of them.

Many women in West Germany at this time do not yet have the courage to separate from their husbands. Often due to material dependence. At some point, the woman in question will take all the blame on herself in order to save the marriage. She even reproaches herself for causing her husband grief. The couple stays together, but things are no longer the way they used to be.

Not only men, but also women cross borders during the kidnapping. One hostage has, as she will later claim, jewellery worth over 48,000 German mark in her luggage. "You can have everything from me", says the woman to the "fat woman" in the terror squad. The hostage opens her necklace and pulls the rings off her fingers. At this moment, "Captain Machmud" slaps her in the face, "I thought my head was going to fall off."[67] The self-proclaimed freedom fighter makes it clear: We Palestinians cannot be bought.

Not even the second terrorist. (…) "And then a lady came to the back and said to him somehow (…) that she would like to speak to him personally. (…) She looked around shyly and probably had the impression that the little girl *(sic) was* listening. Then she offered him money. I'll pay you what you want. (…) But just let me go. (…) So he was deeply offended and I thought he was going to beat her up. And then he caught himself (…) and told her: 'I don't need your money'."[68]

Another hostage offers "Captain Machmud" sex for her release. "Captain Machmud" reacts negatively and angrily. After "Mogadishu", this hostage will struggle for a long time with the fact that she wanted to give herself up, to sell her soul for her survival.

There are also other, positive examples of how hostages behave. When Jutta Knauff (née Brod) threatens to collapse because of the heat, the passenger behind her moves his seat all the way forwards and starts waving a magazine. The breeze does Jutta Brod good. The affection this gesture brings is even

---

[67] Salewski Group discussion I, p. 10.
[68] Salewski Group discussion II, p. 4f.

more so. Jutta Knauff (née Brod) will later say that the hair on the back of her neck stopped growing after the "Landshut" hijacking.

The passengers on a scheduled flight are not the only ones who form a random community; the crew does too. Pulled together for a roster. The "chemistry" between crew members is sometimes more, sometimes less right. Between the purserette and the two stewardesses on this flight, it is not right from the start. This would be irrelevant on the scheduled short-haul flight between Palma de Mallorca and Frankfurt am Main. On an aircraft that has been hijacked for days, it becomes a burden for the crew and the passengers.

"The crew didn't fit together at all", says Gabriele von Lutzau in an interview with psychologist Wolfgang Salewski in the presence of Lufthansa executives.[69] Even on the outward flight, Annamaria and she smirk about the Austrian accent of her superior, who was born in Graz. Her superior didn't find it funny at all. What impertinence, Hannelore Brauchardt (née Piegler) outraged, what are you getting away with?[70]

In fact, the social status of a stewardess, and even more so of a purserette, was much higher in the 1970s than it is today. Flying—including flying personnel—was accorded a high level of respect. Flying did not yet have the trivial character of a train or bus journey. This is also due to the much higher price compared to other means of transport.

The relationship between the purserette and the two stewardesses on the "Landshut" is permanently damaged during the hijacking. Hannelore Brauchart (née Piegler), Annemarie Staringer and Gabriele von Lutzau (née Dillmann) are very different personalities and react very differently in this borderline situation. The youngest of them, Gabriele von Lutzau (née Dillmann), takes on responsibility. Socially gifted and youthfully carefree, she slips into the role of her life. She knows that the kidnappers are dependent on her good English. Gabriele von Lutzau (née Dillmann) used to be in a relationship with a partner whose first language was English.

The stewardess Annemarie Staringer somehow makes herself invisible in this exceptional situation—quite understandably, so to speak. There are no stories of freed hostages about her, only the story of the birthday cake and photos together with her colleagues. "Captain Machmud" took these pictures with a hostage's camera. They show the horror on the young woman's face.

Purserette Hannelore Brauchardt (née Piegler) bases her actions on Lufthansa's regulations in the event of a hijacking. She takes to heart the rules from the instructional film by psychologist Wolfgang Salewski, who

---

[69] Conversation between Lutzau (née Dillmann) / Salewski, vol. 2, p. 16.
[70] Cf. ibid.

is currently accompanying Minister of State Hans-Jürgen Wischnewski. Salewski's advice should be followed when necessary and not ignored.

Hannelore Brauchardt does not engage in conflict with the terrorists like Gabriele von Lutzau (née Dillmann). On this very special flight, too, she treats passengers with detachment—as befits a Lufthansa purserette.

On the hijacked plane, Hannelore Brauchardt (née Piegler) and Gabriele von Lutzau (née Dillmann) have a minor tiff. One insists on the rules and regulations that provide orientation and order, while the other does what it considers right in the specific situation.

However, the three women will later share one thing in common: After their liberation, they will never again board a plane as a purserette or stewardess.

In Dubai, the terrorists believe they are on the road to victory. They have taken control of an almost fully occupied Lufthansa aircraft as planned, startled the world public and confronted the German government with demands. The Palestinian cause is on many people's lips.

"Dubai" gives the kidnappers a breather. They take time to stage themselves as freedom fighters for the Palestinian people. They want to explain their motives to their hostages, whose lives they threaten with guns and hand grenades. To seek understanding. To gain recognition. And, incidentally, from the whole world.

"Captain Machmud" takes a seat in the cockpit and speaks for half an hour about the crimes against the Palestinian people. He does so with a warm heart and in striking images. "Captain Machmud" reports that he has seen pregnant women with torn bellies in Lebanon. And small children, murdered by the Phalangists, members of a Christian party in Lebanon. He has to take this action to save his country.

The man knows his way around vivid linguistic images.

Once the terrorist leader talks himself into such a rage that he fires a shot with his pistol. The bullet penetrates the left backrest of the captain's seat and lodges in it, fortunately. If the bullet had hit the fittings in the cockpit, it would have made it impossible to continue the flight.

The political worldviews of kidnappers and hostages have nothing in common. The Palestinians are among the losers of modern history. Like the Arameans or Kurds, for example. The Palestinians live crammed into the narrow Gaza Strip. Exiled in Beirut or Tripoli. "Captain Machmud" is a terrorist, a criminal, but he is not entirely wrong about the history of his people.

Every time a lecture by "Captain Machmud" comes to an end, the hostages clap. Some may do so out of opportunism, but many are genuinely touched.

They were unaware of the background to the Middle East conflict. One "Landshut" passenger identifies so strongly with the hijackers' cause that she temporarily decides to become a member of a Palestinian organisation.

Captain Jürgen Schumann would presumably never have thought of that. "He always said to me", Monika Schumann would say after her husband's murder, "Send people to the labour camp! People who kill someone else should be shot on the spot, before you spend a lot of money on trials and whatnot. And that was the line" (Fig. 3.1).[71]

> *"On behalf of many of my relatives I ask you to do everything possible to save the life and health of my father and the other kidnap victims human lives should have priority over political calculation and prestige Bernd Reiboldt."*

The terror squad has taken a portable radio on board. In Dubai, "Captain Machmud" wants to listen to the news on the hour. Gabriele von Lutzau (née Dillmann) recalls in conversation with Wolfgang Salewski that "Captain Machmud" missed the news at least twice, but heard it at least twice.[72]

From these messages, he learns that the "Landshut" hijacking team consists of four people—two men and two women. The captain of the plane had smuggled out the relevant information. The young, inexperienced negotiator Sheikh Mohammed Bin Rashid a-Maktum was also responsible for this indiscretion. He blabbed it to journalists.

"Captain Machmud" goes on a rampage. He starts by accusing Jürgen Vietor of betraying him. He still has respect for Jürgen Schumann as the captain of the aircraft. The co-pilot initially pretends to be clueless, saying that he cannot imagine smuggling out information. The terrorist leader is not content with that. When asked repeatedly whether it was him, Jürgen Vietor answers with a "no".

Up until now, the dialogue between "Captain Machmud" and flight captain Jürgen Schuman has been relaxed, even detached. They smoked a lot together. Together they discussed the next technical steps to be taken. The pilot, "Captain Machmud", presumably felt flattered when a Lufthansa captain spoke to him as an equal. Perhaps Jürgen Schumann told him about his time as a "Starfighter" pilot.

The relaxed attitude is now over.

"Captain Machmud" summons Jürgen Schumann into the corridor. Jürgen Schumann has to kneel before the terrorist and confess his "offences". The treacherous radio messages. Thank You FOUR the breakfast. The four

---

[71] Tumler 1978.
[72] Salewski, Group discussion II, p. 25.

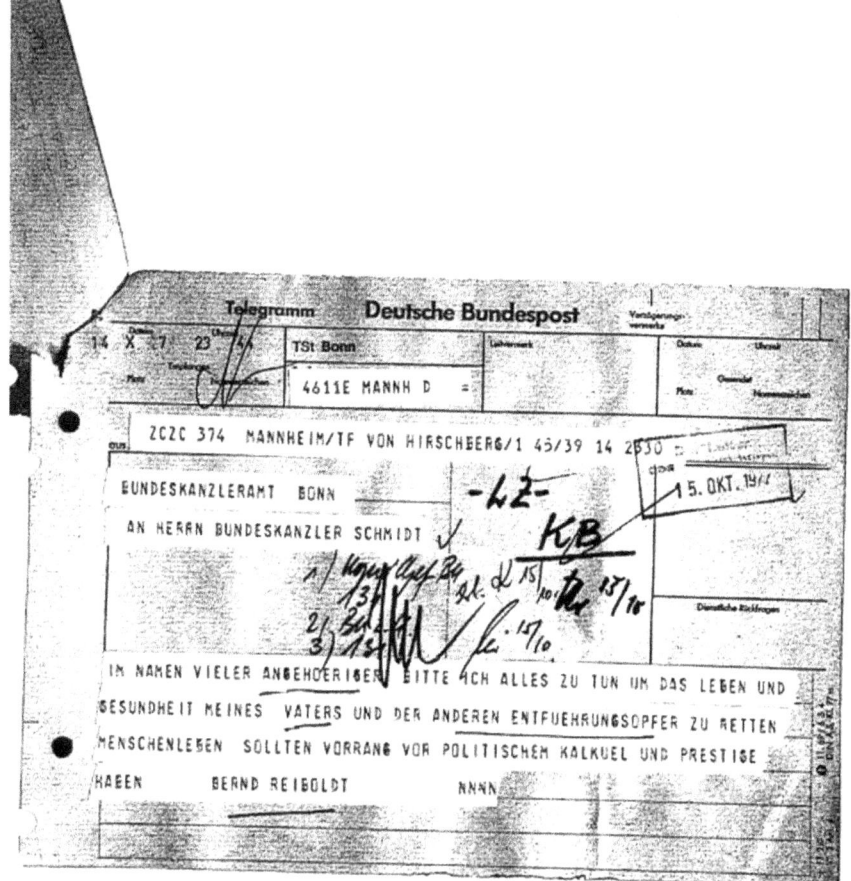

Fig. 3.1 Telegram from Bernd Reiboldt dated 14 October 1977 to Federal Chancellor Helmut Schmidt *Source* BArch B 136/31588

cigars in the rubbish, two of them trimmed. The four newspapers requested. FOUR English and FOUR Arabia Newspapers. The terrorist calls the captain a traitor in front of all the hostages.

Jürgen Schumann has to make U-turns in the dressing room corridor. Walking up and down several times, addressing the terrorist as "Captain". Left, turn left. Right, turn right. A humiliation in front of everyone.

"You are no longer the captain of this aircraft!", shouts the terrorist, "the co-pilot will fly the aircraft as a commander." [73] Then he addresses Jürgen Vietor. "You are the captain from now on."[74]

---

[73] Discussion Vietor/Salewski, vol. S / I, p. 20.
[74] Conversation Vietor/Salewski, vol. S / I – back cover, p. 19.

Jürgen Schumann is sent to one of the back rows of seats. Before that, he has to hand in his captain's hat, which "Captain Machmud" puts on himself. Once in the back of the cabin, Jürgen Schumann says to his neighbour, hostage Cäcilie Meijer-Werner: "They will kill me."[75]

The "trial" against Jürgen Schumann has an effect. Individual passengers show solidarity with "Captain Machmud's" anger towards the captain. They react disappointed about Schumann's behaviour and will speak badly of him after the release.

When "Captain Machmud" realises that he has appointed two new captains on the plane, Jürgen Vietor and himself, he indirectly demotes Vietor again, albeit in a friendly manner. The terrorist leader addresses him as "Charly Papa", a familiar variation of "co-pilot".

On the morning of 15 October 1977—the "Landshut" is now in Dubai for 24 h—Federal Chancellor Helmut Schmidt and Minister of State Hans-Jürgen Wischnewski talk on the phone. The Minister of State proposes what he calls a "decoupling" of the "Landshut" kidnapping case from Hanns Martin Schleyer's kidnapping case. Helmut Schmidt immediately understands. "My personal opinion is that I agree with you. And 88 (sic!) people are more important than one. But that's my personal opinion based on the balance of values at stake."[76]

Helmut Schmidt promises to put this idea up for discussion in the Large Political Advisory Group, which will meet in half an hour.

On 14 and 15 October, there is no question of deploying the GSG9 to storm the aircraft. Nevertheless, preparations for an operation continue. The German Air Rescue Service provides an aircraft "for the horizontal transport of 90 injured people" with a medical team of "5–6 doctors and 10 paramedics or nurses."[77] Unlike the GSG9 aircraft, this aircraft is allowed to land at the British military base on Cyprus.

The Munich State Office of Criminal Investigation receives an anonymous bomb threat this morning. In the event that the German government does not fulfil the terrorists' demands, a "highly explosive, destructive bomb" will go off in the diplomatic quarter in Bonn-Bad Godesberg.[78]

---

[75] Cäcilie Meiyr-Werner in conversation with Ebbo Demant in Demant 1982.
[76] Telephone conversation between Federal Chancellor Helmut Schmidt and Minister of State Wischnewski. Dated 15 10 1977, 08.50 a. m., in: Archiv BK 13–211 20 (2) OTB Bd. 6, p. 151ff.
[77] Telex to the crisis unit of the Federal Government dated 15 October 1977, 12.40 p.m., in: Barch B106/106684d.
[78] Note from the Head of the Situation Centre. Meyer-Sebastian dated 15 October 1977, in: AdsD, 1/HSAA010016; Archiv BK 13–211 20 (3) Additional file 3, no p.

In the "Landshut"

Carrot and stick. The two women of the terrorist squad wave their hand grenades around. When they smoke, they drop the cigarette ash onto the hand grenades. And knock against them so that the ash falls to the ground.

Suddenly the passengers are allowed to undo their seatbelts. Talk to each other. For a while, the atmosphere is as normal as on any scheduled flight. Then another scream, a blow from "Captain Machmud" into the silence. At no time during the 105 h are the hostages allowed to rest.

Nevertheless, there are moments when the kidnappers and hostages get closer. In her memoirs, the purserette Hannelore Brauchardt (née Piegler) writes of good conversations with "the fat one", the older of the two terrorists. They talk about wishes and plans in life. About having children. After one of these conversations, "the fat one" disappears to the toilet and gets back with tear-stained eyes.

The hygienic conditions in the "Landshut" are becoming more appalling by the day. The front toilet is already blocked in Dubai and the rear toilet is close to being blocked. The smallest Boeing only has two. Jürgen Vietor calls in a so-called tamper, which is actually used to crush drinks cans that passengers have drunk empty. The tamper turns out to be too short. Jürgen Vietor then orders a wooden slat. Even with it, he can't clear the toilet. The pilots demand chemicals from the tower to clear the blockage. None are supplied.

Local airport staff manage to drain the collected urine from the aircraft, but not the faeces. A ZDF cameraman captures the urine splashing onto the airfield. These images are not shown in the "heute" news that day. It was only decades later that filmmaker Ingo Helm will come across the ugly, impressive scene in the ZDF archives and includes it in his documentary film.[79]

The hostages' urination stinks more vilely with each passing day. Their foul odour is fuelled by the scorching heat during the day and the high humidity at night. Because nothing can drain away, the urine piles up higher and higher. If you want to get rid of what you have digested, you have to stand.

Jürgen Vietor tries his luck a second time in Dubai, now with a coat hanger. In vain. Urine and faeces are already mixing with blood. Menstrual blood. The women have had their period because the packs of their "pill" are in the luggage compartment. They can't get to them now.

At some point, the menstrual blood seeps through the toilet doors and runs down the corridor.

---

[79] Cf. Demandt/Helm 2012.

No wonder that visits to the toilet are becoming increasingly rare. A 14-year-old girl whispers shamefully to Gabriele von Lutzau (née Dillmann) that she has wet her pants. The stewardess replies: "It doesn't matter. We'll hang the trousers up to dry."

In the desert heat of Dubai, the hostages bathe in their own sweat. Men strip down to their underwear. Women's blouses and dresses made of nylon, i.e. plastic, begin to stink. The passengers accept it apathetically.

The effects of sitting for days on end become apparent from "Dubai" onwards. Many hostages' legs swell up. In some cases, the flesh almost splits open. Hostages' limbs are constricted so severely by the bindings that they turn blue or start bleeding.

The pilot of a Spanish aircraft crew about to take up his duties in Frankfurt am Main is in a particularly bad way when he is tied up. The restraint presses his wristwatch deep into his flesh. Contorted in pain, with tears in his eyes, the Spaniard tries not to let on in vain. Other hostages become aware of his agony and beg the kidnappers for mercy. "Captain Machmud" takes this as an opportunity to show generosity and to have the shackles of all hostages removed.

Later, "Captain Machmud" calls three hostages to him, including Birgitt Röhll, and asks them to report for their execution the following morning at 9.00 a.m. Birgitt Röhll is on board with her ten-year-old son Stephan. Little Stephan encourages his mother over the next few hours. "You're not going to die", he assures her. Stephan sleeps on his mum's lap that night. Birgitt Röhll doesn't sleep a wink.

Early in the morning, "Captain Machmud" is in a calm mood. Perhaps he only wanted to threaten Birgitt Röhll and the other hostages to spread fear of death. Gabriele von Lutzau intuitively recognises his change of mood and gets him to promise that no one will be shot. Birgit Röhll is allowed to stay alive. "Captain Machmud" announces his decision over the on-board microphone.

Birgit Röhll and her son Stephan will suffer from the kidnapping for the rest of their lives. And they remain close to one another. In addition to the family ties, they are united by the shared fate of the hijacked "Landshut".

The women among the hostages have to take off their nylon stockings and hand them in. Stewardess Gabriele von Lutzau (nee Dillmann) wondered what it was all about. When "Captain Machmud" demands fuel and threatens to kill one hostage every five minutes, she realises why: Each of them was not to be shot but strangled in front of everyone! In reality, the stockings were later used to tie up the hostages during the last ultimatum.

Again and again, the tower tries to free individual hostages. Sometimes the sick. Sometimes the women. Sometimes the women and children. "Captain Machmud" doesn't give in to anything. He has obviously been drilled in the training camp to make zero concessions. Frankly and freely, he tells the "Landshut" crew that he will not even allow the dead to be removed from the aircraft. He will make good on his gruesome announcement.

11.27 am. "Captain Machmud" wants the ground power still on the aircraft removed. The "Landshut" should be ready for take-off. He now also reminds of the Chancellor's political responsibility. "Does Chancellor Schmidt realise that there are 87 (sic!) passengers on board? He should decide quickly, otherwise we will honour our warning."[80] The terrorist gives the tower ten minutes.

"Federal Republic had 60 h", "Captain Machmud" addresses the tower again shortly afterwards, "aircraft will take off and will be blown up if conditions are not met by the next target."[81] At 11.59 a.m., a car drives onto the airfield to tow away the generator. It's gone by 12:02 p.m.

"Call from the AA Situation Centre, Mr Westphal: The Finnish and Swedish envoys have spoken to Dr Jesser, Head of Division 31 at the AA, and informed him that the Finnish national (…), 45 years old, is on board the hijacked Lufthansa plane. The two envoys expressed their governments' requests that the Federal Government do everything in its power to protect the life of the Finnish national. At the same time, both expressed their understanding for the difficult situation of the Federal Government" (Fig. 3.2).[82]

> *"it is thanks to your politics that i and the family of my brother hans hasse-beyn (sic!), who is sitting in the lufthansa plane that was hijacked on 13 october, are about to be shot. How many more men do you need on the crisis team and (sic!) nothing to do? don't just allow yourself to be put under pressure, but finally take action one way or another helmut heyn."*

> *"mr federal chancellor the lives of 91 innocent people lie in your power of decision please comply with the demands of the terrorists or is the power of disposal over the baader meinhofs really of higher value? dr brauchart graz fiancé of the austrian chief stewardess hannelore piegler."*[83]

---

[80] Ibid, p. 11 ("Captain Machmud" spoke English, already translated in the log).
[81] Ibid, p. 12.
[82] Note from the Head of Situation Centre Meyer-Sebastian dated 15 October 1977, in: Archiv BK 13–211 20 (3) Additional file 3, no p.
[83] Telegram from Dr Brauchart dated 15 October 1977 to Federal Chancellor Helmut Schmidt dated 15 October 1977, in: BArch B 136/31588.

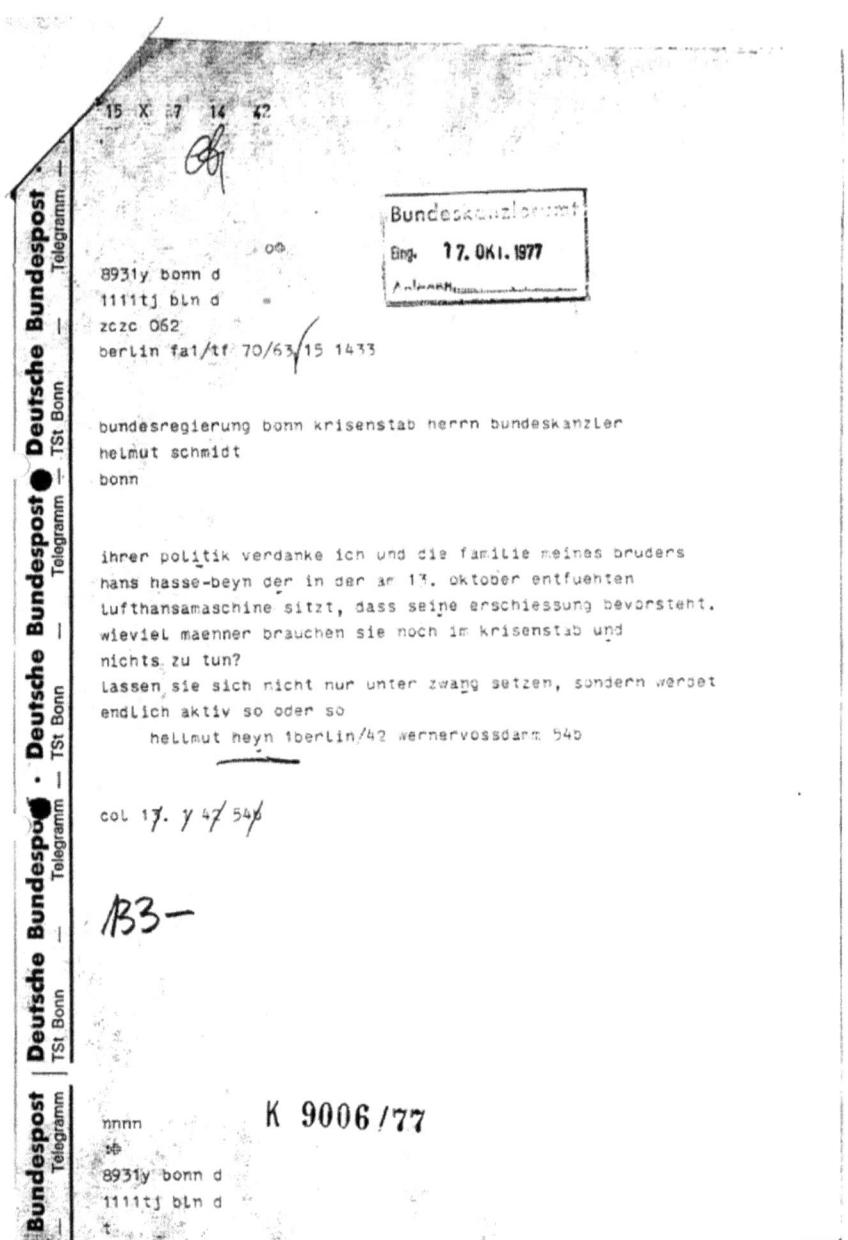

Fig. 3.2 Telegram from Hellmut Heyn dated 15 October 1977 to Federal Chancellor Helmut Schmidt *Source* BArch B136/31588

"(...) my 66-year-old mother is on the lh plane in Dubai. (...) the decision to be taken by the federal government is difficult, there are many pros and cons, as always the decision will have many opponents. But only one thing can be of decisive importance: prioritising the obligation to humanity over all other duties. (...) rolf-meijer-werner caracas/Venezuela."[84]

Things are getting uncomfortable for Ulrich Wegener's men in Ankara. A "PR disaster"[85] had caused the "Tagesschau" news programme to report on the whereabouts of Wegener's men in Turkey. Now the whole world knows that the GSG9 is flying after the hijacked "Landshut".

Defence Minister Sheikh Mohammed Bin Rashid a-Maktum wants to know from the German ambassador to the United Arab Emirates, Hansjoachim Neumann, whether 30 "anti-terror specialists" are on their way to Dubai. Neumann assures him that no specialists are on their way.

Minister of State Hans-Jürgen Wischnewski asks Federal Chancellor Helmut Schmidt in a telephone conversation "that the plane demonstratively flies home".[86] And so it does. Government spokesman Klaus Bölling opts for a forward strategy: He announces the German government's decision to bring the GSG9 home of its own accord. The Second German Television is even allowed to film the landing of the aircraft in Cologne-Wahl. The world should know that the Federal Government is focusing on a negotiated solution.

What Klaus Bölling does not say, of course, is that after a stopover in the Iranian capital Tehran, Commander Ulrich Wegener, his adjutant Frieder Baum and Wegener's deputy Dieter Fox board a small plane bound for Dubai. Employees of the German government and the Federal Criminal Police Office are also waiting in Tehran for this flight.[87]

The situation at Dubai Airport is only outwardly relaxed. On the one hand, Defence Minister Sheikh Mohammed Bin Rashid a-Maktum manages to stall the terrorist leader in the "Landshut". On the other hand, his father has instructed him not to do anything that could jeopardise the life and limb of the hostages. The Emirate of Dubai must emerge politically unscathed from the affair.

Of course, the emirate's political leaders are not acting selflessly. They are using the kidnapping as an unexpected window on the world. But the government is also risking a lot. The images of a massacre of the hostages or an explosion of the aircraft would also go around the world.

---

[84] Telex ibid.
[85] Herzog 2022, p. 169.
[86] Ibid.
[87] Cf. ibid, p. 170.

Bonn

There has long been no other topic of conversation among West Germans than the hijacking of the "Landshut". The terrorist commando's script is just as perfidious as the hostage-taking of Israeli athletes during the Olympic Games in Munich. Back then, the world watched a brutal act by Palestinian terrorists for many hours. Four years later, over many days.

Germans anxiously follow the news on ARD and ZDF. The radio provides news at least every hour. The relatively few programmes available at the time are enough to keep people on tenterhooks day and night about current events. Presumably not only in the Federal Republic, but also in Germany behind the Wall.

At the same time—and this is also part of the historical truth—the kidnapping of Hanns Martin Schleyer disappears from the general radar. The president of the employers' association must presumably feel damned lonely as a hostage in some room, a cupboard. And even more since then. Which is also due to the fact that the trail to him has been lost. In the beginning, the investigators could still assume that the hostage was being held captive not far from where he was kidnapped. Now they are in the dark on this question.

The confidence of finding Hanns Martin Schleyer's hiding place is diminishing day by day. Presumably also among the political decision-makers in Bonn. On the day of the "Landshut" hijacking, it has already sunk massively. BKA chief Horst Herold no longer believes that the hostage is still in the Federal Republic. In fact, the next places of residence are The Hague and Brussels. This makes the search for him or his rescue infinitely more difficult.

Frankfurt Am Main/Karlsruhe

Nevertheless, Hanns Martin Schleyer's family continues to try to do everything in their power to save their father. The Palestinian terrorist commando demanded 15 million US dollars in cash in addition to the release of RAF and PFLP-SC terrorists. Hanns-Eberhard Schleyer raised this sum with the help of West German industrialists. Through the lawyer Denis Payot, he organised a handover of the money at Frankfurt am Main airport.

The role of money in terrorist organisations, whether in Central Europe or the Middle East, should not be underestimated. Not only do their members need to live comfortably, they also need to travel, bribe and buy weapons. Criminal methods of obtaining money include bank robberies and ransom extortion.

BKA President Horst Herold hears about Hanns-Eberhard Schleyer's unauthorised initiative. He cannot and will not allow the family of the kidnapped man to seek a kind of extra-police solution. At the same time, he knows that Hanns-Eberhard Schleyer is putting himself in personal danger with this action. It would be easy for the terrorists to take him into their power as well.

Horst Herold leaks the time and place of the planned handover of money to journalists. When Hanns-Eberhard Schleyer arrives with his suitcase of money, he finds himself in unwelcome company. Terrorists literally fear such company like the plague. The operation failed. It is an example of how the Schleyer family used their father's political network with dedication and success, instead of passively hoping for a successful outcome from the police.

The Schleyer family puts massive pressure on Chancellor Helmut Schmidt, his cabinet and the members of the two crisis teams in many ways. A kind of early showdown of the German Autumn, the final confrontation between Hanns-Eberhard Schleyer's family and the federal government, occurs in the early morning hours of Sunday, 16 October. The reason for this is the presumably last ultimatum of the Schleyer kidnappers, who, in conjunction with the terrorist commando in the hijacked "Landshut", are putting more pressure than ever on the federal government. This ultimatum ends this Sunday morning at nine o'clock.

For the young lawyer Hanns-Eberhard Schleyer and his family, the hour has come to resort to a kind of last resort, the invocation of the Federal Constitutional Court. Hanns-Eberhard Schleyer had already announced to Chancellor Helmut Schmidt in an early conversation after the kidnapping of his father that, if necessary, he would.

The conditions under which the Federal Constitutional Court had to make an urgent decision, presumably about the life or death of Hanns Martin Schleyer, were among the many dramas of the German Autumn. The blackmail by terrorists ultimately reached this power in the state. The federal government and the German Bundestag have been confronted with this for weeks. The same applies to the press and broadcasting media, which are commonly referred to as the "fourth estate". They are subject to the autocratic control of government spokesman Klaus Bölling, who imposes a news blackout. A muzzling decree.

On Saturday, 15 October, the lawyers of the Schleyer family appeal to the Federal Constitutional Court. This is a unique procedure that is not provided for in West German legislation. The court agrees to hear the case because of its special significance. The lawyers argue that Hanns Martin Schleyer's life is in immediate danger. The federal government has not indicated that it will meet the kidnappers' demands, so the lawyers say that Schleyer's existence is now in the hands of the court.

The defence lawyers are opposed to the stereotypical view put forward by the Federal Minister of Justice, Hans-Jochen Vogel, that it is necessary to weigh up the direct danger to a single human life against the potential danger to a great many people as future victims of terrorism. According to the Basic Law, so the argument goes, the constitutional protection of a human life takes precedence over everything.

The Federal Government, in turn, unsurprisingly argues with Hans-Jochen Vogel's dictum. It sees itself confirmed in its view by the bloody history of the Schleyer kidnapping, with kidnappings and murders. Furthermore, it makes it clear that the Federal Constitutional Court must not take over the task of governing from it. It must not restrict the scope of action of a federal government, which could anticipate future decisions in comparable situations.

On Saturday evening at 9:30 p.m.—roughly at the same time as Jörg Zink's "Word of the Sunday"—the oral proceedings begin in Karlsruhe. Representatives of the Schleyer family and the federal government present their positions to the First Senate. At midnight, the judges withdraw to deliberate. At 4:00 a.m., the court announces a verdict at 5:30 a.m. At 5:45 a.m., three and a half hours before the RAF ultimatum expires, the court announces its decision: "The issuance of a temporary injunction is denied."

Hanns-Eberhard Schleyer would later often refer to the political pressure to which the Federal Constitutional Court was exposed by the federal government. The late Ernst Benda, then president of the Federal Constitutional Court, had admitted this to him.

Thirty years after the events, Carsten Polzin takes a critical legal view of the ruling:[88] The federal government behaved unconstitutionally, as did the Federal Constitutional Court, by failing to recognise the significance of human dignity. The court did not sentence Hanns Martin Schleyer to death, but it did create the conditions for his assassination.

Like much of the "German Autumn", the judgement must be seen in its temporal context. It occurred during a period of political and emotional emergency the likes of which this country had never seen since its founding. The members of the First Senate found themselves in a borderline situation in their roles. Presumably, they wrestled with their judgement after the "German Autumn" as did many political decision-makers afterwards.

---

[88] Cf. Polzin 2006.

3 The Brutality of Chance

As the German Autumn progressed, the time available for political decision-making became increasingly shorter. This also applied to the judiciary. The Federal Constitutional Court had to decide on a temporary injunction between the beginning and the end of a night. The same applied to the members of the first senate: Whatever they decided, it would be insufficient, a choice between plague and cholera, as the saying goes.

> *"Decisions will probably be made that night that, whatever they may be, will cast heavy shadows into the future. (...) No one can do so much that they don't miss out on something crucial. And no-one can think so carefully that they don't still have serious debts to pay. No one."*
>
> From Pastor Jörg Zink's "Word for Sunday" on ARD, Saturday, 15 October 1977

On the evening of 15 October 1977, somebody is trying to calm the agitated West Germans. Jörg Zink is a Protestant clergyman and so-called television pastor, he time and again speaks the "Word for Sunday", which is broadcasted on Saturday evenings on ARD and reaches millions of television viewers. By this time, he words of Christians still have social cohesion in the country.

Jörg Zink wants to comfort people in front of the screen and give them hope. He also provides an accurate analysis of the decision-making situation in which Chancellor Helmut Schmidt and his party find themselves.

"Decisions will probably be made that night that, whatever they may be, will cast heavy shadows into the future. (...) No one can do so much that they don't miss out on something crucial. And no-one can think so carefully that they don't commit serious offences. Nobody. Not even those responsible at the top of the state, who have now borne their terrible responsibility for six weeks. There can be no solution that works without a remainder. It is both right and wrong at the same time. (...).

A conflict of this kind is endured in solitude before God and not in public. (...) And that is the core of the Christian faith, that God does not judge those who stand before him in this way. (...) In the end, someone will not say: It was all right. But perhaps rather: I made that decision. I stand by it. God help me."[89]

Chancellor Helmut Schmidt either sees Jörg Zink's "Word for Sunday" himself or is informed of it later. The next day, an employee of the Federal

---

[89] Jörg Zink: The Word for Sunday, ARD, 15 October 1977. Attachment to the letter from Pastor Dr Jörg Zink to Federal Chancellor Helmut Schmidt dated 17 October 1977, in: OTB 13–211 20 (2) Additional file OTB vol. 7, p. 298f. letter from Pastor Dr Jörg Zink to Federal Chancellor Helmut Schmidt dated 17 October 1977, in: OTB 13–211 20 (2) Additional file OTB vol. 7, p. 295f.

Chancellery contacts Zink with the request for the text. This can be seen in a letter from the pastor to Helmut Schmidt dated 18 October 1977. The letter will be referred to later.

This evening the Federal Government activates a telephone number at the Federal Ministry of Defence. An information centre has been set up there for relatives of the hostages. German Lufthansa had previously published a telephone number for those affected.

Dubai

Sunday, 16 October. Since 4.29 a.m., "Captain Machmud" has been negotiating a refuelling of the aircraft by 6.00 a.m. He issues an ultimatum until 6.00 a.m. Otherwise the captain will be shot. The tower, for its part, once again demands the release of sick hostages. Minister of State Hans-Jürgen Wischnewski had gone to bed in the airport guest house. He is woken up and called to the tower.

Shortly before the ultimatum expires, the terrorists select hostages who are to be taken to First Class and kneel down: Jürgen Schumann, Gabriele von Lutzau (née Dillmann), Diana Müll and Dutch passenger Gerry Wetenkamp. "Captain Machmud" gives them numbers. Captain Schumann is given the number 1, Gabriele von Lutzau (née Dillmann) the number 01, Diana Müll the number 2 and the Dutch passenger Gerry Wetenkamp the number 3. Then they are told to return to their seats. Whose number the terrorist calls out must come forward for his or her execution.

Gabriele von Lutzau (née Dillmann) will later surmise in the "Stern" magazine interview with Gerd Heidemann that the numbers were chosen arbitrarily. Gabriele von Lutzau (née Dillmann) is probably right. There is no recognisable systematic approach. The terrorist wants to cause confusion and alarm. Presumably as taught in the training camp that lasted several weeks.

"Captain Machmud" calls "Number 3", Gerry, to the front. Diana Müll and Gerry's fiancée sit next to each other. Diana Müll takes him in her arms. They are forbidden to say anything. Or to cry.

Gerry goes through the curtain into First Class. Many hostages cover their ears in anticipation of a shot. After a while, Gerry emerges unharmed. "Captain Machmud" has asked him to go to Diana to tell her: "You'll be shot first".

Diana Müll gets up and makes her way to "Captain Machmud". She feels like she has a long way to go, at least 50 metres.[90] "Like my feet are standing in a concrete bucket."[91]

The terrorist leader asks Diana Müll, who must kneel again, for her name. He then kicks her in the head with his foot, causing her to fall backwards. "Captain Machmud" and a female terrorist drag Diana Müll to the open cockpit door. The terrorist leader presses his pistol to her head.

"Captain Machmud" threatens the tower to shoot a hostage every five minutes if petrol doesn't arrive immediately.

Bonn

At 5.59 a.m. German time on 16 October, Hans Jürgen Wischnewski calls State Secretary Heinz Ruhnau: "If the plane is not refueled immediately, there are only seconds left. The hijackers have now threatened to shoot the pilots and two hostages."[92] Heinz Ruhnau has the Chancellor woken up. Helmut Schmidt comes to the phone.

Wischnewski: "I am in favour of starting the refueling process".

Schmidt: "Where will that end?[93] A tonne at most.[94] (…) Under no circumstances allow anything that makes it easier or possible for the aircraft to take off. Under no circumstances. It must be accepted if individual people are actually killed. Have you understood me?"

Wischnewski: "Yes, I have understood."

Schmidt: "The killing of individuals must be accepted. Subsequently (…) must be attacked" (Fig. 3.3).[95]

Hans-Jürgen Wischnewski goes back to the tower. Helmut Schmidt calls the West German economic attaché in Dubai, Hubert Lang, again. "The German government instructs Mr Wischnewski to do everything in his power to prevent the aircraft from being supported in its readiness for take-off. At

---

[90] In the following waste 2023.
[91] Ibid.
[92] Conversation between the Federal Chancellor—StM Wischnewski—Sts Ruhnau on 16 October 1977, 5.59 a.m., in: Archiv BK 13–211 20 (2) Additional file OTB Bd. 6, p. 243.
[93] Ibid.
[94] Ibid, p. 244.
[95] Ibid, p. 251.

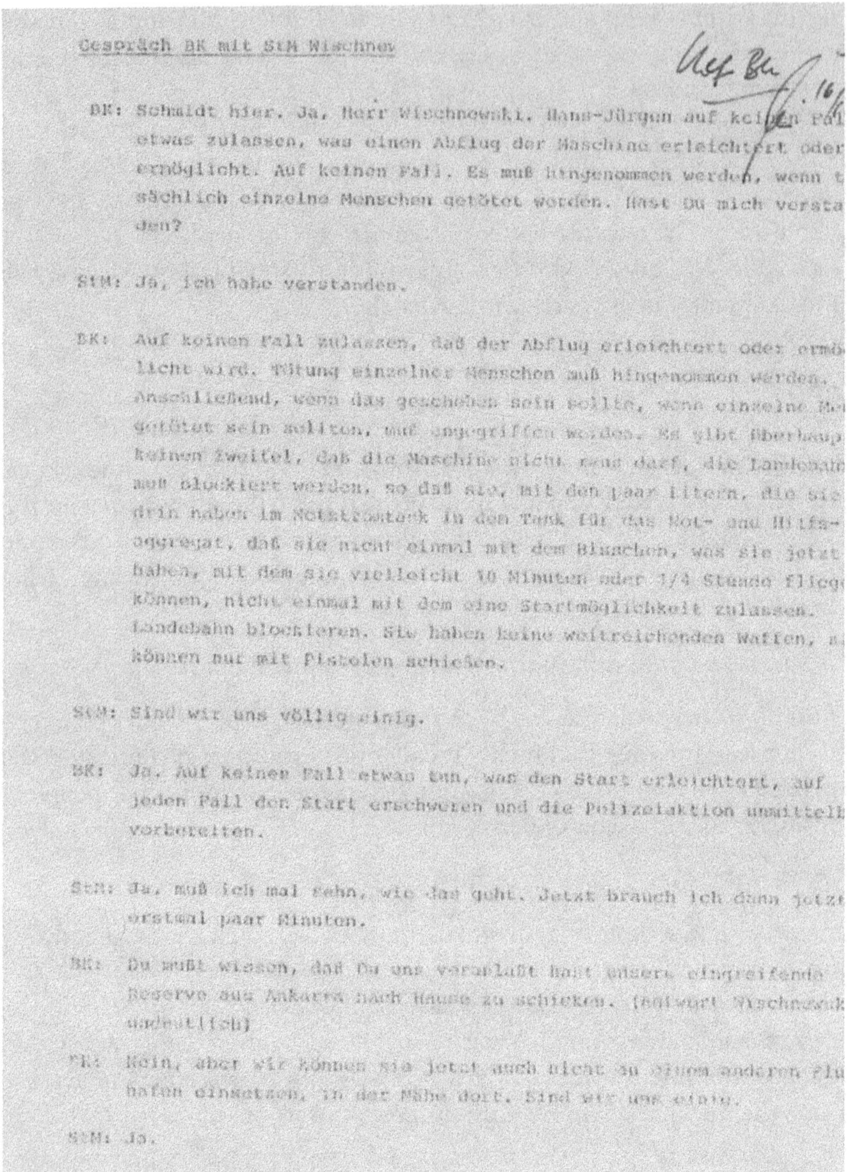

Gespräch BK mit StM Wischnew

BK: Schmidt hier. Ja, Herr Wischnewski. Hans-Jürgen auf keinen Fal
etwas zulassen, was einen Abflug der Maschine erleichtert oder
ermöglicht. Auf keinen Fall. Es muß hingenommen werden, wenn t
sächlich einzelne Menschen getötet worden. Hast Du mich versta
den?

StM: Ja, ich habe verstanden.

BK: Auf keinen Fall zulassen, daß der Abflug erleichtert oder ermö
licht wird. Tötung einzelner Menschen muß hingenommen werden.
Anschließend, wenn das geschehen sein sollte, wenn einzelne Me
getötet sein sollten, muß angegriffen werden. Es gibt überhaup
keinen Zweifel, daß die Maschine nicht weg darf, die Landebahn
muß blockiert werden, so daß sie, mit den paar Litern, die sie
drin haben im Notstromstock in dem Tank für das Not- und Hilfs-
aggregat, daß sie nicht einmal mit dem Bisschen, was sie jetzt
haben, mit dem sie vielleicht 10 Minuten oder 1/4 Stunde flieg
können, nicht einmal mit dem eine Startmöglichkeit zulassen.
Landebahn blockieren. Sie haben keine weitreichenden Waffen, s
können nur mit Pistolen schießen.

StM: Sind wir uns völlig einig.

BK: Ja. Auf keinen Fall etwas tun, was den Start erleichtert, auf
jeden Fall den Start erschweren und die Polizeiaktion unmittelb
vorbereiten.

StM: Ja, muß ich mal sehn, wie das geht. Jetzt brauch ich dann jetz
erstmal paar Minuten.

BK: Du mußt wissen, daß Du uns veranlaßt hast unsere eingreifende
Reserve aus Ankara nach Hause zu schicken. (Antwort Wischnewsk
undeutlich)

BK: Nein, aber wir können sie jetzt auch nicht an einem anderen Flu
hafen einsetzen, in der Nähe dort. Sind wir uns einig.

StM: Ja.

BK: o.k.

Fig. 3.3 Telephone conversation protocol between the Federal Chancellor—StM Wischnewski—Sts Ruhnau on 16 October 1977, 5.59 a.m *Source* Archiv BK 13–211 20 (2) Additional file OTB Bd. 6, p. 243

the risk of human life. (…) Tell Mr Wischnewski: by any means necessary" (Fig. 3.4).[96]

This time, Hans-Jürgen Wischnewski disobeys an order from his superior. He gives the okay to refuel. At 6:35 a.m., a tanker is at the aircraft. "Captain Machmud" lets go of Diana Müll. She faints. She probably owes her life to the energetic initiative of the Minister of State.

Even the Minister of State, who has nerves of steel, the momentary shock runs down his spine. "I have one big request", he calls Heinz Ruhnau shortly after ten, "write down a telephone number, Cologne 407,701, and let them know that I'm doing very well."

The Federal Criminal Police Office has determined that the Minister of State is at risk. Due to his prominent role in the "Landshut" drama, he could be a possible target for an attack. On the same day, Hans-Jürgen Wischnewski receives a telegram with a "list of additional security measures" for his private home in Cologne-Liblar. His personal adviser Peter Kiewitt calls Bonn hours later and conveys Wischnewski's wish to "start installing and implementing the planned measures immediately".[97]

That morning, Chancellor Helmut Schmidt learns—presumably from a Palestinian source—that "the hijackers (…) could try to fly on to Aden."[98] In a further telephone call with British Prime Minister James Callaghan, he reiterates his desire to end the hijacking in Dubai. No matter what the cost. The onward flight should be prevented "even with the possible loss of individual lives."[99]

The Prime Minister convenes a crisis team in London, which liaises with the German government via State Secretary Jürgen Ruhfus. Helmut Schmidt asks the Prime Minister for permission for Ulrich Wegener's men to land on a British military base in Cyprus. The GSG9 wants to be ready there for deployment "in other areas of the Middle East (…) in case the hijackers manage to fly on."[100] James Callaghan wants to think things over. As previously described, Cyprus is politically a minefield. Hours later, the British government will turn the Chancellor down.

Helmut Schmidt resorts to a last resort to keep the "Landshut" in Dubai. He asks the President of the United Arab Emirates, Sheikh Zayed Bin Sultan Al Nahayan, for a telephone call at 11.15 am. It is under bad auspices. The

---

[96] Ibid., p. 252.
[97] Cf. AdD, 1/HSAA010017.
[98] Note. Telephone conversation between the Federal Chancellor and PM Callaghan on 16 October 1977, 08.40/09.00, in: Archiv BK 13–211 20 (2) Additional file OTB vol. 6, p. 293ff.
[99] Ibid., p. 295.
[100] Ibid., p. 294.

Gespräch BK mit Lang (Wirtschaftsattache Deutsche Botschaft)
16.10.1977   6.19 Uhr

BK : Herr Lang, wie weit ist Herr Wischnewski weg von Ihnen?

Lang : Etwa 5 m von mir weg, spricht aber gerade mit dem Verteidigungsminister, soll ich ihn holen?

BK : Nein, sagen Sie ihm, die Bundesregierung beauftragt Herrn Wischnewski, mit allen Mitteln, die ihm zur Verfügung stehen, den dipl. Druckes für notwendig, mit allen Mitteln zu verhindern, daß das Flugzeug in seiner Startbereitschaft gefördert wird.
Unter Inkaufnahme von Menschenleben.

Lang : Ich werde das sofort übermitteln Herr Bundeskanzler.

BK : Ich bin noch nicht fertig. Unter Inkaufnahme von Menschenleben. Zweitens. Mit allen Mitteln Flugbahn, Startbahn blockieren lassen. Drittens. Ich ersuche dringend, Truppen und Polizei um das Flugzeug zu konzentrieren um den Zugriff unmittelbar zu ermöglichen. Ich verlange nicht, daß es sofort ausgeführt wird. Unsere Leute, die sich jetzt wahrscheinlich nicht im Tower befinden, unsere Berater und Hilfskräfte heranziehen. Übermitteln Sie das sofort. Haben Sie mich verstanden?

Lang : Ich habe Sie verstanden, ich habe habe es übergeben, genauso, wie Sie es mir jetzt mitgeteilt haben. Die Antwort war: Inhaltlich weiß der Verteidigungsminister Ihre Antwort oder Ihre Weisung schon.

BK : Sagen Sie Herrn Wischnewski mit allen Mitteln.

Lang : Ich werde es nochmal sagen, mit allen Mitteln.

Fig. 3.4 Telephone conversation protocol between the Federal Chancellor—StM Wischnewski—Sts Ruhnau on 16 October 1977, 5.59 a.m *Source* Archiv BK 13–211 20 (2) Additional file OTB Bd. 6, p. 252

Sheikh does not speak English. The dialogue partners each need translators in their offices, which makes the conversation impersonal and lengthy.

Helmut Schmidt repeats his wishes: Keep the plane on the ground, allow a rescue operation. He emphasises the seriousness of the situation and the consequences if the hijacking is not stopped. The sheikh listens to everything and responds diplomatically.

What the Federal Chancellor cannot know: At 12.12 p.m., Jürgen Vietor starts the engines of the "Landshut". The aircraft taxis towards the runway, stops, taxis again. At 12.23 p.m., it takes off for an unknown destination.

Chancellor Helmut Schmidt is handed a note saying that the "Landshut" has just left Dubai Airport with an unknown destination.

Helmut Schmidt feels stalled and deceived. He is convinced that Sheikh Zayed Bin Sultan Al Nahayan gave the go-ahead for the plane during the phone call. Once again, he has to realise that the Federal Republic of Germany is a tiny player in world politics.

Under no circumstances should it look like a defeat for the Federal Chancellor. Helmut Schmidt instructs Hans-Jürgen Wischnewski on the phone to "put my respect at the feet of Defence Minister Sheikh Mohammed Bin Rashid a-Maktoum. Anything friendly you say to him, say it in my name."[101] The Minister of State should also shower the Sheikh with praise in front of journalists and thank the authorities for their willingness to help for days on end.

According to Helmut Schmidt's version of events, neither the German government nor the Foreign Minister of the United Arab Emirates was responsible for the departure of the plane!

Aden

Standing Time "Landshut": Sunday, 16 October 1977, 03.52 P.M., Until Monday, 17 October 1977, 02.02 A. M.

"Captain Machmud" wants the "Landshut" to land in Salalah on the island of Massora. The island belongs to the Sultanate of Oman. The local authorities refuse to allow the landing. The pilots suggest to the terrorist leader that he land in Mulkalla Ryan, a city in the People's Democratic Republic of Yemen ("South Yemen"). "Captain Machmud" refuses.

---

[101] Conversation BK—StM Wischnewski. 16 October 1977. 1.50 p.m., in Archiv BK 13–211 20 (2) Additional file OTB vol. 6, p. 287ff.

At 03.21 p.m., the "Landshut" is 30 nautical miles from the southern Yemeni capital Aden. The tower there informs the "Landshut" cockpit that the airport is closed. "What should we do?" Jürgen Vietor asks the terrorist next to him. "Captain Machmud" tells him to land in any case.

At 03.37 p.m., Jürgen Vietor reports to the tower in Aden that the aircraft still has 15 min of fuel left. At 2.40 p.m., the tower knows that the "Landshut" has set course for Aden. A fuel line is leaking—presumably the damage already discovered by the "Lufthanseaten" in Dubai. The cockpit is clueless.

Unlike in Dubai, this time there is no air traffic controller who means well with the people in the "Landshut". The runway remains blocked by vehicles and a frequency for the landing approach is refused.

Jürgen Vietor heads for an area next to the runway. It is no longer concreted, there is a mixture of sand and rubble. How deep is the ground, can the aircraft sink into it? It has to be able to roll out. Otherwise, it's over.

The cabin crew prepares the passengers for the emergency landing. Purserette Hannelore Brauchardt (née Piegler) gives Lufthansa's instructions for this eventuality over the on-board microphone.[102] Passengers are told to put jewellery, glasses and dentures between their seats. Gabriele von Lutzau believes that things will then break. She announces over the on-board microphone that she will collect everything and sets off with a large rubbish bag.

The fact that sometimes Hannelore Brauchardt (née Piegler) and sometimes Gabriele von Lutzau (née Dillmann) pick up the on-board microphone—often in immediate succession—does not go unnoticed by the hostages. The crew members give contradictory instructions, even in this dramatic situation.

Jürgen Vietor asks "Captain Machmud" to have his men secure the hand grenades in the cabin. Apparently, the terrorist didn't come up with this good idea himself.

The pilots know that the aircraft could crash on touchdown and that many or all of the passengers could perish. Shortly before landing, Jürgen Schumann and Jürgen Vietor say goodbye to each other with a handshake. They also shake hands with "Captain Machmud". He is now the captain.

Jürgen Vietor realises shortly before landing that "Captain Machmud" is not strapped in. During the hard landing, he could fall forwards onto the throttle and the aircraft could no longer be braked. Both pilots fasten the seatbelt of "Captain Machmud", who has become stiff with fear.

---

[102] Cf. letter from Hannelore Brauchardt (née Piegler) to Christa Schmiedl dated 23 January 1978, in: LH-Archiv.

.52 p.m., the "Landshut" touches down. The impact is hard. Passen- scream in agony. Ceiling panels fall down. The aircraft is badly shaken. spends what feels like an eternity digging through sand and rubble.

Jürgen Vietor activates the aircraft's own fire extinguishers in case an engine catches fire. He himself has no visibility, only sand in front of his eyes. He brakes the aircraft, and it eventually comes to a halt. Its landing gear sinks in. It is the landing of his life. Jürgen Vietor has been flying the "Landshut" since Rome.

Sudden silence in the machine. When the passengers realise that they are still alive, they give the cockpit frenetic applause. And somehow, themselves too. Once again, they have cheated death.

Aden. Aden of all places. Yemen is politically divided like Germany, the island of Cyprus or Korea. Aden. In the north, the Westernised Yemeni Arab Republic, in the south, with Aden as its capital, the People's Democratic Republic of Yemen. The only Marxist regime in an Arab country rule there under the leadership of Salim Rubai Ali.

South Yemen is largely ignored by states beyond the so-called Eastern bloc. It is considered an Eldorado for terrorist groups, including Palestinian splinter groups. "At present, the terrorist splinter group of the PFLP (Popular for the Liberation of Palestine, editor's note) under Wadi Haddad is dominant within this complex", according to a country assessment by the German Federal Intelligence Service dated 23 September 1977.[103] The organisation of Wadi Haddad, aka Abu Hani, originally a doctor, is known as the PFLP-SC. Popular Front for the Liberation of Palestine—Special Command. In the autumn of 1977, the PFLP founders George Habash and Wadi Haddad were already divided, both personally and within the organisation.

On the evening of the Cologne murders and Hanns Martin Schleyer's kidnapping, the Federal Foreign Office had already reported to the Federal Intelligence Service on South Yemen. Training camps for terrorists there had been repeatedly reported and confirmed in at least one case in the Aden area.[104] In the summer of 1976, the "Popular Front for the Liberation of Palestine" was said to be running a training camp in Halma, a two-hour drive from the capital Aden. Many RAF members from West Germany received firearms training there and were recruited for Haddad's infamous "foreign operations"; for example, Brigitte Kuhlmann and Wilfried Böse in Entebbe in 1976.

---

[103] Cf. Archiv BK 13–122 20 (2) Additional file OTB vol. 3, p. 189f.
[104] Memo from the Federal Foreign Office, Division 63, dated 6 September 1977, in: BArch B136/16489.

Members of the "Front for the Liberation of the Moluccans", who carried out two attacks in the Netherlands in the spring of 1977, also allegedly trained in South Yemen. These attacks will be discussed later.

In Aden, the "Landshut" terror squad expects to meet some friends. But to the complete surprise of "Captain Machmud", the comrades are stonewalling. The South Yemeni regime only agrees to pull the "Landshut" out of the sand and supply it with water and fuel. "Captain Machmud" is told by the tower that he should leave with the aircraft as quickly as possible. Also, from a Palestinian, a PLO representative, who negotiates with the terrorist leader for an hour.

"Captain Machmud" is raging. He can't make sense of what he is experiencing.

Afterwards, various scenarios become known as to what "Captain Machmud" could hope for. "The plan was to renew the "Martyr Halimeh" commando with PFLP-SC members on the ground and take the hostages to one of the training camps until the prisoner exchange".[105] This would the claim of former members of the Red Army Faction decades later. There is no scientific evidence for this.

Bonn

The South Yemeni regime also sends a clear message to the German government. The Foreign Office receives a wire report which, transmitted by telex, immediately reaches the head of the Federal Chancellery. "All airports in yemen are completely closed", it says.[106] "Minister Wischnewski is not authorised to land. Please do not attempt to land under any circumstances whatsoever. (…) After initial discussions at the highest level, the government is absolutely determined to make clear its rejection of all terrorism by stating that under no circumstances can terrorists be accepted here. Disembarkation from the aircraft will also be denied."[107]

The pilot of Hans-Jürgen Wischnewski's plane is instructed to fly around Aden. He circled the southern Yemeni border until the plane ran out of petrol and was forced to land in Jeddah, a port city in Saudi Arabia. The Minister of State and his travelling companions are warmly welcomed by the Saudis— not a matter of course for West Germans in the Arab world at that time. In

---

[105] Cf. Geiger 2009, p. 437.
[106] Telex from AA to BK dated 16 October 1977, Boeker. In: AdsD, 1/HSAA010017.
[107] Ibid.

Jeddah, Hans-Jürgen Wischnewski meets the chargé d'affaires of the People's Democratic Republic of Yemen ("North Yemen").

Federal Chancellor Helmut Schmidt authorises Minister of State Hans-Jürgen Wischnewski to "negotiate with the Yemeni government without restrictions".[108] A little later, Helmut Schmidt informs the Minister of State that his authorisation "also extends to talks on development aid for South Yemen"[109]—in other words, money.

At 7.07 p.m., Chancellor Helmut Schmidt instructs the Chargé d' Affaires of the Federal Republic of Germany in Aden, Damm, not to allow the "Landshut" to take off.[110] The authorisation for the Minister of State and the instruction to the chargé d'affaires will once again demonstrate the Federal Chancellor's impotence in the "Landshut" drama.

The GDR maintains diplomatic relations with its communist "brother" South Yemen. Political and economic advisors from the former GDR provide development aid in the country. Employees of the Ministry of State Security train security forces in South Yemen. In September 1976, Willi Stoph, Chairman of the State Council of the former GDR, visited the country.

"In Aden, there is no possibility of co-operating with the security forces", Hans-Jürgen Wischnewski sums it up in a phone call with Helmut Schmidt. The "Landshut" is currently approaching the South Yemeni capital. "Everything there is in the hands of the GDR."[111]

Nevertheless, diplomacy must do everything it can. Minister of State Hans-Jürgen Wischnewski "requests a call to East Berlin for support from the GDR ambassador on humanitarian grounds".[112] In the period that follows, the telephone lines from the Foreign Office to the Soviet Union and the GDR proverbial run hot.

At 10.00 p.m., a meeting is held between Federal Foreign Minister Hans-Dietrich Genscher and his GDR counterpart Oskar Fischer. According to Genscher's request, Fischer should try to persuade the South Yemeni government to seek dialogue with the German government.[113]

The unusual request made at the time by the Foreign Minister of the Federal Republic of Germany to his colleague in the GDR provided the material for a legend that was cultivated well into the 2000s. It goes like this:

---

[108] German Lufthansa, Event-Log, p. 13.
[109] Ibid.
[110] Cf. ibid.
[111] Ibid, p. 287.
[112] Ibid. p. 13.
[113] Note from the Working Group on German Policy dated 17 October 1977, in: PA-AA, Embassy of the Federal Republic of Germany in Abi Dhabi. Abduction Lufthansa (…), Vw 260,30 Pol 300,25 B10/1,5 + 6.

The PFLP wanted to end the "Landshut" hijacking in Aden by moving the hostages to the organisation's camps in the interior. This would lead to difficult, protracted negotiations with the German government led by Helmut Schmidt. This method would be chosen by the new Iranian regime in 1979 after the overthrow of the Shah with the members of the US Embassy in Tehran. With success.

Legend also has it that the GDR regime and its Ministry for State Security prevented the planned abduction of the "Landshut" hostages and urged "Aden" to immediately expel the hijacked aircraft from the airport.

A legend, as long as there is no scientific evidence to prove it. According to currently known sources GDR Ambassador Günther Sanftenberg will indeed make representations to the South Yemeni Foreign Minister Mutia—unfortunately only after the "Landshut" has already left Aden. Whether this was due to the political unwillingness of the GDR regime or the circumstances on the ground, can no longer be clarified today.

Other governments will urge the regime in South Yemen to cooperate in the coming hours. Historically, this has been assured by Finland, the Netherlands, Austria, Denmark and Norway.[114] Saudi Arabia is also in favour of rescuing the hostages—at the request of Bavarian Prime Minister Franz Josef Strauss, who is currently in the country.

All efforts remain unsuccessful. The South Yemeni government pretends to be politically dead the "Landshut" does not seem to exist. It acts as if there were no hijacked aircraft there. Their behaviour seems callous, even cold-blooded towards the hostages, who can only fear the worst from angry terrorists.

Beyond the creation of legends, the South Yemeni regime is fulfilling a promise it made to West German Minister of State Hans-Jürgen Wischnewski, whose machine does not allow it to land in Aden now, the previous month. Only a few people know about the agreement—apart from Hans-Jürgen Wischnewski, for example, Federal Development Aid Minister Marie Schlei. The Federal Chancellor is obviously not privy. Therefore, he cannot know: The talks on development aid, which he authorises Hans-Jürgen Wischnewski to hold on the flight of the "Landshut" to Aden, have in fact already taken place.

But first things first. The German government and the regime in Aden establish diplomatic relations at the end of 1974—Helmut Schmidt is already Chancellor—after an "ice age". From a German perspective, this will prove to be a stroke of luck in spring 1975. Left-wing terrorists kidnap the Berlin

---

[114] Cf. note "LH abduction Aden" dated 17 October 1977, signed. Löschner, in: AdsD, HSAA010017.

CDU politician Peter Lorenz and release imprisoned like-minded people. The South Yemeni government agrees to take in the terrorists—out of consideration for relations with West Germany, as cabinet member Abdallah Khamri will later tell the GDR ambassador in Aden, Günther Scharfenberg.[115] In other words: "Aden" helps in the firm expectation that the German government will show its appreciation with what West Germany mainly has to offer in the 70 s: money.

Perhaps it is due to the Cold War, perhaps to bad diplomacy, that "Bonn" is reacting cautiously to the favour that "Aden" has done it. The Federal Foreign Office suspends negotiations with South Yemen on capital aid totaling 10 million German mark.[116] It wants to prevent the impression that South Yemen has been rewarded for harbouring terrorists.[117] The Federal Republic of Germany is thus giving the cold shoulder to a country that is both willing and in need of help. "This resulted in a certain amount of resentment on the part of the People's Republic of Yemen."[118]

Furthermore, after the Lorenz kidnapping, the Western media label South Yemen a "terrorist stronghold".[119] The Cold War is raging between East and West, and both sides cultivate images of the enemy. The South Yemeni government feels it was being treated ungratefully. It fears for its international reputation and economic cooperation with other states.

The German government in Bonn would like to have seen the South Yemeni government quickly expel the freed terrorists. The cooperation of the Germans with extremist Palestinians in the country might not be stopped, but it would be made more difficult. "Bonn" allegedly promises money for this "concession". "Aden" does not respond to this offer, which in fact formulates a new condition. Not for the time being.

For a long time, the deported terrorists live undisturbed in Aden. And apparently not a bad life. The women among the RAF members are called "the anarchist ladies" in the capital. They regularly frequent a bathing club together. Which means that they don't even avoid public places.

---

[115] See Scharfenberg 2012, p. 82.

[116] Norbert Montfort/Hans-Peter Plischka: Submission to the Secretary of State on an intergovernmental agreement with the People's Democratic Republic of Yemen of 1 December 1977, resubmitted on 20 January 1978, in: Pol AA. 311. subject: 400.11–700.00 YEN. Vol. 2 from 1977 to 1978. Political Archive. Interim archive.119927.

[117] Udo Kollatz (State Secretary in the Federal Ministry for Economic Cooperation): Brief note on the status of e-pol. cooperation with the People's Republic of Yemen dated 16 October 1977, in: Archiv BK 13–211 20 (2) Additional File OTB Bd. 6, p. Ibid., p. 339.

[118] Scharfenberg 2012, p. 82.

[119] Ibid.

One day, as the then GDR ambassador Günther Scharfenberg writes in his memoirs, "the terrorists seemed to have disappeared too". Presumably the South Yemeni regime made them leave. At the end of 1976, the Foreign Office in Bonn resumes talks with South Yemen on economic aid. Federal Foreign Minister Hans-Dietrich Genscher has personally given his approval beforehand.

The Germans continue to act confidently, even arrogantly. Talk ingratitude after the embarrassment Aden helped them out of by taking in RAF terrorists. The Foreign Office goes one better. Unlike in the 1975 talks, it now demands that the South Yemeni government accepts the so-called Berlin clause.

Accepting the clause means accepting that laws passed by the German Bundestag apply not only in the federal territory, but also in West Berlin. De facto, it is a recognition of West Berlin as part of the Federal Republic of Germany.

A big ask of the South Yemeni regime. As a socialist country with close ties to the GDR, this is not at all to its liking. The GDR has declared the eastern part of Berlin to be its capital. "Berlin, capital of the GDR" is the text on the motorway signs in their territory. Anyone who questions this is politically antagonising Erich Honecker and Co.

On the one hand, the hard line taken by the Foreign Office can be criticised as arrogant towards South Yemen as a poor country that is willing to help in a particular situation. Before opening its wallet, the German government asks the crucial question: "Are you for or against us?"

On the other hand, it is long been common practice in the 1970s to tie development aid money to political considerations. Now more than ever. See the Chinese regime's "New Silk Road" project, with billions invested in the distant Balkans and elsewhere.

South Yemeni and West German politicians are negotiating again about money and the Berlin clause. Suddenly, the German Autumn begins. On 17 September 1977—a few days after the President of the German Employers' Association, Hanns Martin Schleyer, fell victim to the violence of his kidnappers—Minister of State Hans-Jürgen Wischnewski travels to Aden. The Red Army Faction prisoners in Stuttgart-Stammheim had named the People's Republic of Yemen among the countries to which they wanted to be flown. As previously reported, Minister of State Hans-Jürgen Wischnewski visits all the places of interest, ostensibly to sound out the respective governments about making concessions. In fact, he wants to get "rejections" to gain time for the search for Hanns Martin Schleyer's kidnappers.

During the talks conducted by Hans-Jürgen Wischnewski in South Yemen, the regime renews its request for financial aid. Wischnewski again offers the regime ten million German mark—no small sum for the Federal Republic at that time. On condition that the regime accepts the Berlin clause. The South Yemenis request time to consider. The Minister of State is staying overnight in Aden for this purpose.

The next day, the South Yemenis agree to the Federal Government's demand to recognise the Berlin clause. In response, Hans-Jürgen Wischnewski suggests that he would be able to "certainly increase the amount, if not exactly double it".[120]

The political leadership of South Yemen also grants the Minister for Foreign Affairs another wish. It assures him that they will never again take in German terrorists who want to be flown in a German matter to their country. This creates clarity in another case that was presumably not considered by the negotiating partners. No aircraft in which foreign kidnappers want to force terrorists in Germany to release will be granted permission to land on South Yemeni soil.

Wischnewski's agreement with "Aden" should be followed by immediate action in the Federal Republic of Germany. "StM Wischnewski has immediately promised the initialing of the KH agreement and is pushing for this offer to be kept."[121] He wants to discuss this as early as Wednesday, 21 September, at a cabinet meeting in Bonn with Federal Development Minister Marie Schlei.

To cut to the chase: The South Yemeni government is in the process of quietly accepting money from a Western system opponent, when a plane hijacked by Palestinians with West German holidaymakers on board is forced to make an emergency landing in Aden. Sooner than hoped for, the promise not to allow any terrorists into the country against the Federal Republic of Germany counts. Consequently, the South Yemeni government refuses the "Landshut" permission to land. And after it landed anyway, it wants it to leave immediately. Unexpectedly, the South Yemeni regime suddenly finds itself caught between two stools—ideologically still anchored in the East, but looking for money in the West. In such a situation, any movement can be fatal. Either scare off the still-partner or the desired one. Or both. Then it's better to see nothing, hear nothing and say nothing.

---

[120] Hans Otto Bräutigam: Note for Sanaa (B. Franke), in: Pol AA: File of the Embassy of the Federal Republic of Abu Dhabi. Subject: Abduction Lufthansa. Bundestag delegation in: UAE. Political situation in the Middle East. Situation in the Indian Ocean. Sahara conflict. Volume D5 from 1974 to 1979.

[121] Ibid., p 2.

Aden

Captain Jürgen Schumann asks "Captain Machmud" to carry out an external check. Is the landing gear intact? Is oil or fuel leaking anywhere? The terrorist leader gives the go-ahead.

Jürgen Schumann leaves the machine. And is gone after a few minutes. How long exactly is remembered differently by the former hostages. They range from 30 to 150 min. In any case, long enough for his absence to become the dominant theme in the "Landshut".

"Captain Machmud" suspects that the captain has gone to the tower, for whatever reason. He asks his interlocutor in the tower to have Jürgen Schumann brought back, otherwise the aircraft will be blown up. Schumann is presumably not there, because the tower is switching on huge searchlights to look for the captain. "They started searching the whole area (…)."[122] Without success.

"Captain Machmud" is getting impatient. He asks Jürgen Vietor to call for the captain at the doors. "Jürgen, return to the aircraft, they want to shoot you!" the co-pilot speaks into a megaphone, as every aircraft has on board. He also calls out of the cockpit window. In vain.

"Yes, and now nothing happened for a long time. I also had to sit in the back. I think it was after that, when he said: 'Now they've found him' or 'Now they've found him and are bringing (him) (…)'".[123]

"Captain Machmud" informs the passengers that the captain has been "seized" via the on-board microphone. He announces that Jürgen Schumann will be shot. "He will be executed". And then, as a kind of encore, he says in English: "Anyone who makes any noise during the execution will be shot immediately afterwards."[124]

One hostage on the "Landshut", Helma van Dreumel, will later tell another one, Diana Müll, that she saw Jürgen Schumann return to the aircraft accompanied by South Yemeni soldiers. The captain climbs the gangway alone. In the cabin corridor, he has to kneel before "Captain Machmud". At this moment, the crew and hostages do not expect Captain Machmud to get serious. The terrorist has already spared the captain once. He's not going to shoot the captain!

Captain Machmud punches Jürgen Schumann several times in the face. He asks the captain twice: "Guilty or not guilty?" Jürgen Schumann tries to avoid the question, to explain himself. Presumably a mistake. As Schumann's head

---

[122] Vietor/Salewski interview, vol. S / I—back cover, p. 11.
[123] Ibid, p. 12.
[124] Discussion Vietor/Salewski, vol. S / I, p. 12.

flies to one side from another blow, Captain Machmud pulls the trigger. The bullet penetrates Jürgen Schumann's left nasal root and kills him instantly. His body falls forwards lifelessly.

Nobody makes a sound. "And there was nothing to be heard during the shooting or afterwards. A very small sigh somewhere or a sound like that, but nobody wrote, nobody cried, at least not audibly."[125]

"Captain Machmud" lights a cigarette. "A girl was eating an apple, I don't know if she ate it when she was shot or only then, and you could hear her laughing from the front of the cockpit."[126]

Jürgen Schumann's head is bleeding profusely, some of his brain matter is leaking out. Someone places a blanket over the corpse. The high humidity causes the corpse to start decomposing after a short time. The hostages sitting next to the dead man start to feel sick. Purserette Hannelore Brauchardt (née Piegler) has to bring them oxygen bottles so that they don't pass out.[127] She will later recount how difficult it was for her to climb over the corpse of her captain.

After some time, two hostages, the teacher Hartwig Faby and the boxing promoter Hans Hasse-Heyn, carry the body of Jürgen Schumann away and place it in the back cloakroom cupboard. Some of Schumann's brain matter remains on the corridor floor. At this sight, one of the kidnappers' faints, as Gabriele von Lutzau will remember a few days after her rescue. Co-pilot Jürgen Vietor is told to sweep the puddle onto a shovel with a broom and pour it onto the airfield. It doesn't work at first. "The pool of blood, they tried to wash it away, it was so gelled, so thick, it was so thick on the carpet (…)."[128] Helpers reach for a bottle of gin and empty it over it. The gin has an effect Jürgen Vietor does what he has been ordered to do.

"Captain Machmud" answered the question as to why Jürgen Schumann's body was not removed from the aircraft in Aden. He announced to the crew: "Even the dead stay on board."[129]

What exactly happened at Aden airport, i.e. where Jürgen Schumann was at the time in question, will probably never be clarified. There are theories, no certainties. In a 2008 television documentary,[130] the film author Maurice Remy offers an allegedly responsible person at Aden airport. The man reminds the captain of someone who tried to resolve a conflict in the tower.

---

[125] Ibid.
[126] Ibid, p. 13.
[127] Group discussion II Crew/Salewski, p. 27.
[128] Conversation Brauchardt (née Piegler)/Salewski, vol. 1, p. 2.
[129] Group discussion III Crew/Salewski, p. 3.
[130] Remy 2008b.

However, his statement lacks any historical context. Remy also provides no evidence for the credibility of his interviewee—such as a contemporary photo of the man at the airport.

The then GDR ambassador in Aden, Günther Scharfenberg, claims in his memoirs that Jürgen Schumann used a patrol on the airfield "to run to the Yemeni line of posts and get through. He was not allowed to pass, he had to return to the aircraft."[131] The diplomat does not provide any proof.

Just like many former SED functionaries who recount their views on historical events after 1989 without providing evidence. Their memoirs are of little use for historical research. This applies, for example, to former SED Politburo member and the last GDR Chairman of the Council of State, Egon Krenz, during the German Autumn. This will be discussed later.

Back to Aden and the "Landshut" cabin. It can be taken for granted that "Captain Machmud" did not shoot the captain in the heat of the moment, but literally with an announcement. The act does not stand on its own, but at the end of a series of events over several days. From the very beginning, the terrorist and the captain were involved in a subliminal conflict that escalated in Aden.

Jürgen Schumann is a captain with courage. He saves Jürgen Vietor's life twice (in Bahrain and Dubai) and uses himself at his own risk for hostages who are also threatened with execution. He informs the political decision-makers in Bonn with valuable information for the storming of the plane. He does all this in great physical pain. Jürgen Schumann had a slipped disc, and sitting in the plane for days on end became a torture for him. Nevertheless, he always remains in control of his behaviour and assumes his responsibility as captain.

On the other hand, Jürgen Schumann appears on the hijack flight as a personality who finds it difficult to subordinate himself to someone, he believes to be a criminal. Co-pilot Jürgen Vietor attributes this to Schumann's pilot training. Jürgen Vietor's notes before the trial against Souhaila Andrawes are quoted here:

---

[131] Scharfenberg 2012, p. 83.

"Food for thought:
Schumann: Starfighter pilot, i.e. lone fighter and one-man decision-maker. Vietor: Breguet Atlantic commander. 12-man crew, absolute teamwork required."[132]

Jürgen Vietor stoically accepts the humiliations and death threats of the terrorist leader. In his career, he has learnt to subordinate himself. To carry out orders against his own convictions. Jürgen Schumann is different. He is a typical, proud Lufthansa captain of the 1970s and former Starfighter pilot. He receives maximum respect, even admiration for his work.

Even on the "Landshut" hijacking flight. "He was constantly thinking", Gabriele von Lutzau (née Dillmann) would later say recognising about him. "He was constantly focused on finding a way out. I knew him (…). And if you didn't know him, you could interpret his concentration as arrogance."[133]

For all his commitment to his co-pilot and the passengers, Jürgen Schumann apparently also had a recurring reflex to shirk his responsibility as captain. According to Jürgen Vietor, he tried to make off several times. "I only told Captain Held and my wife that, and now you're next (…). Mrs Schumann asked me: 'What should we do, my husband—a hero?' And, I say, why not? I then set everything up in such a way that he really is a hero now. That seemed to me to be the better solution."[134]

Declaring Captain Jürgen Schumann a hero is also in the interests of the German government and Lufthansa. A captain who is thinking of leaving does not fit in with the image of this arrogant airline.

A captain who thought about of running away is not suitable as a national hero. At the same time, he thwarts the self-image of the world's safest airline with the most responsible staff. The German government and Deutsche Lufthansa are circulating a kind of language regulation on how the violent death of Captain Jürgen Schumann is said to have occurred. The text was included in Helmut Schmidt's operations diary.

"After the outside check", reads the text entitled "Aktennotiz. LH 181 flight segment Aden—Mogadiscio", "Mr Schumann attempted to contact representatives of the authorities in order to personally explain the impossibility of a restart. The South Yemeni authorities refused to engage in talks and brought Mr Schumann back to the plane (…)". The hijackers assumed that Mr Schumann had given information about the hijackers to the outside world. (…) "The ringleader shot Mr Schumann in front of the passengers."

---

[132] Vietor 1995, p. 4.
[133] Krausz 1978, p. 21.
[134] Discussion Vietor/Salewski, vol. S / I, p. 10.

No wonder that the German government after the German autumn shows only hesitant interest in exploring the reasons for the captain's murder. It was only when Monika Schumann, the wife of the dead captain, persistently presses for investigations that two officers from the Federal Criminal Police Office are to make a stopover in Aden from 12 to 13 January 1978, "following a trip to Mogadishu", to find out the background.[135] It is not clear from the files inspected whether this visit materialised.

Mogadishu

Standing Time "Landshut": Monday, 17 October 1977, 4.34 a.M. To Tuesday, 18 October, 5.10 a.M.

The night in Dubai was terrible. The night in Aden topped the terrible conditions. The humidity is higher because, unlike in Dubai, there is no wind now. The hostages are in shock over Jürgen Schumann's execution.

Nevertheless, fewer passengers pass out that night. They are, as Gabriele von Lutzau (née Dillmann) will put it in an interview with "Stern" magazine reporter Gerd Heidemann, in an "almost coma". Body and psyche have switched to stand-by. The conscious mind fends off the terrible, also bloody reality.

Jürgen Vietor has eaten a banana, a pear and a piece of cake since the kidnapping. The secret piece of cake on occasion of stewardess Anna-Maria Staringer's birthday. He doesn't touch the chicken with mayonnaise in Dubai, served with a so-called Russian salad. Nevertheless, he remains fully focused. Who else is there to fly the "Landshut" now?

The South Yemenis show zero cooperation. Lufthansa has a telephone line to Aden, but the switchboard is balking. It does not connect calls from Frankfurt or Aden. The tower wants the aircraft to disappear as quickly as possible. It makes this very clear to the cockpit.

For aeronautical reasons, Jürgen Vietor wants the "Landshut" to stay in Aden for as long as possible. Four of the five landing lights were broken during the emergency landing. Another possible (emergency) landing at night would presumably result in the death of all passengers. He wants to reach the next airport at dawn, or even better, in daylight.

Jürgen Vietor begins to stall for time. He orders a few 200 gallons each for the right and left tanks—supposedly to make it easier to get the machine

---

[135] Wire decree concerning the hijacking of the LH aircraft of 22 December 1978, in: AuswA, AZ 311, Subject: 400.11–700.00 JEV, Vol.2 from 1977 to 1978.

out of the sand. In reality, he is planning a second, time-consuming refuelling process.

Jürgen Vietor explains that rapid pressurised refuelling of the 400 gallons is impossible because no power supply is connected. False information. The Yemenis fall for it and set off in search of a long hose and a tall ladder.

Jürgen Vietor suggests to "Captain Machmud" that the suitcases be thrown out of the luggage compartment onto the tarmac to make the aircraft lighter and easier to get out of the sand. At first the terrorist is in favour, then against. Shortly after his mortal fear during the emergency landing, he is back to his "old self".

The machine has to get out of the sand. The Yemenis bring in a tugboat, but there is no pole that fits the "Bobby". The "Landshut" has to make it under its own power. To start the engines, Jürgen Vietor fibs again, they need ground power, a mobile power generator. A ground power unit with 230 V is brought in—and sent away by the co-pilot: "We need 115 V". Again, he gains valuable time.

Jürgen Vietor gets the "Landshut" out of the sand and rubble at full throttle. The South Yemenis assign it a place on the tarmac airfield.

The tower continues to be stubborn. Information about the weather is only given when the aircraft is back in the air. But where to on the flight? There is no suggestion from the tower. The main thing is that the "Landshut" flies away again.

Jürgen Vietor doesn't want to, of course. Presumably never before has a civil aircraft taken off again immediately after an emergency landing in sand and rubble. Without any checks. The co-pilot runs through possible scenarios: The sand in the turbines could reduce the air flow, i.e. the engine performance. The tyres could burst on take-off or during the subsequent landing. The fuel line could have been ruptured during the emergency landing. "In the rear cloakroom my murdered captain, to my left a mad hijacker."[136]

After an ultimatum from the tower to take off, the "Landshut" taxies to the runway at 02:00 on 17 October 1977, a Monday. Throttle to full power, let the engine stabilise, release the brakes. Due to the weakened engines, Jürgen Vietor only brings the aircraft up on the last few metres of the runway. Behind them are the mountains.

Captain Machmud's next destination is Mogadishu, the capital of Somalia on the Horn of Africa. It is the last city name on a piece of paper that is later found on the dead terrorist leader. In Mogadishu, the radical Palestinian

---

[136] Jürgen Vietor in conversation with the author.

organisation PFLP-SC, led by Wadi Haddad, is not thought to have a training camp like those in Baghdad or Aden, but it does have an operational base of around 60 men. Wadi Haddad and Somali President Siad Barre know each other personally.

Jürgen Vietor, the Lufthansa pilot on the short-haul flight, asks "Where is Mogadishu?".

The "Landshut", which is as a short-haul aircraft not supposed to leave the European continent, has a "Southwest Asia radio navigation map" on board. Mogadishu is just barely marked on it. Two millimetres before the bottom edge of the map. Jürgen Vietor has the coordinates to get there, but he is flying a dilapidated aircraft. It could catch fire at any time because of the sand in the engines. The fire extinguishers are empty.

The successful emergency landing in Aden was a flying masterpiece. The flight to Mogadishu requires another feat from Jürgen Vietor. This is the co-pilot's fourth night without sleep. "And then we flew, climbing higher and higher because of the storm clouds, up to an altitude of around eleven kilometers", Jürgen Vietor will later recall.[137] Before the "Landshut" reaches Mogadishu, it is dusk, and the sun is rising from the sea. At least the co-pilot doesn't have to land in the dark.

Jürgen Vietor suspects that the airport in Mogadishu does not want the "Landshut" either. The German government has known this in black and white since Sunday. The government "in any circumstances will not allow a hijack-plane owned by the Federal Republic of Germany land or com near the air ot the SBR", reads a telex from the German Embassy in Addis Ababa to the crisis team in Bonn.[138]

Jürgen Vietor obtains permission from "Captain Machmud" to land without prior notice. The runway would presumably be blocked as it was in Aden. The exhausted terrorist leader now seems to be happy with anything. "The choleric, armed captain of the hijackers becomes "the small, grumpy co-pilot", would Jürgen Vietor say later.

Of course, the co-pilot does not know "Mogadiscio Airport". He wants to get an overview—literally—of the airport's location. The pilot flies a circle to see whether the runway is clear or blocked with vehicles. To do this, he hires "Captain Machmud" with tasks that a co-pilot has to complete. Together they plan the approach.

In the building of the German Embassy in Somalia, Bernd Zeitler is on night duty. He looks after the embassy together with Chargé d' Affaires Michael Libal, Head of administration ("Chancellor") Ernst Fischer, a Paying

---

[137] Jürgen Vietor in conversation with the author.
[138] BArch 106/106684.

Agent Manager and Registrar as well as three secretaries. Their boss, the ambassador, has just left the country for another job. A successor is not yet in place.

The embassy staff work under technically backward conditions. There is a radio link to the German embassy in the Ethiopian capital Addis Ababa in the event of a crisis. It is tested once a week. To make a phone call, Wolfgang Libal and his team have to register calls at the main post office in Mogadishu and wait a long time. Just two telephone lines connect Somalia with the world. The lines were set up by the Italians during the colonial era. They are still switched via Rome.

The German chargé d'affaires Michael Libal, temporary administrator of German affairs in Somalia, is awake early. Or is awakened by the noise of an aircraft that is not flying to Mogadishu on schedule. Wolfgang Libal looks out of his bedroom window and sees the "Landshut" in the sky.

So does Bernd Zeitler from the window of the embassy building. Not a little surprised, he informs his diplomatic colleagues in Addis Ababa, who in turn inform the Federal Foreign Ministry in Bonn. From there, a member of staff on duty calls the Federal Chancellery.

Ahmed Dahir, the air traffic controller in the tower, is not expecting an aircraft at this early hour. In any case, not soon enough to raise the alarm. This "merit" changes decisively Ahmed Dahir's life: After landing in Mogadishu, Minister of State Hans-Jürgen Wischnewski will offer him and his family the opportunity to relocate to the Federal Republic of Germany. Ahmed Dahir will accept.

4.34 a.m. German time. Suddenly, the small Boeing that was supposed to fly to Frankfurt am Main is located at the Horn of Africa. In a coastal town on the Indian Ocean. From a West German point of view, it felt like the end of the world. It is already light. The sea is roaring. The sun sparkles on its surface.

Silence on the airfield.

At some point, a young Somali man runs up to the aircraft. "Can we help you, sir?", he asks Jürgen Vietor, who has opened his cockpit window. Vietor calls out in English: "I need the radio frequency from the tower." A few minutes later, the boy returns with a piece of paper and the requested information.

Mogadishu. The authoritarian President Siad Barre sees his country as the southern flank of the Arab world. Somalia is a member of the Arab League. In October 1977, it is at war with its neighbour Ethiopia over a border region. Like the entire economy of his country, Siad Barre finances this war with money from the "Eastern Bloc". The Cold War is also raging on the African continent.

The Soviet Union is currently changing sides in the region. It is supplying weapons to the war opponent Ethiopia because it expects politically more from this partnership. In October 1977, President Siad Barre was already looking to the West but had not yet completed the break with "Moscow". With the landing of the "Landshut" in his capital, events will come thick and fast.

After the plane is on the ground, the stewardesses say to Jürgen Vietor: "Jürgen Schumann's body smells terrible. It has to go." Jürgen Vietor asks "Captain Machmud" to agree. He nods. At the rear door on the left, an emergency chute is filled with air and Jürgen Schumann's body is lowered down. Somalis drive it away in a red ambulance. Kurt Stenzel's cameraman, ARD's Middle East correspondent, films the scene from a distance. On the evening of the following day, the pictures will go around the world.

At 5.40 a.m., the German embassy in Addis Ababa sends a wire report to Bonn:

- "(…) Captain executed; to be removed from aircraft
- Somalis have made 1st contact (badly) with the aircraft. Ultimatum: 14.00 GMT (=15.00 here). Negotiating partner: Qfar Qhaddum (…)"[139]

Initially, Bonn receives contradictory reports about the departure of the "Landshut" in Aden. When the stop in Mogadishu becomes known, the Federal Chancellor is once again provided with country information. Where are the clock hands when it is midnight in Germany? Who governs the distant country and with whom is it politically allied?

The Somali government makes one of its two telephone lines abroad available to the German embassy. A 42-metre high antenna, quickly erected in the Bonn area, picks up the signals. The connection has the quality of a poor radio. What is said is often choppy or does not reach the other party at all. This will make communication between "Bonn" and "Mogadishu" much more difficult.

When the Boeing 727 with Minister of State Hans-Jürgen Wischnewski arrives in Mogadishu at 11.45 a.m., it is an uninvited guest. The Germans are greeted with diplomatic coldness. All crew members have to hand over their passports. Initially, only the Minister of State is allowed to leave the aircraft.

---

[139] Note AA (VLR I Böcker): Wire report from Addis Ababa after crisis radio message from Mogadishu, undated, in: AdS, 1/HSAA010017.

Bonn

The head of the planning staff at the Federal Foreign Office, Klaus Kinkel, now has a key role to play. He was in Somalia in mid-September because the RAF prisoners had also mentioned the Somali capital as a possible target country. Klaus Kinkel got a "basket" in Mogadischu just as Hans-Jürgen Wischnewski did in Aden, among other places. Now he can report on conditions in the distant, unknown country to the Short Briefing and the Large Political Advisory Group.

In autumn 1977, Siad Barre's change of course towards the West became much clearer than that of the South Yemeni regime. Also, because Siad Barre urgently needed money for his war. "That's where we have to start",[140] Klaus Kinkel presents in Bonn in the presence of Federal Chancellor Helmut Schmidt.

Shortly after eight o'clock, Helmut Schmidt meets the Somali ambassador to Germany, Yusuf Adan Bokah. He suggests that "an aircraft with German police specialists" travel to Mogadishu to prevent the plane from taking off again. If the Somali leadership behaves as requested by the German government, "this will have a decisive influence on our behaviour towards Somalia in the long term. Somalia can then count on all the help it can get from Germany."[141]

There is also a lot going on outside the Federal Chancellery this Monday in Bonn. Relatives of the "Landshut" hostages come to the long, high fence of the Federal Chancellery to protest for the rescue of their mothers and fathers, partners, children and siblings. One boy carries a placard reading "Mr Chancellor, I want my mum back." The relatives are by no means alone; hundreds of people are there in their tension before the presumed showdown. "The number plates showed cars from Wilhelmshaven to Starnberg."[142]

The hostage's relatives ask for a meeting at the gate and the Federal Government honours their request. Ernst Haar, State Secretary in the Federal Ministry of Transport, meets with them in a meeting room of the Federal Chancellery. Not a man from the front row, but someone who has himself been the victim of a kidnapping. He can presumably empathise well with the suffering of the "Landshut" hostages and their relatives. More so than the other gentlemen in the Short Briefing or the Large Political Advisory Group.

---

[140] Cf. Herold/Hauser, p. 92.

[141] Note on the conversation between the Federal Chancellor and the Ambassador of Somalia, Bokah, in the presence of Federal Minister Genscher on 17 October 1977, in the Federal Chancellor's study, in: Archiv BK 13–211 20 (2) Additional File OTB Bd. 6, p. 422f.

[142] Carl-Christian Kaiser 1977.

During the discussion, a relative formulates a handwritten declaration. All relatives in the group sign it. The declaration states, among other things:

"The relatives and friends of the Somali hostages present at the Federal Chancellery on 17 October 1977 hereby call on the Federal Government and the crisis management teams,

(a) to declare immediately and irrevocably that they are prepared to extradite the captured criminals.
(b) to bring the eleven criminals together immediately at an assembly point and to provide them with an aircraft" (Fig. 3.5).[143]

In the course of the morning, "Bonn" already knows what aid for Somalia could look like: Technical aid such as lorries and money. No war equipment and weapons. The diplomatic room for manoeuvre of the West German rump state is small. In a telephone conversation with Hans-Jürgen Wischnewski at midday, State Secretary Heinz Ruhnau outlines "the threshold beyond which we cannot cross. (…) But you can give them the means to transport something like that."[144]

Heinz Ruhnau then passes the phone to Helmut Schmidt. "Hans-Jürgen, how are you? I'm glad you're here."

"Excuse me?".

"I am glad that you exist."[145]

Helmut Schmidt reads Hans-Jürgen Wischnewski the text of a telegram he sent to President Siad Barre after a phone call in the morning. In it, he emphasises that he "fully respects" Somali sovereignty. Later in the text follows a ruse: "I would like to point out that the hijackers are obviously three Germans and only one Arab, who is supposed to cover the case as a front man."[146]

The misrepresentation misleads Siad Barre into believing that the kidnapping has nothing to do with the Palestinian cause. The Federal Foreign Office knows that no third country in the world liked to mess with the Palestinians in the 1970s, not even an African president.

Schmidt's order to Hans-Jürgen Wischnewski: Get President Siad Barre to allow the GSG9 to land in Mogadishu and storm the "Landshut". Money should flow in return. "I have already indicated to you that you have authority

---

[143] Rupps 2012, p. 85.
[144] Telephone conversation between Sts Ruhnau and StM Wischnewski on 17 October, 12.00 noon, in: Archiv BK 13–211 20 (2) Additional File OTB Bd. 6, p. 439.
[145] Archiv BK 13–211 20 (2) Additional file OTB, vol. 6, in: OTB, p. 442.
[146] Ibid, p. 443.

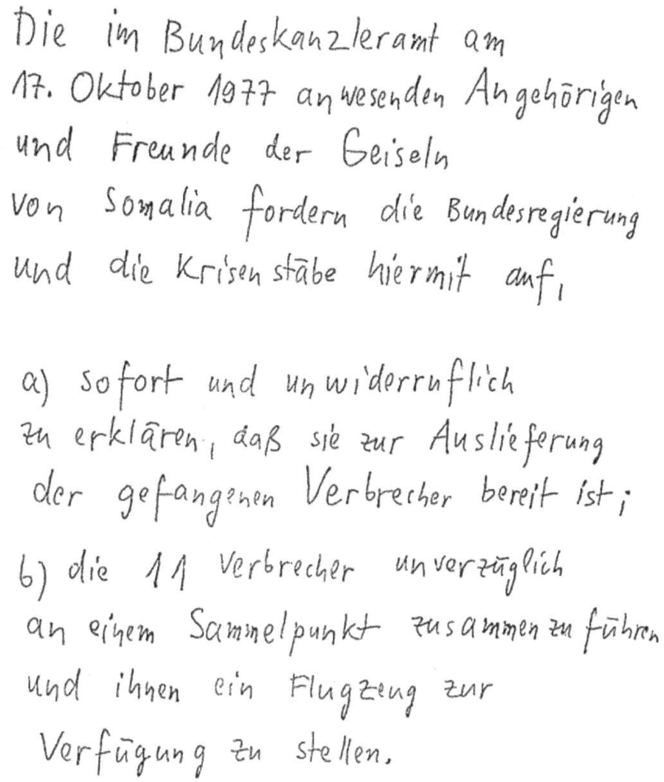

> Die im Bundeskanzleramt am
> 17. Oktober 1977 anwesenden Angehörigen
> und Freunde der Geiseln
> von Somalia fordern die Bundesregierung
> und die Krisenstäbe hiermit auf,
>
> a) sofort und unwiderruflich
> zu erklären, daß sie zur Auslieferung
> der gefangenen Verbrecher bereit ist;
>
> b) die 11 Verbrecher unverzüglich
> an einem Sammelpunkt zusammen zu führen
> und ihnen ein Flugzeug zur
> Verfügung zu stellen.

Fig. 3.5 Text: Statement by relatives of the "Landshut" hostages, who will be received for talks at the Federal Chancellery in Bonn on Sunday, 17 October *Source* Rupps 2012, S. 85

over Hans Apel's portfolio."[147] Hans Apel is the Federal Minister of Finance in Helmut Schmidt's cabinet.

At 12.00 a.m., the tower asks the Landshut cockpit whether lunch should be brought to the aircraft. Captain Machmud refuses with the laconic remark that all the hostages will be free or dead by 3.00 p.m. anyway. They would not need any food until then.

> "Note: Mr Klar Baltes (…) requests the following message to the Federal Chancellor: "I am 64 years old. There is also a young couple from our town on the plane. To save all aircraft passengers, release the terrorists immediately! Sincerely. Karl Baltes."[148]

---

[147] Ibid, p. 444.
[148] Ibid.

"*My daughter and grandchildren are on the kidnapped machine would you also sacrifice your daughter irmgard gruenewald (...)*"[149]

"*as 5 members of one of the hostages in mogadiscio, we appeal to those responsible in the federal government to save the lives of the hostages (...) in every possible way, i.e. to respond as quickly as possible to the conditions of the kidnappers ilse, dr klaus, diplomsoziologin agnes, jochen and juergen hanke and diplomingenieure (sic!) juergen hanke (...)*"[150]

"*one gets (sic!) the impression that the federal government tolerates the execution of death sentences on innocent people relying on the protection of the federal republic, while in the fight against terrorism the death sentence is rejected surely the people who make the relevant decisions have no relatives on the plane helga wihlfahrt as sister of an affected passenger and on behalf of other relatives*"[151]

Lufthansa 737 fleet manager, Peter Heldt, who was on board Hans-Jürgen Wischnewski's aircraft, is asked to identify the dead man from the "Landshut". This proves to be difficult. The body is already in an advanced stage of decomposition. The head shot by "Captain Machmud" has disfigured Jürgen Schumann's face. From the Lufthansa radio traffic between Frankfurt am Mainz and Mogadishu:

Frankfurt: "Lufthansa Frankfurt, go ahead."

(...)

Mogadiscio: (incomprehensible)…identification…

Mr Held himself wanted to comment on this. (...) I can only tell you one thing in advance: Mr Held could not clearly identify Mr Schumann as Captain Schumann, although he knows him well."[152]

Peter Heldt surmises that it is the body of Jürgen Vietor. He will later say to "Stern" magazine reporter Gerd Heidemann: "Maybe they thought it must be the co-pilot. He's not as important as the captain."[153]

Peter Heldt informs the Lufthansa crisis team, which in turn informs the German government. A bearer of the terrible news calls Renate Vietor, the wife of the "Landshut" co-pilot. He then telephones Monika Schumann, whom he assures: Her husband is alive!

---

[149] Ibid. Including a handwritten, crossed-out note "BK". According to this, Helmut Schmidt did not receive the telegram.
[150] Ibid.
[151] Ibid.
[152] Ludwig Hildebrandt: Protocol radio recording Mogadishu on 17 October 1977, typescript.
[153] Jürgen Vietor in conversation with Gerd Heidemann, October 1977.

At some point, a notebook is found in the dead man's clothes. It contains the name and telephone number of Monika Schumann.

Two hours later, the caller contacts Renate Vietor again—this time with the news that her husband is alive. He then calls Monika Schumann and informs her who really has been killed in the "Landshut".

Federal Chancellor Helmut Schmidt immediately sends his condolences to Monika Schumann by telegram. "I was horrified to learn of the terrorist murder (…). I share your grief and offer you my sincere condolences (…)." A very political, not very personal text. The Federal Chancellor later had the wording distributed by the Press and Information Office of the Federal Government.

> *"dear chancellor, after this cowardly murder of mr flight captain schumann, which has just been reported, i hereby urge you for the last time to release the terrorist pigs in order to save the lives of my wife, my son and all other hostages. do you want more human lives on your conscience? Dieter Roehll"*[154]

In Aden, the "Landshut" hijacking costed a first human life. The murder also signals a political turning point in the hijacking drama.[155] German Chancellor Helmut Schmidt has already announced during the plane's stopover in Dubai that he would have the plane stormed if hostages were killed—even at the cost of further human lives. And if necessary, against the will of the local government. "Dubai" and "Aden" have prevented this intention in one case by cunning, in the other by force.

Wherever the "Landshut" would fly from Aden—not only Hans-Jürgen Wischnewski and Ulrich Wegener were to follow in a joint aircraft, but also the men of the GSG9, who had been expelled from the British military base on Cyprus with an unknown destination. At the next airport, the matter has to be "shot out", as a member of the Bonn crisis team put it.

At 3.35 a.m., the German chargé d'affaires on site confirms that the aircraft has taken off with an unknown destination. It is not initially known exactly when.

"1 person is said to have been shot",[156] it says on Monday, 17 October, at 8.20 a.m. German time in the Lufthansa Event-log. At 9.50 a.m., "Captain Machmud" calls for an ambulance—to remove a body, as it turns out.[157]

---

[154] BArch, B136/31588, among others with handwritten note "submitted to Mr Chief BK" (meaning Manfred Schüler).
[155] Cf. Hartmann 2009, p. 47.
[156] German Lufthansa, Event-Log, p. 15.
[157] Ibid.

At 10:10 a.m., the terrorist leader issues an ultimatum. As mentioned, the German government has until 3:00 p.m. to meet the demands, otherwise the aircraft will be blown up.

That morning, President Siad Barre is inundated with requests from all over the world to behave constructively. US President Jimmy Carter personally sends him a message via the American embassy in Bonn.[158] A Somali government has probably never received so much worldwide attention. The hijacked "Landshut" puts Siad Barre in a political quandary, but it also opens doors unexpectedly.

At 2.48 p.m., Federal Chancellor Helmut Schmidt and Minister of State Hans-Jürgen Wischnewski speak on the phone. Wischnewski says that Siad Barre's cabinet has now sat down with the Somali police generals. He speaks of an "unbelievable unease"[159] that has arisen.

"I have one more point to make", the Chancellor says later. "If you can gain time to act independently, you know where our borders are." Wischnewski replies: "That's clear."[160]

At 3.10 p.m., the Federal Chancellery receives a telephone message from Minister of State Hans-Jürgen Wischnewski.[161] According to the message, the Somalis wanted a quick police operation, which the Minister of State has advised against, as it would be hasty and not very successful. "Wischnewski told the kidnappers that he has heard that the prisoners would be brought together in Germany. (…) Given the situation, the ultimatum should be extended until tomorrow morning."[162]

In the "Landshut"

After landing in Mogadishu, Jürgen Vietor tells "Captain Machmud" in no uncertain terms: This is the end. Another take-off of the aircraft is out of the question. The terrorist leader—overtired, exhausted, disappointed by the unfriendly reception in South Yemen—agrees. In Mogadishu, then, the German government must give in.

---

[158] Note. Message from President Carter to President Siad transmitted by telephone from the American Embassy in Bonn on 17 October 1977, in: Archiv BK 13–211 20 (2) Additional file OTB vol. 6, p. 426.
[159] Memo of conversation:—StM Wischnewski, 17 October 1977, 2.48 p.m., in: OTB 13–211 20 (2) Additional file OTB vol. 6, p. 449.
[160] Ibid. p. 450.
[161] Ibid, p. 451.
[162] Ibid.

Knowing that the hijacking will not go any further, the terrorist leader gives the co-pilot a safe passage. The terrorist has known since the emergency landing in Aden that he owes his life to Jürgen Vietor. Now Vietor is given the gift of his own life.

The co-pilot refuses. He will repeat his answer to "Stern" magazine reporter Gerd Heidemann: Either we all go up in the explosion or we all come out. "Thank you, Captain. I will stay here on board." The terrorist nods.

Jürgen Vietor picks up the on-board microphone and tells the hostages about the offer to leave. He fibs about why he wants to stay on board so as not to be seen as a hero. He doesn't want to be shot by "Captain Machmud" as he leaves the airfield. Hostages then would have to take his body back to the aircraft where he would keep his dead captain company in the closet. At this point in time, Jürgen Schumann's body is still on the aircraft.

The hostages may have an idea that flying in Mogadishu is over. In this situation, an ultimatum weighs heavily. A short one like this, till 3.00 p. m., is particularly heavy. "Captain Machmud" is piling on the pressure; he is clearly running out of steam. According to the terrorist leader, the federal government must fulfil the demands by noon.

Stewardess Gabriele von Lutzau (née Dillmann) thinks incessantly about how she can encourage a peaceful solution. She comes up with the idea of sending a radio message to the German government. A brilliant idea. A radio message goes beyond the telegram that Captain Jürgen Schumann sent to Helmut Schmidt in Dubai. Also, beyond a mention of the Chancellor in a radio message from "Captain Machmud", also in Dubai.

Chancellor Helmut Schmidt or other members of the federal government or the crisis teams themselves have not addressed the hostages—presumably for fear of raising hopes that they will not be able to fulfil. In the part published so far, the operation does not indicate that directly addressing the hostages was an issue.

Chancellor Helmut Schmidt presumably relies on the deployment of the GSG9 from the outset. He does not want to talk to the hostages, to encourage them, but to have them taken out of the machine. If he succeeds in this—so his presumed calculation—the children, women and men will not hold a grudge against him.

The passengers on the hijacked "Landshut" feel anger and disappointment at the silence of the German government. Friedrich Christian Delius will get to the heart of this anger in his novel "Mogadishu Window Seat".

"The day passed and I wished the men in the government saw us and heard what was happening. But they didn't care. But they didn't care. They didn't even send us a message. Greetings from the relatives, a consolation, a friendly appeal, a helpful lie. (...) Perhaps they thought of us too, perhaps they had already made the decision to exchange us, but they left us alone."[163]

Stewardess Gabriele von Lutzau (née Dillmann) asks "Captain Machmud" for permission to make an announcement. She speaks English so that he understands her words immediately and doesn't feel betrayed.

"We know now that this is our end. We know we have to die. It will be very hard for us, but we will die as bravely as we can. We are all too young to die, even the old people among us are all too young. We only hope that it goes quickly, that we won't be in too much pain. But perhaps it is better to die than to live in a world where human lives count for so little (...)."

The world public is unaware of the radio message. In historical retrospect, it represents a landmark in this hijacking drama because it represents a change of perspective. Until now, the hostages have been suffering in complete isolation. The stewardess Gabriele von Lutzau creates this public in the form of a tower and the Federal Chancellery in one fell swoop. At the same time, she documents the desperation of the people in the machine for posterity in case the "Landshut" is blown up. Gabriele von Lutzau, with her initially political and later personal thoughts, impressively reminds the po that the "Landshut" is full of people in mortal fear, not an anonymous political pawn of terrorists.

Gabriele von Lutzau (née Dillmann) still hopes that the German government will give in, but she expects the plane to be blown up. The radio message now would bring salvation or become a posthumous testimony to her desire to survive. She knows about the moral power of her appeal. Her strategy resembles the calculation of Hanns Martin Schleyer's kidnappers, who put the employer president in front of a video camera every few days to get the German government to give in.

The kidnappers tie up the hostages. First the men, then the women, then the children. They pour the entire supply of whiskey and schnapps on board onto the cabin carpet—not over the heads of the hostages, as is often written later. The fire from the detonated hand grenades is supposed to travel quickly to the rear with the help of the escaping oxygen.

The hijackers also pour out the perfume that passengers are supposed to buy in the "Bobby". Now the smell in the "Landshut" is even more terrible than before—if it is possible to increase it at all. At 2.49 p. m., "Captain Machmud" announces to the tower that the aircraft will be blown up in eleven minutes. The tower asks for a delay so that surrounding aircraft can be moved away. "Captain Machmud" puts his command to the vote. Three votes

---

[163] Delius: Mogadishu Fensterplatz 1987, p. 115.

in favour, one against an extension.[164] The terrorist gives another 30 min. Speak by 3:30 p.m.

The head of the Somali police, Abdallah Mohammed Hassan, occasionally offers the kidnappers free passage if they let the hostages go. "Captain Machmud" refuses.

At 3.33 p.m.—the ultimatum has passed, preparations to blow up the aircraft are almost complete—"Captain Machmud" is called into the empty cockpit. It can be heard over the radio loudspeaker that the tower wants to speak urgently. Back on the ground, the terrorist finally hears what he has been trying to force for days: The German government agrees to fulfil his demands. To fly the RAF terrorists out to Mogadishu.

The bound, terrified hostages notice a sudden whispering among the men and women of the terror squad. A flurry of activity in First Class. "Captain Machmud" storms up to Jürgen Vietor: "How long does it take to fly from Frankfurt to Mogadishu?" Mogadishu is on the equator, the co-pilot begins to calculate, Frankfurt is about 50 degrees north from the equator. One degree of latitude equals 60 miles. 50 times 60 equals 3000 miles. A commercial aircraft flies at an average speed of 420 kilometres. "Around seven to eight hours", Vietor answers.

It is the turning point. About eight hours, a representative of the federal government also gives this time frame. Jürgen Vietor is not bluffing. "You are free!", shouts "Captain Machmud" several times in the cabin and gives the order to release the hostages. The detonators on the explosives are removed.

"I and the members of my command will also be released", is a subliminal message in "Captain Machmud's" euphoric exclamation. We will survive! We will come back in our homeland of Palestine and be celebrated as heroes!

Captain Machmud" immediately reverts to his authoritarian ways. The tower asks for an extension of the ultimatum until 7.00 a.m.[165] The hijackers grant a time corridor until 1.30 p.m.[166]

In the following hours, Wolfgang Libal, chargé D' affaires of the Federal Republic of Germany in Somalia,[167] and psychologist Wolfgang Salewski alternately inform the terrorist commando about what is supposedly happening in West Germany to fulfil the demands. At 6.54 p.m., for example, that the RAF prisoners were on their way to Mogadishu in an aircraft.

At no time do "Captain Machmud" and the three other members of the terror squad express any doubts about what they are hearing from Salewski

---

[164] Cf. ibid.
[165] Event log of German Lufthansa, p. 17.
[166] Ibid.
[167] The post of ambassador in Mogadishu is currently vacant.

and Libal. They react with gratitude to every supposedly full report. All aggression, all mistrust has fallen away from the terrorist leader. He and his commando members appear exhausted but happy. The assumption that everything is going according to plan is based on the kidnappers' wishful thinking. Their desire to stay alive.

Nevertheless, the great negotiating skills of Wolfgang Libal and Wolfgang Salewski are needed during these hours. The commander remains capable of short-sighted reactions. Everything can change from one second to the next.

"Urgent Federal Chancellor Helmut Schmid (Sic) Federal Chancellery Bonn

We hereby prohibit you from attempting to forcibly free the kidnapped lufthansa passenger Georg Reiboldt

On behalf of Bernd Reibodt and Isabella Reiboldt"[168]

"Mr Erich Bender, brother of one of the Lufthansa passengers, from Kierspe/ Sauerland, asks you to inform him that as a Christian he appeals to your Christian responsibility to do everything possible to free the hostages (...)."[169]

Bonn

Helmut Schmidt has an appointment in the Chancellor's bungalow at 3.30 p.m. He receives three writers and a publisher. The meeting with Heinrich Böll, Max Frisch, Günter Grass, Siegfried Lenz and Sigfried Unseld, the head of the Frankfurt Suhrkamp publishing house, had long been arranged. The gentlemen wanted to meet in Hamburg. Helmut Schmidt did not cancel in the German Autumn but arranged a new date in Bonn.

Günter Grass is unable to attend because he is celebrating his 50th birthday that day. Government spokesman Klaus Bölling, Federal Research Minister Hans Matthöfer and Federal Labour Minister Herbert Ehrenberg also take part in the discussion—in other words, only SPD colleagues, none from the coalition partner FDP. Unlike his predecessor Willy Brandt, Helmut Schmidt feels a deep mistrust of his coalition partner. A particularly deep mistrust of FDP Chairman and Federal Foreign Minister Hans-Dietrich Genscher.

---

[168] Telegram from Bernd and Isabella Reiboldt dated 17 October 1977 to Federal Chancellor Helmut Schmidt, in: BArch B136/31588.

[169] Note from the Head of the Situation Centre to the Federal Chancellor dated 17 October 1977, in: AdD 1/HSAA010017.

Helmut Schmidt greets his guests with a compliment, telling them that they are the only "normal" people he has spoken to since the abduction of Hanns Martin Schleyer.[170] "In the face of Böll and Frisch, that was quite bold."[171] For 30 min, the Federal Chancellor informs the audience about the current state of affairs without revealing what was to come.

Then Heinrich Böll speaks. Also, for 30 min. He laments—as Siegfried Unseld will later describe him—the situation of insecurity and fear in the Federal Republic, "every citizen must fear a house search like his son".[172] According to Unseld's impression, Böll develops a growing understanding of Schmidt's attitude in the hours that follow—the conversation lasted five and a quarter hours in total, and the Chancellor had to leave the meeting twice for 30 min each time. Max Frisch says to Siegfried Unseld on the journey home to Frankfurt that he doesn't want to be stuck in his, Schmidt's, role.

Max Frisch will also make notes about the conversation. "Unfanatic, great presence"[173] is what he writes about the Federal Chancellor, whom he had already accompanied on his trip to China in 1975. "Without posturing. (…) Presence to the point of composure. He can listen to everyone, questions out of understanding, he comes back to what is implied. In between to the crisis team and back".[174] But then he also has doubts. "Does he want us as witnesses (in case everything goes wrong)?".[175]

Until now, intellectuals in this country have reacted to RAF terrorism in a sometimes alarmed, sometimes prudent manner. In German Autumn, historian Golo Mann gives many people a voice when he talks about a civil war and the death penalty for terrorists. Golo Mann is one of the most brilliant minds in his profession, but he is not insensitive to the political moods of the day.

Gert Kalow, the deputy chairman of the PEN Club, the German section of an international authors' organisation, stands for a level-headed, understanding attitude. Gert Kalow addresses the Federal Chancellor at the beginning of October. "The memories of the Weimar period, as they are now appearing in the press, especially in our friendly western neighbours, unfortunately do not appear to be far-fetched", writes Gert Kalow.[176]

---

[170] 2010, p. 101; this and the following quotes also in the abridged version in Fellinger/Reiner 2014, p. 187f.
[171] Ibid, p. 102.
[172] Ibid., p. 104. In fact, the flat of one of Böll's sons had been searched shortly before.
[173] Citizen 2010, p. 109.
[174] Ibid.
[175] Ibid, p. 110.
[176] Letter to Federal Chancellor Helmut Schmidt dated 8 October 1977, in: AdsD, 1/HSAA010016.

We would not understand "the terrorists of Ulrike Meinhof's ilk (and run the risk of reacting wrongly to them), if we did not recognise the sincere madness of their moral fanaticism". In this context, the author quotes a sentence by the philosopher Charles de Secondat, Baron de Montesquieu: "The higher the ideals, the more terrible the practices."[177]

Mogadishu

Minister of State Hans-Jürgen Wischnewski and later GSG9 commander Ulrich Wegener negotiate with President Siad Barre about the possibility of storming the aircraft.[178] The president insists that Somalia's territorial sovereignty be respected. Ulrich Wegener states openly and frankly that it would be better if German forces, rather than Somali ones, stormed the machine. This provokes the president's pride. We'll see about that! Siad Barre tells the German, essentially. We have good people, too! No police force from another country should "shoot" the matter on their territory.

The clever Minister of State Hans-Jürgen Wischnewski refrains from saying, "You can't do it!" Instead, he plays it diplomatic. "Yes, that's fine. You don't know the plane that well. Our people know it. We will show you how to do it."[179] President Siad Barre agrees. In secret, Hans-Jürgen Wischnewski and Ulrich Wegener want the GSG9 to storm the plane on its own.

On the military part of the airport, there is a Boeing 707 and two very old aircraft. Somali rangers and skydivers show Ulrich Wegener what they can do. "And then they tried to get up the plane. The one ladder (…) swayed very precariously (…) They couldn't get to the door, couldn't get to the handle, couldn't open the door."[180] They finally succeed with a lot of noise.

After that, Ulrich Wegener, his adjutant and Dieter Fox show them how it's done. Dieter Fox climbs the ladder in seconds and opens the door without a sound. He obviously makes an impression with this. The Germans' better training cannot be denied.

Hans-Jürgen Wischnewski and Ulrich Wegener suggest to President Siad Barre, who has since come to the airport together with his cabinet, that they divide the work. Wegener says: "If you take over the cordon outside in the dunes and the outer cordon, we feel safe. Then we know that we can work

---

[177] Ibid.
[178] See Fox 2023.
[179] See Hauser/Wischnewski, p. 20.
[180] See Fox 2023.

in peace." The Somalis are also to start a fire to distract the hijackers. Immediately after the storm, sovereignty over the aircraft passes to the Somalis. Unspoken agreements are made to plunder the passengers' valuables in the cabin and baggage hold.

Siad Barre and Ulrich Wegener have established a good relationship. Siad Barre, a soldier with the rank of colonel, likes Wegener's no-nonsense manner. Ulrich Wegener is not a soldier himself, but he leads the GSG 9 like a military unit.

The president gives his okay. This joint solution appears to preserve the country's territorial sovereignty and actively involves its own people. Later, GSG 9 troops will nevertheless form an outer cordon in the dunes.

There is a danger lurking there that does not need bullets. The dunes around the "Landshut" are teeming with poisonous snakes, as Dieter Fox vividly recounts to this day.

Minister of state Hans-Jürgen Wischnewski asks the president about how to deal with possible prisoners, that is, terrorists who do not die during the storming: To which Siad Barre replies: "What, you want to take prisoners too?" The remark proves Barre's political instinct: In fact, the only surviving terrorist will be a diplomatic headache for many years to come.

To Hans-Jürgen Wischnewski—and also to Helmut Schmidt after a telephone conversation they had that same day—the head of state of the African country comes across as an approachable, cooperative politician. President Siad Barre does not cheapen himself for a political price that is as high as possible. He knows that he can get something out of this situation for his country. No more, no less. In historical retrospect, this also counts as one of the "miracles of Mogadishu".

Helmut Schmidt, too, is impressed by Siad Barre. In Schmidt's eyes, he is a reliable man. In the years to come, Helmut Schmidt would often mention the generosity and courage of the president, for example in his speech at the 1980 SPD party conference in Essen.

At the time, the Iranian government was holding the staff of the US Embassy in Tehran hostage. "One must imagine, in view of the hostage situation in Iran", says Helmut Schmidt in Essen, "what it meant for a black government of a black country to allow us, with our white border police, to country to free hostages from the hands of criminals by force."[181] The determination, with which the Chancellor will show his appreciation of the

---

[181] Helmut Schmidt: Wir werden den Frieden nach innen und außen bewahren. Speech at the Essen SPD party conference on 9 June 1980, in: Neue Gesellschaft/Frankfurter Hefte Nr. 27/1980, p. 584.

situation in Somalia, is rooted in this deep respect, even in the face of domestic political resistance.[182]

The last head of state and party leader of the GDR, Egon Krenz, would later claim that GDR foreign minister Oskar Fischer has not only mediated in Aden, but also in Mogadishu. Without this mediation, "Bonn" would not have encountered friendly conditions at the Horn of Africa and would certainly not have been allowed to free the hostages.[183]

Egon Krenz's claim is not supported by the files of the Federal Chancellery and the Foreign Office, at least not the accessible ones. Just as little as contacts between Minister of State Hans-Jürgen Wischnewski and GDR diplomats in Mogadishu. Egon Krenz contributes as little as former GDR diplomat Günther Scharfenberg to the historical clarification of events. Both exaggerate the diplomatic role of their state in retrospect.

Now Ulrich Wegener's men, who have been circling over Djibouti, a Somali neighbour, for hours, are also allowed to land in Mogadishu. The pilot breaks the plane hard after touchdown so that the terrorists do not notice anything. In fact, the landing goes unnoticed.

It is now accepted as historical fact that the GSG9 team would have landed in Mogadishu even without the consent of President Siad Barre. Presumably with the lights switched off after dark. Helmut Schmidt would later indirectly concede[184] and Ulrich Wegener would openly state[185] that the GSG9 had a "Plan B" for storming the "Landshut" at night without Somali involvement. The German government wanted a storming in Mogadishu at all costs.

Later that afternoon, GSG9 commander Ulrich Wegener, his adjutant Frieder Baum and Wegener's deputy Dieter Fox narrowly escape being shot.[186] Accompanied by a Somali major, they are driven to their hotel to collect personal belongings that they had been forced to leave behind as a guarantee. On the way from the hotel back to the airport, the jeep driver does not take the main road but takes a shortcut. At a barrier, the men are asked for a password, which—of course—they don't know.

Within seconds, three guards point their Kalashnikovs at Wegener and his men. After another unsuccessful request for the password, the first guard loads his Kalashnikov, i.e. unlocks the safety, and says to the others: "If they don't

---

[182] Cf. Geiger 2009.
[183] Cf. Krenz/Kunze 2016, p. 84f.
[184] "In the defence against the attempted murder of 90 airline passengers hijacked to East Africa, we were very fortunate not to have been forced to violate international law." In: Helmut Schmidt: Speech on the award of the Franz Josef Strauß Prize 2003 to former Federal President Prof. Dr Roman Herzog, p. 17, typescript.
[185] Cf. Holger Schmidt 2016.
[186] In the following see Fox 2023.

answer, we'll shoot!" A loud exchange of words begins between the threatened and the threatened.

Fortunately, an officer appears at this moment and wants to know what the shouting is all about. The officer allows himself to be led to the jeep with the Germans. By chance, the officer and the Somali major in the car know each other. They are able to clear up the matter. The leaders of the GSG9 get away with the scare.

> *"one gets the impression that the federal government tolerates the execution of death sentences on innocent people who trust in the protection of the federal republic, while in the fight against terrorism the death sentence is rejected—surely the people who make the relevant decisions have no relatives in the machine.*
>
> *Helga wihlfahrt as sister of an affected passenger and on behalf of other relatives"*[187]

Among the assembled federal police officers, GSG9 commander Ulrich Wegener puts together several groups for the storming. A few of his men suddenly get cold feet. They declare: "I'm out." The commander still has enough manpower, but some of his ready-to-go men are overtired from various flights and on-call duties over the last few days. Among them is Wegener's deputy Dieter Fox.

The commander sets the start of the operation, called "Fire Magic", for 2.00 a.m. local time—midnight in Germany. Then the Somali sky is as dark as possible. And the members of the terror squad in the "Landshut" would hopefully be in night mode.

Bonn

"The highest degree of loneliness is loneliness of conscience, which can increase infinitely; to measure it, think of borderline situations in which even the neighbour can no longer give advice, he can only ask, pray and regret, whereby the question always remains as to whether he has the right to do so. Such borderline situations are those of the hero; he is completely on his own."[188]

---

[187] Telegram from the German Federal Post Office to the Federal Government, Crisis Staff of Federal Chancellor Schmidt, Bonn, dated 17 October 1977, 4.51 p.m. Delivered at 18.56, in BArch B136/31588.
[188] Hans Richtscheid: Existence in this time. Munich 1965, p. 69.

Helmut Schmidt has presumably never read the writings of the philosopher Hans Richtscheid. Nevertheless, these lines could speak to him, the German Chancellor, on this Sunday as an apt description of his situation.

Far to the south of Bonn, in Stuttgart, a Protestant pastor reflects on the spiritual dimension of this day. A day that would make history in whatever way, for joy or sorrow. And if not this one, then the next one or the one after that.

There has already been talk of Jörg Zink as the "TV pastor". He spoke the "Word for Sunday" when the "Landshut" had already been in the hands of Palestinian hijackers for a few days. He comforted the West Germans in their hopes and fears for a good outcome.

After the Federal Chancellery requested the aforementioned "Word for Sunday", it received the published version. Jörg Zink would now like to send Helmut Schmidt the actual wording together with an accompanying letter. In it, he thanks Helmut Schmidt for his "focused, calm and consistent leadership in recent weeks."[189] And asks him to "maintain this clear course unwaveringly."[190] Zink's message is twofold. Someone considers himself called upon to strengthen the Chancellor's soul. And at the same time knows that the man might need it.

The pastor writes, "When Golda Meir (Israeli Prime Minister between 1969 and 1974, editor's note) was threatened with kidnapping by the PLO, she declared in the Knesset: 'If they catch me, forget me.' (...) She was never kidnapped."[191] Zink continues: "I would give a lot if one of the leading men in our state stood up and said: 'If I am kidnapped, I don't want to be replaced. The state is more than my person.' Those who value the democratic rule of law more than their own lives cannot be held hostage by terrorists."

Helmut Schmidt feels understood. As he reads the letter, he underlines the word "unwavering" with his green felt-tip pen. Green is the colour of the boss. He answers Pastor Jörg Zink personally and without beating about the bush. "In the event that I were the victim of a hostage situation, I would expect those responsible to make the necessary decisions without taking my person into consideration." He has considered saying this publicly but has so far rejected the idea—partly out of concern that he would be misunderstood.

"Anyone who (...) would publicly declare that he does not want to be replaced in the event of a kidnapping would expose himself to the misinterpretation that he is actually concerned with inappropriate publicity. The

---

[189] Letter from Pastor Dr Jörg Zink to Federal Chancellor Helmut Schmidt dated 17 October 1977, in: OTB 13–211 20 (2) Additional file OTB vol. 7, p. 295.
[190] Ibid.
[191] Israeli Prime Minister from 17 March 1969 to 3 June 1974.

Federal Chancellor in particular would certainly have to reckon with such a misunderstanding."[192]

A rare moment when Helmut Schmidt gives an insight into his most personal thoughts.

On Monday, 17 October 1977, another pastor appears at the Federal Chancellery: Helmut Frenz, internationally renowned human rights activist and Secretary General of the Amnesty International Section of the Federal Republic of Germany, is given a quarter of an hour's interview time.[193] A speaker, Dr Kern, takes notes. He, Pastor Frenz, is personally acquainted with Hans-Heinz Heldmann, Andreas Baader's lawyer. The lawyer has asked him to mediate between the lawyers of the RAF terrorists in Stuttgart-Stammheim and the Federal Minister of Justice, Hans-Jochen Vogel. In addition to Hans-Heinz Heldmann the other lawyers involved are Otto Schily (Gudrun Ensslin's defence lawyer), Karl-Heinz Weidenhammer (Jan-Carl Raspe's defence lawyer) and Jutta Bahr-Jendgens (Irmgard Möller's defence lawyer).

Pastor Helmut Frenz is allowed to dictate a few lines himself in order to present his request as authentically as possible. "In view of the murder of the airline captain Schumann in Mogadishu (…)" the defence lawyer and the three defence attorneys wanted to have a conversation with their clients as quickly as possible "with the intention of persuading them to take a step that could put an end to the murders in the Lufthansa plane."[194]

He, Pastor Frenz, had a conversation with the colleague and his colleagues. After the death of the flight captain, they became convinced that they "had to help stop the hostage-taking."[195] He and the defence lawyers he named, the transcript of the conversation continues, "believed they could influence their clients to refuse to fly out". If, contrary to expectations, the terrorists were to reject the request, the defence lawyers would be willing to take the "ultimate consequences". Which probably means: Resignation of their mandates. They ask the Federal Minister of Justice, via Pastor Frenz, to lift the ban on contact between defence lawyers and clients "for this one conversation".

State Secretary Manfred Schüler receives the note at 6 p.m. Shortly after 6 p.m., he has already passed it on to Hans-Jochen Vogel. The Federal Minister

---

[192] Letter from Helmut Schmidt to Pastor Jörg Zink dated 7 November 1977, in: OTB 13–211 20 (2) Additional file OTB vol. 7, p. 300.

[193] Cf. note by Mr Chief BK. Re: Presentation by Pastor Helmut Frenz, Secretary General of Amnesty International on 17 October 1977 from 5.30 p.m. to 5.45 p.m. AL1, in: Archiv BK 13–211 20 (2) Additional file OTB vol. 6, p. 473f.

[194] According to dictation by Pastor Frenz (Secretary General of Amnesty International) on 7 October 1977, 5.30 p.m., n.d., in: Ibid., p.475.

[195] Conversation note from 17 October. AL II, in: OTB, p. 473.

of Justice promises that a ministerial director from his office will meet with Pastor Frenz.

It would be pointless to speculate on the chances of success of this initiative. It is worth mentioning because it illustrates the emotional escalation that takes place this weekend. The population, the police, political decision-makers, the families of Hanns Martin Schleyer and the "Landshut" hostages, their kidnappers and also the RAF terrorists and their defence lawyers sense, that the showdown is near.

The German autumn before the showdown. The politicians of Helmut Schmidt's generation, the so-called war generation, do not write diaries. They keep their feelings to themselves. They locked them away in the storerooms of their hearts. "Talking about emotions such as fear or insecurity was not intended, as it could be interpreted as a sign of weakness or influenceability."[196]

Helmut Schmidt reads a lot during the German autumn. Statements from the major churches and articles on the spiritual situation of the times. He always has a green felt-tip pen in his hand. He uses it to underline sentences and make comments in the margins.

Some of these "shredded" texts—such as the declaration of the General Assembly of the German Bishops' Conference on terrorism of 21 September 1977 or an article in "Die Zeit"—end up in the archives. Time and again, the Federal Chancellor instructes his staff to pass on passages from them to his speechwriters for further use. Helmut Schmidt does not describe himself as a devout Christian, but regularly seeks dialogue with Protestant clergymen. Women and men in top politics also feel the need to reassure themselves of their ethical standards. And to have their actions confirmed.

So far, the Federal Chancellor has not made any of his decisions in the German autumn alone. Everything has been discussed and approved by the small and big group of political advisors and the cabinet. As the lone pilot of the government ship, the man only appears resolutely decisive when making statements in the German Bundestag or in television speeches. Then there is Helmut Schmidt, the state actor, the equal of none in the old Federal Republic.

On this evening, however, before the showdown in Mogadishu, the responsibility lies solely with him. And under gruelling conditions. Someone will later calculate that Helmut Schmidt slept at best twelve hours in the five nights between the hijacking of the "Landshut" and the "fire magic" operation.[197]

---

[196] Maren Richter: Life in a state of emergency, p. 246.
[197] Cf. Kaiser 1977.

Only the Federal Chancellor can order the storm. He does so in a telephone conversation with GSG9 commander Ulrich Wegener on the afternoon or evening of 17 October 1977, the exact time is not known. Perhaps on one of the two occasions when he leaves the round table with the intellectuals.

The conversation between the two men is short and military. They click because, like Schmidt, Wegener has also experienced the "steel bath" of the World War, having been drafted into the army at the age of 15. Helmut Schmidt asks Ulrich Wegener what percentage he believes in the success of the operation. 100 per cent, the commander replies. The answer satisfies the Chancellor. He gives the go-ahead.

The way in which Helmut Schmidt makes this decision characterises him as a follower of critical rationalism, which was founded by the Austrian philosopher Karl Popper. Popper recommends that politics should not seek to implement desirable scenarios, visions, but rather minimise risks and dangers in everyday life. Not blindly rushing ahead but taking one step at a time. The "fire magic" campaign is a highly risky endeavour. However, it is well prepared and theoretically has a high chance of success. Anything can go wrong. Nothing needs to go wrong.

Shortly before his death, Helmut Schmidt will confess that he believed 50 per cent in success and 50 per cent in failure.[198] And that the tragedy of the events would burden him with guilt in any case.

In this interview, Helmut Schmidt also mentions his motive for not releasing the members of the Large Political Advisory Group till the end of "fire magic". In the event of failure, no one should issue a statement blaming others. Especially not on him, the Federal Chancellor. The common term for this is "levelling up".

Helmut Schmidt's decision to storm the machine is, strictly speaking, twofold. The Chancellor's actions put the life of the President of the Employers' Association, Hanns Martin Schleyer, in immediate danger. The kidnappers will assume that the hostages will not be released. In addition, Helmut Schmidt puts the lives of the GSG9 commandos and all the hostages on the "Landshut" at risk. A decision whose harshness was recently pointed out by the historian Helmut Stubbe da Luz.

"88 people are more important than one", said the Federal Chancellor to Hans-Jürgen Wischnewski on the phone in Dubai. The sentence is only half-finished. In full, it should read: "88 people are more important than one and 61.35 million Germans are more important than 88."

---

[198] Cf. Stubbe da Luz 2022, p. 198.

Helmut Schmidt knows what he is doing. He will later affirm that he would have resigned from office if there had been a larger number of dead "Landshut" hostages—ten? 20? That sounds noble. Responsible. Nevertheless, to this day no one has seen the alleged letter of resignation which is said to have been in his jacket (according to other accounts, in a desk drawer in the Federal Chancellery) that Sunday evening.

"Helmut Schmidt would have resigned", CSU politician Friedrich Zimmermann will be certain in his personal retrospective.[199] Hans-Jochen Vogel would also later report that the Chancellor's resignation had been an issue since the "Landshut" hijacking.[200] Zimmermann and Vogel may or may not know.

Alea iacta est. The head of the Federal Criminal Police Office, Horst Herold, will later talk about the atmosphere of that evening in a meeting room of the Federal Chancellery in Bonn. There was nothing more you could do, things moved forward on their own. One person drank coffee. Helmut Schmidt was playing chess with Klose (First Mayor of Hamburg and party colleague, M. R.'s note), both bored and not interested in the game.

And then Mr Schmidt gave up and sat down next to me and asked: "Tell me, how do they actually live in the cells?" And then I had to tell him: "Mr Chancellor, I've never seen a cell. I don't even know the Stuttgart prison."[201]

For the first time at a meeting of the Large Political Advisory Group, there is not just coffee, water and juices, but alcohol. "I had quite a lot to drink that night", Friedrich Zimmermann recalls in conversation with Dorothea Hauser, "but it still enabled me to formulate precise statements at two in the morning."[202] Friedrich Zimmermann is one of the authors of a joint press release by the German government, the opposition and the minister presidents of the "detention countries". Klaus Bölling reads it out after the happy "Landshut" release.

The former Wehrmacht soldiers experience flashbacks as mentioned. Helmut Schmidt and Friedrich Zimmermann play "Present arms!"[203] Presumably a valve to "release" the internal tension. For the worry about the abducted people in the "Landshut". Everyone knows that the "war" will be

---

[199] Cf. Zimmermann/Hauser, p. 5.
[200] Cf. Vogel/Hauser, p. 35.
[201] Herold/Hauser, p. 63, referring to the cells of the RAF terrorists in the Stuttgart-Stammheim prison.
[202] Zimmermann/Hauser, p. 3, referring to the joint declaration by the Federal Government and the governments of the states in which imprisoned RAF terrorists were to be ransomed. Government spokesman Klaus Bölling reads out this declaration at a late-night press conference shortly after the successful release of the "Landshut" hostages in Mogadishu.
[203] Cf. Stubbe da Luz 2022, p. 194.

decided with this "battle". Without them having any direct influence on the events themselves. The outcome would have political consequences for them. His personal future is also at stake.

On this evening, GSG9 commander Ulrich Wegener also knows that it's all or nothing. About the future of his unit. Before the German autumn, politicians were half-loudly contemplating disbanding his expensive unit. Ulrich Wegener knows that success on this night will silence the debate. And that if the GSG9 fails, it would be disbanded "that very night".[204].

In the early evening, Rüdiger von Wechmar, German Ambassador to the United Nations in New York, calls the Federal Chancellery. The telephone message states that "the AP news agency has just received a report from an Israeli journalist in Mogadishu who had observed a Boeing 707 with dimmed lights landing on the runway at Mogadishu airport and who had previously intercepted radio traffic from this aircraft".

A radio amateur in Tel Aviv has indeed listened in on the tower's radio communication. Euphoric about his coup, he informs Israeli television that an unidentifiable aircraft has landed at Mogadishu airport without lights. It was possibly a special commando unit.[205] An employee of the news agency agence-france-presse sees the message read out on television and sends a telex to the Paris headquarters. This is how the news spreads across radio stations and news agencies in Europe.

Government spokesman Klaus Bölling presents Helmut Schmidt with a proof copy of the daily newspaper "Die Welt" from 18 October 1977 with an editorial according to which the Somali government is said to have rejected an attack by German forces.[206] The Federal Chancellor is alarmed. The indiscretion could jeopardise the operation at the last moment! Hans-Jürgen Wischnewski is warned in advance. In the event that the Somali president "falls over", the Minister of State and GSG9 commander Ulrich Wegner agree to storm the plane even without the approval of the Somalis.[207]

Helmut Schmidt calls "Die Welt" and is put through to the editor on duty, Wilfried Hertz-Eichenrode, who is also the author of the editorial. The Chancellor hurls threats and curses, which he would later refuse to quote. The journalist reacts quickly. "If we want to do anything else, we have to end our conversation now." Wilfried Hertz-Eichenrode looks round at his colleagues: "How much money do we have with us?" Some of them take taxis to the

---

[204] Wegener 2012.
[205] Press and Information Office of the Federal Government, p. 113.
[206] Cf. memo from Division 131 dated 27 October 1977, subject: Schleyer kidnapping case. Reference: Yesterday's Cabinet meeting, in: OTB 12–211 20 (2) vol. 4, p. 288.
[207] See Holger Schmidt 2016.

station kiosks where the evening edition of "Die Welt" is already on display. They buy the copies back. At the same time, the printing of later editions is stopped and Hertz-Eichenrodes' editorial is replaced by another text.

Wilfried Hertz-Eichenrode would call the story spread by Helmut Schmidt that the Federal Chancellor had made threats and curses towards him a legend. Throughout his life. Helmut Schmidt, on the other hand, insists on his own personal recollection. To avoid the reputation of having violated the freedom of the press that evening, he has his version of the events recorded in the minutes of the next cabinet meeting.[208]

Mogadishu

Hans-Jürgen Wischnewski does something that evening "that I don't do very often".[209] He retreats to a quiet corner on the airport grounds and prays. "Because I've told myself that I've done everything I can do here in terms of preparation, but the risk is so great. If someone else doesn't help, the risk is very high."[210]

It is not known whether Commander Ulrich Wegener prays. He and his men have to do it now. They have been preparing for this baptism of fire for almost five years. The mood is focused, but not tense. German Lufthansa has sent them copies of the flight tickets. They know which hostages are sitting in which seats. (They have no way of knowing that the hijackers have repeatedly moved passengers). When planning the operation, the door where the "beauty queens" are supposedly sitting proves to be particularly coveted. Competition between men prevails even before a dangerous mission like this.

The GSG9 members go through the procedures again in their heads. They are fully aware of the risk they are taking. The operation takes place with a lot of people in a very small space. The behaviour of hostages and kidnappers is unpredictable. A hostage which doesn't duck in time can die in a hail of bullets, as in previous rescue operations—for example on a train hijacked by Moluccans in 1977. This kidnapping will be discussed later.

At the same time, Wegener's people are aware of their excellent training. And that they joined the GSG9 for such missions. The GSG9 sees itself as an elite unit. Its members must and want to prove this now.

Shortly before midnight, reconnaissance troops and GSG9 precision marksmen take up positions around the aircraft. At a distance so as not to

---

[208] Hildebrandt 1977, p. 2.
[209] Wischnewski/Hauser, p. 53.
[210] Ibid.

be seen by the terrorists. At the same time close enough to reach the aircraft quickly if necessary.

The GSG9 task forces for the storm sneak up on the "Landshut". Without cover. Protected only by the darkness of the night. All the task forces are in radio contact with each other. The radio traffic is recorded. Two GSG9 members photograph and film the operation.

Wegener's people set off, divided into six groups. Each group is to reach one door. The two doors at the front and rear as well as two emergency exits at wing level. The squads are labelled 310, 320, 330, 340, 350, 360.

They manage to reach the "Landshut" unnoticed. The six ladders are placed as quietly as possible at the doors. Co-pilot Jürgen Vietor, who has been dozing in a seat at the front of the aircraft, hears noises on the outside wall of the aircraft. His intuition tells him to find a seat further back.

Ulrich Wegener sees Jürgen Vietor standing up and waits until the co-pilot has taken his new seat. It can start. Somalis ignite a fire in some distance—a diversionary manoeuvre for the hijackers. Irritated, everyone runs to the front and looks outside.

Now the British special forces set off their stun grenades, which checkmates the kidnappers for seconds. Wegener's men blow open the doors. Each squad—in turn, each man in the squad—has his own zone in which he is allowed to move. The interior of the "Landshut" is divided into so-called penetration sections and security positions. Some of the comrades hunt down the terrorists, while others provide them with cover. No GSG9 man should be hit by a bullet from one of their own men.

Dieter Fox is one of the first of Wegener's people in the machine. He shouts "Heads down! Where are the pigs?" "In the front of the cockpit!" replies hostage Birgitt Röhll from the last row of seats. Dieter Fox and Co. open fire. Whoever is still standing now is a terrorist.

Almost everything works like clockwork, only the front door on the right does not open. It only leaves a gap because of the piled-up hand luggage. A terrorist, the "fat one", fires shots through the gap. A bullet hits the GSG9 man holding the ladder on the airfield—he is shot through the neck. He is brought to safety by a comrade and given medical treatment.

The other members of the squad jump down the ladder, pass under the aircraft and storm through the door opposite into their zone. A fierce firefight rages between Wegener's men and the terrorists. Wegener and Co. shoot their way down the aisle to the cockpit, as they have practised many times before.

Riddled with bullets, "Captain Machmud" collapses in the cockpit and falls onto the throttle. A terrorist has locked herself in the front toilet, the

GSG9 men sift through the door. The second terrorist is also fatally shot. The second terrorist suffers serious injuries.

After seven minutes, the "fire spell" is over.

Some "Landshut" passengers are not in such a hurry to be rescued—despite the explosives and the highly flammable alcohol that has been spilt. They run into First Class and rummage through the piled-up luggage in search of their bags and valuables. After one woman finds her handbag, she continues to rummage. For a straw bag with vegetables.

The freed hostages are led by the GSG9 men to a sandpit at a safe distance from the aircraft. A car with a water tank in tow also arrives there.

At 00:17 German time, Commander Ulrich Wegener radios the code word "Springtime" (end of mission) to his men. He informs Minister of State Hans-Jürgen Wischnewski.[211]

"90 hostages freed,

Three hostages slightly injured,

three terrorists killed,

a terrorist seriously injured,

A member of the GSG9 was slightly injured by a bullet to the neck,

Order executed."

The fact that all the hostages and liberators survive the "fire spell" is nothing short of a miracle. Ulrich Wegener's men were one protective waistcoat short during the storm. Ulrich Wegener leaves his to a comrade who is hit by a bullet. The waistcoat consists of 16 layers of fabric, and the bullet penetrates 14 of them.

Technical specialists from the GSG9 enter the aircraft to render the explosive devices unusable if necessary. Afterwards, photographers from the Federal Criminal Police Office are allowed into the "Landshut" to preserve evidence. They document the terrible state of the aircraft. The hopeless disorganisation. Rubbish everywhere. One of their picture motifs is "Captain Machmud", who is lying badly injured on the throttle levers.

The terrorist leader is carried out of the aircraft and laid out on the airfield. There he bleeds to death. Officers from the Federal Criminal Police Office photograph the dying or the dead. A shot deer after the hunt. The motif is featured on the cover of the next issue of "Stern". Former "Landshut" hostage Jutta Knauff (née Brod) will keep a copy of the magazine for decades.

---

[211] Herzog 2022, p. 216f.

In the airport building, five Italian doctors look after the completely exhausted hostages. Many of them are too weak to stand. They lie on the floor and are given drinks. There is a commotion when first aiders carry in the seriously injured terrorist Souhaila Andrawes.

When Souhaila Andrawes sees a cameraman filming, she raises an arm in a victory sign. She shouts in her own language "Kill me, we will win!" Then her voice chokes and she loses consciousness.

The cameraman is part of the team of ARD correspondent Kurt Stenzel. He collects sound bites (in television jargon, for original sound bites). Jutta Brod (née Knauff), the winner of the beauty contest in the "Graf Zeppelin", says into the camera: "I would never have thought that a person could endure so much."

Jürgen Vietor lost almost four kilos during the five days he was kidnapped without sleep. In the airport hall, he is initially in a joking mood. He jokes with Gabriele von Lutzau (née Dillmann), who was injured in the foot by a hand grenade: "If that was a hand grenade, it must have been from Woolworth's (a low-priced department stores' chain with branches in West Germany, note M. R.)." When he finds out that his wife has been given the wrong death notice, he almost keels over. A doctor gives him a shot to boost his circulation.

Jürgen Vietor later returns to the machine once again. He has lost not only kilos but also his "hair", the toupee. In the turmoil of the "fire spell" it remained in the cockpit. Vietor also reaches for the bunch of keys in his jacket, which is hanging in the cockpit. He needs it to pick up his car at Frankfurt Airport. Having just been in mortal fear, the trivial topics of life return.

The freed hostage Dieter Coldewey also has to return to the "Landshut". His eight-year-old daughter Gaby has forgotten her rag doll in there. The doll that she always carries with her and clutched to her chest during the kidnapping. Fortunately, her father finds it. He comes across a dog that had been left in the machine. Dieter Coldewey takes him to the sandpit, where her owner gratefully embraces it.

After her lucky escape from the "Landshut", Gaby Coldewey will sleep with the rag doll under her pillow for decades. She develops a strong sense of empathy for victims. Her professional biography will include an interview project with Holocaust survivors.

Hostage Brigitte Paul associates a different image with her rescue. "After the happy rescue", former hostage Brigitte Paul (née Pittelkow) will write decades later, "what I remember most is the tropical starry sky above

Mogadishu airport at night and the reunion with my child, parents and sister in Germany."²¹²

Bonn

Hans-Jürgen Wischnewski calls the Federal Chancellery. Helmut Schmidt is called into his office.

"Schmidt here!—Schmidt here! I'm listening!"

"Speak slowly and loudly, please!."

"The aircraft is cracked!."

"Not understood."

The job. The job is done. Three dead terrorists."

"Three dead terrorists."

"A GSG9 man wounded."

"Not understood."

"A GSG9 man wounded."

"One."

(…)

"Wait a few more minutes. The lorries are leaving now."

"Yes, now the lorries are driving (…)."

"And then the people are taken out first."

"I give back, Hans-Jürgen. I can hardly understand you."

Hans-Jürgen Wischnewski talks to Ulrich Wegener. Afterwards Ulrich Wegener talks to Helmut Schmidt. The Chancellor doesn't seem to believe what he hears from the technically distorted conversation.

"How many dead, how many injured?"

"We have no casualties. One of my people is slightly injured, that's all. Among the terrorists, one survived seriously injured and three are dead. Everything went very well."

---

[212] Brigitte Paul (née Pittelkow): The tropical starry sky over Mogadishu. Report for a history project at the Ludgerusschule Heiden, 2002, in: Rupps 2012, p. 226.

"Colonel…"

"I understand that you're saying that to me now. But I am a lieutenant colonel."

"That will change."[213]

Helmut Schmidt is on the phone to Hans-Jürgen Wischnewski again. It is simply too good to be true. When the Minister of State confirms that there were no casualties, Helmut Schmidt is in tears. He returns to the conference room with wet eyes. There he says: "The work is done. All the hostages have been freed." Then he hugs his secretary Lieselotte Schmarsow.

At first, the men in the Large Political Advisory Group find it as hard to believe as the Federal Chancellor himself. As former Wehrmacht soldiers and top politicians in the Federal Republic of Germany, they do not hug each other, but congratulate Helmut Schmidt with a handshake. Just don't show any unruly feelings now. We are soldiers after all!

As previously announced, government spokesman Klaus Bölling will address the press after 1:00 a.m. When he appears in the press conference room, the journalists applaud him—presumably a unique event in the history of the old Federal Republic. Bölling, like Helmut Schmidt a master of self-control, is unable to suppress groaning press sounds this time, he is so exhausted. He then presents the joint statement by the federal government, the leaders of the parliamentary groups in the Bundestag and the prime ministers of the "detaining countries". It proves that a release of the imprisoned terrorists was never considered.

Mogadishu

Deep in the night, the hostages, their liberators and Hans-Jürgen Wischnewski's entourage have to leave Mogadishu. The Minister of State had to promise Somali President Siad Barre that the Germans would be gone before sunrise. The de facto violation of Somali sovereignty cannot stand the light of day.

The injured stewardess Gabriele von Lutzau (née Dillmann) can be treated as an outpatient in a hospital in Mogadishu. Other hostages cannot. They are too exhausted for the return journey and have to stay in a clinic for a few days, together with their only surviving kidnapper. The following day, radio and television will not mention—presumably not even notice—that passengers are missing.

---

[213] Ibid, p 217.

Hans-Jürgen Wischnewski meets Somali President Siad Barre again at the airport. Presumably, the president reminds the Germans that they promised to leave before dawn.

Hans-Jürgen Wischnewski goes to some trouble to put the exhausted hostages back on an aircraft so soon after their rescue. In the hustle and bustle of the departure, it almost goes unnoticed that the passports of Hans-Jürgen Wischnewski's entourage have been confiscated. The Minister of State's personal assistant, Peter Kiewitt, remembers this just in time. He also remembers the silver suitcase containing 100,000 German mark, which he took to Mogadishu as a precaution and left in the tower.

Two planes with the Germans take off at 5.10 a.m. bound for Frankfurt am Main (the freed hostages) and Cologne-Wahn (Hans-Jürgen Wischnewski's staff and the GSG9). Now the Somalis take over the abandoned "Landshut" as agreed between President Siad Barre and Minister of State Hans-Jürgen Wischnewski. In other words, they are going all out. They plunder the valuables in the cabin and rummage through the suitcases in the luggage compartment.

Apparently, there is no art expert among the soldiers and policemen. Pablo Picasso's tapestry is staying where it is.

4

A Night of Life and Death

Tuesday, 18 October 1977, 00:58. "This is Deutschlandfunk with important news: the 86 hostages kidnapped by terrorists in a Lufthansa Boeing have all been happily freed."[1]

> *"re: deployment of the gsg 9 in modagischu, here: congratulations from the population*
>
> 1. *On 18 October, 01.00 a.m., a citizen from Karlsruhe came to the bverfg karlsruhe after the success report became known and embraced the two security guards of the bgs. He handed them a bottle of cognac, left with his car and returned a short time later with his wife. He also handed over a crate of beer. At 0.15 a.m. a woman handed over a bunch of flowers.*
> 2. *On 18 October, 08.20 a.m., a large bouquet of flowers with a card was handed in at the bgs station in haar near munich. Wording of the card: 'thanks to the bgs for the operation 17/18 October 77, 00.00 h, a citizen of haar.'"*[2]

Church bells ring throughout Germany in the morning. Newspaper publishers distribute extra sheets. Complete strangers who learn of the successful liberation are hugging each other. Commentators in the press and on the radio thank God for his help. Suhrkamp publisher Siegfried Unseld

---

[1] Quoted from Herzog 2022, p. 224.
[2] Telex to 03 St. Augustin bgs (gsg 9), in: BArch B106/371617.

is congratulated by a taxi driver in Brussels for his "president"—meaning the Federal Chancellor.³

> *"Chancellor schmidt federal chancellery bonn*
>
> *We would like to take this opportunity to thank you from the bottom of our hearts for our liberation from the hands of the terrorists we still cannot believe the courage and the extent of the help and sympathy we have received julia and dietrich filius."*⁴

In the days that follow, the Federal Chancellery receives "around 2,500 letters and around 1,000 replyable telegrams (plus another 2,500 telegrams without sender details)",⁵ counts a staff member or has counted with a reference date of 24 October 1977. Helmut Schmidt himself edits the text of a printed card, with which is thanked by the majority of letter writers.

Celebrities such as actress Romy Schneider and heads of state from all over the world choose personal words to thank and congratulate Chancellor Helmut Schmidt. The diplomatic exchange with punched phrases is suspended for a short time because of the general feeling of genuine relief. The GSG9's successful "fire magic" campaign evokes admiration around the globe. Just German virtues. Thorough preparation. Discipline. Responsibility.

The general tenor is that "Mogadishu" sets global standards in the fight against terror. Police forces have sought direct combat with terrorists. In a few Boeing square metres. In a broken aircraft. In a full risk shoot-out. They have prevailed.

"Mogadishu" signals nothing less than a turning point in the struggle of Western democracies against their enemies. The brutality of the "Red Army Faction" radiated far beyond the Federal Republic of Germany. Although "Mogadishu" is not the final blow against the group, it is a historic one.

The outcome of the "German Autumn", which was marred by fatalities but was nonetheless mild, briefly suspends the political dispute in the Federal Republic of Germany. For once, even "Der Spiegel" does not write derisively about Bonn politics and the man in the most important office. The cover of the issue after "Mogadischu" features Federal Chancellor Helmut Schmidt, wearing a black, red and gold sash. Next to it is the text: "After Mogadishu: the admired German". Presumably the highest possible praise from the Hamburg news magazine for a German chancellor.

---

³ Bauer/Hacke 2006, p. 106.
⁴ Ibid, B136/31588.
⁵ Letter from BK Division 133 (Dr Melzer) to the Federal Chancellor dated 24 October 1977, in: AdsD, 1/HSAA010018.

In the night of 17 to 18 October, all 86 hostages and the four crew members of the "Landshut" are rescued. A few hours later, three of the eleven terrorists who were to be ransomed by kidnapping Hanns Martin Schleyer and the people on the Lufthansa plane "Landshut" kill themselves: The *Stammheimer* Gudrun Ensslin, Andreas Baader and Jan-Carl Raspe. Irmgard Möller also wants to commit suicide there. With a knife she inflicts serious but non-fatal stab wounds on herself.

The unexpected, even the unimaginable happens. Chancellor Helmut Schmidt goes berserk ("Shit!") when he hears about the suicides. He intuitively recognises the political damage. So-called sympathisers will publicly express doubts that they were suicides. They will blame the "shitty state" for this, in their parlance.

West Germany is immediately preoccupied with the question of how the unexpected could happen. In the aftermath, unprecedented sloppiness in dealing with the terrorists in Stuttgart-Stammheim prison comes to light. Despite regular searches of their cells, a pistol in a record player and one in the cavity of a wall remained undiscovered. Baader and Raspe, prisoners in the so-called high-security wing of what was supposedly the most modern prison building in West Germany, had weapons and ammunition![6]

They apparently listened to the radio and even communicated with each other personally during the "German Autumn". Among those in charge in Stuttgart-Stammheim, there was a momentous naivety—see the telephone logs of the prison director with the head of the Federal Chancellery and the Federal Prosecutor General—a momentous naivety. Presumably more so than the fear of being denounced in the media as allegedly inhumane prison conditions.

In fact, Baader and his cohorts enjoyed comfortable prison conditions that the other inmates in Stuttgart-Stammheim could only dream of. At the same time, the RAF terrorists' political influence was still greatly underestimated behind bars. This also applied to their intentions to go to extremes, to commit suicide for their own cause.

As far as the suicide intentions are concerned, perhaps not one person believed in it: Siegfried Nusser, as head of the Stuttgart-Stammheim prison, or Federal Public Prosecutor General Kurt Rebmann. In the closing phase of

---

[6] And that's not all. On 11 November 1977, 360 g of explosives and three electric detonators were found behind the plaster moulding in the cell of RAF terrorist Ingrid Schubert, who had been in the high-security wing of Stuttgart-Stammheim prison between 25 June and 18 August 1977. On 18 November, in the former cell of RAF terrorist Helmut Pohl, who was in the high-security wing of Stuttgart-Stammheim prison between 6 July and 12 August, investigators discovered a Colt Detective Special revolver, calibre 38, No. 41530, under the plasterwork, along with six cartridges. Also a box with a quick-loading strip containing twelve cartridges.

the German Autumn, however, political decision-makers such as Chancellor Helmut Schmidt and presumably his most important advisor, the head of the Federal Criminal Police Office, Horst Herold, at least did not completely rule it out. This will be discussed later.

The day after the "fire magic" and the Stammheim suicides, employer president Hanns Martin Schleyer has served his time as a political pawn. His kidnappers could let him go. His fate is no longer relevant to the failed "Offensive 77".

In a televised speech on the evening after the "Landshut" has been successfully stormed, Federal President Walter Scheel urgently appeals to the hijackers. "Release Hanns Martin Schleyer". The urgency of his appeal will remain in the collective memory of many West Germans.

On television, the Federal President recalls the eternal validity of fundamental values in the Federal Republic of Germany. At the same time, he expresses a certain understanding for the motives of Hanns Martin Schleyer's kidnappers, who have presumably taken a wrong turn in life and must now be deeply disappointed about the failure of their political goals. They are criminals, according to Scheel's message, but they are also human beings.

They have kidnapped the employer president as a representative of a supposedly shitty state. In their personal encounters, they experienced him as an open-minded, self-critical person. Perhaps they have developed sympathy for the man, or at least empathy.

Hanns Martin Schleyer's kidnappers decide nonetheless on his senseless death. Perhaps to play the winners even in their defeat. Or out of a false, cynical sense of camaraderie. Or out of fear that Hanns Martin Schleyer's clues could lead to their capture.

Hanns Martin Schleyer is driven into a forest in Mühlhausen in Alsace and shot with a pistol held to the back of his head. Executed. The terrorists stow his body in the boot of a green Audi 100. One and the other are supposed to completely strip the man of his dignity in front of the world.

The forensic examination of Hanns Martin Schleyer's body is fully documented in the operation diary. The Federal Criminal Police Office still keeps the car to this day.

Hanns Martin Schleyer's eldest son, Hanns-Eberhard Schleyer, learns during the night that his father has been found dead, not from the police but from "Stern" magazine boss Henri Nannen.[7] Nannen gets in touch at 1.15 a.m. and the two talk on the phone for three hours. Hanns-Eberhard

---

[7] Oral information provided to the author by Hanns-Eberhard-Schleyer.

Schleyer is amazed at how well informed Nannen is. He obviously has excellent contacts with the Federal Criminal Police Office. This now presumably proves to be a thank you for Nannen, together with Rudolf Augstein the most important magazine maker in the republic, accepting the government's ban on news after a brief flinch.

5

On the Catwalk

On 13 October 1977, 86 holidaymakers and businesspeople boarded a Lufthansa twin-engine short-haul aircraft to fly from Palma de Mallorca to Frankfurt am Main in 135 min. They reach their destination 105 h later after a diversion of thousands of kilometres. For six passengers, the journey takes even longer. They are reportedly too weak for a return flight and have to stay in a hospital in Mogadishu.

During the "Landshut" hijacking, the German government and German Lufthansa worked together. When the "Landshut" passengers are on their way home, the harmony is over.

On the morning of 18 October, Heinz Ruhnau, State Secretary in the Federal Ministry of Transport, asks the management of German Lufthansa to organise a joint press conference with Federal Transport Minister Kurt Gscheidle for that day. Venue: Frankfurt am Main Airport.[1] German Lufthansa invites journalists to attend. Hours later, State Secretary Heinz Ruhnau—allegedly on the instructions of the Federal Chancellor—announces,

(a) "The press conference may not be held.
(b) a large event was to be organised for the return of the rescued passengers. The instruction also covered the details of the event."[2]

---

[1] Cf. internal memo from Franz Cesarz to Dr Cullmann (Chairman of the LH Executive Board, note M. R.) dated 19 October 1977, p. 3, in: Archiv German Lufthansa Frankfurt am Main.

[2] Ibid.

This has led to considerable annoyance in the press and intensive direct questioning of passengers.[3]

The Federal Government's about-turn gives the impression that it wants to claim the happy ending of the "Landshut" drama for itself.

Tuesday, 18 October 1977, 1.57 p.m., at Frankfurt Rhine-Main Airport. The Boeing 707 with the freed hostages from Mogadishu reaches its stopping position. Sweaty, dishevelled, wrapped in blankets, the women, men and children descend the gangway. The Second German Television is focusing its cameras on them, as are hundreds of photographers on a specially erected grandstand. On the airfield, they are not greeted by their relatives, but by politicians with bouquets of flowers in their hands. They hand out the bouquets at random so that they can be photographed with the recipients.

Second German Television shows live how buses drive the freed hostages from the airfield to the terminal. There they finally meet their relatives—without television cameras but surrounded by photographers. The pictures of weeping ex-hostages and their equally weeping parents, partners and children will provide the tabloids with material for many weeks.

Freed hostage Cäcilie Meijer-Werner does not know what is happening to her. After the gruelling days, she—and presumably not only she—wants to go home. Instead, she encounters a crowd of people at the gangway. And a grandstand with photographers in sight.

Many relatives of the "Landshut" hostages made the acquaintance of the tabloid press in the days leading up to the incident. Journalists rang the doorbell and, when they were answered, put one foot in the door. They hung up family photos in the hallway or ransacked photo albums. They drove Gabriele von Lutzau's grandmother (née Dillmann) to the hairdresser before the "Landshut" returned. Freshly styled, she arrives with reporters in the airport hall. There she embraces her rescued granddaughter—with the cameras clicking, of course.

The freed hostages are given fresh clothes in the Lufthansa canteen at Frankfurt Airport. They change behind screens that don't really offer any protection from curious photographers. Some climb onto chairs and are given the motifs of their choice.

The welcoming ceremony then takes place in Maintenance Hall 5, the largest on the airport site. It is supposed to be a celebration for the rescued hostages and a memorial service for the dead captain. A lopsided concept. It

---

[3] Ibid. p. 4.

would be better if the completely exhausted people would be shielded from the public and receive psychological counselling.

The German national anthem is played. During the entire days of the hijacking, no member of the German government or any other politician spoke to the people in the "Landshut". Encouraged them, promised them the best possible help. Not even after Gabriele von Lutzau (née Dillmann) desperately called for help from Mogadishu. Now some representatives of this country are sitting in the front rows, clearly visible to millions of television viewers, celebrating the liberation—but actually they are celebrating themselves.

The beautiful staging is "disturbed" by the widow of the murdered captain. Jürgen Schumann's wife was not invited to the party. She goes anyway. To "pick up my husband's coffin", as she explains at the airport.

At the funeral service, Monika Schumann sits next to the Hessian Minister President Holger Börner, who is visibly uncomfortable with this. The usually talkative politician only exchanges a few words with her. During the ceremony, he consistently avoids Monika Schumann's gaze.

Federal Transport Minister Kurt Gscheidle makes his grand entrance. He gives a poor speech full of linguistic platitudes. He speaks too loudly and in an almost thunderous voice. A wrong man in the wrong place. A brass band plays. When Beethoven's funeral march is intoned, Gabriele von Lutzau (née Dillmann) suffers a crying fit. All the tension and exhaustion of the past few days come pouring out.

The freed "Landshut" hostages travel home after landing in Frankfurt am Main and the joint celebration. The political decision-makers in the German autumn believe they have done everything possible for the 86 people. They sent a special commando after them to the Horn of Africa to get them out of the plane unharmed. For the political personnel, the German Autumn is over, the crisis has been overcome.

In his government statement to the German Bundestag on 20 October 1977, Helmut Schmidt recalls the suffering of the hostages and their bravery. It will remain so. The freed "Landshut" passengers were allowed to attend the award ceremony for the Federal Order of Merit for the men of the GSG and the "Landshut" crew in the Chancellery—as onlookers. They are denied their own honour.

Other television images that day do not include exhausted people wrapped in blankets and their relatives with teary eyes. They form the basis of the heroic epic of "Mogadishu". GSG9 commander Ulrich Wegener and his men do not land in Frankfurt am Main, but at Cologne-Wahn Airport. It is closer to their home base in Hangelar near Bonn.

The GSG9 is a unit of the Federal Border Guard, i.e. a police unit, but Ulrich Wegener lets the men compete like soldiers. They stand at attention in front of Federal Minister of the Interior Werner Maihofer and give the military salute. The message is that the liberation operation in Mogadishu was not a police success, but a military victory. A decisive defeat was inflicted on the enemy.

The liberation of the Olympic hostages in 1972 was a miserable failure. Five years later, the wound is still bleeding. The "miracle of Mogadishu" is supposed to heal the wounded soul of the people. Just like the "Miracle of Bern" in 1954.

Federal Minister of the Interior Werner Maihofer also gives a speech that is too loud and barking. A victory song over RAF terrorism with the help of German virtues. We are somebody again!

The press and radio readily accept the interpretation of "Mogadishu" as a decisive battle against terrorism. As mentioned above, "Stern", the most influential magazine in the country alongside "Der Spiegel", prints photos of the dead terrorists on its cover and on double-page spreads. We have defeated them, is the message. The journalists' choice of words is also borrowed from the language of war. They unapologetically choose terms such as stun grenades, close combatants, precision shooters.

German Lufthansa has an image problem since the hijacking drama. The airline, spoilt by success and offended in its pride, has resorts to a PR trick to restore its good reputation. The airline brings the prominent faces of the "Landshut" drama, co-pilot Jürgen Vietor and stewardess Gabriele von Lutzau (née Dillmann), to "Stern" magazine for interviews. With the help of heartbreak stories, the injured Lufthansa crane is supposed to recover.

Jürgen Vietor is in shock, when Lufthansa chief pilot Martin Gaebel and fleet chief B-737 Peter Heldt ring his doorbell on day two of his return. A third person, the "Stern" magazine reporter Gerd Heidemann, is sitting outside the house in a VW Beetle.

Lufthansa executives ask Jürgen Vietor to answer the reporter's questions about the dramatic days. The airline wants the story to be told from the Lufthansa perspective. No shadow should fall on the airline. The Lufthansa captain Jürgen Schumann who was killed is to be honoured posthumously for his courageous behaviour.

LH employee Jürgen Vietor doesn't really have a choice. He wants and has to be loyal to his employer. In addition, "Stern" magazine beckons with a with a five-digit German mark amount. Jürgen Vietor agrees. Gerd Heidemann is invited in and conducts the first of several interviews with him and, at times, in the presence of Vietor's wife. Vietor and Heidemann will sit together for a total of eight and a half hours.

For this book, Jürgen Vietor has made the recording of the talks available for the first time.

The second heartbreak story is created by German Lufthansa with the placement of "Landshut" stewardess Gabriele von Lutzau (née Dillmann) with "Stern". Including the Lufthansa co-pilot Ruedeger von Lutzau, who proposed to his girlfriend in the airport hall in Mogadishu. A story that only life itself can write.

Gabriele von Lutzau also receives a five-digit amount, a much lower one. Probably because she is a woman and not a man and she was "only" a stewardess on the hijacked aircraft. 1975 was the international year of women, but two years later, equality between women and men still seems a long way off.

The young woman is beautiful. She is also very intelligent. German Lufthansa and "Stern" magazine make her a figure of identification for the drama. Later, a newspaper would coin the term "Angel of Mogadishu". The title recognises her great achievement during the days of the kidnapping. At the same time, it puts a lifelong label on her.

For this book, a recording of a conversation between Gabriele von Lutzau (née Dillmann) and her future husband Ruedeger von Lutzau together with Jürgen Vietor and Gerd Heidemann was available for the first time.

On the available tapes, the conversation partners of "Stern" reporter Heidemann appear to be heavily burdened by the events. Present and absent at the same time. Jürgen Vietor has a hard time with the chronology of events, Gabriele von Lutzau (née Dillmann) speaks in a tone-less voice. Ruedeger von Lutzau once says that he hardly recognises his girlfriend's voice.

The magazine "Stern" uses the interviews for a lurid story that—cobbled together in a short time—contains many misrepresentations. Also supposedly invented quotations. The tenor: Co-pilot Jürgen Vietor saved the hostages in an aeronautical way, Gabriele von Lutzau (née Dillmann) saved them in an emotional way. That's a gross generalisation. But it was all much more complicated. Sadder.

The reason the "Stern" project is discussed in such detail here is because it becomes the "mother legend" of the German Autumn. Its stories, always the same ones, are told again and again in the decades to come and embellished with fiction.

When the series of articles start, Gabriele von Lutzau (née Dillmann) understandably disagrees with the way in which her statements were used. She claims never to have made a few of the statements reproduced.

She travels with her partner to Hamburg to see "Stern" magazine author Peter Koch, who greets her with a roar.[4] Koch says: "I've set aside 15 min for this interview. You are ten minutes late, so you still have five minutes to say what you want to say." Gabriele von Lutzau (née Dillmann) responds: I don't think it's good that you have exploited every drop of blood.

Peter Koch continues to shout. In his own words: "What an outrage! You can be glad that you got anything at all for the story! With the stammering you spoke on the tape for that kind of money. I can still hold my head in my hands today!.."

The five minutes are up, the conversation is over.

The episode sheds light not only on the power, but also the self-importance of the influential magazines in the old Federal Republic. With an almost infinite amount of money at their disposal, they not only report on events, but also create themselves the collective memory of them. This self-importance would six years later take its revenge—on Gerd Heidemann himself, once an interviewer for Jürgen Vietor and Gabriele von Lutzau. Heidemann would organise the purchase of the alleged Hitler diaries. They turn out to be fake. The old Federal Republic of Germany has its biggest media scandal.

After the GSG9 men return, the Federal Chancellor announces to Commander Ulrich Wegener that the Federal President intends to honour him with the Federal Cross of Merit.[5] Ulrich Wegener asks which other GSG9 man will receive the honour. Helmut Schmidt replies: "Well, just You."[6] The commander insists that all members of his squad should be honoured—even those where not ordered to Mogadishu or who had flinched before the mission. The Chancellor responds: "Are you crazy? We've never had that before."[7] To which Ulrich Wegener replies glibly that yes, there has probably never been such a rescue operation in the Federal Republic of Germany.[8]

All or none—after this success, GSG9 boss Ulrich Wegener even defies a German chancellor. And gets away with his blackmail. Federal President Walter Scheel signs no fewer than 62 certificates for the awarding of Federal Crosses of Merit. Another five for the freed "Landshut" crew and posthumously for the captain. Co-pilot Jürgen Vietor will carry Jürgen Schumann's Federal Cross of Merit at his funeral. There, Monika Schumann, the widow

---

[4] For Gaby von Lutzau's (née Dillmann's description of the meeting, see Krausz 1978, p. 33.
[5] See Herzog 2022, p. 238.
[6] Ibid.
[7] Ibid.
[8] Cf. ibid.

of the murdered captain, refuses to shake Vietor's hand. "An insult that I have never forgotten",[9] Jürgen Vietor will note years later.

After landing in Cologne-Wahn, Minister of State Hans-Jürgen Wischnewski is driven to the Federal Chancellery in Bonn. Once there, Helmut Schmidt throws his arms around his neck. "Stop it", says Hans-Jürgen Wischnewski, "you don't look that nice."[10] The members of the so-called war generation are not very good at expressing their feelings.

Federal Chancellor Helmut Schmidt announces a government statement for the session of the German Bundestag on Thursday, 20 October. He spends a long time working on the text—until every word is perfect (Fig. 5.1).

He knows that not only the people of the Federal Republic of Germany will be listening, but also diplomats from all over the world. The liberation in Mogadishu was a coup. Now it has to be explained and justified by the man who took the great risk.

The explanatory statement turns out to be one of Helmut Schmidt's most personal and best speeches—probably because the Federal Chancellor has not yet shaken off the depressing events after the end of the German Autumn. Helmut Schmidt shares his feelings of concern and hope during these weeks in a way that he will never do again on any other occasion.

Firstly, the Federal Chancellor mourns Jürgen Schumann and Hanns Martin Schleyer and his companions. He thanks the governments of other states for their moral and active support, above all the Somali President Siad Barre. He thanks the members of the GSG9 for winning a battle against national and international terrorists.

Helmut Schmidt thanks the two major churches for their respective statements on the German Autumn. He calls them important testimonies of sympathy. What he presumably thinks, but of course does not say: I am glad that the explanations did not ask me to make any particular decision, such as the release of terrorists in exchange for Hanns Martin Schleyer.

The Federal Chancellor tries to explain his government action rationally, in the spirit of the philosopher Karl Popper, the founder of critical rationalism. The eleven terrorists who were to be ransomed account for 13 deaths and 43 attempted murders. The terrorists released after the kidnapping of Peter Lorenz and flown out to Aden subsequently killed nine people and carried out four attempted murders.

---

[9] Vietor 1996.
[10] Wischnewski/Hauser, p. 56.

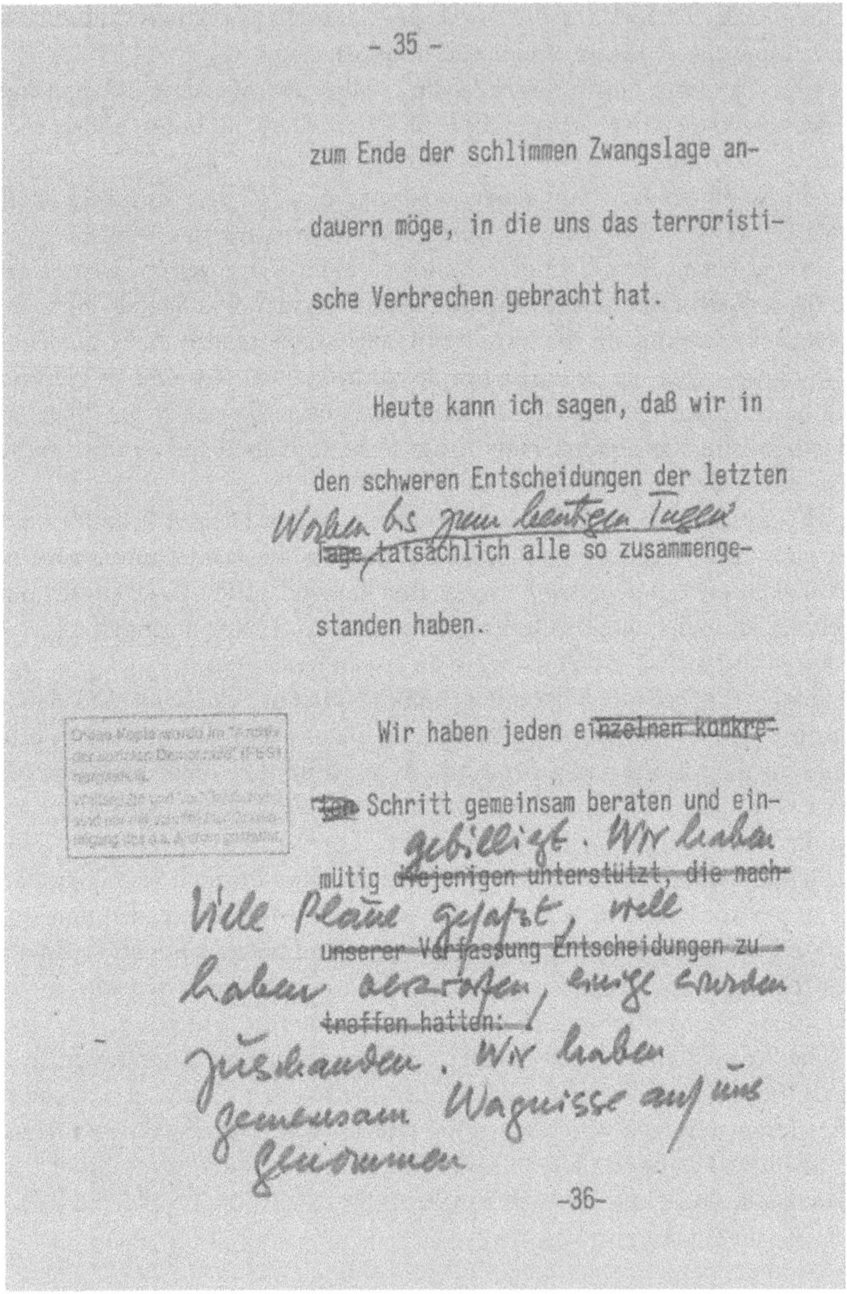

> – 35 –
>
> zum Ende der schlimmen Zwangslage andauern möge, in die uns das terroristische Verbrechen gebracht hat.
>
> Heute kann ich sagen, daß wir in den schweren Entscheidungen der letzten ~~Wochen bis zum heutigen Tagen~~ ~~Tage~~ tatsächlich alle so zusammengestanden haben.
>
> Wir haben jeden ei~~nzelnen konkre-ten~~ Schritt gemeinsam beraten und ein~~mütig diejenigen unterstützt, die nach unserer Verfassung Entscheidungen zu treffen hatten:~~ gebilligt. Wir haben viele Pläne gefaßt, viele haben beraten, einige wurden zustanden. Wir haben gemeinsam Wagnisse auf uns genommen.
>
> –36–

Fig. 5.1 Manuscript of Helmut Schmidt's government statement to the German Bundestag on 20 August, as edited by him. Statement actually delivered, in the minutes of the German Bundestag of 20 October 1977, 8th legislative period/50th session, pp. 3756–3760

The Chancellor makes it clear that the protection of the population from further victims, whose numbers cannot be estimated, goes beyond the sacrifice of a single human life in the hands of kidnappers. After a failure in Mogadishu, he might speak of "a few" lives.

It is a very personal speech and at the same time very typical of Helmut Schmidt's generation. He, the "trained democrat"[11], speaks of "orders of the Basic Law" that must be obeyed. Twice he addresses the young people in West Germany directly, whose intellectual alienation obviously did not escape him. Initially, he expresses understanding for the fact that they are questioning material prosperity as the goal of life. The well-intentioned gesture then fizzles out with a lecture how young people have to appreciate German democracy.

It is also typical of the generation that Helmut Schmidt, as mentioned, says little about the freed hostages. He thanks them for taking on the hardships of the kidnap flight. He emphasises even more the efforts of five Italian doctors who provided first aid to the hostages at Mogadishu airport.

The Federal Chancellor received text proposals from several cabinet members for his important government statement. He took up some of these proposals, but not others. Not included is a draft text by Antje Huber, the Federal Minister for Youth, Family and Health, which states, among other things:

"Throughout these days, the Federal Government was always aware of how fearfully both the passengers of the 'Landshut' and their relatives at home in Germany and in some other countries looked at the political leaders in our state and how little concrete information could be conveyed to them about the government's constant efforts to rescue the hostages as a result of the news blackout necessary for the success of the rescue."[12]

One example of a supply that was taken into account, on the other hand, is the final sentence of Helmut Schmidt's government declaration—it heads this book. It expresses the dilemma in which the political decision-makers found themselves in the German autumn. They suspected or knew that whatever they did, they would bring guilt upon themselves. That would weigh heavily on her soul from now on.

"Those who know that, despite all their endeavours, they will be burdened with neglect and guilt, however they act, will not want to say of themselves that they have done everything and that everything was right. He will not try to blame others for his failings and omissions, because he knows that others are facing the same inevitable entanglement. But he will be allowed to say:

---

[11] Stephan 1988.
[12] Letter from the Federal Minister to the Head of the Federal Chancellery dated 19 October 1977, the text proposal in the appendix, in: AdsD, 1/HSAA010351.

We decided this and that. We failed to do such and such a thing for such and such a reason. We are responsible for all of this."

The manuscript of Helmut Schmidt's statement, which had previously been given to journalists, ends with this sentence. In his speech to the German Bundestag, Helmut Schmidt adds the words: "God help us."

The next day, a Friday, the Federal Chancellor will return to his constituency in Hamburg. He has announced that he will be speaking at the SPD rally in Kirchwerder-Fünfhausen. The first opportunity for a "Schmidt snout" speech for many weeks. Helmut Schmidt seems relieved of the weight of responsibility that has been weighing on him. He is presumably also pleased to be back in his hometown of Hamburg and to be speaking to ordinary people. Even more ordinary than writers and a publisher.

At the beginning of his speech, Helmut Schmidt wittily apologises for "not talking about the agricultural market organisation and about cut flowers and vegetables" (…), "although these are very important topics here", but "about the course of the last seven weeks (…)".[13] Even more detailed and in more comprehensible terms than the day before ("Orientation was given"), he interpreted the German government's perseverance as a militant and at the same time morally exemplary act. The chancellor, who has a reputation as a cold "doer", assures: "We didn't do anything inside our country that we weren't allowed to do, and we didn't do anything outside our borders that we weren't allowed to do."[14] This case has shown that democracies are "not powerless and sapless(…)". "Even democracies need not allow themselves to be brought to their knees by criminals and blackmailers."[15]

With regard to the suicides in Stuttgart-Stammheim, Helmut Schmidt predicts "that a great legend will be created (…) as if the state government in Baden-Württemberg or its officials had deliberately put a gun in someone's hand or even shot them."[16] The Chancellor will be right with this prediction.

A little later, Helmut Schmidt says a sentence that he will not repeat. "Baader and Ensslin had already threatened to commit suicide ten days earlier."[17] The Federal Chancellor publicly revealed that the politicians in Bonn did not only know the last statements by Baader and Co. but also seemed to have understood the implications contained therein.

Apparently, this speech fades away without a critical journalist asking critical questions.

---

[13] Helmut Schmidt: Speech at an SPD rally in Hamburg (Kirchwerder-Fünfhausen) on 21 October 1977. Unedited version, not intended for the public! Typescript, in AdsD 1/HSAA10690, p. 1.
[14] Ibid, p. 38.
[15] Ibid, p. 41.
[16] Ibid, p. 40.
[17] Ibid.

6

Mr Vietor, We Make You Captain

On Tuesday, 18 October 1977, three obese men sit in the hall of the Federal Press Conference to report on their achievements during the "Landshut" hijacking and answer questions from journalists. Minister of State Hans-Jürgen Wischnewski, who is speaking on behalf of the Federal Government, is an old acquaintance here, as is Federal Minister of Justice Werner Maihofer.

The third in the group, Lufthansa board member Werner Utter, represents an airline which was traumatised by the "Landshut" hijacking. This trauma will last for decades. The airline that claims to be the safest in the world was the scene of a hijacking that put passengers and crew in mortal danger. And in which a Lufthansa captain was killed.

Of course, Lufthansa has no part in the lax security checks at Palma de Mallorca Airport. Nevertheless, the airline could have known about it, because it was no secret. Just a few months earlier, this airport had been declared the world's least secure in a study. It is quite possible that the planners of the "Landshut" hijacking were aware of the results of this study.

But now that 91 innocent people were in mortal danger and the pilot has been shot, the airline is directly affected. What's more, Lufthansa officials on the ground—keyword: power generator in Dubai—behaved amateurishly an put themselves in danger. The history of Lufthansa cannot go back to this debacle.

The hijacking of an aircraft for days on end hits an airline harder in some respects than when a plane crashes. A crash occurs suddenly and almost always without witnesses. It is a tragedy with fatalities and bereaved families. After a few days, or weeks at the latest, public attention dies down. The grief of relatives also shifts into the private sphere. After that, media attention is only focused on half or full anniversaries of the disaster.

An aircraft hijacking, on the other hand, takes place in public from start to finish in the second half of the 1970s. The television images go around the world in black and white or colour. Criminal acts in the air are therefore a frequent, spectacular means of fighting for a political cause.

Women and men on all continents fear for the lives of the "Landshut" hostages. Images of the drama dominate the news for days. For days, the Boeing with the crane on its tailplane stands lonely and seemingly godforsaken at the desert airport in Dubai. This image will become iconographic for the drama.

Lufthansa's management positions are held by pilots—intellectually strong, technically excellently trained minds to steer an aircraft. An elite circle of highly paid men who are not only aware of their responsibility, but also their high social status. Political intuition and diplomatic tact are often not among their strengths.

The Lufthansa esprit de corps overrides the simple rules of psychology. Ruedeger von Lutzau, who fears for the life of his girlfriend Gabriele, is allowed to fly a plane to Mogadishu as a co-pilot in this stressful situation. This also contradicts the airline's claim to ensure the greatest possible safety.

In addition, the Chairman of the German Lufthansa Executive Board, Heinz Cullmann, who holds a doctorate in law, does not appear during the "Landshut" hijacking. He had been seriously injured in a car accident three years earlier. The strong man in the company is board member and captain of the B-747, Werner Utter. He heads the Lufthansa crisis team during the "Landshut" hijacking.

Once captain to German President Heinrich Lübke and Lufthansa chief pilot, Utter seems to be born for his leadership role at LH. A brawny, powerful man. The company's image must not be tarnished. Werner Utter leads the staff with a strict regiment. This spirit will also characterise the internal handling of the "Landshut" hijacking.

One episode may serve to illustrate the corporate culture at Lufthansa at the time. There is great *Schadenfreude* over the dreaded boss when Werner Utter "loses" himself on his way to the USA. How can something like this happen? A brief explanation is in order.

To this day, aircraft crossing the Atlantic still require a clearance to fly in the North Atlantic region. There is an entry and an exit point. The flight route has a latitude component for each degree of longitude. This is how it reads: "LH420 cleared to Boston via DOGAL 54N20W 54N30W 53N40W

52N50W 51N60W ALLRY, from DOGAL maintain Flight Level three six zero, Mach decimal eight two."

Nowadays, you receive this clearance in written form, but in the 70's, you had to request it over shortwave, which meant in super-poor audio quality.

After that, the pilot and co-pilot always check together whether these points have been entered correctly into the aircraft's navigation system. In Utter's day, they had to be entered manually when the clearance was received. On the day in question, Werner Utter and his crew repeatedly fly over the wrong latitude. Either the men misunderstood the clearance or entered it incorrectly.

This has certainly happened to other colleagues (as mentioned, at that time still no female colleagues) and still happens, very rarely, today. But the fact that it happens to the flight operations manager Werner Utter several times—which means that he flies 60 miles "height"—attracts a lot of ridicule. A new "currency" is born—a degree flown is now called "an Utt" in pilot circles.

Before the welcoming ceremony for the rescued hostages on 18 October 1977, Werner Utter and "Landshut" co-pilot Jürgen Vietor speak briefly. "Mr Vietor, we're making You captain!" Utter whispers to the "Landshut" co-pilot. The seniority principle applies strictly in the company—the most senior employee (at that time not yet the most senior) takes over from a colleague who is leaving. Werner Utter tells Jürgen Vietor that he will suspend the seniority principle in recognition of his service.

The board member is obviously serious about this, because the next day he tells his intention to the Filius couple, two hostages from the "Landshut" mentioned earlier. The couple wants to thank the chief pilot for the rescue. "It was important to him", writes Dietrich Filius in an email to the author, "to let his two thanking visitors know that he wanted to prematurely promote the co-pilot to captain (…)."[1]

It doesn't come to that. At some point, Werner Utter calls the co-pilot of the "Landshut" hijacking flight to him and informs him that he has to renege on his promise "because of objections from colleagues (…) and to avoid setting a precedent."[2]

The pilots' union Cockpit, which then as now has a strong position vis-à-vis the Executive Board, presumably puts up resistance. When pilots go on strike, the airplanes stay on the ground. Nobody can replace the pilots. That builds self-confidence.

The Cockpit chairman at the time Hans-Dieter Gades does not want Jürgen Vietor to be favoured—not even for him, who brought a "Bobby"

---

[1] Dietrich Filius: Mail to the author dated 30 May 2023.
[2] Notes Vietor, p. 13.

with people on board to Mogadishu who have been kidnapped. Perhaps he fears that this could generate envy among pilots. And the beginning of the end of the seniority principle.

Shortly before Christmas 1979, Hans-Dieter Gades approaches Jürgen Vietor on the subject. He wants to talk to him in peace after he had returned from a Lufthansa flight to Johannesburg. This would not happen. Hans-Dieter Gades dies in a swimming accident in South Africa.

Jürgen Vietor, the aviation hero of the "Landshut" hijacking, remains in line behind his more senior colleagues. Almost 13 years were to pass before he willl be appointed captain on 4 September 1990. He remains loyal to the "Bobby" even as captain. The "Bobby" remains the airplane in which his life took a tragic turn.

Gabriele von Lutzau (née Dillmann), the young stewardess who excelled herself during the hijacking flight, also has to experience the ingratitude of her employer Deutsche Lufthansa. She protected and comforted hostages with never-ending energy. She calmed terrorists. She appealed to a German chancellor.

Her superior on the hijacked flight, purserette Hannelore Brauchart (née Piegler), initiates disciplinary proceedings against her at German Lufthansa. The criticism: allegedly improper behaviour. One of the reproaches is that Gaby von Lutzau (née Dillmann) touched passengers contrary to regulations. The young woman also concedes: "I held people in my arms."

Hannelore Brauchardt (formerly Piegler) continues a conflict on the ground during the hijacking flight. From a letter she wrote to the Lufthansa board: "Ms Dillmann has repeatedly discussed political issues (…) and thus exacerbated the already dangerous situation on board." (…) "Ms Dillmann (…) resolutely carried out her solitary decisions and thus contributed to our further endangerment."

Gabriele von Lutzau (née Dillmann) has to answer questions from the head of Lufthansa cabin crew. The stewardess sees it as a tribunal. She feels denounced by her boss on the kidnapping flight. And ungrateful by her employer because she was treated formally. With Gabriele von Lutzau's decision to no longer work in her profession and to leave LH, the proceedings come to nothing.

Later, Hannelore Brauchardt (née Piegler) will use a memoir[3] to repeat the accusations against Gabriele von Lutzau (née Dillmann). An employee of German Lufthansa, who is supposed to read and evaluate the book for the

---

[3] Piegler 1978.

Executive Board, finds the author's accusations inappropriate. The publication has no internal Lufthansa consequences for Hannelore Brauchardt (née Piegler)—she is no longer working for the airline at the time.

Franz Cesarz is one of the few Lufthansa executives who openly empathises with the "Landshut" victims. He knows all about aviation mishaps, because he analyses the causes of near-crashes or crashes of LH fleet. Shortly after the "fire magic" campaign, on 19 October 1977, Franz Cesarz proposes a "German Solidarity Fund" to the Lufthansa Executive Board. Franz Cesarz names the purpose as "the possibility of providing assistance where the solidarity of the whole nation is required (…)." The widow and children of Jürgen Schumann are to receive money from the fund. German Lufthansa itself was to pay 200,000 German mark into the fund, and other companies such as Daimler-Benz and Dresdner Bank were to be recruited.[4]

Such a fund, into which the federal government could also pay, is not being established.

In October 1977, the Lufthansa Executive Board was not only concerned about the company's scratched reputation but its economic success. After the "Landshut" hijacking, booking figures fall for a few weeks, on "peak days" by up to 40 per cent. The US airline Pan Am benefits most from this.

Company managements are advising employees not to fly with German Lufthansa. Many people are now afraid of this themselves. In addition, there are rumours that terrorists are in possession of old Soviet SAM-7 surface-to-air missiles. They could use them to shoot down Lufthansa aircraft in retaliation for the failed hijacking. Such a threat is received by news agencies on 7 November 1977 and an attack announced for 15 November 1977.[5]

The German Press Agency refrains from publishing the news, AFP and Reuters do not. On 13 November, "Bild am Sonntag" and "Welt am Sonntag", Sunday papers of the conservative Springer publishing house, take up the issue. The announced rocket fire does not materialise. However, a launch pad for SAM-7 missiles is later discovered in a forest above Stuttgart Airport, the so-called *Weidacher Höhe*. The *Weidacher Höhe* is one of the flight paths where aircraft are already at low altitude.

German Lufthansa is spending a lot of energy and money on making the "Landshut" hijacking a thing of the past as quickly as possible. The aircraft should soon be flying again in a state as if nothing has ever happened. A team of mechanics makes makeshift repairs to the aircraft in Mogadishu. Because

---

[4] Franz Cesarz: Memo to the Lufthansa Executive Board dated 19 October 1977. 2320/9 Fund idea, in: Lufthansa-Firmenarchiv Frankfurt am Main.

[5] For the following information, see the "Landshut" hijacking file in the Lufthansa company archive in Frankfurt am Main.

the pressure equalisation in the cabin no longer works, the Boeing is flown at low altitude to Lufthansa Technik in Hamburg, with a stopover in Cairo.

Lufthansa technical staff photograph the damage to the aircraft—countless bullet holes inside and out, filthy toilets, blood, alcohol and urine everywhere. The photos will disappear forever into the Lufthansa company archives in Frankfurt am Main. Nobody should see what the kidnapped "Bobby", badly wounded and riddled with bullets, looked like. A wounded, bleeding, half-dead whale that had only just managed to escape its captors.

At a reception to mark the decommissioning of "Bobby" from the Lufthansa fleet in 2016, the mechanics of the time come together once again. They vividly recount the terrible condition in which they found the "Landshut". A task in their professional life that they would never forget.

When the repaired "Landshut" rolls out of a Lufthansa Technik hangar in Hamburg, it looks brand new. A camera team from what was then Südwestfunk (now Südwestrundfunk) on the initiative of former Südwestfunk editor Ebbo Demant is allowed to film the exterior and interior of the aircraft the following year. The film reels that have been preserved to this day show: Lufthansa Technik has done an outstanding job.

On 18 November 1977, the "Landshut" returns to the airline's regular operations with a flight from Hamburg to Barcelona. That does not go unnoticed by passengers. Lufthansa customers complain to the airline that the aircraft is still called "Landshut". Presumably a bad omen after the kidnapping drama.

The surviving co-pilot of the hijacking flight, Jürgen Vietor, is also supposed to go back to work. After only a few weeks' break—much too short, as we know with today's psychological knowledge[6]—he initially accompanies other crews on short-haul flights—in the seat behind the captain, just as "Captain Machmud" as on the hijacking flight did when Jürgen Schumann was still alive. Jürgen Vietor's employer wants to clarify whether Vietor is psychologically stable again.

Everything is going smoothly. On 29 December 1977, Jürgen Vietor boards a Lufthansa aircraft as co-pilot again. For this first flight, he is deliberately only given the aircraft's position on the tarmac, not its designation. He only finds out that it is the repaired "Landshut" when he is standing in front of it. "Sink or swim" is the message from his airline.

The day before, Lufthansa board member Werner Utter tried to erase the hostages' memory of the "Landshut" trauma. He has a letter drafted by a

---

[6] Flight captain Chesley Sullenberger, who successfully ditched an Airbus A320 in New York's Hudson River on 15 January 2009, returned to the cockpit on 1 October 2009.

member of staff.[7] It says that "this year, which I very much hope will now end for you too with peaceful and happy holidays, has imposed a tough test on you and Lufthansa in its last quarter."[8]

Elsewhere, Werner Utter expresses his confidence that "the depressing nature of what you have suffered may fade more and more in your memories in favour of the lasting joy of the happy outcome of this serious experience." In the meantime, with the help of the German government, Lufthansa has reached worldwide agreements and precautions "that additionally secure our flights in an unprecedented way. I wanted to say that to you, who trusted in our services."[9]

A promotional letter for the airline. Not a word of apology. Not a word about compensation.

Their bosses will soon find out what those affected actually think about the supposedly safest airline in the world. When Minister of State Hans-Jürgen Wischnewski invites the former hostages to Bonn on 24 and 25 June 1978, Lufthansa employees also take part. One of them, "FRAU EX 1 F. Schoiber", writes a memo for the Executive Board.[10]

"In all discussions", it states, "it was established, however, that the occupants of the 'Landshut' had expected a 'generous gesture' from LH - irrespective of the material claims". This was particularly true in view of the fact that generous assistance had been provided by many uninvolved third parties, such as an invitation from the state of Carinthia for a free holiday. "Many had expected lump-sum compensation from the federal government in the form of a kind of 'compensation for pain and suffering'."

The author of the memo ponders "whether LH should offer a final generous gesture in the form of a free European flight for all inmates and one relative, even if it is delayed". The German government could pay for the respective shore leave.

F. Schoiber proposes the following language for a proposal by the airline: "LH is also one of the victims in order to achieve a clearer differentiation in the claims and the demarcation from the federal government."

Werner Utter's hope of keeping the people on the hijacked flight as customers of German Lufthansa will only be partially realised. Many of the freed "Landshut" hostages will not board an aircraft again for many years. Some of them for the rest of their lives.

---

[7] See the original in the Lufthansa-Archiv Frankfurt am Main.
[8] Cf. ibid.
[9] Ibid.
[10] F. Schoiber: File note on the meeting of the occupants of the "Landshut" on 24/25 June 1978 in BNJ, in: "Landshut" abduction file, German Lufthansa company archive.

Regardless of voluntary payments, there is a need for clarification between the airline and the freed hostages. The first point of contention is the reimbursement of costs for lost items. The Somalis, to whom the German government handed over the aircraft after the storming, presumably helped themselves to the suitcases. However, some of the hostages' claims appear exorbitantly high. Presumably, they want to get compensation for pain and suffering through the back door.

One hostage demands over 1000 German mark for new "third teeth" after, as he claims, his third teeth fell out of his mouth during the emergency landing in Aden and broke on the ground. Another, very young hostage claims to have lost a ring worth 9000 German mark. A third hostage makes claims of 5700 German mark for lost documents, a tax licence, a bunch of keys, late meetings and additional long-distance calls.[11]

Claims from businesspeople who were allegedly deprived of business, i.e. sales because of the kidnapping are particularly problematic. These freed hostages are demanding reimbursement of the allegedly lost sums.

German Lufthansa only fulfils most of the claims in part. Some of those affected who have registered claims will not receive a penny. The airline claims to have checked the plausibility of claims and decided in favour. Many of those affected react bitterly to what they perceive as the snooty, stingy attitude of an airline whose customers they were.

Deutsche Lufthansa is acting strangely, to say the least, in its efforts to "show its appreciation" to the men of the GSG9, as Franz Cesarz writes in an internal memo dated 1 February 1978. "With the approval of the Lufthansa Executive Board, we have provided the commander of the GSG9 with a copy of the book 'GSG9—Kommando gegen Terrorismus' (GSG9—Commando against Terrorism), which has just been published by Wehr & Wissen, for each member of the GSG9."

Apparently, LH believes that Ulrich Wegener's people are unable to get hold of a copy of the book about their own unit themselves—presumably also free of charge.

---

[11] Letter from the Federal Minister of Transport to Ministerial Dr Jabcke, Federal Chancellery, dated 21 June 1978, regarding the "Landshut" hijacking. Here: Measures taken by DLH for the passengers, pp. 1–4, p. 4, in: BArch B136/12963.

7

Congratulations on Your Rebirth

2 December 1975: Seven South Moluccans[1] hijack a Dutch regional train on its way from Groningen to Zwolle. The train comes to a halt near the village of Wijster. The action is spontaneously flanked by South Moluccans who occupy the Indonesian consulate in Amsterdam on 4 December 1975. Negotiations between the government and the kidnappers lead to a bloodless end to the hostage-taking on 14 December 1975 in Wijster and shortly afterwards in Amsterdam.

A report from the German embassy in The Hague to the Federal Ministry of the Interior[2] reconstructs the beginning, course and end of the double kidnapping. It also deals with the psychological aftercare of the hostages by the Dutch government. The report describes their motive as follows: "Experience with the victims of protracted hostage-takings has taught us that the hostages may suffer after-effects as a result of their harrowing experiences."[3]

Dutch victim awareness is far ahead of its time. Local police authorities and technical staff, including police psychologists, report to the situation centre.

---

[1] In 1950, the South Moluccan people proclaimed their own state. Five years later, it was occupied by Indonesian troops, whereupon many Moluccans fled to the former colonial power, the Netherlands. Like the Palestinians, terrorist acts of violence were intended to pave the way for a state of their own (again).

[2] Report on the events surrounding the train hijacking in Beilen and the attack on the Indonesian Consulate General in Amsterdam Annex to: The Federal Minister of the Interior. Gesch.-Z. ÖS 9—626 535 / 6, Dr Brockmann. Subject: Hostage-taking by Ambonese in the Netherlands on 1 June 1977, in: BArch B 136/15685.

[3] Ibid, p. 29.

Reception centres for family members are set up near the crime scene, where doctors, psychologists and social workers are on duty. This is also where the freed hostages will later receive initial treatment.

Representatives from local social hygiene and social work organisations, the occupational health service and the Dutch railway company set up a working group to provide further support. The municipal health department is responsible for organising help in Amsterdam.

The rapporteur(s) of the German Embassy describe(s) in detail the immediate therapeutic measures in so-called trauma outpatient clinics. These are the first stages of a detailed aftercare concept. Therapists will regularly visit those affected at home for at least twelve months. The aim is to prevent psychological damage as far as possible.

23 May 1977: Nine South Moluccans take 54 passengers hostage on a regional train near De Punt in the Netherlands, a border town between the provinces of Groningen and Drenthe. On the same day, four South Moluccans hijack a primary school in Bovensmilde, ten kilometres away, where five teachers and 100 pupils are staying.

The schoolchildren are released four days later due to an outbreak of an epidemic. On 11 June, the police storm both kidnapping locations. The teachers are freed unharmed, and the terrorists are captured. Six of the nine South Moluccans and two hostages die during the rescue operation on the train. The other terrorists are arrested.

A report by the German ambassador in The Hague is received by the Foreign Office on 16 June 1977.[4] It describes the Dutch government's hard line. "The terrorists remained unyielding; the government therefore had no choice but to use force." The storming of the train by marines is bloody.

A train is a difficult object to access and one that terrorists choose with care. The rescue operation at the school was much easier. "The operation, in which no one was injured, took less than ten minutes."[5]

It is interesting to note the mental link that the authors of the report make to RAF terrorism in West Germany. Before the hostage-takings, many Dutch people had pointed a disdainful finger at West Germany. In their view, the German government had reacted too nervously to acts of terrorism by the Baader-Meinhof group. The people had shown themselves to be indifferent.

After the kidnapping dramas of 1975 and 1977, the Dutch psychotherapist Jan Bastiaans took care of the freed hostages. In 1975, he offered counselling to the 100 schoolchildren who were released early and their parents.

---

[4] Report of the Embassy The Hague of 16 June 1977 concerning the end of the hostage drama in North Holland, in: BArch B 136/16489.
[5] Ibid, p. 3.

The parents were told what the children would go through mentally in the coming weeks and months. On their own initiative, the parents organised neighbourhood help for the children and themselves.

In 1977, when the hostages were still on the hijacked train, Jan Bastiaans predicted psychological damage to the victims. The government in The Hague was receptive to his predictions. The State Secretary of the Ministry of Public Health set up a working group to write a kind of script for the care of the freed hostages.

Jan Bastians had a special ward set up for the victims in the Academic Hospital of Groningen, a normal hospital. Quite deliberately not in a psychiatric hospital, as his German colleague Andreas Ploeger would do after the "Landshut" abduction. Bastians knows that in his day, psychiatric wards were seen as a place for the insane.

In July 1977, a few months before the "Landshut" kidnapping, psychiatrists, including Jan Bastiaans, criminologists and senior police officers meet for a conference in Evian, Switzerland. They discussed defence strategies and defence mechanisms that people in hostage situations develop. And what a survived hostage situation does to them. The topic has finally arrived in Europe from the USA.

Presumably not yet in the Federal Republic of Germany. The Federal Foreign Office forwards the German embassy's report on the hostage-taking in 1977 to the Federal Chancellery, which receives it on 11 October, in the middle of the German Autumn. Chancellor Helmut Schmidt's personal advisor, Jochen Busse, receives the report, as does—probably on Busse's initiative—the head of the Federal Chancellery, Manfred Schüler. It is not documented whether Chancellor Helmut Schmidt also gets it or at least a summary of it.

There is historical evidence that the Federal Chancellor is aware of his Dutch neighbour's successful ambulance concept. In a telephone conversation with Dutch Prime Minister Den Uyl on 23 September 1977, the Federal Chancellor praises the concept, saying that the German government was "benefiting from the behaviour of the Dutch government during the hostage-taking in Bovensmilde and Assen and trying to do the same as the Dutch in terms of psychological control of this case."[6]

It is quite possible that Helmut Schmidt is reading the words from a prepared speech slip. None of this will be implemented by the federal government he leads.

---

[6] Note on the telephone conversation between the Federal Chancellor and the Dutch Prime Minister Den Uyl on 23 September 1977 of the same day, in: OTB 13–211 20 (2) Additional file OTB vol. 4, p. 16X (not legible).

You can't blame him for that. The man leads the country through its most serious crisis to date. Others could and should think of that the Dutch are setting an example in this area. But there is no one in Bonn politics far and wide. At Frankfurt am Main Airport, where the freed hostages from Mogadishu return, there is no trauma centre waiting for them. Even less thought is given to aftercare for the important months ahead.

> *"congratulations on your rebirth a quick forgetting and a healthy life wishes heidi morinez née schwarz"*[7]
>
> *"Best wishes for your birthday (text on the front of the greetings card) My heartfelt congratulations on the rebirth of your daughter in all friendship Your Otto Fehmke (text on the back of the greetings card)"*[8]
>
> *"Dear Mr Chancellor, following the successful rescue of the Lufthansa aircraft in Mogadishu, I would like to take this opportunity to express my heartfelt thanks to you. My wife and son have now arrived safely in Berlin and are trying to recover from the difficult days. Unfortunately, however, we have received a phone call with a death threat, which is putting a further strain on their mental state."*[9]
>
> *"Dear Mr Federal Chancellor! I would like to warmly congratulate you on your decision in the hijacking cases. Never before have I listened to or watched all the news programmes on radio and television as regularly as I did during the days of the hijacking. But despite all the joy about the happy outcome of the hijacking, I am disappointed. (...) For Mr Schleyer, 3 minutes of silence were even ordered on Tuesday, 25 October 77. There was not even a "public" minute's silence for Captain Schumann. Isn't Mr Schumann worth just as much as Mr Schleyer (...)?"*[10]

Of course, at the airport and in the home village, in the hometown, the joy at the return of the people is enormous. The freed hostages are met by a sea of flowers and congratulatory cards. To overjoyed relatives and friends. The head of the village, mayor or mayoress organises a reception, which is also attended by complete strangers out of genuine sympathy or curiosity.

The joy doesn't last long. Neither the returnees nor their relatives and friends, colleagues and bosses are prepared for the situation. Everyone means well for the women and men, girls and boys who have narrowly escaped

---

[7] Telegram to the family of the freed "Landshut" hostage Beate Keller (née Zerbst). Private property Beate Keller.
[8] Congratulations card privately owned by Beate Keller (Zerbst).
[9] Letter from Dieter Röhll to the Federal Chancellor dated 26 October 1977, in: BArch B136/31588.
[10] Letter from Claudia Böhl, 15 years old, dated 27 October 1977 to the Federal Chancellery, in: BArch B 106/103790.

death. But well-intentioned does not automatically mean well done. They cannot be blamed for this either.

What makes it even more difficult is that people react very differently to trauma. And very different things help them to cope. Hostages like Beate Keller (née Zerbst) benefit from going back to work after two weeks. They get their daily rhythm back. Others, like the freed hostage Matthias Rath, fail at this. He also goes back to the office to read the newspaper. His ability to work seems to have gone.

Awareness of mental suffering was well developed in the USA at the end of the 1970s. US scientists were the first to diagnose post-traumatic stress syndrome, as it would later be called. There and in other Western countries, word quickly spread in scientific and medical circles.

Not in the Federal Republic of Germany. Here, post-traumatic stress disorder makes it into the "red book", but GPs are not trained to react appropriately to their patients' emotional upheavals. Rescued "Landshut" hostages are complimented in the surgeries on how splendid they look despite the days of exertion. Many doctors measure their blood pressure, which is fine, prescribe a sleeping pill and issue a sick note for a fortnight.

In the Federal Republic of Germany, a wounded soul traditionally has a hard time. After losing two wars, West Germans don't have it so good with the psyche. Moving on after the catastrophe means moving forward. The West Germans put all their energy into work. Into rebuilding the country. They become hard-working creators of a better future. Some things are neglected, such as their own soul.

This harshness towards oneself has a social price, for example in dealing with those who have suffered mental damage. Historian Svenja Göltermann has evaluated medical records of those returning from war. Those affected felt perpetually tired and listless, unable to find their way back into civilian life. Their doctors had no prescription for this despondency. Physically, the patients appeared healthy. The medical profession does not see that her soul is suffering. Or it is suppressed.[11]

The returnees from the war already have an experience that the freed "Landshut" hostages will share decades later: They are accused of faking mental illness out of laziness. To avoid work. To get an early, undeserved pension. Only those who have lost their minds need a psychotherapist, are ready for the "loony bin".

Diana Müll, a former "Landshut" hostage, hides her mental illness from her own family. She is ashamed of her depression. Diana Müll takes a

---

[11] Cf. Göltermann 2009.

part-time job at a nightclub to start psychotherapy without her parents' knowledge. At some point, she no longer has the strength for the round-the-clock double burden. She has to stop her therapy due to a lack of funds.

The traumatisation continues unintentionally in the partnership, in the family and among friends. They can no longer get along with each other. Rhett Waida's family goes on holiday, but there is no sign of relaxation—on the contrary. The Waidas spend their time off work thinking about the kidnapping from morning till night. They go home early, back to the pub. There, the day has a fixed structure. There they are reasonably distracted from work and from their guests.

Nonetheless, the topic sticks in the craw. In his doctoral thesis, a doctoral student of psychotherapist Andreas Ploeger quotes sentences that freed "Landshut" hostages would have been told after their return. One of those affected is said, "You could have taken the weapon and been like Rambo, right?"[12]

Envy arises. "You just want a cheap holiday in the Baltic Sea, you don't want to pay for it", is what another victim has to listen to.[13] When the couple Edelgard and Everhard Wolff buys a new car sometime after the "Landshut" drama, neighbours rumour that the federal government had certainly paid for it.

Partners show their true colours. Even before Jutta Knauff (née Brod) gets home, her husband, branch manager of the local savings bank, has sold his wife's drama to the newspaper "Münchner Abendzeitung". Jutta Knauff only has to sign the contract.

In a television interview, with his wife and son sitting wordlessly next to him, the husband boasts that he has negotiated with several newspapers. The highest offer of 10,000 German mark tipped the scales in favour of the "Abendzeitung".

Decades later, Jutta Knauf (née Brod) will not only speak badly about the interview project. It was an opportunity for her to express herself. To share what she had experienced with someone. However, her trust in her enterprising husband is gone. Jutta Knauff (née Brod) divorces soon after the abduction, which is not accepted in the Hessian province at the end of the 1970s. Her former circle of friends and acquaintances disown the renegade.

It is the second expulsion from her home in Jutta Knauff's life. After the war, she was expelled along with her family from the eastern territories of Germany. During the flight, Jutta Knauff's grandmother was shot dead by a

---

[12] Ibid.
[13] Cf. Hagenkötter 1993, p. 84.

bullet. In her old age, the images of the expulsion and the hijacking haunt her, as she repeatedly reports in conversations with the author.

Many of those affected do the same to Jutta Knauff (née Brod) sooner or later and leave their girlfriend or husband. The young woman whose husband drank her water will not remain in the shared household for another year. Another woman, whose husband reached for her plate, feels the same deep disappointment. Ultimately, at her advanced age, she shies away from a new beginning.

In October 1977, Simone Regelmann (née Liedtke) goes on holiday to Mallorca, in El Arenal. She is sixteen and a half. An intelligent, beautiful girl who is one of the best young swimmers in Germany. She excels in the strokes and backstroke, as her future husband will tell the author Ralph Regelmann.

Simone Regelmann (née Liedtke) takes part in the beauty contest at the "Graf Zeppelin" discotheque. She also just manages to catch the plane back to Frankfurt am Main with great holiday memories in her head.

Then the shock. The days of agony. Simone Regelmann (née Liedtke) witnesses the murder of Captain Jürgen Schumann at close quarters. The captain's blood splatters on her dress. In the "Landshut", the young woman's heart and soul are damaged.

Simone's parents are innkeepers who run the "Löwenbräu-Quelle" in a neighbourhood of Dortmund. They understandably have neither the energy nor the knowledge to help their distraught daughter. Let alone seek help themselves as distressed relatives.

After her liberation in Mogadishu, Simone Regelmann (née Liedtke), as her future husband Ralph Regelmann will tell the author, initially seems to be in high spirits. With more energy than ever. At some point, this energy fades. Simone withdraws completely and no longer wants to see anyone.

At school, her classmates empathise with Simone's suffering, but not her teachers. "Don't make such a fuss!" is the recurring message when the girl is once again unable to concentrate. Simone Regelmann (née Liedtke) drops out of school and starts an apprenticeship as a travel agent. She quits it after a short time.

Her parents employ her as a waitress in the pub. They give her a fixed daily rhythm, provide her with social contacts. And earn good money with her. The "Löwenbräu-Quelle" is a men's pub. The guests enjoy the sight of the beautiful woman. Sometimes for a beer, sometimes for a schnapps, so that Simone can sit at their table. "Her parents abused Simone", her future husband Ralph Regelmann would say decades later.[14]

---

[14] Conversation with the author.

What nobody knows: After her abduction and liberation, Simone Regelmann (née Liedtke) is plagued by the fear of dying of thirst. Apparently, she kept coming up short in the "Landshut" hostages' struggle for water. Soon Simone no longer drinks water, but alcohol.

Simone Regelmann (née Liedke) spent the last wonderful days of her life, full of light-heartedness and Mediterranean sunshine, on the island of Mallorca. The desire to return to this time before the abduction will become a mania. She travels there frequently and wins the title of "Miss Mallorca" eleven times by 1987. Always at the "Graf Zeppelin" disco in El Arenal.

Simone Regelmann (née Liedtke) doesn't look after her health and must pay for it with her life early on. She dies on 19 August 2020. "Unforgotten! (Mogadishu 1977)" is written at the top of her obituary. Ralph Regelmann also refers to the event in his thank-you card after Simone's funeral: "Time does not heal all wounds, it only teaches us to live with the incomprehensible."

8

Guinea Pig

The German government simply sends the freed, traumatised "Landshut" hostages home. This therapeutic vacuum is recognised by the ambitious psychotherapist Andreas Ploeger and the equally ambitious psychologist Wolfgang Salewski. Both find the men and women from the "Landshut" scientifically fascinating. The hostages were exposed to an existential borderline experience. What has it done with them?

It starts with the psychologist Wolfgang Salewski, who advised the German government during the "Landshut" abduction and accompanied Minister of State Hans-Jürgen Wischnewski to Mogadishu. He writes to those affected on the letterhead of the "Institute for Conflict Research and Crisis Counselling", which he founded. In a letter to the freed hostages Edelgard and Everhard Wolf, he states that "my negotiations with the hijackers of the 'Landshut' were somewhat successful, mainly because our institute has been conducting research in the field of terrorism and hostage-taking for several years."[1]

That seems exaggerated. Minister of State Hans-Jürgen Wischnewski found Wolfgang Salewski's involvement helpful, as he will assure after the German autumn. Salewski stalled the completely exhausted, no longer suspicious "Captain Machmud" until the plane was stormed.

Wolfgang Salewski asks Mr and Mrs Wolff, among others, for an interview "exclusively for scientific purposes". It is intended to supplement and expand the Institute's research work. The Wolffs are not even asked for their consent.

---

[1] Letter from Wolfgang Salewski to Everhard Wolff, Kempen, dated 13 January 1978, in: Persönlicher Nachlass Edelgard und Everhard Wolff.

Wolfgang Salewski announces that he or one of his employees will approach them to arrange an interview.

Just five days later, a ministerial director of the Federal Minister of the Interior, Werner Smoydzin, writes "to the crew members and passengers of LH 181 'Landshut'".[2] He "politely" asks them to answer Prof. Dr. med. Dipl. Psych. Andreas Ploeger from the Faculty of Medicine at the Rheinisch-Westfälische Technische Hochschule Aachen "a few questions relating to the behaviour of individuals during the hijacking of LH 181 'Landshut'".[3] The Ministerial Director also askes "for your understanding if the questioning reminds you once again of the terrible events that you had to witness".[4]

Newly traumatised people have always been of scientific interest to the neurologist. In 1963, Andreas Ploeger visited the miners of Lengede in hospital, who were declared dead after a mining accident, before the search continued and brought the trapped people up. Andreas Ploeger later interviewed survivors of severe earthquakes in all parts of the world.

As he once put it himself,[5] the psychotherapist is interested in researching forms of interpersonal terror. In the longer term, it should provide an insight "into the way in which people react to threats and seek to process them, threatening the existential foundations of their humanity."[6]

Andreas Ploeger pursues his personal scientific interest. He spent between two and six hours interviewing a total of 46 freed "Landshut" hostages (as of June 1978), bringing back fresh memories of the terrible days. The interviews are used by Research associates for his own studies and those of his colleagues. The focus is always on post-traumatic stress syndrome in kidnap victims.

Andreas Ploeger has commissioned at least one academic doctoral thesis on the results. He will give lectures in specialist circles on the question of how many partnerships and marriages were broken up as a result of the "Landshut" abduction.

A letter from Professor Andreas Ploeger dated 20 March[7] to the Wolff couple shows that he had asked them and also visited them. In the letter, he thanks them for their "detailed reports on your experiences and the difficulties of coming to terms with them (…). Your information was of particular value

---

[2] Letter from Werner Smoydzin dated 18 January 1978 to Edelgard and Everhard Wolff. Subject: Investigation into the behaviour of people during and after extreme emotional stress, in: Estate of Edelgard Wolff.
[3] Ibid.
[4] Ibid.
[5] Cf. Ploeger & Schmitt 1982, p. 182.
[6] Ibid.
[7] Letter from Professor Andreas Ploeger to Mr Eberhard and Mrs Edelgard Wolff dated 20 March 1978, in: ibid.

to our enquiry (...)." In the days that followed, the professor sent further questions to Edelgard and Everhard Wolff by letter, which both answered.

After interviews with Edelgard Wolff in February and September 1978, Ploeger's psychological findings were as follows: "Significant psychopathological traumatisation as a result of the stress she experienced, with phobic reactions, anxiety, sleep disorders and startle reactions."[8]

Everhard Wolff obviously suffers even more from what he had experienced. The findings report by Andreas Ploeger states "Psychopathological: tendency to depressive moods with difficulty in processing the experience, especially the traumatisation, significant slowing down of all mental functional processes, irritability with phobic and anxiety reactions on the occasion of certain situational stresses that mobilise the traumatising contents of the experience."[9]

Nine months after the stressful event, Andreas Ploeger proposes psychotherapy services for those affected to the Federal Ministry of Labour and Social Affairs. Andreas Ploeger tells the freed "Landshut" hostages that it took him some effort to be entrusted with this task. This seems credible given the low awareness of mental illness at the time.

From today's perspective, on the other hand, the argumentation with which he pandered to the officials of the Federal Ministry of Labour and Social Affairs reads fatally. As a rule, it is not to be assumed "that psychological disorders remain in the long term (...)".[10]

Andreas Ploeger also argues that "it is to be warned against discussing the question of granting a pension with those affected (...)."[11] In other words: Pay for my services once, then the people concerned won't be on your back in the future!

At the start of therapy, the kidnapping was more than a year ago. Now only a dozen of the freed "Landshut" hostages accept the offer. Andreas Ploeger forms two groups, each of which comes to his clinic in Aachen for five days and a few months later to a spa clinic in the Baltic resort of Damp 2000.

Edelgard and Everhard Wolff say yes together—an exception to the rule. Of the married couples in the "Landshut", almost only the women take part. They get involved in the re-enactment of the stressful events, while the men dismiss it as a "soul striptease".

---

[8] Andreas Ploeger's letter to the Düsseldorf Pension Office - Medical Service - dated 30 November 1978: Psychological findings on Ms Edelgard Wolff (...), in: BArch B149/99967.
[9] Ibid.
[10] Note on a discussion on the implementation of the Act on Compensation for Victims of Violent Crime (OEG), here: Care for the victims of the hijacking of the Lufthansa aircraft "Landshut", in: BArch B136/12963.
[11] Ibid.

The different ways of dealing with the trauma will alienate other spouses from each other. In the Coldewey family, for example, the wife travelled there, and the husband stayed at home. The couple will later also become estranged over their different approaches to conflict resolution and end up getting divorced.

Andreas Ploeger informs the Wolff couple at the beginning of November 1978 that the psychotherapeutic measure will take place in Aachen from 5 to 13 December.[12] Beforehand, their general practitioners have to justify to the local pension office why such a therapeutic measure is necessary—the prerequisite for the costs to be covered by the pension office.

The procedure may be understandable from the point of view of the pension office, i.e. the state. It is about benefits for private individuals from public funds. For the freed "Landshut" hostages and other groups of people suffering from trauma, it means running the gauntlet, as will be discussed later.

In Aachen, the ordeal follows the ordeal. Andreas Ploeger puts the traumatised people in quarantine. During the entire stay, any contact with relatives or friends is forbidden.

It just so happens that people with disabilities live on the same floor as Ploeger's clients. In the 1970s, the topic of disability had not yet reached the centre of society. Non-disabled people often looked away in shame when they saw people in wheelchairs. In turn, many disabled people and their relatives felt socially excluded.

Some of the freed "Landshut" hostages are burdened by the sight of neighbours with disabilities. They feel that they have already been put under maximum strain by the trauma of the kidnapping itself. They threaten to leave if they are not allowed to move. Andreas Ploeger honours their request.

The psychotherapist plays impromptu games with the participants. They are asked to relive the humiliations they experienced on the hijacking flight. A pretend "Captain Machmud" beats a "hostage" once again or announces that they will be shot the next morning.

"We were guinea pigs", Gabriele von Lutzau would later say. In other words, the scientist is testing a method for its effect. He doesn't seem to realise that he is doing more harm than good for some people.

Andreas Ploeger also remains unimpressed by the side effects of the therapy. One patient stands out because "she doesn't attend her treatments regularly—she lies in her room in the morning (…). The room is almost

---

[12] Cf. letter from Andreas Ploeger to Mr Everhard and Mrs Edelgard Wolff dated 2 November 1978, in: Nachlass Edelgard und Everhard Wolff.

trashed."[13] The clinic staff find the woman disorientated during a room inspection.

Another patient "often sleeps all morning because she has been partying all night. Despite repeated reminders and intensive discussions, she could not be persuaded to comply with the house rules."[14]

After the first week of therapy in Aachen, Andreas Ploeger reports on his clients to the relevant pension office. In Edelgard Wolff's case, an extremely profound processing of her experiences came to light, which "caused her to react in a lively emotional-affective manner and at the same time revealed an intensive effort to overcome the traumatising experiences".[15]

The diagnosis for Everhard Wolff is less favourable. Andreas Ploeger diagnoses him with an "organic cerebral syndrome unrelated to the abduction", which is characterised by a "tendency to poor memory and an urge to speak, as well as a general slowing down of thinking and a possible onset of dementia".[16]

The Wolffs also travel to the second therapeutic measure from 22 to 30 May 1979 in Damp 2000. Professor Andreas Ploeger does not want to treat his clients to a holiday but wants to bring the project to a successful conclusion. This time, even family members are allowed to join them.

A particular challenge for the Berlin Senate Administration is a request from a victim to take his nine-year-old son to Andreas Ploeger's therapy days. The parents have been on holiday alone in Mallorca and wanted to return to Germany on the "Landshut". The son was staying with his grandparents at the time. During the "Landshut" abduction days, he was very afraid for his parents, a fear that still haunts him. He seems unfocused and distraught.

The Berlin Senate Administration is struggling with the question of whether the boy, as a non-hostage, can come with them for free. The Senate passes the issue on to the Federal Ministry of Labour and Social Affairs. Someone there takes heart and comes up with a clever reason for his okay. The success of the father's cure was not guaranteed without the son's participation. The son was needed as his father's "permanent companion".[17]

---

[13] Patient protocol of the Ostseeklinik Damp, 2335 Damp 2000, in: BArch B 149/99967.
[14] Ibid.
[15] Andreas Ploeger's letter to the Düsseldorf Pension Office—Medical Service—dated 18 December 1978, medical report following psychotherapeutic treatment between 5 and 13 December 1978 in Aachen, in: BArch 149/99967.
[16] Ibid.
[17] Cf. minutes of a meeting at the Berlin State Welfare Office at the request of the Federal Ministry of Labour and Social Affairs on 8 May 1978 concerning: Implementation of the OEG, here: Care for the victims of the hijacking of the Lufthansa aircraft "Landshut", in: BArch 149/99968, p. 3.

Things are not running smoothly in the Baltic seaside resort of Damp 2000 either. A couple and their two children have to stay in a one-bedroom flat for several days because the clinic is fully booked. Presumably a massive reduction in the success of the therapy.

Andreas Ploeger and his team dictate only successes in their medical findings and final reports. The participants always feel better after two five-day "cures". This is important for the pension offices and health insurance companies, so that they are sticking with follow-up therapy. Besides, it's always nice to give yourself a good report card.

Five years after the "Landshut" kidnapping, Jutta Duhm-Heitzmann takes stock of the hostages' experiences after their liberation in "Die Zeit". She wants to know how they are doing today.[18]

The journalist writes about people who can no longer stand closed rooms, avoid lifts or are afraid of Arab-looking people. "And the broken marriages?" Jutta Duhm-Heitzmann asks rhetorical questions, (such as) "The fear of going to work alone? The shy isolation? The outbursts of hatred? The excessive smoking? Even today, five years later, some of them are still taking psychotropic drugs."

Coincidentally, the article is published just over a month after the Social Democrat Federal Chancellor Helmut Schmidt was ousted by a constructive vote of no confidence in the German Bundestag and Helmut Kohl, a member of the Christian Democrat Party, was elected as his successor. The generation of decision-makers in the German Autumn, whose "Mogadishu" narrative only knows heroes, had to take their political hats off.

The historian Golo Mann is to be proved right with a prophecy that he wrote to the Romance philologist Hans-Martin Gauger in a letter dated 5 April 1980, seven months before the federal election: "If there is no change (in the office of the Federal Chancellor from Helmut Schmidt to Franz-Josef Strauß, note M. R.), and I don't think it will come to that, then there will be a crisis within two years, be it within the SPD, be it between the SPD and the FDP, be it between Helmut Schmidt and the entire SPD. That is my prophecy, although I have always been careful not to make any prophecies."[19]

Helmut Schmid's deselection is more than the loss of office for one individual. The generation of decision-makers in the German Autumn, whose "Mogadishu" narrative only knows heroes, had to resign politically. They were expelled from the government by members of the subsequent, "skeptical generation".

---

[18] Jutta Duhm-Heitzmann: What they are left with is fear, in: Die Zeit v. 05 November 1982.
[19] Letter from Golo Mann to Hans-Martin Gauger, 5 April 1980, in: Lahme/Lüssi 2006, p. 262.

Decades later, the youngest crew member Gabriele von Lutzau (née Dillmann) would say that the hijacking of the "Landshut" had a "terrible impact" on her life. All those affected, including the wife and children of the murdered captain Jürgen Schumann, had to or have to find an individual way to live with the trauma.

Monika Schumann, widow of the murdered "Landshut" captain, chooses a different path from most relatives who have lost a loved one to the RAF. On the anniversaries of the crimes, Monika Schumann visits talk shows on television. Together with camera teams, she meets Barry Davies, one of the two British soldiers in Operation Fire Magic, the freed hostage Birgit Paul (formerly Pittelkow) and the only survivor of the kidnapping commando, Souhaila Andrawes.

Monika Schumann. A woman who did not retreat from the public eye with her fate and that of her two children but instead fought for decades for the memory of her husband, who was the only one not to return from the kidnapping flight. Today, schools, a Lufthansa and a Bundeswehr institution, as well as a road at the capital city airport BER, are named after Jürgen Schumann.[20]

---

[20] Cf. e.g. Warncke 2021.

9

A Red Bicycle from Mr Federal Chancellor

"When you stand before me and look at me, what do you know of the pain that is within me and what do I know of yours? And even if I were to fall down before you and weep and tell you, what would you know of me that you do not know of hell? When someone tells you that hell is hot and dreadful, you know nothing of it. For that reason alone we should stand before one another with as much reverence and love as we do before the entrance to hell."
From a Letter by Franz Kafka to Oskar Pollak, 8 November 1903[1]

Ernst K. H. Schmidt from Hamburg is also relieved about the happy liberation of the "Landshut" hostages. "Dear Chancellor", he types into his typewriter on 18 October 1977, "please allow me to send you—without further comment—a cheque for 1,000 German mark for your free disposal." The donor goes on to inform his namesake that he was born in 1909 and had already crossed both polar circles at the age of 27.

An employee of the Federal Chancellor notes on the letter the idea of giving the money to Monika Schumann and her children. "Purpose is good, amount too little", Helmut Schmidt writes underneath and asks for "another suggestion".

At the beginning of November 1977, a purpose is found for the 1,000 German mark. Eight girls and boys from the abducted "Landshut", aged

---

[1] Quoted by former "Landshut" hostage Gaby Coldewey in an email to the author on 18 October 2012.

between six and 14, are to receive a bicycle from the Federal Chancellor and three-year-old Steffen Waida a Kettcar. A tenth child, who lives in the USA, will receive nothing because of the high transport costs.

An employee of the Federal Chancellery sets off to buy the bikes and the Kettcar. To do so, he visits a Kaufhof shop in Bonn. Despite a discount from the department stores' management, he doesn't quite make the donation. Kaufhof charges him 1268 German mark. The Federal Chancellery collects the 268 German mark from the taxpayer.

Gaby Coldewey—the hostage with the rag doll—is one of the lucky ones. Like all the girls and boys, she receives the bike along with a letter personally signed by Federal Chancellor Helmut Schmidt.

"Dear Gaby, obviously out of joy at the successful rescue operation at Mogadishu airport, a fellow citizen has sent me a cheque. The value of the cheque is enough to bring a little joy to the children who were on the hijacked Lufthansa plane. So a parcel will also be sent to you in the next few days, the contents of which I hope you will enjoy and which should be a small 'consolation' for the terrible days on the plane. Yours sincerely, Helmut Schmidt."[2]

Gaby is surprised, but not pleased. "The 'parcel' was huge and contained a red bike. Someone hadn't thought it through. Of course, when you're almost nine years old, you have one and the second one just stands around. My old one simply rode better and was a nice blue colour. I've never liked red. With so few children, maybe you could have asked the parents beforehand."[3]

One did not. And presumably didn't pay for the goods straight away either. Four weeks after the invoice was issued, the Kaufhof branch wrote to the Federal Chancellery, "It can certainly happen that you overlook paying an invoice. (…) We are convinced that you will make up for the omission (…)." On 22 November 1977, an employee of the Federal Chancellery instructs the amount as noted on the Kaufhof payment reminder.

Money now also plays a role in other contexts. After the end of the German Autumn, the accounts are settled. The Geneva lawyer Denis Payot, mediator between the kidnappers of Hanns Martin Schleyer and the German government, sends "Monsieur Helmut Schmidt" his final invoice dated 28 November 1977.[4] This includes the fees for the staff in his office. The total amount was 473,752.25 Swiss francs. Denis Payot had already received 180,000 Swiss francs as an advance payment. This means that 293,752.25

---

[2] Letter from Federal Chancellor Helmut Schmidt to Gaby Coldewey dated 28 October 1977, privately owned by Gaby Coldewey.
[3] Letter from Gaby Coldewey dated 30 July 2012 to the author.
[4] AdsD, 1/HSAA010019.

Swiss francs (approximately 608,000 German mark at the time) are still outstanding. The amount will not be paid from the budget of the Federal Chancellery, but from that of the Federal Ministry of the Interior.

In December 1977, the same ministry endeavours to ensure that the men of the GSG9 receive their overtime pay ("overtime compensation") before Christmas. Which GSG9 member was in Ankara, which in Mogadishu? And for how long in each case? A list entitled "Secondment/secondment of the GSG9 to the BKA and payment of overtime compensation by the BKA"[5] lists the exact overtime hours worked.

The principle of equal treatment also applies here—as with the award of the Order of Merit of the Federal Republic of Germany. Everyone is paid as if they had been part of the storming of the machine. A noble solution—and the most expensive.

Money is now also at stake for the freed hostages. In 1976, the German government introduced a "Victims' Compensation Act" for people who have been victims of acts of violence, both private and political. This law was first referred to by German Lufthansa and later by the German government.

On the one hand, the law represents socio-political progress in terms of how victims are treated. For the first time in its history, the West German state is granting benefits to people who have suffered psychological or physical injury through no fault of their own. It does not pay much, but it does pay. In most cases for a limited time, but at least for that time. An indirect admission that there are not only heroes in the land of the economic miracle, but also victims.

On the other hand, the path to recognition is quite German. Those affected have to submit an application, i.e. take the initiative themselves. Many former hostages from the "Landshut" only feel able to do so much later. By then, the application deadlines have passed.

The state pension offices responsible for the application have no experience with the OEG. When "Landshut" hostages want to submit applications, many places do not have forms. And if they do, they do not provide for the case of political kidnapping. "Are you related to the perpetrator by blood or marriage?" is a stereotypical question.

Medical examinations are seen as humiliating. The freed "Landshut" hostage Jutta Knauff (née Brod) has to walk on a white line in front of the public health officer. He wants to determine whether she can walk in a straight line. Jutta Knauff sees this as running the gauntlet.

---

[5] BArch B106/373626.

The "Landshut" hijacking in the German autumn is gradually occupying not only the Federal Government, German Lufthansa and pension offices throughout the country, but also the lawyers of those affected and the courts.

Of course, no amount of money in the world can heal the injustice suffered—in this case the mental torture of the hijacking flight. But many hostages want a gesture of recognition from German Lufthansa or "the state"—in this case in marks.

There is no law or regulation to decide on such recognition. Over time, most of the enquiries from those affected or their lawyers end up on the desk of Minister of State Hans-Jürgen Wischnewski. If anyone can help us, the common hope is that it will be him!

The Minister of State may personally understand the sometimes understandable, sometimes bizarre requests of former hostages—but he does not have his own coffers. He does what is in his limited power: He uses his good name for the concerned. He asks the authorities for re-examinations or goodwill solutions. A favourable decision due to the seriousness of the case. Also because of the historically unique occasion—hopefully it will remain a one-time thing.

The fact that the German government has not set up a central working group—possibly together with Lufthansa—after "Mogadishu" is now coming back to haunt it. Authorities and airlines interpret the regulations individually. Very often to the detriment of those affected.

Reimbursements are made, but not enough from the point of view of those affected. At the end of January 1978, "CGN LS 1" Klein lists the cash payments made to the Executive Board of German Lufthansa.[6] According to this list, 70 claims totalling 151,302 Deutsche Mark had been made by the former hostages. The airline paid 90,191 German mark to 68 passengers, an average of 1,288 German mark per person. The mentioned hostage, who claimed 48,000 German mark for lost jewellery, received 10,000 German mark.

The German government and Lufthansa always react with alarm when freed hostages seek publicity. Every mention of the subject in the media is closely monitored by Bonn politicians. Dorothea Konwiarz was on board the hijacked "Landshut". A TV magazine devotes an article to the set designer of Wim Thoelke's ZDF programme "The Grand Prix."[7] In these as in other "public" cases, the German government exerts pressure on the pension offices to ensure that the proceedings are processed quickly.

---

[6] Note from CGN LS1 to FRA VS dated 22 January 1978, subject: LH 181/13 October 1977, pp. 1–2, in: Lufthansa-Archiv Frankfurt am Main.
[7] TV Hören und Sehen No. 52 of 30 December 1978, in: BArch 149/99968.

It also does this with freed hostages who turn to SPD member of parliament Gert Weisskirchen (SPD) shortly before Christmas 1977. The comrade formulates a question to the German government asking whether Helmut Schmidt's cabinet "has so far failed to offer psychotherapeutic counselling to the hostage victims of the Lufthansa plane 'Landshut' hijacked to Mogadishu after their release, and if so, what are the reasons for this?"[8]

A Swiss journalist had already asked such a question at the first press conference of the federal government after the return of the hostages. "The Swiss radio journalist Steiner was referred to LH (Lufthansa, editor's note) by the Federal Press Office, the Ministry of the Interior and the Ministry of Transport when he asked whether the freed hostages would receive psychological care along the lines of the Dutch model (months of psychological monitoring and care)."[9]

The enquiry by MP Weisskirchen takes the usual official route. The responsible Ministerial Director in the Federal Ministry of Labour and Social Affairs, Leonhard Trometer, urges German Lufthansa to inform the freed hostages about "medical treatment claims under the Act on Compensation for Victims of Violent Crimes (OEG) of 11 May 1976 (Federal Law Gazette I p. 1181)".[10] With this in mind, the Ministerial Director also appeals to the Ministers and Senators for Labour and Social Affairs of the federal states.

The State Secretary in the Federal Ministry of Labour and Social Affairs, Anke Fuchs, replies to Gert Weisskirchen MP on 19 January. "German Lufthansa AG" (…), it says, "has informed all passengers of the Lufthansa aircraft 'Landshut' (…) that they are entitled to medical treatment—including, of course, psychotherapeutic treatment—for all health problems caused by the hijacking and related events in accordance with the Act on Compensation for Victims of Violent Crimes (OEG)."[11]

We have done nothing wrong, is the tenor of the letter. As officials in Bonn's ministries always emphasise. Anyone who has a heart for those affected, like Ministerial Director Leonhard Trometer, a recognised man in his field, would not get far. Like Minister of State Hans-Jürgen Wischnewski, he too can do no more than appeal, urge and invite people to "round tables". He would be the right mediator between politicians and hostages because of

---

[8] BArch B136/12963.
[9] Internal memo from Lufthansa spokesman Franz Cesarz to Dr Cullmann (Chairman of the LH Executive Board, note M. R.) dated 19.10.77. Subject: Letter from the Federal Minister of Transport dated 17.10.1977, p. 5, in: Archiv German Lufthansa Frankfurt am Main.
[10] BArch B136/12963.
[11] Ibid.

his rank and his empathy. Nobody would think of that. It would also lead to jealousies between the federal and state governments.

Minister of State Hans-Jürgen Wischnewski is also known to have a heart for the hostages. He has to accept that his boss Helmut Schmidt rejected Wischnewski's proposal to pay each hostage 5,000 German mark in compensation. That could set a precedent![12] On other occasions, however, the Minister of State successfully takes sides with those affected.

At the beginning of February 1978, Hans-Jürgen Wischnewski tells the *Kleeblatt*—a group of Schmidt's closest colleagues—that the criticism of former "Landshut" hostages can no longer be ignored. Hans-Jürgen Wischnewski heard that OEG applications from those affected and applications for support measures are being held up for a long time. The Minister of State suggests that he invites the former hostages to a meeting in Bonn. The "cloverleaf" agrees.

In the meantime, the Minister of State receives a report from the Federal Criminal Police Office, whose officers have interviewed all of the freed "Landshut" hostages.[13] "The mental anguish suffered by a considerable number of the hostages left some of them with very serious psychological disorders."[14]

As far as the OEG is concerned, the authors come to a damning judgement. "The 'Act on Compensation for Victims of Violent Crimes', which came into force on 16 May 1976, does not provide sufficient protection in this area beyond the provisions of the Federal Compensation Act." There is no provision for compensation in the form of damages for pain and suffering. Victims could also not receive compensation for the loss of valuables for justified claims, "as the Victims Compensation Act also does not provide a legal basis for compensation for financial losses".[15]

CDU member of parliament Lieselotte Berger is also committed to helping freed hostages. Although only for those from West Berlin, where the MP has her constituency, her initiative attracts nationwide attention. In mid-April 1979, Lieselotte Berger meets with those affected. Monika Schumann is also there. Lieselotte Berger then begins some correspondence with the Petitions Committee of the Berlin House of Representatives, which she makes available to Hans-Jürgen Wischnewski. The Minister of State considers sending the petitions committee's statement to all former hostages.

The mindset in the Federal Chancellery is revealed in a memo to Manfred Schüler and Minister of State Hans-Jürgen Wischnewski in the winter of

---

[12] Cf. Wischnewski 1989.
[13] BArch B136/12963.
[14] Ibid, p. 4.
[15] Ibid. p. 5.

1979. Ministerial Counsellor Peter Jabcke, Head of Division 43,[16] bluntly advises against passing on the correspondence to the hostages. The response from the Petitions Committee convincingly demonstrates that there can be no preferential treatment for the Mogadishu hostages compared to other victims (…). Sending the reply to all Landshut passengers would.

- "make the Berlin case nationwide.
- Dealing with problems that are none of their business, perhaps not even of interest to them
- For some, this may lead to them having something to criticise themselves."[17]

The note shows a lack of empathy on the part of the senior official. And the frequent practice of nipping debates in the bud before they become public. Minister of State Hans-Jürgen Wischnewski follows Peter Jabcke's suggestion and does not send the Berlin Petitions Committee's response around after all. The Minister of State also acts with all due empathy nevertheless within the logic of the political system. Ideas "out of turn"? Initiatives for his own account? Not a chance.

Between 18 and 21 April 1978, eight Berlin women and men from the hijacked "Landshut" are in Bonn together with the widow of the slain captain Monika Schumann. They were invited to this second meeting by the aforementioned member of parliament Lieselotte Berger. Heinrich Dieburg, a member of the Bundestag, also joins them.

His report to Minister of State Hans-Jürgen Wischnewski is unambiguous. It can be concluded that the Federal Government "is not interested in an in-depth investigation of the events, is content with the findings available to date and is sparing the costs".[18]

Officials in the Ministry of Labour and Social Affairs have no influence on the OEG procedures in the federal states but follow developments closely. By mid-May 1978, 36 applications have been received. The husband of a married couple in the hijacked "Landshut" applies to the Berlin pension office for OEG because of his permanent psychological damage. The application is rejected, and the appeal is also dismissed. "The proceedings regarding Mrs.

---

[16] Responsible for the Federal Ministry of Labour and Social Affairs; social and societal policy; labour market policy, health.
[17] Note from Division 43, Dr Jabcke, dated 9 February 1979 on (…) Mr Head of the Federal Chancellery. Mr Minister of State. Concerning Landshut passengers. Here: Reply from the Petitions Committee of the Berlin House of Representatives to Mrs L. Berger, MdB, in: BArch B136/12963, pp. 1–2.
[18] BArch B136/12963, p. 2.

(…)s objection are still ongoing. She has also subsequently claimed gynecological complaints (…). As this finding is based on the medical history of a neurologist, the BMA (Federal Ministry of Labour and Social Affairs, note M. R.) has asked the Berlin pension administration to obtain a special expert opinion from a gynecologist."[19] The observation stands: "Bonn" has no legal recourse.

Incidentally, nobody is asking about the freed hostages who did not apply for OEG benefits.

On 30 May 1978, ZDF broadcasts the documentary "106 Hours— Between Palma and Mogadishu" by Ruprecht Eser and Wolfgang Salewski. As never before and never since, former "Landshut" hostages express their disappointment at the behaviour of the German government. At a time when West Germans only receive three television channels, Eser and Salewski's film is sure to attract a great deal of attention. The failings of the federal and state governments are publicised on a large stage. The radio and the press then would take up the issue.

On 24 and 25 June 1978, 66 former "Landshut" passengers came together in Bonn at the invitation of Minister of State Hans-Jürgen Wischnewski. Including the crew on the hijacked flight and relatives who are allowed to come along, the number of guests totalled 74. The Federal Government does not let itself be outdone, at least for these two days. It accommodates the participants in the noble "Bristol" hotel in Bonn. Minister of State Hans-Jürgen Wischnewski takes them on a boat trip on the Rhine.

Representatives of the German government and Lufthansa seek dialogue with those affected, but both sides, it seems in retrospect, are talking past each other. Minister of State Hans-Jürgen Wischnewski sees himself as a helper with bureaucratic issues. OEG applications to the pension office are to be processed more quickly. On the second day, he assures the audience that the federal government would endeavour to resolve all outstanding cases positively.

Many of the freed hostages have no ear for the usual political phrases. They are still burdened by their disappointment that the German government did not seek contact with them during the days of the kidnapping. A former hostage and participant in the meeting will later summarise: "A steamboat trip with coffee and cake, a cold buffet, and then they slapped us on the shoulder, now you're all calm again, now you can go home."[20]

Just a few days later, the issue raises again in Bonn. Heinz Ricken, a judge at the Federal Court of Justice, writes to the Federal Chancellor under the

---

[19] BArch B136/12965.
[20] Ploeger & Schmitt 1986, p. 72.

impression of a radio programme[21] in which former "Landshut" hostages and the aforementioned psychotherapist Prof. Jan Bastiaans have their say.

"The abduction victims", Heinz Recken says verbatim, "complain about uncomprehending bureaucracy—you can't see suffering!—and a disappointing lack of interest on the part of the German government, which rightly celebrated the liberation at the time as a victory for reasons of state. You, Mr Chancellor, are still living off this glory today (...). The successful liberation campaign also benefited "the existence of this federal government."

Heinz Recken advises "to make up for what is still possible today: a written, but not only formal recognition (of the hostages' suffering, note M. R.); an honourable gratuity (...); an unbureaucratic guarantee of further psychotherapeutic treatment."[22]

Chancellor Helmut Schmidt receives the letter and decides not to answer it himself. He instructs Minister of State Hans-Jürgen Wischnewski to do so. He in turn orders a draft reply from the aforementioned head of Division 43, Peter Jabcke. "I have personally pursued the granting of an honourable gratuity with vigor", it says. As heard, Hans-Jürgen Wischnewski suggested to the Chancellor that each freed hostage should receive 5000 German mark in compensation—in vain.

With warm sincerity, Jabcke continues his draft text for Hans-Jürgen Wischnewski. "The Victims Compensation Act has proven to be the biggest obstacle on the way to a more flexible regulation of the material problems."[23] A clear admission, that the strategy of the federal and state governments in dealing with the freed "Landshut" hostages has failed.

Not even the committed, empathetic Minister of State Hans-Jürgen Wischnewski wants to express that much remorse. He cancels the ministerial councillor's draft response, and the submission is filed. Heinz Recken does not receive a chancery grill from him after all, but from the mentioned ministerial council Jabcke.

The Ministerial Councillor writes a short letter on a report by the Federal Ministry of Labour and Social Affairs "in which it comments on administrative action under the Victims' Compensation Act".[24] The report is "thoroughly self-critical". Peter Jabcke points out that some inmates of the

---

[21] Krausz 1978.
[22] Letter from Dr Heinz Recken to Federal Chancellor Helmut Schmidt dated 18 February 1979, pp. 1–2, in: BArch B136/12963.
[23] Draft reply from Hans-Jürgen Wischnewski to Dr Heinz Recken dated March 1979 (no date entered), in B136/12963.
[24] Letter from Dr Jabcke dated 9 July 1979 to Dr Heinz Recken, in: BArch B136/12963.

"Landshut" are still undergoing group therapy with Professor Plöger (sic), Aachen. "Of course, this treatment is free of charge for the patients (…)."

Heinz Recken has approached the Federal Chancellor with his biography and life's work. He is fobbed off by a high-level official in the Federal Chancellery with a cover letter for an official report.

It is worth reading how tenaciously former "Landshut" hostages fight for justice and with what tenacity the other side keeps creating new hurdles.

Helma Van Dreumel

A foreign passenger on the hijacked flight, Dutchwoman Helma van Dreumel, writes Hans-Jürgen Wischnewski a handwritten letter dated 25 January 1979.[25] The Minister of State receives it together with a "rough translation" into German.[26] During the emergency landing in Mogadishu—probably referring to Aden—y teeth have been so seriously damaged that I am now forced to have part of my front teeth replaced. The associated costs are so high that I cannot afford them myself (…)."[27]

Hans-Jürgen Wischnewski passes the matter on through official channels but wants to reply to the former hostage personally. Undersecretary Peter Jabcke at the Federal Chancellery passes the letter on to his colleague at the Federal Ministry of Labour and Social Affairs, Undersecretary Leonhard Trometer.[28]

The Ministerial Director in turn declares that he is not responsible. "In the case of (…) the Dutch national Helma van Dreumel, the Minister of Labour, Health and Social Affairs of the State of North Rhine-Westphalia (…) has been asked to have the request of the sender examined by the competent pension office."[29]

The experienced civil servant Leonhard Trometer already knows the outcome of the examination. In the present case of a Dutch woman, she is basically entitled to care under the OEG. "The federal government is the payer in this case."[30]

---

[25] BArch, B 136/12965.
[26] Ibid.
[27] Ibid.
[28] Ibid.
[29] Letter from Ministerial Director Leonhard Trometer to Ministerial Councillor Peter Jabcke dated 2 March 1979, in: ibid.
[30] Letter Leonard Trometer (o. U., on behalf of Ruh. Notarised: Employee Ruh to the Minister for Labour, Health and Social Affairs of the State of North Rhine-Westphalia dated 2 March 1979. Re:

A few days later, State Minister Hans-Jürgen Wischnewski's personal advisor, Peter Kiewitt, sends Helma van Dreumel an interim notification. "The examination of your claim (...) will take a few more weeks. In principle, you have the same legal claims for physical injuries suffered as your German fellow sufferers."[31]

In a letter dated 13 August 1979—five and a half months after Helma van Dreumel's submission—the Minister for Labour, Health and Social Affairs of the state of North Rhine-Westphalia agrees. Dr Delitz, an employee of the authority, writes to the Federal Minister for Labour and Social Affairs that the Münster Pension Office has recognised the health disorders "damage to teeth 11 and 21" as a consequence of injury within the meaning of § 1 OEG in its decision of 11 July 1979.[32] Shortly afterwards, the head of the Federal Chancellery is also informed.[33]

Presumably no topic that the closest employee of the Chancellor of the Federal Republic of Germany has to deal with.

This is by no means the end of the matter. On 22 January 1979, Helma van Dreumel submits a cost estimate for 2,500 Dutch guilders. This cost estimate is not specific enough for the Münster pension office. "If the dentures have not yet been fitted, you will be asked to submit a more specific cost estimate."[34] An employee of the North Rhine-Westphalia Ministry of Labour also writes to the Federal Minister of Labour and Social Affairs along the same lines.[35] And the Federal Minister of Labour and Social Affairs in turn writes to the head of the Federal Chancellery.[36]

On 23 November 1979, the responsible employee at the North Rhine-Westphalia State Employment Office is able to notify the Federal Minister of Labour and Social Affairs of the completion of the application.[37] On 2 November 1979, the Münster pension office grants an application for

---

Benefits under the OEG to Landshut passengers; here: Submission by Mrs Helma van Dreumel, Nijmegen, Netherlands. AZ VI a 1—516.01 (OEG) -/79, in: ibid.

[31] Letter from Peter Kiewitt to Helma van Dreumel dated 8 March 1979, in: BArch, in: ibid.

[32] Letter from Dr Delitz to the Federal Minister of Labour and Social Affairs dated 13 August 1975, Gesch-Zeichen II B 1—4371 -, in: ibid.

[33] Letter from the Federal Minister of Labour and Social Affairs. On behalf of Ruhan to the Head of the Federal Chancellery dated 1 August 1979. Via 1—5196.1 (OEG)—van Dreumel, in: ibid.

[34] Letter from the Versorgungsamt Münster to Helma van Dreumel dated 3 September 1979, in: ibid.

[35] Letter from the Minister for Labour, Health and Social Affairs of the State of North Rhine-Westphalia (on behalf of Sträßer) dated 18 September 1979, Geschz. II B 1—4371 -, in: ibid.

[36] Letter from the Federal Minister of Labour and Social Affairs (on behalf of Ruh) to the Head of the Federal Chancellery dated 21 September 1979. Via 1—5196.1 (OEG)—van Dreumel, in: ibid.

[37] Letter from the Minister of Labour of North Rhine-Westphalia (on behalf of Dr. Delitz) to the Federal Minister of Labour and Social Affairs dated 2 November 1979, in: ibid.

reimbursement of dental prosthesis costs and transfers an amount of 970.30 German mark.

Helma van Dreumel also applies for another dental prosthesis, which is paid for by the pension office. On 5 December 1979, the Federal Minister for Labour and Social Affairs is able to inform the Head of the Federal Chancellery about this.[38] In a letter dated 6 May 1980, Manfred Schüler receives a report on the execution and reimbursement of the additional dentures.[39] The matter was thus "to be regarded as settled".

Livia Vamos

The Victims Compensation Act applies not only in the Federal Republic of Germany, but also in the Netherlands, Great Britain, Ireland and Sweden, as mentioned above. The Austrian hostages from the "Landshut" are left empty-handed. These include Livia Vamos, whose Jewish origins were concealed from "Captain Machmud" by the skillful tactics of stewardess Gabriele von Lutzau (née Dillmann).

At the end of December 1979, more than two years after the "Landshut" abduction, a Munich law firm writes to Ministerial Director Leonhard Trometer at the Federal Ministry of Labour and Social Affairs on behalf of Livia Vamos. An OEG application in the Federal Republic of Germany has previously been rejected because of her citizenship.

"The consequential damages", the law firm claims, "were particularly serious for Mrs Vamos, because she was politically persecuted during the years 1933 to 1945. The traumas she suffered as a result of her imprisonment in a concentration camp at that time have been fully actualised by the incident of October 1977 (...). We suggest that in this undoubtedly special case, the Federal Ministry (...) should do something for our client within the framework of hardship compensation."[40]

An employee of the Federal Ministry of Labour and Social Affairs, Wesel, presumably sees political explosives in the case and writes on 1 February 1980 "to the head of the Federal Chancellery, the Federal Minister of Justice,

---

[38] Letter from the Federal Minister of Labour and Social Affairs (on behalf of Ruh. Angestellte) to the Head of the Federal Chancellery dated 5 December 1979, in: ibid.

[39] Letter from Ders. (on behalf of Au. Angestellte) to the Head of the Federal Chancellery dated 6 May 1980, in: ibid.

[40] Letter from lawyers Oskar Möhring et. Al. To Ministerial Director Leonhard Trometer, Federal Ministry of Labour and Social Affairs, 27 December 1979, in: BArch B136/12965.

the Federal Minister of Finance and the Foreign Office."[41] The rejection of any compensation payment by the Federal Government would probably once again meet with a lack of understanding from the public. "Mrs. Vamos' fate (as a Jew she was imprisoned in a concentration camp) is also likely to contribute to this".[42] The author of the letter "would therefore like to exhaust all possibilities to help Mrs Vamos, who is certainly affected by the event in a special way (… e.g. by paying a one-off sum of money) (…)."[43]

In the Federal Chancellery, the letter reaches the desk of Werner Jabke, a ministerial councillor already known here. He writes to the Federal Minister for Labour and Social Affairs that it would be "not unimportant to know which specific benefits have been applied for. It may turn out that certain benefits for the consequences of the attack (…) have already been granted by (Austrian) social insurance institutions."[44]

The Federal Foreign Office, which is presumably also involved in the matter, does not believe that the freed "Landshut" hostage is entitled to benefits, but considers it "for humanitarian reasons"[45] to be right that Livia Vamos receives compensation for pain and suffering. The Federal Ministry of Justice shares this view, but not at its own expense. "However, budget funds for this cannot be made available from section 07."[46]

Three ministries point out that Livia Vamos is not legally entitled to benefits.

The head of the Federal Chancellery, Manfred Schüler, asks the Federal Ministry of Finance to check whether Mrs Vamos can receive a one-off payment. "According to the results of my examination", a Mr Kaiser writes to Manfred Schüler, "I regret to inform you, however, that grants of the kind requested cannot be awarded from federal funds."[47]

---

[41] By order of Wessel. Notarised: (name not legible), employee. Subject: Care of Landshut hostages. Here: Austrian citizen Mrs Livia Vamos from 1 February 1980. V1a 2—5234–02, in: BArch B 136/1295.

[42] Ibid.

[43] Ibid.

[44] Chief BK. On behalf of Dr. Jabke to the Federal Minister for Labour and Social Affairs dated 21 February 1980. Subject: Care for victims of the Lufthansa aircraft "Landshut". Here: Austrian citizen Mrs Livia Vamos, in: BArch 136/12965.

[45] Foreign Office, Dr. Jestaedt, to the Federal Minister for Labour and Social Affairs, 27 February 1980, regarding the care of Landhut hostages; here: Austrian citizen Ms Livia Vamos, in: BArch B 136/12965.

[46] The Federal Minister of Justice. By order of Schätzler. Certified by Dudell to the Federal Minister of Labour and Social Affairs dated 55 March 1980. Subject: Compensation for victims of 'acts of violence. Here: Austrian citizen Livia Vamos, in: BArch B 136/12965.

[47] The Federal Minister of Finance. By order of Dr Kaiser. Notarised by Pohne. To the Federal Minister of Labour and Social Affairs. Subject: Care for victims of the Lufthansa aircraft "Landshut". Here: Austrian citizen Livia Vamos of 2 June 1980, in: BArch B 136/12965.

On 4 July 1980, an official from the Federal Ministry of Labour—presumably Leonhard Trometer, with a capital "T" as his signature—writes a note stating that he had spoken to Livia Vamos' lawyer on the phone that same day. "I informed him about the legal situation and advised him to submit an application to the Vienna State Disability Office, 1010 Vienna, Badenbergstrasse (…) The lawyer (…) was very grateful for the information and explained that a written reply was no longer necessary after this detailed information."[48]

Edelgard and Everhard Wolff

Like all passengers on the "Landshut", the Wolffs receive only part of their luggage back. Everhard Wolff files a claim with German Lufthansa for a material loss of 4809.70 German mark for his wife and himself. The airline recognises the claim minus an amount of 400 German mark.

Everhard Wolff will soon be back at the typewriter. He demands compensation from the Federal Ministry of Justice. On 2 December 1977, the Ministry informs him that the hijackers' crime did not give rise to "any claims against the Federal Republic of Germany or any of its states that go beyond the compensation claims under the Victims Compensation Act".[49] The Wolffs are advised to apply for OEG benefits at the Düsseldorf pension office.

Independently of this, German Lufthansa informs the Wolff couple at the beginning of 1978 that "we have been asked by the Federal Minister of Labour and Social Affairs to confirm to you that, according to the Act on Compensation for Victims of Violent Crimes (OEG), psychotherapeutic treatment is also one of the benefits under the Federal Pension Act (…)."[50]

In spring 1978, the Wolffs go on a cure. The costs are reimbursed to them under the Victims Compensation Act.

Everhard Wolff sits down at his typewriter again. He demands from the German government and Lufthansa "compensation for the almost five days of deprivation of liberty under threat and torture and for the loss of use of our holiday due to the events". He encloses medical reports for his wife and himself with the letters.

---

[48] Note by Leonhard Trometer (presumably), Department VI BMA, dated 4 July 1980, regarding the care of victims of the hijacking of the Lufthansa aircraft "Landshut". Here: Austrian national Livia Vamos dated 4 July 1980, in: BArch B 136/12965.

[49] Letter from the Federal Minister of Justice (on behalf of Schätzler) dated 2 December 1977, AZ 4226/1-II-26 509/77 in: Personal papers of Edelgard and Everhard Wolff, p. 2.

[50] Letter from German Lufthansa (Klein, Pocke) to Edelgard and Everhard Wolff dated 11 January 1978, in: Ibid.

In a letter to Edelgard Wolff, German Luftpool, which covers Lufthansa's insurance claims, rejects any claims. According to the Luftpool doctors, "the extent and duration of your husband's illness, in particular, are largely due to ailments that already existed before the hijacking. (…) In the opinion of our company doctors, it has also not been proven that the ulcer in your lower leg was actually caused by a hand grenade splinter (…)."[51]

The Lufthansa insurer then writes, "We cannot help but get the impression that N.N. (it follows the name of one of Edelgard or Everhard Wolff's family doctors, Note M. R.) has largely issued a certificate of favour." German Luftpool agrees to make a payment of 3,000 German mark to the couple, "provided that this brings the matter to a close".[52]

Edelgard and Everhard Wolff sign the declaration of the German Air Pool and receive the money in mid-October.

On the first anniversary of the "Landshut" kidnapping, Everhard Wolff also addresses the office of Minister of State Hans-Jürgen Wischnewski. He recalls the minister's meeting with former hostages in Bonn, which the Wolffs attended as mentioned.

"I do not believe", says Everhard Wolff in the letter, "that the horror of the five days and the consequences that have remained with each of us can be compensated for with material things. On the other hand, a certain goodwill on the part of the government can be a consolation to us".[53] Everhard Wolff encloses an invoice from his lawyer for 356.16 German mark "with a request, appealing to your goodwill, for settlement of the same."[54]

There is no reply from Bonn. On behalf of his wife and himself, Everhard Wolff reminds the office of Minister of State Hans-Jürgen Wischnewski of the letter of 14 October in a letter dated 11 January 1979.[55] The Minister of State reacts. He takes sides with the former "Landshut" hostages. "Something like this should not be allowed to go on for so long", he writes in large letters on Everhard Wolff's letter.

Hans-Jürgen Wischnewski replies to Mr and Mrs Wolff immediately and with particular care. Not only is this letter preserved in the Federal Archives in Koblenz, but also the draft by his staff. In addition, the Minister of State's handwritten requests for changes.[56]

---

[51] Letter from German Luft Pool to Edelgard Wolff dated 20 September 1978, in: ibid.
[52] Ibid.
[53] Letter from Everhard Wolff to the office of Minister of State Wischnewski/Personal Advisor dated 14 October 1978, in: ibid., p. 2.
[54] Ibid.
[55] Letter from Edelgard and Everhard Wolff dated 11 January 1979 to the office of Minister of State Wischnewski. Personal adviser. Subject: My letter of 14.10.78, "Landshut passengers".
[56] BArch 136/12965.

Hans-Jürgen Wischnewski accepts his organisation's advice that the state cannot reimburse private legal fees. He rewrites the rest of the draft reply.

With regard to Hans-Jürgen Wischnewski's late reaction, the draft states that "the blame does not lie with me, but politicians are also responsible for such failures". Hans-Jürgen Wischnewski deletes this line. Instead, he feigns persistent activity. It is important to him "to ensure that no stone was left unturned in order to possibly take your concerns into account".[57]

The same "fate", the deletion, befalls an entire paragraph in the draft reply. It reads: "However, to ease my sense of obligation towards you somewhat, I am taking the liberty of sending you 10 (sic) bottles of wine in the hope that the wine will help you get over the annoyance of having spent your legal fees for nothing."

At the end of April 1979, Everhard Wolff sits down at his typewriter again. It was "not only the events of the hostage-taking that bothered us", the letter writer declares verbatim,[58] "but also the behaviour of the government since our return". It was undeniable "that we all did not return home the way we boarded the 'Landshut'."

Then Everhard Wolff gives a hint that also comes from other freed hostages—the aforementioned "suspicion" among friends and acquaintances that the German government has paid high compensation to those affected. "We have been estimated by these people with compensation sums of up to 40,000 German mark", says Everhard Wolff in his letter.

In a TV interview with Südwestfunk editor Ebbo Demant, his wife Edelgard Wolff says that after buying a new car, she and her husband were told: "You got the money for it from the federal government!.."

At the end of June 1979, Minister of State Hans-Jürgen Wischnewski receives a letter from a comrade in the German Bundestag, Erwin Stahl. Edelgard and Everhard Wolff live in Erwin Stahl's constituency and have written to him.[59]

A quarter of a year later, Minister of State Hans-Jürgen Wischnewski takes the Wolff case to the head of the Federal Chancellery, Manfred Schüler.[60] "I would be very interested in a settlement", says Hans-Jürgen Wischnewski about Wolff's request for reimbursement of her legal fees.

---

[57] Letter from Hans-Jürgen Wischnewski to Eberhard and Edelgard dated 5 February 1979, in: ibid.
[58] Letter from Edelgard and Everhard Wolff to Minister of State Wischnewski dated 26 April 1979, subject: Your letter of 5 February 1979, in: ibid.
[59] Letter from Erwin Stahl MdB dated 26 June to the Minister of State in the Federal Chancellery. In person. Mr Hans-Jürgen Wischnewski. Subject: Correspondence with Mr E. Wolff from Kempen 3, Helmeskamp—passenger on the hijacked Lufthansa aircraft "Landshut", in: BArch 12,965.
[60] Letter from Hans-Jürgen Wischnewski to Manfred Schüler dated 25 September 1979 regarding Lufthansa passengers; here: Mr and Mrs Wolff, in: ibid.

In mid-October, Everhard Wolff sits down at his typewriter again. He repeats to Hans-Jürgen Wischnewski an earlier argument that the German government has avoided paying a sum in the millions in the German Autumn. This refers to the hand money demanded for the terrorists to be flown out.

Everhard Wolff chooses pretty much every channel available to him in Bonn at the end of the 1970s. On the second anniversary of the "Landshut" storming, he turnes to the Petitions Committee of the German Bundestag.[61] In their long letter, the Wolffs offer a glimpse of the emotional distress two years after the drama. "One has the impression of having to be glad that we were taken out of the plane at all."[62]

In fact, many of the freed hostages the Wolffs spoke to feel that "apart from the personal conflicts that affected everyone, (…) the behaviour of the government was very offensive". Again, the couple expresses its desire for reimbursement of its legal fees. The Wolffs also ask for compensation for the holiday in Majorca that preceded the kidnapping.

At the beginning of November 1979, the Petitions Committee of the German Bundestag askes the Federal Ministry of Labour and Social Affairs for a statement, which the Ministry provides at the end of January 1980.[63] According to this, "the petitioners' request to be reimbursed by the administrative authority for the legal fees incurred in the administration proceedings cannot be granted."[64] The benefit system of social compensation law also does not provide for compensation for loss of holiday use or loss of holiday enjoyment. "As the administration is bound by law, it cannot provide such benefits as a gesture of goodwill (…)."[65]

There is no reply from the Petitions Committee to the Wolffs in the file.

In April 1980, two and a half years after the "Landshut" hijacking, an official from the Federal Ministry of Labour and Social Affairs contacts the head of the Federal Chancellery, Manfred Schüler, and makes a proposal for kindness. "I would like to point out", writes a Mr Baader, "that 400 German mark was paid to other passengers of the Landshut (Mr and Mrs Wolff) after

---

[61] Letter from Edelgard and Everhard Wolff dated 17 October 1979 to the Petitions Committee HAT 1418 of the German Bundestag. Subject: Claim for recourse against the Federal Government in connection with the hijacking of the Lufthansa aircraft "Landshut" on 13 October 77, in: ibid.

[62] Ibid. p. 3.

[63] Letter from the Federal Ministry of Labour and Social Affairs to the German Bundestag—Petitions Committee—dated 31 January 1980, regarding: Provision under the Act on Compensation for Victims of Violent Crimes; here: Petition by Edelgard and Everhard Wolff, Kempen 3, dated 17 October 1979, in: ibid.

[64] Ibid, p. 2.

[65] Ibid.

the Petitions Committee intervened as compensation for legal fees incurred 'from another pot' without any legal basis."[66]

The Federal Ministry of Finance is annoyed about this. A Mr Kaiser writes a handwritten note to Ministerial Councillor Peter Jabcke in the Federal Chancellery complaining that the Federal Ministry of Labour "wants to pass the buck to us. We have already expressed our views on the special payment of 357 German mark (Wolff). So the BMA's handling of this matter is not at all helpful."[67]

Mr Kaiser attaches a condition to the payment: "If we do not want to rule out a special payment (…), MD Trometer would have to be 'heard' again beforehand (…)."[68]

---

[66] Letter "Baader" to the Head of the Federal Chancellery. Subject: Care of victims of the Lufthansa aircraft "Landshut"; here: Austrian citizen Livia Vamos, pp. 1–2, in: BArch B136/12965.

[67] Handwritten note from Kaiser, employee in the Federal Ministry of Finance, to Dr Jabcke, Federal Chancellery, undated, in: BArch B136/12965.

[68] Ibid.

10

Our New Friends, the Sheikhs

"Mogadishu" opens a gateway to the world for the German government. Since it was founded 28 years ago, its political horizons have mainly focused on the West and the East. Relations with allies in the West and the so-called Eastern bloc, including a second German nation state.

Since the "Landshut" hijacking, Chancellor Helmut Schmidt has caught up with some heads of government, such as the sheikhs in the Arab world. He can't do world politics there with his rump Germany, but he can do good business. The Federal Republic of Germany is politically a dwarf, but economically quite far ahead.

A German government becomes a fully fledged dialogue partner in other parts of the world, not only out of gratitude for its steadfastness against terror, but also out of genuine respect. This was preceded by a tragic event, the German Autumn, which claimed several lives, but the Chancellor was able to use it politically to make new partners.

Nevertheless, the assessment of which governments have supported the Federal Chancellor in these difficult weeks is mixed. So-called allies behaved little or not at all in a spirit of partnership. Countries which were in no or loose connection. Saw themselves as responsible.

Great Britain

Even before 1977, the year of terror, the British government is one of the closest allies. During the "Landshut" hijacking, contrary to the later hymns of thanks from German Chancellor Helmut Schmidt to Prime Minister James Callaghan, it does little to earn its support.

It costs Callaghan nothing politically when he sends GSG9 commander Ulrich Wegener the plans of the airport buildings in Dubai to plan a rescue operation. The politically delicate request from the German Chancellor, which is important for a police operation, for the GSG9 to be allowed to land on a British military base on the island of Cyprus, is turned down.

The two special forces, Major Alastair Georg Angus Morrison and Staff Sergeant Barry Davies, members of the British equivalent of the GSG9, contribute their expertise and glare grenades. The bright light blinded the "Landshut" hijackers and put them out of action for precious seconds.

The morning after the "fire magic" operation, Federal Chancellor Helmut Schmidt receives British Prime Minister James Callaghan for a state visit in Bonn. The first meeting has been postponed due to the Schleyer kidnapping. This time, both sides are sticking to it regardless of the kidnapping cases.

As planned, Helmut Schmidt and James Callaghan discuss the future location of a European test facility "Joint European Torus" (JET), which is to develop nuclear fusion reactors. Germany wants to build JET on the site of the Max Planck Institute in Garching near Munich, Great Britain in Culham, a village on the north bank of the Thames. Both countries are competing for a prestigious scientific project worth billions of euros.

The minutes of the talks between the two delegations can be found in the published files on the foreign policy of the Federal Republic of Germany in 1977.[1] Politicians and diplomats politely exchange their points of view. There is no indication in the minutes as to whether it will be Garching or Culham. This suggests that the actual decision is or was made in a much smaller circle—Helmut Schmidt may have promised JET to the British Prime Minister the morning after "Mogadishu". The decision in favour of Culham is—presumably for tactical reasons—only formally decided and announced later.

The spokespeople in favour of the Garching site react angrily to the decision including Federal Minister of the Interior Werner Maihofer. In historical retrospect, his anger seems understandable because the price for the involvement of two Britons in Mogadishu very high.

Chancellor Helmut Schmidt would like to honour the two British special forces involved in the "Landshut" rescue with the Order of Merit of the Federal Republic of Germany. He even intends to attend this honour in person. The Federal Foreign Office is to clarify whether "London" agrees.

Prime Minister James Callaghan himself has proposed the deployment of the major and sergeant to the Chancellor. Now it is not convenient

---

[1] Cf. Institute for Contemporary History 2008.

for Callaghan's Foreign Secretary that the special forces receive their due thanks. "London" does not want special treatment for the two. Envy could arise among the men of the British GSG9. That was also the concern of Ulrich Wegener, the commander of the German GSG9, after the operation in Mogadischu.

When German Chancellor Helmut Schmidt is in London for a historic speech, the birth of the so-called NATO Double-Track Decision, the British Foreign Secretary takes Schmidt aside and asks him to refrain from honouring him. The chancellor immediately agrees. Instead, the German government is having a thank-you card made for the entire force. The plate is placed on a wall in the common room.

Sergeant Barry Davies, one of those involved, feels that his efforts have been dishonoured. He will write a book[2] and years later meet Monika Schumann, the widow of the murdered "Landshut" captain, for a television documentary.

Palestine Liberation Organisation (PLO)

The "Landshut" abduction marks a new start in the German government's relationship with Yasser Arafat's Palestinian organisation, the PLO. Yasser Arafat was at least aware of the crime committed by the Palestinian terror subgroup "Black September". Arafat subsequently approached the GDR regime in his endeavours to obtain diplomatic advocates for a Palestinian state of his own. It was a win–win situation, as the new "friends" in East Berlin were themselves looking for ways to achieve international recognition for their state. Arafat's organisation came in handy. Erich Honecker was suddenly able to make Middle East policy, i.e. world policy.

In 1973, the PLO leader takes part in World Youth Day in East Berlin as if he were the representative of an independent Palestinian state. In the same year, he is allowed to address the United Nations General Assembly in New York—a historic event for his people scattered across the globe. However, he owes this not to Erich Honecker, but to US Secretary of State Henry Kissinger. Yasser Arafat renounces terrorism. He wants to achieve his goal politically. It will be decades before a so-called Palestinian Authority is formed in the West Bank, but a start has been made.

---

[2] Davies 1994.

The social-liberal federal governments under Willy Brandt (1969–1974) and Helmut Schmidt (1974–1982) recognise the Palestinians' right to self-determination. Brandt und Schmidt are in favour of a separate Palestinian state. Nevertheless, they cannot play an active role as peacemakers in the Middle East out of consideration for Israel, to whose historical debt the Federal Republic of Germany is indebted. The protection of Israel is indelibly part of its raison d'être.

The bloody Olympic bombing of 1972 showed what Palestinian terror is capable of. Palestinians are considered to be the most dangerous terrorists in the world because they are the best trained and supplied with plenty of weapons. If you want to break the chain of violence, you have to get along with Yasser Arafat.

As the story goes, the "Landshut" kidnapping is not the work of Arafat's PLO, but of George Habash and Wadi Haddad, the leaders of the radical Palestinian splinter group PFLP. Different strategies, but even more personal vanities, lead to that the leaders of the different groups do not see eye to eye.

At some point, even George Habasch and Wadi Haddad no longer see eye to eye,[3] but continue to pull in the same direction. Wadi Haddad repeatedly deploys terrorists from other countries, including members of the German "Red Army Faction", for his notorious "foreign operations", which will include the "Landshut" kidnapping. RAF terrorists are prepared for terrorist actions in PFLP training camps in Beirut, Damascus or Aden. Even before the kidnapping of Peter Lorenz in spring 1975, rumours had been circulating that the PFLP was planning to hijack a plane in order to free imprisoned RAF terrorists. Two and a half years later, these rumors became certainty.

The deep divisions between political and terrorist Palestinian organisations created an open flank. Immediately after the "Landshut" kidnapping begins, the Federal Foreign Ministry asks the PLO representative in Bonn, Abdallah Frangi, to phone Yasser Arafat. "Bonn" wants to know whether Arafat is involved in the affair. Through Frangi, Yasser Arafat is assured that there is no connection whatsoever between the PLO and the "Landshut" hijacking. The PLO would do everything in its power to rescue the hostages.[4] Helmut Schmidt receives a note about this and signs it.

Already in Cyprus, a PLO representative seeks a dialogue with "Captain Machmud" as told—with a different tenor than the terrorist expects. The PLO representative calls on him to release the hostages. "Captain Machmud" rages. German Chancellor Helmut Schmidt is told by Palestinian circles that

---

[3] Cf. Skelton-Robinson 2006.
[4] Memo Loeck GL 21 dated 14 October 1977 regarding: Aircraft hijacking, BArch B136/16982.

the hijacked plane could fly on from Dubai to Aden. Later, the German Middle East correspondent for ARD, Kurt Stenzel, receives a tip that the "Landshut" is heading for Mogadishu from Aden. He also has a Palestinian source.[5] Stenzel flies to Mogadishu with a camera team on the eve of the "Landshut" arrival. He will be the only journalist in the world on the ground.

Yasser Arafat keeps his promises. The files of the Federal Chancellery and the Foreign Office contain further evidence that the PLO repeatedly provided the German government with information during the days of the kidnapping.

The PLO does this with its own interests in mind. The PLO is doing this with its own interests in mind. It wants its rivals George Habash and Wadi Haddad to fail with their kidnapping operation—planned and prepared by Haddad. At the same time, Arafat sees an opportunity for a restart in relations with West Germany, one of the richest industrialised nations in the world.

Presumably on 14 October 1977, a Friday, an employee of the Federal Chancellery draws up a list of telephone numbers on which the politicians Egon Bahr (SPD), the FDP parliamentary group leader in the Bundestag Wolfgang Mischnick (FDP), Helmut Kohl (CDU) and Friedrich Zimmermann (CSU) can be reached on Friday night, Saturday and Sunday. There is also a private and a professional number for Abdallah Frangi, the head of the PLO office in Bonn.

On Sunday, 16 October, 4.30 p.m., an unknown person writes a memo for the head of the Federal Chancellery, Manfred Schüler. It says in English that Wadi Haddad knew the time of Hanns Martin Schleyer's kidnapping. "A joint operation involving the kidnapping and hijacking as simultaneous events"[6] has been planned. "For reasons not clear to our source, the hijacking was delayed".[7]

A "reliable source with excellent connections to Fedaijn circles"[8] reports in much greater detail that the hijacking of the Lufthansa plane from Mallorca and the Schleyer kidnapping were coordinated operations "led by Wadi Haddad in collaboration with the Baader-Meinhof gang".[9] The Lufthansa hijackers "have (…) instructions not to kill any passenger (…), regardless of whether their demands are met or not."

Hanns Martin Schleyer's kidnappers had similar instructions. However, the people holding Schleyer in custody questioned their instructions. They feared their arrest because the released employer president could identify them.

---

[5] Interview with the author on the occasion of filming for Helm2011b.
[6] Archiv BK 13–211 20 (3) Additional file 3, no p.
[7] Ibid.
[8] Archiv BK 13–211 20 (3) Additional file 3, p. 2.
[9] Ibid. Skelton-Robinson 2006 on the connection between the PFLP and the RAF in detail.

The Lufthansa hijackers "have instructions to proceed to Aden. Somalia and Vietnam were included in the destination list, simply to avoid emphasising the role played by the Den regime in collaboration with Haddad."[10] In retrospect, this source proves to be prophetic.

Definitely, the hijackers must have expected to be treated favourably in Aden. They are likely to know what the German government has known since a report by the Federal Intelligence Service on 23 September 1977: The People's Democratic Republic of Yemen is considered a sought-after target country for radical PLO splinter groups. "According to the report, the terrorist splinter group of the PFLP under Wadi Haddad is currently dominant within this complex (...)."[11]

In other words, the German government needs helpers on the ground. "Al-Fatah intends to persuade the South Yemeni government to release the passengers without the government responding to the kidnappers' demands."[12]

As early as the end of August 1977, the federal government learns of "subversive activities by radical Palestinian groups" in Dubai, which are mainly "associated with supporters of wadi haddads."[13]

Years later, former RAF terrorists will reveal the background to the "Landshut" hijacking. Before the German Autumn, Wadi Haddad makes two proposals to the Germans to reinforce the demands of Hanns Martin Schleyer's kidnappers and to pursue his own interests. Wadi Haddad thinks of taking hostages in the German embassy in Kuwait City or hijacking a German passenger plane.[14]

The increased protection of foreign missions since the hostage-taking in Stockholm speaks against "Kuwait". Furthermore, a handful of diplomats appear to be a weak bargaining chip compared to a well-booked Lufthansa aircraft with innocent people from many nations on board. The choice falls on suggestion two. The hijacking was to begin in Palma de Mallorca, where security checks presumably are considered to be particularly lax.

Federal Chancellor Helmut Schmidt will expressly thank the PLO after the "Aktiofire magic" operation. "Incidentally, it should not be overlooked", says Helmut Schmidt in his government statement in the German Bundestag on

---

[10] Ibid.

[11] Federal Intelligence Service (BND): Länder-Beurteilung zur Frage der Aufnahmebereitschaft von Terroristen vom 23. September 1977. KKK - TgbNr. 267/VS-NfD, in: Archiv BK 13–211 20 (3) Bd. 1 OTB, p. 63f.

[12] Note for State Secretary Dr Schüler dated 16 October 1977, in: Archiv BK 13–211 20 (2) Additional file OTB vol. 8, no p.

[13] Telex to the Federal Chancellery dated 14 October 1977, in: OTB, p. 92.

[14] Cf. Geiger 2009, p. 424.

20 October, "that the head of the PLO, Yasser Arafat, also clearly distanced himself from the action of the kidnappers long before it came to an end." A passage that is missing from the speech manuscript distributed to journalists beforehand. Perhaps the thought occurs to Helmut Schmidt spontaneously or—more likely—he does not want to bring the explosive sentence to the market earlier.

Helmut Schmidt's words of thanks are heard by the PLO and received "with great satisfaction".[15]

Souhaila Andrawes

"What, you want to take prisoners too?" is the horrified exclamation of Somali President Siad Barre to Minister of State Hanns-Jürgen Wischnewski on 17 October 1977. The president agrees to the police action of another state on his territory in the expectation that the Germans will shoot all the members of the terror squad. He doesn't want any trouble with the Palestinians or with governments that have an ear for the Palestinian cause.

Siad Barre's wish is not granted. "Captain Machmud" must bleed to death on the tarmac, "the fat one" and "the boy" die in a hail of bullets. Souhaila Andrawes is lucky and survives. Politically, she is now a burden. Palestinians are homeless and stateless. One Palestinian terrorist in particular.

A telex from the German embassy in Mogadishu reveals that the seriously injured Souhaila Andrawes is still in the police hospital in mid-December.[16] "The Somali government has obviously not yet decided on her fate."[17] A delegation of Palestinians belonging to the PLO is travelling to Mogadishu in order to obtain the extradition of the terrorist. The Somali government refuses.

Souhaila Andrawes has barely recovered from her gunshot wounds, when she is to be deported to the Federal Republic of Germany. The Federal Chancellor the Federal Ministers of the Interior and Justice, the Federal Public Prosecutor General and the President of the Federal Criminal Police Office discuss the matter on 5 December 1977. They decide "that extradition should

---

[15] Cf. telex from Beirut No. 300 to AA dated 29 October 1977, n.d., in: BArch 136/16982.
[16] Telex from Mogadishu to the Federal Foreign Office dated 27 December 1977, reference: RK 530.35 Subject: Aircraft hijacking. Here: Surviving terrorist, in: Archiv BK 13–211 20 (3) Vol. 1, p. 169.
[17] Ibid.

not take place".[18] The reasons for this include the fact that "criminal proceedings in the Federal Republic of Germany would face considerable difficulties in terms of evidence" and that "the tactics and actions of the GSG9 and its officers would have to be exposed". Furthermore, a trial in Germany would open up "undesirable opportunities for international terrorism to present itself."

It is presumably not the enforcement of the rule of law against a violent criminal that guides action of the German government, but the state's political need for protection. A convicted Palestinian woman in a German prison could give rise to revenge actions. For this reason, Chancellor Helmut Schmidt did not want the terrorists deported to Aden back two years earlier.[19]

Regardless of the cabinet's decision, the Federal Criminal Police Office in Wiesbaden is still in charge of the investigation into Souhaila Andrawes. The terrorist is considered "wanted for arrest".[20] She remains on the radar, so to speak.

In the summer of 1978, the Federal Criminal Police Office files the "Landshut" kidnapping and the supposed manhunt for the surviving terrorist.[21] Almost four years later, on 25 February 1982, a member of the special commission responsible states that Souhaila Andrawes has been sentenced to 20 years in prison in Somalia on 25 April 1978. However, it is suspected that she has been released from prison and deported to Iraq.[22]

It is not so much the Germans as the Italians who have a criminal interest in the terrorist. Italian investigators feel formally responsible because the hijacked "Landshut" touched solid ground in Rome for the first time. In aviation, this is considered the "beginning" of a crime. On 2 June 1981, a court in Rome sentences Souhaila Andrawes in absentia to 30 years' imprisonment for hijacking an aircraft, violating the Weapons Act and deprivation of liberty.[23]

---

[18] Letter from BKA President Horst Herold dated 30 January 1978 to the Federal Minister of the Interior - ÖS 9, regarding the extradition of the Iranian national Soraya Amari from Somalia to Germany, in: BArch B136/12963.

[19] Cf. Geiger 2009, p. 425.

[20] Cf. BArch B 131/1173.

[21] Annotation Noltsch. ED 1 LH 181. file No. 174//. Ref. GBA 1 BJs 122/77 of 22 August 1978, in: BArch B131/1173.

[22] Note from the Federal Criminal Police Office, Hauer, dated 25 February 1982, subject: Hijacking of the Lufthansa aircraft "Landshut" on 13.10.77, here: Souhaila SAYEH, born 1053 in Hadath/Lebanon alias Soraya ANSARI, in: BArch B 131/173.

[23] Attachment to a memo from the Federal Criminal Police Office, Hauer, dated 25 February 1982, subject: Hijacking of the Lufthansa aircraft "Landshut" on 13.10.77, here: Souhaila SAYEH, born 1053 in Hadath/Lebanon alias Soraya ANSARI, in: BArch B 131,173.

Nevertheless, the terrorist remains unmolested. She later lives in Beirut, Damascus and—after being expelled from Syria—on the island of Cyprus. In 1991, she is granted political asylum in Norway together with her husband and the common daughter. The northern European country is considered to be particularly friendly to Palestinians. It is no coincidence that an agreement between Israeli Prime Minister Yitzchak Rabin and PLO leader Yasser Arafat is reached in its capital Oslo in the 1990s. The last one to date.

It is not until 13 October 1994—exactly 17 years after the start of the "Landshut" kidnapping—that Souhaila Andrawes is arrested in the Norwegian capital Oslo, presumably at the instigation of the Federal Public Prosecutor's Office and the Federal Criminal Police Office in Karlsruhe and Wiesbaden respectively. An understanding between the German and Norwegian governments—with whatever political background—must have preceded. On 25 November 1995, Andrawes is transferred to Hamburg, the first suitable place of jurisdiction in Germany from Scandinavia.

The trial turns into a media spectacle. The defendant insists on only being photographed or filmed with crutches as a sign of the permanent injuries she suffered in Mogadishu. Souhaila Andrawes pours herself into self-pity. She minimises her role during the "Landshut" kidnapping. I was young and politically immature, according to the tenor. Many former "Landshut" hostages, including the then co-pilot Jürgen Vietor or Beate Keller (née Zerbst), testify at the trial. They know better.

On 19 November 1996, the Hamburg Higher Regional Court sentences Souhaila Andrawes to twelve years in prison. After one year, she receives permission to be transferred to a Norwegian prison. The convict is released early on 30 November 1999. On this day, the Ministry of Justice in Oslo announces that Souhaila Andrawes has been granted a permanent residence permit in Norway.

By all accounts, her harshest sentence—a life sentence—is only now coming. Instead of appearing as a fighter for the Palestinian cause during the trial, she stole away from her responsibility in court. She is said to have fallen out of favour in her Palestinian community as a result. She even lost her husband and child.

Arab Emirates

Some of the countries with which the German government is involved during the "Landshut" hijacking, are located in the Arab world. This is not easy diplomatic terrain. On the one hand, Germany is pursuing economic interests there. It wants to export weapons and obtain oil. In the 1970s, petrol was the lubricant of prosperity in each Western European country.

On the other hand, there are political incompatibilities between the West Germans and the Arabs. The Arabs regard Israel as a mortal enemy; according to a charter, all Jews should be driven into the sea. An absolute no-go for the Federal Republic of Germany. After the Holocaust, the historical responsibility for the security of the State of Israel is part of the German raison d'état, the basic political understanding of every federal government.

Even before Helmut Schmidt's chancellorship, these policy objectives rub up against each other. For example, in relations with the Arabs after it becomes known that West Germany has secretly supplied weapons to Israel. Because the Federal Republic of Germany sides with Israel in the 1973 Yom Kippur War, the oil tap is also turned off.

The sheikdom of Dubai does not want to allow the hijacked "Landshut" to land, but when it arrives at the desert airport, the defence minister gets personally involved. Over 55 h of diplomatic negotiations with the "Landshut" hijackers are not to be expected from a government that previously has little to do with the Federal Republic of Germany so far.

The leadership of the Sheikdom of Dubai behaves inconsistently during the time that the "Landshut" is at its airport. Defence Minister Mohammad Sheikh bin Rashid Al Maktoum stalls "Captain Machmud". He raises hopes in Bonn of a rescue operation by the German GSG9. His boss, Sheikh Zayid bin Sultan Al Nahyan, allows the aircraft to be towed.

In the summer of 1978, the German embassy in Abu Dhabi suggested inviting the United Arab Emirates' Minister of Defence, Mohammad Sheikh bin Rashid Al Maktum, to Bonn. Together with Minister of State Hans-Jürgen Wischnewski, he is to meet the former "Landshut" hostages.

The Federal Foreign Office replies by coded telex: "However, an invitation to the Federal Republic (…) should not be considered. (…) He would certainly present requests for arms deliveries that we would have to refuse."[24] Even today, the Federal Government considers it inappropriate to allow itself

---

[24] Submission by the Federal Foreign Office, Dr Lahn in the Montfort Division, to the State Secretary dated 25 October 1977, here: Stocktaking and assessment of the behaviour of the countries concerned and the consequences to be drawn from this behaviour, in: AsD, 1/HSAA010018, pp. 1–3.

to be forced into military or arms policy cooperation by inviting the defence minister of an Arab country.[25]

Abu Dhabi returns with a dashing reply: Sheikh Mohamad bin Rashid Al Maktoum had no intention of "pressurising us into military or arms policy cooperation." Nor, it continues, does the Emir of Abu Dhabi, Zayid bin Sultan Al Nahyan, "who would also like to use Abu Dhabi's money to buy weapons in Germany (which the German government was happy to do in the case of the speedboats)".[26]

Seven months after the "Landshut" kidnapping, Sheikh Mohamed is to receive a high honour. It is not until the medal ceremony that it emerges that although the person to be honoured is described as a "gentleman" in the first (unusable) certificate, he is otherwise regarded as female by the relevant authorities.[27] The neck cross is missing from the medal box. The existing medal is attached to a longer, narrow ladies' shoulder strap. The author requests that "a male version of the Grand Cross of Merit with star and shoulder ribbon" be sent immediately.

Finally, there is the complaint—not unjustified in view of the aid provided—that that German Chancellor Helmut Schmidt never again seeks talks with the defence minister of the United Arab Emirates after the German Autumn.

Saudi Arabia

In the old Federal Republic of Germany, boys dress up as cowboys or Indians for carnival. After the so-called oil crisis in 1973, they also dress as sheikhs. Before this crisis, the men in their white robes, headgear and dark sunglasses were unknown to them. These gentlemen, the crisis teaches, turn the oil tap on or off in Western Europe. They decide whether dad gets petrol at the filling station. And at what price.

At the beginning of the 1970s, sheikhs stand for a distant culture that is deeply alien to Europeans. The Arab states are to provide the West with the lubricant for its flourishing prosperity, no less and no more. Luxury Tourism

---

[25] Cf. telex from the Federal Foreign Office to Embassy Abu Dhabi dated 7 June 1978, in: PA-AA, Folder D5 VW 260.30 Pol 300.25 310.10/1.5 - 6.

[26] Telex from the German Embassy in Abu Dhabi to the Federal Foreign Office dated 10 June 1978, in: ibid.

[27] Telex from Hansjoachim Neumann to Minister of State Wischnewski dated 4 June 1978 regarding the Lufthansa hijacking to Dubai. Here: Thanks to Sheikh Mohamed, in: Pol AA. Embassy of the Federal Republic of Germany Abu Dhabi. Subject: Lufthansa hijacking (…). Vol. D5 from 1974 to 1979. Vw 260,30. Pol 300, 25. 310/1,5 + 6.

for normal West German holidaymakers, for example in Dubai, does not yet exist.

The Western states side as mentioned with Israel and against its Arab neighbours in the so-called Yom Kippur War of 1973. In doing so, they antagonise the sheikhs. And in the winter of 1973, millions of Germans do likewise. They have to queue up for petrol. The German government, led by the Social Democrat Chancellor Willy Brandt, decides on car-free Sundays—an initiative of his cabinet member Helmut Schmidt.

During the "Landshut" hijacking four years later, the German government seeks dialogue with the most important state in the region, Saudi Arabia. However, it is not a government representative who flies to King Khalid ibn Abd al-Aziz, and Crown Prince Fahd in Riyadh, but the Bavarian Minister President Franz Josef Strauß. He enjoys travelling far and wide to countries where he receives more and, in his opinion, deserved recognition for his political genius.

King Khalid and Crown Prince Fahd of Saudi Arabia promise the Bavarian Prime Minister to speak up in favour of the German government in Aden. The Federal Chancellor will expressly thank the rulers for this in his government statement in the German Bundestag on 20 October.

In April 1981, Chancellor Helmut Schmidt takes advantage of the established dialogue and pays a state visit to Riyadh. He emphasises his interest in economic cooperation between the two countries. The Saudis turn this interest—not to the surprise of the German government—into a military one: We have the oil, you have the Leopard II tank! Helmut Schmidt cannot decide on a delivery alone. He is personally in favour and presumably lets the sheikhs know this. Back in Germany, his "party friends" will thwart such considerations.

Shortly before that, on 7 October 1980, the German government and the Kingdom of Saudi Arabia meet in a different way. The German government agrees to help the Saudis set up a Special Security Forces anti-terror organisation with 76 men.[28] There is no doubt that the successful "fire magic" operation of Ulrich Wegener's men has made a worldwide impression. Ten GSG9 people are going to Riyadh as trainers for ten months. Germany is also supplying equipment and weapons or the new special force.

Soon afterwards, a second, equally strong unit is to be formed at the Saudi request. This time too, the German government will provide equipment and

---

[28] Note Volker Busse. Group Leader 13 of 13 July 1981 to the Head of the Federal Chancellery. Subject: Co-operation with Saudi Arabia in the field of internal security. Reference: Your enclosed instruction of 8 July 1981, in: BArch AZ n. b.

weapons. A total value is given for the second delivery: Approx. 7.5 million German mark.

The German company Thyssen plays a key role in the deal. Thyssen is supplying "several armoured vehicles" as equipment for the "mechanised unit". For the second project, GSG9 personnel will again send to Riyadh for a few months. This time, their personnel costs will be borne by Thyssen.

On 7 July 1981, Federal Chancellor Helmut Schmidt receives Commander Ulrich Wegener for talks. Also present are Manfred Schüler, Head of the Federal Chancellery, and Helmut Schmidt's personal advisor Jochen Busse.[29] Ulrich Wegener describes his experiences with the Special Security Forces, the Saudi Arabian equivalent of the GSG9, which he trained. According to Wegener, the Saudis want to work with him to develop a far-reaching concept for internal security. Helmut Schmidt explains that "there is great interest in continuing to support Saudi Arabia in this area".[30]

A further memo from the dialogue reveals that Ulrich Wegener is already advising the governments of Singapore, the USA, Great Britain and Israel. Cooperation with the government of Kenya, one of the West's few reliable partners on the African continent, is to be started soon.

The GSG9 is becoming an "export hit",[31] whereby Ulrich Wegener advises governments on a very individual basis—sometimes with more, sometimes with less time and energy.

In the conversation, Helmut Schmidt also discusses the security of the Federal Chancellery by the GSG9. The Chancellor asks the commander to "pay attention to the behaviour of the BGS officers".[32]

Israel

Helmut Schmidt is the only German Chancellor not to have travelled to Israel during his term of office. Never has the relationship between the Federal Republic of Germany and Israel been as icy as during the Schmidt era. The reasons for this are the rapprochement between West Germany and the Arab states during and after the "Landshut" kidnapping and Helmut Schmidt's interest in trade. The closer the economic ties, the less likely a second "oil shock".

---

[29] O. A.: Note dated 8 July 1981 - sealed -.AZ 13 - 211 02 - Bu 101 (NA 1), in: BArch AZ n. b.
[30] Ibid.
[31] Herzog 2022, p. 279.
[32] Ibid.

At the end of the 1970s, there is as mentioned mortal enmity between most Arab states and Israel. Then as now, the political doctrine is to drive all jews into the sea. This can no longer be taken literally at the time, but it expresses the relationship between Israel and its neighbours.

Nevertheless, in September 1978, US President Jimmy Carter is able to broker a "cold peace" between Israel and its former wartime enemy Egypt. The historic Camp David Accords are still in place today. It ended the Middle East conflict at least on this border—but no more.

In 1981—Israel is in the middle of an election campaign—German Chancellor Helmut Schmidt declares the Palestinians' moral claim to their own state during his state visit to Riyadh. He does so there on television so that no Arab ruler misses his message.

The incumbent head of government of the conservative Likud party, Menachem Begin, is furious. Presumably for election campaign purposes, he claims that Helmut Schmidt was once a loyal officer of Hitler. Menachem Begin wants to know from the Chancellor what he did to the Jews on the Eastern Front.[33]

Perhaps the Prime Minister is just misinformed. Menachem Begin points out that Helmut Schmidt attended a trial day of the Nazi People's Court against the men of 20 July. According to Begin analogous, this visit illustrates Schmidt's attitude. The Federal Chancellor himself claims throughout his life that he had been sent there as a kind of intimidation. Prior to this, he claims to have engaged in political blasphemy on several occasions.

For his part, Helmut Schmidt lets it be known that he does not want Begin to be Israeli Prime Minister. The Federal Chancellor could also refer to a Jewish ancestor—his biological grandfather was Jewish—but refrains from doing so. He presumably fears the effect of such a confession in his own country. And in an earlier Bundestag election campaign, he witnessed how his predecessor Willy Brandt was vilified as a candidate for chancellor because of his illegitimate birth.

South Yemen

The South Yemeni regime is not prepared to cooperate in any way during the "Landshut's" stay in Aden. Captain Jürgen Schumann is shot in Aden, for reasons that will probably never be fully clarified. No wonder the German government puts the planned capital aid agreement mentioned here earlier

---

[33] Cf. cover story Der Spiegel No. 20 of 11 May 1981; Bergmann 1998.

with the People's Democratic Republic of Yemen on ice. Minister of State Hans-Jürgen Wischnewski postponed the decision until 1978 presumably in order to put pressure on the government to cooperate in the investigation into Schumann's death.

The South Yemenis continue to stonewall, as a telex from the West German chargé d'affaires Werner Michel shows. It states: "I had the opportunity today to discuss questions relating to the murder of Captain Schumann in a lengthy conversation with the State Secretary in the Foreign Ministry of the DPR Yemen. She repeatedly assured me that documents from South Yemeni authorities contain no evidence that Captain Schumann was forced to return to the aircraft."[34] There was no evidence of conversations between Yemeni security forces and the captain.

The chargé d'affaires was personally at the airport during the events. As he emphasises, he "did not notice whether Captain Schumanns (sic) got off the plane".[35] Since only very few members of the local security forces speak English, it cannot be ruled out "that Captain Schumann's shouts were not understood and for this reason alone it must be assumed that South Yemeni authorities will not be able to provide any additional information."[36]

Mogadishu

Until 17 October 1977, Somalia is in the consciousness of the federal government one of many African countries for the Federal Republic of Germany. For 1977, the development aid ministry earmarks eight million German mark in capital aid and technical equipment worth five million German mark.[37]

In May 1977, the Somali ambassador to the Federal Republic of Germany, Yusuf Adan Bokah, invites German Development Aid Minister Marie Schlei to visit his country. The Federal Foreign Office had previously rejected a visit by Hans-Dietrich Genscher to Somalia. It did not want to honour a socialist police state regime.[38] Marie Schlei is travelling to Mogadishu and brings the

---

[34] Michel, Werner: Telex to the Federal Foreign Office, section 311, dated 8 November 1978, AZ 530.36-JEV, in: PA-AA, Embassy of the Federal Republic of Germany in Abi Dhabi. Abduction Lufthansa (…), Vw 260,30 Pol 300,25 B10/1,5+6.
[35] Ibid.
[36] Ibid.
[37] Cf. Udo Kollatz (State Secretary in the Federal Ministry for Economic Cooperation and Development): Brief note on the status of political cooperation with Somalia, in: Archiv BK 13–211 20 (2) Additional File OTB Bd. 6, p. 476ff.
[38] Cf. Geiger 2009, p. 441.

message from there that more money from Germany could accelerate the regime's shift towards the West.

As heard, Feder Chancelor Helmut Schmidt and Minister of State Hans-Jürgen Wischnewski promise the Somali government civilian equipment and money on the day the hijacked "Landshut" touches down in Mogadishu. Unexpectedly, in this way they continue the talks started by Marie Schlei and led by Klaus Kinkel weeks before.

After their hospitality for the GSG9, the Somali government wants to strike while the iron is hot. On 30 October 1977, around two weeks after the "fire magic" operation, the German government receives a request from President Siad Barre for political and military assistance. At this time, Barre has submitted his request for political support and arms aid to the USA, Great Britain and France.[39]

On the same day, Helmut Schmidt's cabinet decides on an emergency programme, which includes a credit assistance framework and technical equipment worth millions. Millions in cash will be added later. The German government cannot export weapons itself. The Federal Chancellor will persuade Egyptian President Anwar es-Sadat to supply arms to the Somalis. Siad Barre pays for the weapons with German money.[40]

On 3 November, Yusuf Adan Bokah, the Somali ambassador to Germany, visits Helmut Schmidt in his office. On 30 November 1977, a government delegation led by Somali Vice President Major General Hussein Kulmie and Foreign Minister Abduraman Jama Barre arrives in the German capital. They are also received by Helmut Schmidt. In the evening, there is a dinner for the guests at Palais Schaumburg, where the Federal Chancellor gives a speech at the table.

Historian Tim Geiger has described the Federal Chancellor's tenacious endeavours to keep his word to the Somali government after "Mogadishu". The longer the Somali concession was delayed, the more the will to turn words into deeds dwindled in the German capital. Helmut Schmidt personally spends a lot of time and energy on action. He wants to be seen as reliable by Siad Barre. Just as Barre has shown himself to be reliable towards him.

Outside Bonn, the new friendship with Somalia blossoms into folklore. Six weeks after the "Landshut" hijacking, Gerhard Höper, German honorary consul to Somalia in 1977, the year of terror, travelled to the Lower Bavarian city after which the hijacked plane happened to be named. He wants to persuade Lord Mayor Josef ("Dick") Deimer to sign a friendship pact with

---

[39] Cf. telex from Mogadishu to the Federal Foreign Office dated 27 October 1977, reference: POL 321 VS-NFD, in: AdS 1/HSAA008748.
[40] Cf. ibid., pp. 450–455.

the Somali capital. A town twinning over 6000 kilometres? At the time, that seemed complicated and expensive. Nevertheless, the city administration is prepared to "maintain friendly relations with Mogadishu out of gratitude".[41]

The enterprising honorary consul organises with his own money a big party in Landshut to mark the occasion. The Somali National Ballet happens to be on tour in Germany and is engaged for an additional performance in the State Hall of Landshut Town Hall in front of 600 invited guests.

At the end of October 1977, the German-Arab Travel Agency in Cologne reminds travellers that it has been possible to book package tours to Somalia for a year now. The price per person, including flights and accommodation in First-Class hotels, is 2550 German mark. The East African country is particularly recommended for a beach holiday in the months of September to March and late April to June.

In June 1978, German Lufthansa establishes a direct flight between Frankfurt am Main and Mogadishu. Lower Bavarian *Schuhplattler* dancers are on board the first aircraft. They are to familiarise their new friends in the Horn of Africa with their culture. Later in the year, the Somali ambassador to Germany, Yusuf Adan Bokah, takes part in the "Landshut Wedding", a folklore festival, with the country's tourism chief, Ahmed Hussein Bulbul.

The political ties between the two capitals also remain strong. At the end of June 1980, a delegation from the German government led by Federal Minister of the Interior Gerhard Baum travelled to Mogadishu. The Federal Chancellor gives Baum a personal letter to President Siad Barre in which he promises further "humanitarian aid"—that means money.

The diplomatic relations between the Federal Republic of Germany and Somalia end abruptly with the overthrow of Somali President Siad Barre in January 1991. Soon afterwards, the country sinks into civil war. Tribes divide the territory among themselves. Since then, people have fled from there for their very survival—including to the Federal Republic of Germany.

---

[41] O. A.: The alliance with Mogadishu. Partnership as a duty of gratitude, in: Die Zeit of 7 April 1978.

11

Triumph and Decline of a Generation

Helmut Schmidt derives a great deal of personal esteem from the success of "Mogadishu", but no political credit. He will soon learn this.

At the invitation of the Federal Chancellor, the writer Max Frisch comes to Hamburg as a guest speaker at the SPD party conference on 17 November 1977. In other words, shortly after the German Autumn. In the 1970s, SPD party conferences provide seismographic data about the mood not only in the party but also in the country as a whole.

Max Frisch does not forget Helmut Schmidt for taking the time to talk to him on Sunday 16 October, the day of the decision for a "Landshut" storm. In his greeting, Frisch expresses his respect and even admiration for Helmut Schmidt's strong nerves. He shares the Chancellor's tough stance on the matter. "If one affirms—and I do—the rigorism of the government", says Max Frisch in his party conference speech, "which led to human sacrifice in Alsace and to success in Mogadishu—also with human sacrifice there—the logic continues—then this very government, dependent on ethical legitimisation for its rigorism, can no longer give up the great promise of more democracy."[1]

He links his okay to an accusation that must have been a sour grape for Helmut Schmidt and the politicians of his generation. "I ask: How much room for manoeuvre was given to this generation to shape their era

---

[1] Frisch 1977, p. 380. Max Frisch alludes to a sentence by Helmut Schmidt's Social Democratic predecessor in office Willy Brandt, "We want to dare more democracy".

together with their fathers? (…) Their devotion was expected, their submission was expected. (…) Apart from the invitation to cheerful consumption as a prerequisite for economic growth—what do they find, the adolescents, what goal—beyond themselves -, what sense of existence?"[2]

In other words: Mr Chancellor, you and your colleagues were great in the German autumn. But now it's time to put an end to your generational lack of interest in the personal wishes and social ideas of young people!

After the half-tragic, half-happy outcome of the German Autumn, everyday life seems to be returning to political Bonn. The Chancellor's party is divided into left and right wings. The coalition partners SPD and FDP are arguing about substantive issues. The CDU/CSU, as the opposition party in the German Bundestag, demonises pretty much everything the federal government decides.

There is already a row over the creation of a documentary on joint action in the German autumn. The CSU state leader in the German Bundestag, Friedrich Zimmermann, until recently paraded with the Federal Chancellor. He now feels that the federal government has provided far too little insight into the political work of the past few weeks. In other words, it is keeping quiet about the role and involvement of the CDU.

The general hysteria among the population, followed by the euphoria over the successful "fire magic", is subsiding. At the same time, the enormous pressure that the Federal Government exerted on the public and the other pillars of this state in the German autumn is decreasing. On the legislature and judiciary, the German Bundestag and the Federal Constitutional Court. On the colloquial "Fourth estate", the media.

Speaking of legislature: The federal government rushed the "Contact Blocking Act" through parliament. It is still in force today. In the opinion of critics, the federal government and the opposition jointly violated fundamental rights.

Keyword judiciary: The Federal Constitutional Court gave the Federal Government a free hand in the Schleyer kidnapping case. The judges did so under massive pressure from Bonn. Of course, court judgements are never made in politically free space. And yet a stale aftertaste remained.[3]

Keyword media. With the so-called news blackout—the press and radio were not to report on the Federal Government's search measures—the constitutionally enshrined freedom of the press was cancelled.

In the collective consciousness of West Germans, the German Autumn of 1977 remains a time with the character of a police state. The Federal Ministry

---

[2] Ibid. p. 381.
[3] Cf. Polzin 2006.

of the Interior had pretty much every police car in the country swarm out for identity checks. The police searched more flats and houses than ever before or since. In the vast majority of cases, the result was: nothing.

Pressure creates counter-pressure. The harshness of the war generation in the German Autumn calls on advocates of a liberal state. Like Max Frisch at the SPD party conference, they demand a serious examination of the causes of terrorism. What has gone wrong in this state when young, often highly educated people believe they have to bomb it away at all costs—even at the cost of their own lives?

One of the "Stammheim women", RAF terrorist Gudrun Ensslin, came from a Protestant parsonage. During her studies, she was a scholarship holder of the German National Academic Foundation. The foundation supports intellectually brilliant women and men and creates future elites.

The protagonist of this new way of thinking is the Federal Minister of the Interior, Gerhard Baum, successor to Werner Maihofer, who resigned over the Stammheim suicides. He is no longer part of the war generation. His understanding of political freedom was shaped without the burden of a world war. Baum's way of communicating is also new—a modern way of speaking. The Free Democrat has been involved in politics since a young age and does not speak legal German. He listens carefully in discussions and is willing to learn.

His manner of dealing with the Federal Chancellor also appears progressive. In a lecture in 2024,[4] Gerhard Baum recalls conversations with Helmut Schmidt about the latter's China policy. Schmidt considered it presumptuous "to teach other peoples how they should live."[5] Baum replied: Serious violations of human rights challenge us to defend the ethical foundations of the international community.[6]

The new Federal Minister of the Interior, Gerhard Baum, and the head of the Federal Criminal Police Office, Horst Herold, belong to different generations and represent different world views. It is no wonder that there is friction between the two from the outset. This is presumably exacerbated by the fact that the serious mishap in the Schleyer manhunt occurs with Herold, the inventor of the "dragnet investigation". Before the German Autumn, the intellectually brilliant, unusually political policeman, a social democrat, was considered the data genius of his guild. Now, because he could not save Hanns Martin Schleyer, as the nation's top snoop.

---

[4] Gerhard Baum: Leadership is leadership, in: Kellerhoff/Stubbe da Luz 2024, pp. 6–13.
[5] Ibid., p. 10.
[6] Ibid., p. 11. See also Rupps 2022.

Horst Herold, a tragic hero in the aftermath of the German Autumn. With his methods, he came quite close to uncovering Hanns Martin Schleyer's hiding place. A presumably careless police officer ruined his chances. Shortly after the "German Autumn", Horst Herold resigned from his post, allegedly for health reasons. Federal Minister of the Interior Gerhard Baum does not want to dissuade him from his decision.

Horst Herold will spend his retirement in a house on a barracks site of the Bundeswehr. For his personal safety. He will speak with bitterness until the end of his days about how badly he was treated by the political establishment in Bonn. He wants to write a book, for which he presumably had a copy of Helmut Schmidt's "war diary" made. It doesn't come to that.

The way of Horst Herold's departure seems to presage the departure of his generation, the war generation. The morning after the "Landshut" liberation, Helmut Schmidt and his generation celebrate a political triumph. From day two onwards, things will go downhill for them politically.

This is presumably due less to them than to the political succession of generations since the founding of the Republic in 1949. When Konrad Adenauer became Federal Chancellor, he was an old man. Since then, the members of each political leading generation—in the federal government and the German Bundestag—have been older on average than the respective social generation. That is to say, the women and men in leading economic, social or cultural positions.[7]

As intellectually brilliant as Chancellor Helmut Schmidt is—he no longer understands many developments in the present. For example, the new social movements that had been emerging since the mid-1970s. In his government declaration on 20 October 1977, he calls the so-called young people to order in a preachy manner. A change in values is gradually breaking through. Helmut Schmidt cannot see any good in it.

As a member of the war generation who grew up in Hitler's Germany with a compliant Reichstag, he sees the German Bundestag as the heart of democracy. Anything that happens politically outside of it, at universities and on the streets, will always remain suspect to Helmut Schmidt and his ilk. Dangerous.

On top of that, the West German economic miracle has been running out of steam since 1979/80. After the fall of the Shah of Iran, oil exports, which after all account for ten per cent of total demand, dry up. Prices skyrocket. The 1973 oil crisis was harmless by comparison.

---

[7] See Rupps, Twilight of the Chancellor 2017.

At the end of the Schmidt era, West Germany is undergoing a profound industrial transformation. The flagship companies "Made in Germany" are still at the forefront of technology, but in view of high wages and new, cheaper competing products from the Far East, they are no longer competitive. Dual, Grundig, Saba, Telefunken. The flagship companies in consumer electronics are falling like dominoes.

Agfa, Rollei, Bauer. Camera mechanics of world renown. It's over. Because of Canon or Nikon. Toyota, Datsun, Nissan, Honda. Suddenly, West Germans are buying Japanese cars, which don't look particularly European at first, but impress with an unbeatable price-performance ratio. With "the Japanese", you don't have to buy every extra, as you do with VW or Opel. They offer full equipment including electric windows, fleecy carpets and door panels made of fur.

In 1982, the American company IBM launches its largest and at the same time last ball-head typewriter. A technical marvel. Unbreakable. But unfortunately, mechanical. The next generation is equipped with electronics, the precursor to the personal computer.

The type cases disappear from the printing houses. Many of these type cases survive as odds and ends shelves in West German hallways. The former typesetters henceforth glue newspaper pages together from electronically created images and texts.

For decades, West German fathers captured family celebrations on film, first on standard 8 mm and later on super 8 mm. Now, St. Nicholas is coming to video formats such as Betacam (Sony), VHS (JVC) or Video 2000 (Grundig). VHS is catching on because the porn film industry in the USA relies on the format. Grundig's fate is sealed.

This is bitter and yet not surprising. Even Helmut Schmidt's predecessor in office, Willy Brandt, was confronted with the death of entire industries. In the 1960s, coal mines began to close. In the 70 s, the death of farms. The steel industry was also severely hit during this decade.

The autumn of Helmut Schmidt's war generation also brings many things to an end in terms of everyday culture. Ilja Richter ends his "Disco" programme on Second German Television. Even before that, ZDF discontinues Rainer Holbe's "Starparade". The pop group Abba, the musical and commercial Beatles of the 70 s, takes a break for the next 40 years.

In everyday design, bright colours such as yellow, orange and green are disappearing from wallpaper and upholstery as the generation of Helmut Schmidt leaves the stage. German living rooms, caravans and motorhomes are sinking into rustic brown. The era of the "sceptical generation" with its protagonist Helmut Kohl is on the horizon. Kohl and Co. will wear the most conservative suits and ties of any West German politicians before or since.

West Berlin. A provisional solution. The place that keeps the German question open, both bravely and anarchically. With no prospect of a solution. It can't go on like this forever, its people think. I won't live to see it, they say.

A city of contrasts like no other in the so-called federal territory. In districts like Reinickendorf, residents accumulate riches. This can still be seen in online classifieds, where furniture and design items from this period are for sale. At the same time, the dirty, miserable West Berlin mainly exists near the Wall. Kreuzberg.

West Berlin. A political powder keg (both good and bad at the same time). The so-called student movement started in West Berlin in 1967/68. It spread to West Germany and liberated Adenauer's Germany from its proverbial stuffiness. At the end of the 1970s, in the autumn of the war generation, the island city is once again becoming a driving force for social development.

This time, the young people do not take to the streets in protest like in 1967/68 but dye their hair and hung around. "Punk music" spills over from the British Isles and brings with it shrill fashion. The young people provoke with half-shaven heads. They were clothes full of rivets. A telephone cable around their neck. Their message is: We are against it. We want to live differently. Man does not live by bread alone.

West Berlin. Anyone who still goes to school is often a "latchkey kid" like Christiane Felscherinow. She lives in Gropius-Stadt, one of the satellite towns in West Berlin. In 1978, as "Christiane F.", she presents a life story about her slide into the drug and hustler scene. The biography of an extreme life, but for reasons that many young people can identify with.

Many of the 15, 20, 25 year olds reject political Bonn. Chancellor Helmut Schmidt's rigid course in the German Autumn presumably reinforced this rejection. This state wants to be a democracy, but it disregards basic rights. In fact, it is a police state that arbitrarily searches and spies out people.

The disappointment of young people in West Berlin spreads to the rest of the country. To both young people and adults alike. "Christiane F."'s book has a circulation of millions. It becomes a schoolbook and the basis for a feature film. For the first time, the affluent society in the Federal Republic of Germany is holding a mirror up to itself.

One year after the German Autumn, with the publication of Christiane F.'s life confession, the gentlemen in the political Bonn have grown old in their offices. Helmut Schmidt has been a member of the German Bundestag since 1953, the second parliamentary term. Franz Josef Strauß, who wants to replace Helmut Schmidt as Federal Chancellor in 1980, has been in office since 1949, the first ever.

The power dismantling of the men who lead the country through the German Autumn is already beginning in these weeks. On 29 September 1977, the German Bundestag debated the draft of a so-called Contact Prohibition Act. I was already mentioned. In certain cases, the judiciary and police can impose a ban on contact between imprisoned men and women and their lawyers.

In the Bundestag debate on 29 September 1977, Social Democrat member of parliament Wolfgang Coppick recalls that the possibility of meeting a lawyer of one's own choice in the event of arrest was one of the fundamental conditions of a constitutional criminal procedure. "I doubt", Manfred Coppick says verbatim, "whether the exclusion of this possibility is at all compatible with the provisions of the Convention on Human Rights."[8]

Manfred Coppick is already one of the outsiders in his group at the time. With his left-wing positions, he is provocative. Coppick is a man with an unconventional way of thinking who speaks plainly regardless of his political future. He says what quite a few men and women in the House presumably think but are afraid to say.

Manfred Coppick and another rebel, Karlheinz Hansen, are expelled from the SPD parliamentary group in the current legislative period. Coppick and Hansen may be out, but the rebellion within the party against the Chancellor's policies does not die down. And it soon skips over into the streets with historic force. Helmut Schmidt himself provided the impetus for the so-called NATO double-track decision on the stationing of new medium-range weapons in Western Europe.

In retrospect, it must come as a surprise that such an abstract topic triggered the largest protest movement in the old Federal Republic. Presumably this was because the political component—people were afraid of nuclear war—was joined by a generational one. A surfeit of the war generation, which has determined the political fate of West Germany for so long.

The German Autumn also set the course for the country in the medium term. Its subsequent swing towards more liberalism and self-criticism opens the party system to women and men who would presumably not have had a chance before.

Before the German Autumn, it would have been unthinkable that Joschka Fischer, a left-wing sponti with no professional qualifications, can first become Hessian Environment Minister and later Federal Foreign Minister

---

[8] Minutes of the session of the German Bundestag on 29 September 1977, p. 3372.

and Vice-Chancellor. Or the former lawyer of RAF terrorist Gudrun Ensslin, Otto Schily, first making a career with the Greens, later with the Social Democrats and makes it to the position of Minister of the Interior.

Hans-Christian Ströbele, who defended RAF terrorist Andreas Baader, enters the German Bundestag for the Greens. There he will become a legend with his intellectual independence.

Klaus Uwe Benneter, who was expelled from the SPD as a suspected communist in the year of the German Autumn, is now, decades later, the General Secretary of the same party.

Fischer, Schily, Ströbele, Benneter—they represent life journeys and ruptures that are being given space in politics for the first time. As the chastened and the minds with political passion at the same time. The Republic is making amends for the harshness of the "German Autumn". Fischer and Co. can consider Helmut Schmidt their political mentor.

12

Expansion

Presumably no other political event affected the politician Helmut Schmidt as much emotionally as the murder of Hanns Martin Schleyer. For the rest of his life. Political reason, which he valued so highly, assures him that he had acted correctly. And yet he is plagued by feelings of guilt. With a different policy, he would probably have saved this human life. A person he knew personally and valued politically.

Even in his old age, Helmut Schmidt will still have nightmares about images from the German Autumn. This is all the more serious as he does not become more sentimental or self-critical with age. By his own confession, he does not need God to forgive his sins. Nor does he feel any fear of death.

Helmut Schmidt is deeply moved when the Schleyer family extend their hand to him in reconciliation. But first things first.

Helmut Schmidt telephones his wife Waltrude the day after Hanns Martin Schleyer is kidnapped. She thanks him sincerely for this gesture. It remains with this one conversation.

After Hanns Martin Schleyer's body was found, the Federal Chancellor has a three-page letter drafted by his office delivered to Waltrude Schleyer at midday on 20 October. The letterhead is a simple "BRD—Der BK". A gesture of humility from the most politically powerful man in the country.

The text of the typewritten letter reads less like it is addressed to Waltrude Schleyer than to the public. The public is immediately taken into consideration. In the evening, the letter of condolence is sent to the press.

The copy to Waltrude Schleyer contains the publicly distributed text, with a handwritten note from the Federal Chancellor. The addendum is:

"Honoured, dear Mrs Schleyer!

Perhaps it will help you a little to know what we all know here in Bonn: Your husband gave his life for the liberal order in which he believed and for which he stood up all his life.

I wish you comfort in God.

Your devoted.

Helmut Schmidt."[1]

On 25 October 1977, the funeral service for Hanns Martin Schleyer is held in St. Eberhard's Cathedral on Königstrasse in Stuttgart. Men in black suits with submachine guns at the ready stand at the entrance. In the cathedral itself, Waltrude Schleyer and Helmut Schmidt sit next to each other in the first pew. Waltrude Schleyer has previously asked that the Federal Chancellor will not be giving a speech.

Helmut Schmidt watches the funeral service with his head bowed, visibly shaken. Waltrude Schleyer and he have nothing to say to each other. The murder of Hanns Martin Schleyer is the first and only time they meet in person. Helmut Schmidt would later describe this moment as the most difficult of his political life.

Waltrude and Hanns Martin Schleyer have four sons, Hanns-Eberhard, Arndt, Dirk and Jörg. While their father is held hostage, 32-year-old lawyer Hanns-Eberhard Schleyer acts as spokesman for the family. He cuts an excellent figure. He speaks on an equal footing with the politicians who have to decide the father's fate. Exerts public pressure with the help of the "Bild" newspaper. He appeals to the Federal Constitutional Court for an urgent legal decision.

Hanns-Eberhard is particularly close to his father. He is the only one—because he is by far the eldest—of the four Schleyer children to develop a reflective relationship with him. Father and son engage in political discussions. Also about Hanns Martin Schleyer's behaviour in National Socialist Germany.

For the younger brothers Arnd, Dirk and Jörg, their father is an absent father, as is usual for fathers in top political positions at the time. He always takes time for the family on holiday; the Schleyers own a holiday home in Meersburg on Lake Constance. Political friends also come there. Super 8 films shot by Hanns-Eberhard show Kurt Georg Kiesinger in casual clothes and Helmut Kohl in swimming trunks. Waltraud Schleyer took spontaneously the swimming trunks out of her husband's wardrobe for him.

---

[1] Archiv BK 13–211 20 (2) Additional file OTB vol. 7, p. 132.

After the assassination of his father, on 12 March 1978, Arnd Schleyer writes a letter to Chancellor Helmut Schmidt. "I am not calling for your resignation (…), but perhaps you now realise that such a decision must be the last resort, which—if at all—is only morally justifiable if everything (emphasis A. S., note M. R.) has been done to save the endangered life. (…) I am not accusing you of recklessness, but I am accusing you of having self-righteously comforted yourself in your decision by saying that everything had been done (to find H. M. S., note M. R.)."[2]

Arndt Schleyer expresses what his mother and older brother Hanns-Eberhard presumably also think. And the youngest Dirk and Jörg at least feel the same way. But neither Waltrude nor Hanns-Eberhard Schleyer ever expresses themselves in a comparable emotional, authentic way in letters or in public. Not during the German Autumn and never afterwards.

Asked about his personal restraint, Hanns-Eberhard Schleyer says in historical retrospect that, as the family spokesperson, he was keen to engage in constructive dialogue with the Federal Government. Waltrude and Hanns-Eberhard Schleyer wanted to follow the personal style that their father stood for—a calm, rational dialogue partner who wanted to convince with arguments.

Helmut Schmidt chickens out of responding to Arnd Schleyer's letter. He writes "Chief BK" on it. Meaning: Manfred Schüler should reply. Schmidt is presumably worried that Arnd Schleyer would make the answer public. Or Hanns Martin Schleyer's murder weighs so heavily on the Chancellor's mind that he feels unable to answer. Perhaps it is just more comfortable to entrust someone else with it.

"The circumstances that have come to light in the handling of information about the flat in Erftstadt have deeply affected the Federal Chancellor", Manfred Schüler assures in his reply. "The fact that it was nevertheless not possible to follow up the information about the flat in Erftstadt in the necessary manner must be a cause for concern."[3] The Federal Chancellor had worked hard to ensure that the fundamental goals that had been set were constantly and intensively pursued.

Arnd Schleyer's accusation that Helmut Schmidt acted self-righteously will not be accepted by his most important colleague. "The Federal Chancellor's actions were guided by a constant and unwavering responsibility to the values of our constitution."

Waltrude Schleyer never forgave Helmut Schmidt for the rest of her life. Her sons will try to cope with the trauma in different ways. Losing a father

---

[2] AdsD, 1/HSASA010020.
[3] Ibid.

at an early age is terrible. Seeing him suffer in public for weeks before his murder is even worse.

It is only after the death of Waltrude Schleyer in 2008 that a reconciliation between the family and Helmut Schmidt comes into question. Hanns-Eberhard suggests to his brothers that the former Federal Chancellor should receive the Hanns Martin Schleyer Prize. This is an honour for important personalities from politics, business, science and society. Not all of the Schleyer brothers immediately agree. Hanns-Eberhard Schleyer is finally able to convince them.

On 26 April 2013, former German Chancellor Helmut Schmidt will be awarded the Hanns Martin Schleyer Prize in Stuttgart's White Palace. The laudatory speech will be held by former French President Valery Giscard d'Estaing, a political and personal friend of the Chancellor from the mid-1970s to the present day.

Helmut Schmidt appears visibly moved by this honour. In his short acceptance speech,[4] he confesses that he was able to understand the complaint made by Waltrude Schleyer and her children to the Federal Constitutional Court at the time. "They placed the fundamental right to life of their husband and father above all other basic values." However, those responsible in Bonn could not have once again allowed "criminals who had been set free to continue their murderous activities. (…) I am deeply moved today by the fact that the Schleyer family has publicly expressed their respect for my attitude at the time."[5]

After the ceremony, selected guests are invited to a reception. Helmut Schmidt and his partner Ruth Loah attend, as do the Schleyer brothers with their partners and CDU politician Wolfgang Schäuble. Also those affected by the "Landshut" hijacking, Jürgen Vietor and his wife Rosi and Gabriele and Ruedeger von Lutzau.

For Gabriele von Lutzau (née Dillmann) and Helmut Schmidt, it is the first reunion since the 1977 reception at the Federal Chancellery in Bonn. The atmosphere is relaxed, even cheerful, as Gabriele von Lutzau recalls. She uses her gift to help people who are tongue-tied to speak and laugh. Ruth Loah talks about the support stockings she puts on Helmut Schmidt in the morning.

As trivial as the topics of conversation may be, the encounter is of historical significance. The Schleyer family, who lost its father in the German Autumn, former Federal Chancellor Helmut Schmidt as the decision-maker at the time

---

[4] Cf. Schmidt 1986.

[5] Ibid, p. 42.

and freed hostages, who indirectly owe their lives to Helmut Schmidt, at a joint celebration. Meeting now also means an opportunity for coping.

Helmut Schmidt and Hanns-Eberhard Schleyer talk to editors of the "Süddeutsche Zeitung Magazin" on the occasion of the award ceremony. "88 people (sic!) are more important than one", Helmut Schmidt once said to Hans-Jürgen Wischnewski when the hijacked "Landshut" was in Dubai. Almost 36 years later, he would repeat this sentence in this very conversation.

Helmut Schmidt and Hanns-Eberhard Schleyer recall their personal rapprochement in the decades following the German Autumn. The first encounters failed because of a mutual bias. The two men did not click. Not even in the decades that followed, when they met by chance on various occasions.

As in his acceptance speech in Stuttgart, Helmut Schmidt shows understanding for the Schleyers' actions during the German Autumn. That they mobilised the media to save her husband and father. And that she appealed to the Federal Constitutional Court as the final legal authority. The tenor: I would have done the same in your place.

At the same time, the former Chancellor leaves no doubt that he would make the same decision today as he did back then. No giving in to Schleyer's kidnappers. No release of terrorists. Even if it costs a human life.

Helmut Schmidt and Hanns-Eberhard Schleyer continue to part ways with different positions, but with mutual understanding. Two lives that were fatefully intertwined during the German Autumn of 1977.

13

State Raison

The chapter is preceded by an unwieldy word. Reason of state. The Federal Government was confronted with it even before the German Autumn had come to an end. Relatives of the "Landshut" hostages ask the State Secretary in the Federal Ministry of Transport, Ernst Haar, in a conversation on Monday, 17 October 1977, whether reasons of state are more important to the Federal Government than saving so many lives.[1]

The term "reason of state" has its origins in Prussian history. It stands for the actions of rulers for the good of the state. For the stability of the state order. The welfare of the state takes precedence over the individual welfare of its citizens. The state order must be protected as a solid framework for people to live together. At all costs. Even at the cost of human life.

"Räson" means reason. In reference to the German Autumn: The voice of the heart demands that everything be done to save Hanns Martin Schleyer. Reason demands that the demands of his kidnappers not be met. The released terrorists would continue to kill in order to shake the state order.

In his government statement to the German Bundestag on 20 October, Chancellor Helmut Schmidt seeks to dispel the impression that his government has placed the interests of the state above those of Hanns Martin Schleyer. He provides a spiritual, value-oriented foundation for his decisions. "Guidance was given". In other words: By remaining firm, the Federal Government has set an example in defence of democracy.

---

[1] Cf. Kaiser 1977.

"What is reason of state?" asks Carl-Christian Kaiser in "Die Zeit" the next day. He doesn't give an answer himself but predicts that the question will occupy many authors after the German Autumn. He will be right with this prediction.

On 21 January 1978, Helmut Schmidt is awarded the 1978 Theodor Heuss Prize. The memory of the German Autumn is still fresh. "The freedom we defend is a moral and a political good",[2] physicist Carl-Friedrich von Weizsäcker explains the decision. According to von Weizsäcker, we must "defend our real social order. If we lose it, we won't get a better one."[3] The FDP politician Hildegard Hamm-Brücher then praises the Federal Chancellor for his "exemplary, radiant and convincing democratic leadership" during the German Autumn.[4]

In his acceptance speech, Chancellor Helmut Schmidt himself recalls the qualities that the sociologist Max Weber has prescribed for a politician: Passion, a sense of proportion, a sense of responsibility. "In my understanding, politics is pragmatic action for moral purposes (…)."[5] Max Weber is one of Helmut Schmidt's "in-house pharmacists", as he himself called the teachers of his political thinking; Marcus Aurelius, Immanuel Kant, Max Weber and Karl Popper.

The awarding of the Theodor Heuss Prize to Helmut Schmidt is a statement. In retrospect, the political, social and scientific elite of the Federal Republic of Germany approves of Schmidt's persistence in the German Autumn. It explicitly clears him of possible accusations such as violating fundamental rights.

At the same time, it is a statement to the Germans. The German government's rigid policy should go down in the history books as politically cured. In the collective memory as a success.

The acquittal remains half an acquittal. On the same occasion, Stuttgart's Lord Mayor Manfred Rommel is also awarded the Theodor Heuss Prize. He ordered that Andreas Baader, Jan-Carl Raspe and Gudrun Ensslin be buried next to each other in Stuttgart's forest cemetery. "All enmity must end in death", was his courageous credo, endeavouring to achieve domestic peace.

The double award ceremony also marks a generational change. Manfred Rommel no longer belongs to Helmut Schmidt's wartime generation. Manfred Rommel stands for a new, liberal understanding of politics. It is to be recognised and strengthened with Rommel's honour.

---

[2] Theodor Heuss Foundation 1978, p. 10.
[3] Ibid.
[4] Ibid, p. 19.
[5] Ibid, p. 2.

The political history of the old Federal Republic of Germany has many happy moments. The liberation of the women, men and children from the hijacked "Landshut" on 17 October 1977 and the fall of the Berlin Wall on 11 November 1989. Helmut Schmidt cried on both occasions, as he would later confess.

The episode of Schmidt's tears of joy after "Mogadishu" has many variations. Sometimes the Federal Chancellor's eyes get wet to moist, in other articles or books tears roll down to the point of profuse weeping. The topic would not be worth mentioning if Helmut Schmidt does not immediately regret his confession and dismiss his tears as a "fact of life". By then, the "facts" are already out in the world and the sympathy of many West Germans is won.

In June 1981, the Federal Chancellor visits the Protestant Church Congress in Hamburg. During a panel discussion on the topic of "How Christian can politics be?", he talks about his personal decision-making situation in "Mogadishu".

The former Governing Mayor of Berlin, Heinrich Albertz, assures him that he deeply empathises with what Helmut Schmidt has been going through these days. "There was just one difference that made me think: After a similarly terrible situation, when he used force to free the hostages on the train, your colleague said: 'I am ashamed that I had to use force? I haven't heard such tones here but have read about the Heroes of Mogadishu'."[6]

Despite his tears, Helmut Schmidt still owes something important after the German autumn. A speech, a confession, even an admission that goes beyond his government declaration in the week after "Mogadishu". A big word that also names failures in the "German Autumn" and before. A speech of humility and pride.

20 years after the German Autumn, Heinrich Breloer's "Todesspiel", produced by Westdeutscher Rundfunk, stages the events. One episode focuses on the kidnapping of Hanns Martin Schleyer, the other on the errant flight of the Lufthansa plane "Landshut". Heinrich Breloer cuts together scenes and interviews with contemporary witnesses. For the first time, the Germans are given a staged demonstration of how Hanns Martin Schleyer must have fared in his RAF prison and how the "Landshut" hostages must have fared on their hijacking flight.

The response after the broadcast is huge.

---

[6] Luhmann/Neveling 1981. What is meant is the previous hijacking by Moluccans in the Netherlands, as mentioned here.

The "Todesspiel" is less about historical clarification than letting the protagonists tell how they experienced the events of the time. After 20 years, it all sounds very quotable for the history books.

Of all the contemporary witnesses, Helmut Schmidt once again presents himself best—thanks in part to Heinrich Breloer's lighting design, which makes Schmidt's face reminiscent of the Commendatore in Mozart's "Don Giovanni". Every word from the Mogadishu decision-maker would be a gift to the world. As always, the former chancellor masterfully uses pauses in his speech. He takes a deep drag on a cigarette. He sighs and says, "I have incurred guilt". It is a scene that is sure to be remembered, along with the sentence.

On another occasion, the former chancellor says: "I am entangled in guilt".[7] Another dramatic sentence. An interpretable one. Does he not only feel politically guilty about Hanns Martin Schleyer's death? But also, personally responsible? Self-pity shines through.

Until the end of their lives, the political decision-makers in the German autumn will claim that they did not pay homage to any reason of state. That, in this crisis situation, they did not revert to the ruling mindset of a non-democratic, absolutist state.

Only one of the political decision-makers, Helmut Kohl, takes a break for a moment. Born in 1930, Helmut Kohl no longer belongs to Helmut Schmidt's wartime generation, but to the "sceptical generation", as the sociologist Helmut Schelsky called Kohl's cohort. Its members were politically moulded in the late phase of the world war and the post-war period.

On 18 January 1977, the German Bundestag convenes for the first time after the Christmas break. Over the holidays, Helmut Kohl presumably reviewed the terrible events of the German autumn. When he takes the floor on this January day, he does not keep his conflict of conscience and his own feelings of guilt to himself.

Hanns Martin Schleyer, says the opposition leader of the CDU/CSU, "was expected to make the heaviest possible sacrifice as a result of the joint decision in the Large Political Advisory Group".[8] Elsewhere in his speech, he reminds us—directly addressing Federal Chancellor Helmut Schmidt—"that we have expected him (H. M. S., author's note) to make a sacrifice, and that this is no longer a political question, but a moral question to us personally as to how we face up to this responsibility."[9]

---

[7] Cf. Schmidt 2007.
[8] Kohl 1978, p. 4983.
[9] Ibid, p. 4985.

Helmut Schmidt himself will reject the accusation with the reason of state for life. In truth throughout his life, the stability of the state order would be more important to him than saving human lives. This is obviously the old Helmut Schmidt, who after his retirement from politics says and writes bluntly what he thought. See his trivialising attitude towards the Chinese regime's Tian'anmen massacre in June 1989.[10]

The world power China has interested, even electrified Helmut Schmidt since his state visit in October 1975, the first visit by a German chancellor to China. Helmut Schmidt can meet the terminally ill Mao Zedong. He would later write about this encounter with great respect for this world revolutionary.

Throughout his political life, Helmut Schmidt feels drawn to charismatic personalities. These include the Swede Olof Palme, the Egyptian Anwar es-Sadat and Mao Zedon. Outside of politics, he calls personalities such as Siegfried Lenz, Leonard Bernstein and Justus Frantz his friends.

Mao Zedong is already decrepit, as Helmut Schmidt will remember in his memoirs. The Chancellor is not even sure whether the host understands what he is saying. Together with his two interpreters. Nevertheless, Mao Zedong receives the head of government of a politically small but economically strong country in the centre of Europe.

The Chancellor manages to establish a common bond with Mao Zedong's successor Deng Xiaoping. He is interested in West Germany's so-called social market economy. Perhaps it contains elements that the government of the giant empire can learn from. Helmut Schmidt, for his part, wants to know from Deng Xiaoping how his regime is coping with the country's huge population. With the difficulty of keeping such a large number of people together politically.

Helmut Schmidt has always thought big. International. He is both admired and ridiculed for his proverbial "World Economic Opera"—an analysis of the global economy in 20 or 30 min. Helmut Schmidt originally wanted to become an urban planner out of an interest in large dimensions. This came to nothing because of his long years in the Wehrmacht.

Schmidt's trips to China, where he meets masses of people in a small space, draw his attention to the growth of the world's population. At a meeting with Pope John Paul II, he sharply criticises the Catholic Church's stance on birth control.

Also as a book author. "Europeans or Americans, John Paul II and Ronald Reagan at the forefront, may condemn the Chinese regulation of the birth

---

[10] For the following, see Rupps 2022.

rate as an infringement of individual freedom or as unchristian—but what else can the moralist recommend to control the population explosion?."[11]

In his books *Menschen und Mächte* ("People and Powers") and *Weggefährten* ("Companions"), Helmut Schmidt talks in detail about the German chancellor who held talks with Mao Zedong and Deng Xiaoping on equal terms. The massacre on Tiananmen Square—in June 1989, the regime had protesting students crushed by tanks—is mentioned in passing.

In one of the few footnotes in the book—and therefore all the more striking—Helmut Schmidt casts doubt on the figure of up to 400 dead in the massacre that has been cited in Western publications. "The German embassy in Beijing gave me much lower figures."[12] In other words: It wasn't all that bad. On another occasion, he criticises "how the event is referred to in the West (…)." The word "massacre" seems exaggerated to him.

Helmut Schmidt deplores "Western judgements and commentaries (as) overly self-righteous when they apply Western democratic constitutional standards to China and Deng Xiaoping and claim human rights. Those who apply Chinese standards (…), on the other hand, know that there have been mass sacrifices in China before."[13]

In other words, the fundamental right to life and physical integrity, as set out in the catalogue of basic rights in the German constitution, has no equivalent in China. Neither in the tradition nor in its political practice. Helmut Schmidt expressly defends the Beijing regime against criticism from the West.

Helmut Schmidt's attitude appears to be incompatible with the concept of universal human rights, which underlies the political principles of democratic states—including the state that Helmut Schmidt governed politically between 1974 and 1982.

It is unlikely that the Chinese interlocutors downplayed the massacre to the frequent guest from Germany. It is based on the political characterisation of Helmut Schmidt himself. He knew full well what he was writing about. To put it bluntly, what are a few dozen or a hundred or a thousand dead students compared to over a billion people who need to be kept in check politically? The stability and ability of the state to act take precedence over a person's right to physical integrity. Keyword reason of state.

In order to explain the Chinese situation, reference is often made to the spiritual foundation of its people, Confucianism, which is over 2000 years old. Helmut Schmidt takes up this reference. He reminds us that "hierarchies

---

[11] Helmut Schmidt 1987, p. 395.
[12] Helmut Schmidt 1996, p. 320.
[13] Schmidt, *Weggefährten*, 32.

are not a communist invention, but a Confucian one (...)."[14] In contrast to the European Enlightenment, the role of the individual is relatively small.

The so-called war generation is no stranger to this kind of thinking. Born around 1918, Helmut Schmidt and his family became "Hitler Youth" after 1933 and later NSDAP members. Nolens volens, they were part of the National Socialist "people's community". Helmut Schmidt was told: "You are nothing, your people are everything."

Even during the world war, instigated by the Nazi regime, the Schmidts and Herolds remained numbers. Never individuals. Personalities. Their "falling" in the war, as this way of dying is still called today, meant nothing ethically and politically to the "national community". They only received recognition as a collective.

The so-called war generation was only able to free itself from the ideological thinking of the Nazis after 1945. The imprint of authoritarian and totalitarian thought patterns in the decisive years of their lives remains. Helmut Schmidt and Co. will occupy the political control centres of the West German state as "learned democrats"[15]. They undoubtedly learnt the trade, but they never completely shook off the influence of a fascist state.

For Helmut Schmidt, as a member of the war generation, a situation in which citizens had to fear a terrorist gang was an expression of a weak state that was no longer fulfilling its protective function. In other words, it had lost its legitimacy. State authority had to be restored at all costs. Even at the cost of a human life, Hanns Martin Schleyer, or of the kidnapped hostages in the "Landshut".

Not for a second did the Federal Chancellery, the Federal Government and the crisis teams seriously weigh up the requirement of the Basic Law to place the dignity of the individual above all else against the threat posed by released terrorists who would presumably commit new murders. The matter was already decided on the evening of Hanns Martin Schleyer's abduction. Not only, as Helmut Schmidt would claim decades later in an interview with the oldest son of the president of the German Employers' Association, when the Lufthansa aircraft "Landshut" was hijacked.

After the German Autumn, Helmut Schmidt will fondly recall the supposedly difficult conflict of conscience of Bonn's leading politicians at the time. "We wrestled with ourselves for a long time—deeply moved and at the same

---

[14] Frank Sieren, *Nachbar China: Helmut Schmidt im Gespräch mit Frank Sieren* (Berlin: Ullstein, 2007), 257.
[15] Cf. Stephan 1988.

time under all our reason",[16] said the Federal Chancellor at the Protestant Church Congress in 1981.

No, Helmut Schmidt and his team did not. In fact, the political leaders act consistently from the beginning to the end of the German Autumn. Tough as nails.

The Federal Constitutional Court, to which the Schleyer family appealed, approved this hardship in its urgent ruling of 16 October 1977. The presiding judge, Ernst Benda, would later concede to Hanns-Eberhard Schleyer that members of the German government had exerted massive pressure on the court.

There is no doubt that Federal Chancellor Helmut Schmidt was hard on the constitutional organs during the German Autumn. The federal government muzzled the press and broadcasting in Germany, combined with blatant threats. In the German Bundestag, it rushed through the so-called Kontaktsperregesetz (law on the interruption of contacts). Another example is the harshness with which it made it clear to the Federal Constitutional Court: We still govern this country!

In another way, the generational influence of Helmut Schmidt and his peers in the "steel bath" of the Second World War is fortunate. Through the lens of war, they never underestimated the terrorists' willingness to use violence. BKA boss Horst Herold delved deeply into the mind of the "opponent". His method of computer surveillance almost succeeded in tracking down Hanns Martin Schleyer's hiding place.

Without hesitation, Helmut Schmidt and Co. sent German police forces after the hijacked "Landshut". It took courage to actually allow the GSG9 to storm. Only the Israelis had been so determined in Entebbe before. Helmut Schmidt proves that courage.

With the miraculous success of the "Feuerzauber" operation, the German government inflicted a historic defeat on the RAF. The suicides in Stuttgart-Stammheim wiped out the RAF leadership of the first generation. This was not the end of RAF terror in the Federal Republic of Germany, but it could no longer shake the Federal Republic as much as it did during the German Autumn.

Chapeau, Helmut Schmidt and his team! Probably no future generation of politicians in the Federal Republic of Germany, moulded in peacetime, would have held their nerve in a comparable way. In retrospect, the former Federal Chancellor proved to be a man with great strengths, but also weaknesses.

---

[16] Luhmann/Neveling 1981, p. 685.

The Austrian filmmaker Wolfgang Tumler, author of a documentary about the family of "Landshut" captain Schumann, took part in a television discussion with Helmut Schmidt in the 1960s. Both were guests in an edition of "Das Seepferdchen", a series produced by the Austrian Broadcasting Corporation. It was about the Hamburg storm surge of 1962 and the role of Helmut Schmidt, who was Senator of the Interior at the time.

Helmut Schmidt was asked how he would have dealt with looters in the abandoned houses. He answered: "I would have had them shot."

Sources

Conversations/interviews

Former "Landshut" Hostages

Hannelore Brauchart (née Piegler), died in September 2022.

Gaby Coldewey

Hartwig Faby

Beate Keller (née Zerbst)

Jutta Knauff (née Brod)

Mike Brod

Diana Müll

Gabriele von Lutzau (née Dillmann)

Brigitte Paul (née Pittelkow)

Birgit Roehll

Stefan Roehll

Jürgen Vietor

Talks with relatives of former "landshut" hostages

Mike Brod, son of former "Landshut" hostage Jutta Knauff (née Brod).

Agnes Hanke, daughter of the former "Landshut" hostage Karl Hanke.

Eva Filius-Joepgen, daughter of the former "Landshut" hostages Julia Sost (née Filius) and Dietrich Filius.

Dorothe Köster, daughter of former "Landshut" hostage Matthias Rath.

Felicitas and Jörn von Lutzau (children of Gabriele von Lutzau, née Dillmann, and Ruediger von Lutzau, co-pilot of the Lufthansa plane from Frankfurt am Main to Mogadishu on 17 October 1977, died on 2 August 2021.

Hedwig Rath, widow of former "Landshut" hostage Matthias Rath, died on 11 November 2011.

Ralph Regelmann, husband of Simone Regelmann (née Liedtke). The former "Landshut" hostage died on 19 August 2020.

Horst Meijer-Werner, son of the former "Landshut" hostage Cäcilie Meijer-Werner.

Daniela Schiefner, executor of the estate of former "Landshut" hostage Edelgard Wolff.

Interviews with former members of the Border Guard Force 9 of the Federal Border Guard

Dieter Fox, Deputy Commander.

Aribert Martin.

Ulrich Wegener, Commander.

They also support the project through their willingness to talk or help with research

Volker Busse, employee in the office of Chancellor Helmut Schmidt and recorder of the so-called Operation Diary in the German autumn of 1977.

Hanns-Eberhard Schleyer, Son of Hanns Martin Schleyer

Sophie Hartmann, historian.

Dorothea Hauser, historian.

Michaela Huber, graduate psychologist and licensed psychological psychotherapist.

Carola Kapitza, former Head of Corporate Archives at German Lufthansa.

Peter Kiewitt, personal assistant to Minister of State Hans-Jürgen Wischnewski. He accompanied his boss to Mogadishu on 17 October 1977.

Wolfgang Kraushaar, political scientist at the Hamburg Foundation for the Advancement of Research and Culture.

Rosvita Krausz, radio journalist specialising in trauma and its consequences.

Prof Paula Lutum-Lenger, Director of the House of History Baden-Württemberg Initiator of the exhibition "RAF—Terror in the Southwest" 2013/14 in Stuttgart (later also Berlin).

Anne Ameri-Siemens, book and film author.

Kurt Stenzel, Middle East correspondent for ARD Süddeutscher Rundfunk in 1977 (died on 3 April 2012).

Bernhard Vogel, former Minister President of Rhineland-Palatinate and Thuringia.

Barbara Wüsten, Victims' Rights Officer at the White Ring, Mainz Federal Office.

Bernd Zeitler, member of the German Embassy in Mogadishu/Somalia in 1977.

Unpublished Sources

Recording of parts of the radio traffic between the Lufthansa crisis team in Frankfurt am Main and Lufthansa employees at Mogadishu airport by amateur radio operator Ludwig Hildebrand.

Files of the Federal Chancellery: Released part of the so-called Operation Diary, the minutes of discussions and materials from the Short Briefing and the Large Political Advisory Group in the Federal Chancellery in autumn 1977. As of October 2021, Berlin.

Files of the Federal Ministry of Labour and Social Affairs and the Federal Ministry of Justice in the Federal Archives in Koblenz.

Files of the Helmut and Loki Schmidt Foundation, Hamburg.

Files in the Helmut Schmidt Archive in the Archive of Social Democracy of the Friedrich-Ebert-Stiftung, Bonn.

Gerhard Baum: Transcript of a conversation with Südwestrundfunk editor Martina Treuter on 30 March 2017 in Cologne. Typescript (excerpts in Treuter 2017b).

Interviews by Dorothea Hauser with former politicians as part of a contemporary witness project for the Helmut and Loki Schmidt Foundation, Hamburg. In detail:

Conversations with Horst Herold on 29 November 1995 and 8 March 1996 in Rosenheim. OH12, Vol. 1–164, Folder 1/1.

Conversation with Heinz Ruhnau on 15 May 1995 in Bonn. OH20, B. 1 1–17, folder 1/1.

Conversation with Hans-Jochen Vogel on 17 October 1995 in Munich. HSA: OH29, B. 1–49, folder 1/1.

Conversation with Hans-Jürgen Wischnewski on 15 September 1995 in Bonn. HSA: OH30, B. 1–58, folder 1/1; temporarily present: Heinz Ruhnau.

Conversation with Friedrich Zimmermann on 19 September 1995 in Munich. HSA OH31, B. 1–26, folder 1/1.

Conversation with Klaus Bölling on 15 September 1994 in Berlin. HSA: OH4, B. 1–164, folder 1/11.

Sophie Hartmann: The hijacking of the "Landshut" in 1977—How close is the medium of film to historical reality? Term paper for the Master's degree in October 2009 at the History Department of the Ludwig-Maximilians-University Munich, typescript.

German Lufthansa: 0Z1-Ereignis-Log. Event: Hijacking LH181/130ct B737C DABCE 13 Oct. 1977–18 Oct. 1977, typescript, undated.

Personal notes by Jürgen Vietor on the preparation of a witness statement in the trial against Souhaila Andrawes, typescript, 1996.

Excerpts from the investigation file of the Federal Criminal Police Office on the trial against Souhaila Andrawes (1996), in: BArch B131/1173.

Conversations between Jürgen Vietor and "Stern" reporter Gerd Heidemann on 19 October 1977 at Jürgen Vietor's private home (together with Renate Vietor) in Bensheim and on 22 October 1977 at the "Steigenberger Airport Hotel", Frankfurt. There temporarily together with Gabriele von Lutzau (née Dillmann) and Ruediger von Lutzau.

Transcripts of conversations between psychologist Wolfgang Salewski and the "Landshut" crew members and Ragna Albrecht, Lufthansa flight attendant and passenger on the hijacked flight (commissioned by German Lufthansa). Most of the conversations—including the group discussions—took place during a meeting between Lufthansa executives and two officials from the Federal Criminal Police Office in Frankfurt on 13 and 15 December 1977. Further individual discussions took place during the same period; the date and location can no longer be reconstructed. In detail:

Conversation Brauchardt (née Piegler) / Salewski.
Interview Staringer/Salewski.
Conversation Vietor/Salewski. Volume S/I.
Conversation Vietor/Salewski Volume S/I. Back cover.
Conversation Vietor/Salewski Volume S/II.
Conversation by Lutzau/Salewski.
Group discussion I Crew/Salewski.
Group discussion II Crew/Salewski.
Group discussion III Crew/Salewski.

Interview Ragna Albrecht (flight attendant travelling privately) /Salewski.

Minutes of the interrogation of Peter Heldt, head of the B737 fleet department of German Lufthansa, at the Federal Criminal Police Office in Wiesbaden on 25 October 1977, in: Lufthansa-Archiv Frankfurt am Main.

Excerpt from the minutes of a Lufthansa board meeting on 26 October 1977, in: Lufthansa-Archiv Frankfurt am Main.

(...)) Seemann: File note. Abduction LH 181/13 October 1977 dated 16 December 1977, typescript, in: Lufthansa-Archiv Frankfurt am Main.

Caesar, Heino: CF analysis of the "Landshut" hijacking, 19 December 1977, typescript, in: Lufthansa-Archiv Frankfurt am Main.

Fox, Dieter: Interview with the journalist Christian Stücken on 14 March 2023 in Düsseldorf, typescript.

Müll, Diane: Interview with the journalist Christian Stücken on 9 March 2023 in Friedrichshafen, typescript.

Vietor, Jürgen: Preparation for testimony in the Andrawes trial, typescript, undated (presumably 1986, the year of the Andrawes trial).

Wegener, Ulrich: Interview with SWR journalist and ARD terrorism expert Holger Schmidt and the author on 5 December 2016 in St. Augustin-Windhagen.

Personal collections of material from the former "Landshut" hostages Diana Müll, Beate Keller, Jutta Knauff and Birgit Röhll.

Unpublished Film Material

Fully filmed conversations between Südwestrundfunk (née Südwestfunk) editor Ebbo Demant and former "Landshut" hostages (1980). These include:
Hannelore Brauchart (née Piegler)
Gabriele von Lutzau (née Dillmann)
Hartwig Faby
Karl Hanke
Beate Keller (née Zerbst)
Cäcilie Meijer-Werner
Matthias Rath
Rhett Waida
Edelgard Wolff
Ebbo Demant conducted these interviews in 1980 for the television documentaries "Menschen und Straßen. Mogadishu Airfield" (Demand 1981), and "Mogadishu. Memories and Assessments" (Demand 1982).

Printed Sources

Recording of the radio traffic between the tower of Mogadishu airport and the "Landshut" cockpit (recorded by the American secret service CIA). Supplement in: Hermann, Kai/Koch, Peter: Decision in Mogadishu. The 50 days after Schleyer's abduction. Documents—Pictures—Witnesses, Hamburg 1977.

An audio copy of the recording can be found in the radio database of Südwestrundfunk (née Südwestfunk).

Institute of Contemporary History at the Federal Foreign Office (ed.). Möller, Horst (main ed.), Hildebrand, Klaus; Schöllgen, Gregor (co-ed.): Akten zur Auswärtigen Politik der Bundesrepublik Deutschland 1977. vol. II: 1 July to 31 December 1977. doc. 284, 289–295, 299. Pautsch, Ilse Dorothee (scientific editor), Munich 2008.

Bibliography

Albrecht, Henning: 'Pragmatisches Handeln zu sittlichen Zwecken'. Helmut Schmidt and Philosophy, Bremen 2008.
Ameri-Siemens, Anne: For the RAF he was the system, for me he was the father. The other history of German terrorism, Munich 2007.
Bärnthaler, Thomas/Hein, Theresa: 'Man hat sich nicht um uns gekümmert', in: Süddeutsche Zeitung Magazin 15/2024, Munich.
Bahners, Patrick: In the Cloak of History. Helmut Kohl or Immortalisation, Berlin 1998.
Bauer, Martin/Hacke, Jens (eds.): Schmidt, Bonn, Suhrkamp. From Siegfried Unseld's 'Chronik', in: Zeitschrift für Ideengeschichte Heft IV/4 Winter 2010. Autorität. Munich 2010, pp. 99–106.
Belz, Christopher: 30 years after Mogadishu: What happened to the 'Landshut'? In: transmission, October 2007, pp. 8f.
Bergmann, Werner: Realpolitik versus Geschichtspolitik. Der Schmidt-Begin-Konflikt von 1981, in: Jahrbuch für Antisemitismusforschung 7 (1998), pp. 266–287
Biesenbach, Klaus (ed.): Zur Vorstellung des Terrors. Die RAF (2 vols.), Göttingen/Berlin 2005.
Blank, Ulrich/Darchinger, Jupp: Helmut Schmidt. Bundeskanzler, Hamburg 1974
Bönisch, Georg/Röbel, Sven: Fernschreiben 827. Der Fall Schleyer, die RAF und die Stasi, Cologne 2021.
Bösch, Frank Dahlke, Matthias: Zwischen Schah und Khomeini. Die Bundesrepublik Deutschland und die islamische Revolution im Iran, in: Vierteljahreshefte für Zeitgeschichte, Heft 3./2015, pp. 319–349.
Borgmann, Wolfgang: Boeing 737. Die Flugzeugstars, Stuttgart 2018.

Botzat, Tatjana u. a.: Ein deutscher Herbst. Zustände 1977, Frankfurt am Main 1979.
Breloer, Heinrich: Todesspiel. Von der Schleyer-Entführung bis Mogadischu. Eine dokumentarische Erzählung, Köln 1997.
Brunner, José: Die Politik des Traumas. Gewalterfahrungen und psychisches Leid in den USA, in Deutschland und im Israel/Palästina-Konflikt. Frankfurter Adorno-Vorlesungen 2019, Berlin 2014.
Busse, Volker/Hofmann, Hans: Bundeskanzleramt und Bundesregierung. Tasks. Organisation. Functioning. 5th, revised and updated edition, Heidelberg 2010.
Dahlke, Matthias: 'Nur eingeschränkte Krisenbereitschaft', in: Vierteljahreshefte für Zeitgeschichte, Issue 4/2007, pp. 641–678.
Davies, Barry: Fire Magic, London 1994.
Ders.: 'Wie ein Sechser im Lotto. Nur umgekehrt'. Interview with Hans Dieter Coldewey, in: Ibid., pp. 4–6.
Ders.: Die Entführung der 'Landshut' in Zeitzeugenberichten, Stuttgart 2021.
Ders./Stubbe da Luz (eds.): Role Model Helmut Schmidt? Political Leadership in Crises and Disasters, Hamburg 2024.
Ders/Joachim Schmitt: The hostage-taking and its consequences, in: Faust, Volker (ed.): Fear – Anxiety – Panic, Stuttgart 1986, pp. 177–183.
Ders.: The Pilot. Helmut Schmidt and the Germans, Zurich 2015.
Ders.: More than a Machine, in: der Freitag, 9 February 2017.
Ders.: Kanzlerdämmerung. Wer zu spät kommt, darf regieren, Zürich 2017
Ders.: Die Brutalität des Zufalls, in: Süddeutsche Zeitung vom 3. August 2017.
Ders.: Nur eine wehrhafte Demokratie ist stabil – das zeigt die 'Landshut'. Gespräch mit Sven Felix Kellerhoff, unter: https://www.welt.de/geschichte/raf/article23 1279251/Mogadischu-1977-Die-Landshut-und-die-wehrhafte-Demokratie.html (abgerufen am 24. April 2024).
Ders.: Entscheidungsschlacht. Das emotionale Schema der Generation Helmut Schmidt im Deutschen Herbst 1977, in: Hendrik W. Ohnesorge/Xuewu Gu (Hg.): Der Faktor Persönlichkeit in der internationalen Politik. Perspektiven aus Wissenschaft, Politik und Journalismus, S. 275–292, Wiesbaden/Berlin 2021, pp. 275–292
Decker, Julia/Siemens, Anne: Bühne frei! 30 years after the German Autumn. A conversation between Gabriele von Lutzau and Claus Peymann about crime and forgiveness, in: Süddeutsche Zeitung Magazin No. 13/2007, at: http://sz-magazin.sueddeutsche.de/texte/anzeigen/2637 (accessed on 24 April 2024).
Dehm, Diether (ed.): 'Ich will hier nicht das letzte Wort'. Heinz Rudolf Kunze and Egon Krenz in conversation, Berlin 2016.
Delius, Friedrich Christan: Mogadischu Fensterplatz. Novel, Reinbek 1987.
Ders.: Die Dialektik des Deutschen Herbstes. Drei Thesen über das Terrorjahr 1977 und die Folgen, in: Die Zeit, 25 July 1997.
Ders.: Gewissensentscheidung im Konflikt. Dankesrede bei der Verleihung des Hanns Martin Schleyer-Preises 2012 am 26. April 2013 in Stuttgart, in: Hanns

Martin Schleyer Foundation: Hanns Martin Schleyer Prize 2012/13 (Publications of the Hanns Martin Schleyer Foundation; Vol. 83), Düsseldorf, pp. 41–43.
Ders./Hanns-Eberhard Schleyer: 'Ich würde wieder genauso handeln', in: Süddeutsche Zeitung Magazin Nr. 30/2013, Munich
Deutsche Lufthansa (ed.): Bobby. Die Boeing 737 bei Lufthansa, Mainz 2016.
Dunz, Kristina: Überleben und Leben. Ex-Stewardess von Lutzau, at: https://www.n-tv.de/politik/dossier/Ex-Stewardess-von-Lutzau-article235538.html (accessed on 24 April 2024)).
Fellinger, Raimund/Reiner, Matthias: Siegfried Unseld. His Life in Pictures and Texts, Berlin 2014.
Frisch, Max: Frisch, Max: Greeting at the Party Conference of the Social Democratic Party of Germany on 17 November 1977 in Hamburg, in: SPD-Parteivorstand (ed.): Parteitag der Sozialdemokratischen Partei Deutschlands vom 15. bis 19. November 1977. Congress Centrum Hamburg. Protokoll der Verhandlungen. Anlagen, Bonn no year given (1977/78), pp. 378–383.
Geiger, Tim: The 'Landshut' in Mogadishu. The German government's crisis management in terms of foreign policy in the face of the terrorist challenge in 1977, in: Vierteljahreshefte für Zeitgeschichte 3/2009, pp. 413–456.
Glotz, Peter: Campaign in Germany. Political diary 1981–1983. Hamburg 1986.
Götschenberg, Michael: GSG9. Terror im Visier. Mythos und Realität einer Spezialeinheit, Berlin 2022.
Goltermann, Svenja: Die Gesellschaft der Überlebenden. Deutsche Kriegsheimkehrer und ihre Gewalterfahrungen im Zweiten Weltkrieg, 2. ed. Munich 2009 (2007).
Hachmeister, Lutz: Schleyer. Eine deutsche Geschichte, Munich 2004.
Häntzschel, Jörg: Word cotton in the winter wonderland, in: Süddeutsche Zeitung v. 18 November 2021.
Hagenkötter, Beate: The victims of a hijacking in the follow-up examination. Evaluation approach according to the model of learned helplessness (Seligman), dissertation. Supervisor: Dr. med. Dipl.-Psych. A. Ploeger, typescript 1993.
Hanke, Karl: Five Days as a Hostage. In: Die Zeit, 5 May 1978, Hamburg.
Haus der Geschichte Baden-Württemberg: RAF – Terror in the Southwest, Aalen 2013.
Hauser, Baader and Herold: Description of a Struggle, Hamburg Berlin 2007 (Frankfurt am Main 1998).
Herbert, Ulrich: Drei politische Generationen im 20. Jahrhundert, in: Reulecke, Jürgen (ed.) with the collaboration of Elisabeth Müller-Luckner. Generationalität und Lebensgeschichte im 20. Jahrhundert. Schriften des Historischen Kollegs. Kolloquien 58, Munich 2003.
Hermann, Kai/Koch, Peter: Entscheidung in Mogadischu. Die 50 Tage nach Schleyers Entführung. Dokumente – Bilder - Zeugen, Hamburg 1977.
Herzog, Martin: GSG 9. Ein deutscher Mythos, Berlin 2022.
ibid.: Xuewu Gu, Helmut Schmidt and Mao Zedong. How a Chinese-German Professor made it into the 'ZDF heute-show', in: Hendrik W. Ohnesorge: Power

and Power Shift. Key phenomena of international politics – Festschrift for Xuewu Gu on his 65th birthday, pp. 25–36, Berlin 2022, pp. 25–36.

ibid.: Menschen und Mächte, Berlin 1987

ibid.: Weggefährten. Erinnerungen und Reflexionen, Berlin 1996,

ibid.: Wir werden den Frieden nach innen und außen bewahren. Speech at the Essen SPD Party Conference on 9 June 1980, in: Neue Gesellschaft/Frankfurter Hefte No. 27/1980, Bonn, pp. 566ff., Bonn.

(in conversation with Giovanni di Lorenzo) 'Ich bin in Schuld verstrickt', in: Die Zeit, 30 August 2007, Hamburg.

Jürgs, Michael: Der Tag danach. Vom Verlust der Macht und dem Ende einer Liebe, vom schnellen Tod und von einem neuen Leben. Deutsche Biografien, Munich 2005.

Kellerhoff, Sven Felix: A Short History of the RAF, Stuttgart 2020.

Koch, Peter: The Duel. Franz Josef Strauß versus Helmut Schmidt, Hamburg 1979.

Kohl, Helmut: Speech in the 65th session of the German Bundestag on the occasion of the debate on the government statement on the domestic and foreign policy situation on 19 January 1978, Plenary Protocol 8/65, pp. 4973–4987, Bonn 1978.

Kühn, Alexander: The Dead Captain and Honour, in: Stern of 30 November 2008, at (https://www.stern.de/kultur/tv/tv-drama--mogadischu--der-tote-kapitaen-und-die-ehre-3746150.html (accessed on 24 April 2024).

Kortner, Tim: Mogadischu. Das Entführungsdrama der 'Landshut', Munich 2009.

Kraushaar, Wolfgang: Der nicht erklärte Ausnahmezustand. Staatliches Handeln während des sogenannten Deutschen Herbstes, in: Ders. (ed.): Die RAF und der linke Terrorismus, vol. 2, Hamburg 2006, pp. 1011–1025

Lahme, Tilmann/Lüssi, Kathrin (eds.): Golo Mann. Briefe 1932–1992, Göttingen 2006.

Leber, Hubert: Arms Exports and the Memory of the Holocaust. Saudi Arabia, the Leopard 2 and the secret Israel clause of 1982, in: Vierteljahreshefte für Zeitgeschichte, No. 3/2020, pp. 337–373

Leonhardt, Rudolf Walter: Escaped from the Hell of Somalia. How people react when they face death, in: Die Zeit no. 44 of 28 October 1977, Hamburg.

Luhmann, Hans-Jochen/Neveling, Gundel (eds. Presidium of the German Protestant Kirchentag): German Protestant Kirchentag Hamburg 1981. Documents, Stuttgart/Berlin 1981.

Metzler, Gabriele: 'Denen musste es mal gezeigt werden'. Antiterrorpolitik als Politik der Männlichkeit. Contribution to the thematic focus 'European History – Gender History', in: Themenportal Europäische Geschichte (2014), at: https://www.europa.clio-online.de/essay/id/fdae-1644 (accessed on 24 April 2024).

Münkel, Daniela: Who was the 'Generation Godesberg'? In: Schönhoven, Klaus/Braun, Bernd (eds.): Generations in the Labour Movement, Munich 2004, pp. 343–358.

Musoff, Andreas: Terrorism in the public discourse of the FRG. Its interpretation as an act of war and its consequences, in: Weinhauer, Klaus/Requate, Jörg/Haupt,

Heinz-Gerhard: Terrorism in the Federal Republic of Germany. Media, state and subcultures in the 1970s, Frankfurt/New York 2006.

Nannen, Henri (ed.): Das war 77, Hamburg 1978.

Neumann, Hans Joachim: The Hijacking of the 'Landshut' 1977, in: Bettzuege, Reinhard: On Duty... Reports and Memories from 50 Years of German Foreign Policy, p. 185–191, Munich/Landsberg am Lech 1996, pp. 185–191.

Ohler, Norman: Der totale Rausch. Drogen im Dritten Reich, Cologne 2017

Peters, Butz: 1977. RAF gegen Bundesrepublik, Munich 2017.

Piegler, Hannelore: Entführung. Hundert Stunden zwischen Angst und Hoffnung, Vienna 1978.

Ploeger, Andreas/Schmitz-Gielsdorf, Rosemarie: Depth-psychologically based psychotrauma therapy for the hostages of the Lufthansa aircraft 'Landshut' freed in Mogadishu, in: Gruppenpsychotherapie und Gruppendynamik 15/1980, pp. 353–361, Göttingen, pp. 353–361.

Polzin, Carsten: No exchange! The constitutional dimension of the Schleyer decision, in: Kraushaar, Wolfgang (ed.): The RAF and left-wing terrorism, vol. 2, Hamburg 2006, pp. 1026–1047

Press and Information Office of the Federal Government: Documentation on the events and decisions in connection with the kidnapping of Hanns Martin Schleyer and the Lufthansa aircraft 'Landshut', Cologne 1977.

Rau, Johannes: Speech at the event to commemorate the victims of the terrorist attacks of 1977 on 18 October 2002 in Berlin, at: https://www.bundespra esident.de/SharedDocs/Reden/DE/Johannes-Rau/Reden/2002/10/20021018_ Rede.html (accessed on 24 April 2024).

Richter, Maren: Life in a State of Emergency. Terrorism and Personal Protection in the Federal Republic of Germany (1970–1993), Frankfurt/New York 2014.

Rommel, Manfred: Despite Everything, Cheerful. Memories, Stuttgart 1998.

Rupps, Martin: The Survivors of Mogadishu, Frankfurt/M 2012.

Sarasin, Philipp: 1977. A short history of the present, Berlin 2021.

Scharfenberg, Günther: Jahre am Bab el-Mandeb. Als Botschafter in der Volksdemokratischen Republik Jemen, Berlin 2012

Schmidt, Helmut: Die Kriegsgeneration. Mein Weg zur Sozialdemokratie, in: Neue Gesellschaft/Frankfurter Hefte, Nr. 6/1988, Bonn 1968, S. 479ff.

Schmidt, Holger: Terrorabwehr in Deutschland. A critical balance, Zurich 2017.

Schmitt, Joachim: Extreme seelische Belastung. Verarbeitungsprozesse während einer Flugzeugentführung und ihr Zusammenhang mit längerfristigen Folgewirkungen, Diss. TU Aachen 1987, Typoskript.

Schrep, Bruno: 'Mogadischu hat an meiner Seele gezerrt', in: Der Spiegel No. 9, 26 February 1996, Hamburg.

Stauch, Günter (ed.): Das große Buch der Lufthansa. From 'Auntie Ju' to the Super Jumbo, Munich 2003.

Steffahn, Harald: Helmut Schmidt with self-testimonials and image documents presented by Harald Steffahn, Reinbek 1990.

Stephan, Klaus: Gelernte Demokraten. Helmut Schmidt und Franz Josef Strauß, Reinbek 1988.
Strömsdörfer, Lars/Niemann, Wolfgang: Einsatz in Mogadischu. Der Irrflug der 'Landshut' und die Befreiung der 86 Geiseln durch die GSG 9, Bergisch Gladbach 1977.
Skelton-Robinson, Thomas: Im Netz verheddert. Die Beziehungen des bundesdeutschen Linksterrorismus zur Volksfront für die Befreiung Palästinas (1969–1980), in: Kraushaar, Wolfgang (ed.): Die RAF und der linke Terrorismus, vol. 2, S., Hamburg 2006, pp. 828–904.
Stubbe da Luz, Helmut: Extreme Situationen, schnelle Entscheidungen. Helmut Schmidt gegen Sturmflut und RAF-Terror (Ed.: Bibliothek der Helmut-Schmidt-Universität), Bremen 2022.
This.: Opfer. Die Wahrnehmung von Krieg und Gewalt in der Moderne, Frankfurt am Main 2017.
The same: Laudatio for Roman Herzog on the occasion of the presentation of the Willy Brandt Prize on 29 March 2003, typescript.
Terhoeven, Petra: German Italian Counter translations. One Plane and Three Dead Too Many. The Italian 'Government of National Solidarity' and the German Dilemma, in: Diess. (ed.): Deutscher Herbst in Europa. The Left-wing Terrorism of the 1970s as a Transnational Phenomenon, pp. 505–530, Munich 2014.
Theodor Heuss Foundation: Theodor Heuss Prize 1978. Defence of Freedom, n. a.
Vowinckel, Annette: Aircraft Hijackings. A Cultural History, Göttingen 2011.
Warncke, Finn: Air Force base officially renamed, in: Quickborner Tageblatt, 25 November 2021.
Weinhauer, Klaus. Generationen, Jugenddelinquenz und innere Sicherheit. Die 1960er und frühen 1970er Jahre in der Bundesrepublik, in: Jörg Requate (ed.): Recht und Justiz im gesellschaftlichen Aufbruch (1960–1975). Bundesrepublik Deutschland, Italien und Frankreich im Vergleich, Baden-Baden 2003, S. 33–58.
Wiegrefe, Klaus. 2008. 'Terrible State of Affairs'. Der Spiegel 10 (08), pp. 68f, Hamburg.
Weisswange, Jan-Phillipp/Sünkler, Sören: GSG9. The Special Unit of the Federal Police. Spearhead in the Fight against Terrorism, Bad Ems 2017.
Zander, Ulrike/Biermann, Harald (eds.): Ulrich Wegener. GSG9. Stronger than Terror, 2nd revised and expanded edition, Berlin 2018.

Radio Productions

Current reporting by Südwestrundfunk (formerly Südwestfunk) Baden-Baden on 17 and 18 October 1977.
Diess.: The Second Liberation or the Dreams of the Survivors. On the psychotherapy of hostage victims, typescript, Hessischer Rundfunk 1980.
Hortenbach, Kristina: On Board the 'Landshut'. Co-Pilot and Passenger, Part 1: Co-pilot Jürgen Vietor, Südwestrundfunk 2008.

hostage-taking, in: Tuesday Editorial, 30 January 1979, Süddeutscher Rundfunk.
Koch, Thomas Friedrich: On Board the 'Landshut'. Co-Pilot and Passenger. Part 2: Passenger Julia Sost, Südwestrundfunk 2008.
Krausz, Rosvita: Five Days in October. A psychological profile of a hostage situation, typescript, Südwestfunk 1978.
Krause-Burger, Sybille: In conversation with Hans-Jürgen Wischnewski, Süddeutscher Rundfunk 1987.
Nagel, Petra: Gabriele von Lutzau. The Angel of Mogadishu, Südwestrundfunk 2007.
Rein, Gerhard: The Dreams of the Survivors. On the long-term effects of hostage victims, in: Dienstags reduction of 30 january 1979, Süddeutscher Rundfunk.
Reissenberger, Michael: The 'Landshut' was his destiny. A victim of the hostage crisis in Mogadishu remembers, Süddeutscher Rundfunk 1988.

Television and Film Productions

Adelhardt, Christine/Munz, Martin/Semler, Ulrich: Anne Herr Schmidt hat Geburtstag. Der Bundeskanzler a. D. wird 85, Norddeutscher Rundfunk 2003.
Ameri-Siemens/Rütten, Henning: Wer gab euch das Recht zu morden. Die Geschichte der RAF-Opfer, Rundfunk Berlin-Brandenburg 2007.
Aust, Stefan/Büchel, Helmar: The RAF (Part 1/2: The War of the Children of the Bourgeoisie; Part 2/2: The Autumn of Terror), Norddeutscher Rundfunk 2007.
Bechert, Hilde: The Hijacking to Mogadishu. Monika Schumann and
Beckmann, Reinhold: Beckmann, with Monika Schumann among others, Norddeutscher Rundfunk 2007.
Boers, Eva: Live or die in Entebbe, 2013, self-distribution.
Bott, Gerhard: The most precious weeks of the year. Film protocol of an average holiday, Norddeutscher Rundfunk 1973.
Brauburger, Stefan/Helmburger, Oliver/Vogel, Stephan: The Miracle of Mogadishu, Zweites Deutsches Fernsehen 2007.
Breloer, Heinrich: The Death Game (two parts), Westdeutscher Rundfunk 1997.
Brustellin, Alf: u. a., Deutschland im Herbst, 1977/1978, Studiocanal S. A. 1978.
Demant, Ebbo: Menschen und Straßen. Flugplatz Mogadischu, Südwestfunk 1981.
Ders., Mogadischu. Erinnerungen und Bewertungen, Südwestfunk 1982.
Ders./Helm, Ingo: Im fliegenden Sarg. The 'Landshut' hijacking from the perspective of the hostages, Südwestrundfunk 2011.
Diehn, Timur: Retrospective view of a trauma. The Germans and the RAF, Deutsche Welle TV 2007.
Diezemann, Kai: Life and Work in the Wittlich Prison. Jobs Behind Bars, Südwestrundfunk 2023.
Ders.: Mogadishu. Days of Terror, Norddeutscher Rundfunk 1997.
Diess.: The Hostages of Mogadishu. Life after the 'Landshut' Hijacking, Südwestrundfunk 2017.

Eichinger, Bernd: The Baader-Meinhof Complex (two parts), Norddeutscher Rundfunk 2009 (theatrical version 2008).
Eser, Ruprecht/Salewski, Wolfgang: Mogadishu. 106 hours between Palma and Mogadishu. The 'Landshut' passengers today, Zweites Deutsches Fernsehen 1978.
Froidevaux, Marc/Obermann, Emil: To Mogadishu. The night of the hostages, Süddeutscher Rundfunk 1977.
Gensch, Goggo: 30 Years Later. The German Autumn in Stuttgart, Südwestrundfunk 2007.
Gressmann, Hans et al.: Violence from the Darkness – Terrorism in Germany. The Consequences (Part 2/2), Südwestfunk 1978.
Her New Life, Radio Bremen 1993.
Hegetusch-Weißenbacher, Constanze: Hostage in Mogadishu, Bayerischer Rundfunk 1995.
Heldt, Peter: Witness Interrogation Protocol at the Federal Criminal Police Office. File reference EO 1-LH-181 dated 25 October 1977.
Helm, Ingo: The Day of Decision. Mogadishu, 17 October 1977, Südwestrundfunk 2011.
Jamin, Peter: The Angel of Mogadishu, Westdeutscher Rundfunk 1995.
Jeans, Chris: Caught by the Past. The Terrorist of 'Mogadishu' and the Widow of the Pilot, Westdeutscher Rundfunk 1996.
Kienzle, Ulrich: World Power Terrorism? Ten Years after Mogadishu, Radio Bremen 1987.
Klünder, Irene: Die Witwe und der Mörder. Die vergessenen Opfer der RAF, Südwestrundfunk 2011.
Kölmel, Andreas/Stolpe, Jörg: Daparture for Holiday (Part 1/2), westdeutscher Rundfunk 2011.
Koch, Egmont R.: Deadly Chocolate. A Mossad Poisoning and the Hijacking of the 'Landshut', Südwestrundfunk 2010.
Luxus war; Part 2/2: Von Düsseldorf an den Strand), Westdeutscher Rundfunk 2011.
Laborey, Claire: Christiane F. – We Children of Bahnhof Zoo. Lost Generation, Arte 2022.
Nachtarock. Studio discussion with Jutta Knauff, Horst Gregorio Canellas, Prof. Andreas Ploeger and Ulrich Wegener; discussion leader Christoph Deumling, Bayerischer Rundfunk 1990.
Reimer, Thomas et al.: Violence from the Dark. Terrorism in Germany. The Causes (Part 1/2), Südwestfunk 1978.
Remy, Maurice Philip: Mogadishu. The Documentary, Südwestrundfunk 2008.
Richter, Roland Suso/Remy, Maurice Philip: Mogadishu, Südwestrundfunk 2008.
Sanchez, Roberto/Schaaf, Stefan: Late Revenge for Mogadishu? The 'Landshut' Kidnapper on Trial, Süddeutscher Rundfunk 1996.
Schoen, Hartmut: In the prime of life, Westdeutscher Rundfunk 2011.
Tagesschau and heute editions between 13 and 22 October 1977 (ARD/ZDF).

Sprengel, Bernhard: Barracks bears name of terror victim, in: Pinneberger Tageblatt, 25 November 2021.
Treuter, Martina: The Return of the 'Landshut', Südwestrundfunk 2017.
Tumler, Wolfgang: Vorbild Schumann? A portrait of the murdered captain of the Lufthansa aircraft, Sender Freies Berlin 1978.
Walther, Connie: Schattenwelt, Bayerischer Rundfunk 2006.
Warncke, Finn: Luftwaffenstandort offiziell umbenannt, in: Quickborner Tageblatt, 25 November 2021.
Will, Anne: Terror in the Air. Mogadishu and the Lessons Learned, Norddeutscher Rundfunk 2008.
Wortmann, Michael: Mogadishu Hostages Today, in: Journal 3 of 10 November 1980, Westdeutscher Rundfunk.

Online Productions

Haus der Geschichte der Bundesrepublik Deutschland (ed.): Portal Flug LH-181. Die fünftägige Entführung der "Landshut", erzählt aus der Sicht von Zeitzeugen, available online at: https://www.landshut77.de/de

GPSR Compliance

The European Union's (EU) General Product Safety Regulation (GPSR) is a set of rules that requires consumer products to be safe and our obligations to ensure this.

If you have any concerns about our products, you can contact us on

ProductSafety@springernature.com

In case Publisher is established outside the EU, the EU authorized representative is:

Springer Nature Customer Service Center GmbH
Europaplatz 3
69115 Heidelberg, Germany

www.ingramcontent.com/pod-product-compliance
Lightning Source LLC
LaVergne TN
LVHW010337260326
834688LV00036B/759